Life and Labor:
Dimensions of American
Working–Class History

A Volume in the SUNY American Labor History Series
Charles Stephenson and Robert Asher, General Editors

Life and Labor: Dimensions of American Working–Class History

Edited by

CHARLES STEPHENSON AND ROBERT ASHER

State University of New York Press

Permissions

Patricia Cooper's essay is drawn from her book *Smoke and Fire: Gender, Class and Work Culture in American Cigar Factories, 1900-1919* (forthcoming) and appears here with the kind permission of the University of Illinois Press.

Melvyn Dubofsky's essay first appeared in *Amerikastudien/American Studies* (24:1, 5-20) and appears here with the kind permission of that Journal.

Earlier versions of Brian Greenberg's essay appeared in *The Maryland Historian* (8:2, 38-53), and in his book *Worker and Community: Response to Industrialization in a Nineteenth-Century American City—Albany, New York, 1850-1884* (State University of New York Press, 1985), and appears here with the kind permission both of *The Maryland Historian* and of the State University of New York Press.

Walter Licht's essay contains excerpts from his book *Working for the Railroad: The Organization of Work in the Nineteenth Century*, copyright 1983 by Princeton University Press, and is reprinted here with the kind permission of Princeton University Press.

Earlier versions of Roy Rosenzweig's essay appeared in *Radical History Review* (9:1, 66-81) and as Chapter Five of his book *Eight Hours for What We Will* (Cambridge University Press, 1983), and appears here with the kind permission both of *Radical History Review* and of Cambridge University Press.

Published by
State University of New York Press, Albany

For information, address State University of New York
Press, State University Plaza, Albany, N.Y., 12246

Library of Congress Cataloging-in-Publication Data

Stephenson, Charles.
    Life and labor.

    (American labor history series)
    Includes index
    1. Labor and laboring classes—United States—History.
2. Industrial sociology—United States—History.
3. Trade-unions—United States—History.   I. Asher,
Robert. II. Title. III. Series.
HD8066.S73 1986   305.5'62'0973   86-14362
ISBN 0-88706-173-7
ISBN 0-88706-172-9 (pbk.)

    4   5   6   7   8   9   10

To Mitchell and Colin
and
To Sam and Tanya

Contents

A Note to Students

The editors of this volume have designed it to be used by undergraduates as well as by graduate students. Our contributing authors have written self-contained essays that provide the background necessary for a reader who has not studied history to be able to learn from each piece. We strongly suggest that all readers begin with the Introduction, which defines many of the terms and explains many of the concepts employed by the historians whose work appears in this volume.

Historians use a variety of sources in their work. They examine letters and diaries, testimony at government hearings, transcripts of trials, newspapers, autobiographies, census returns, minute books, business ledgers, and archaeological remains (including old machinery and furniture), seeking information about the way people lived and thought in the past. Readers interested in understanding the way historians move from primary source evidence to written narrative and analysis should look at the footnotes to each article in this book.

Acknowledgments

We would like to express our thanks to Mike Nash and Kathy Claspell for reading the Introduction, to Malcolm Willison, our very thorough and conscientious copy editor, and to Michele Martin, for her encouragement and support throughout this project.

CHAPTER 1

Dimensions of American Working-Class History

CHARLES STEPHENSON AND ROBERT ASHER

Life and Labor presents a series of essays on the experiences of American working people during the industrial epoch that began almost two centuries ago. These essays portray and analyze the historical record of the work and leisure-time activities of millions of American men and women—most of them proletarians who sold the labor of their minds and bodies to employers. The central motif that runs through these essays is the struggle of working people to achieve—both individually and collectively—as much autonomy and control as possible over their work lives and their leisure-time worlds.

All the authors whose work appears in this volume are professional historians, accustomed to examining patterns of change and continuity. It is the study of society as time passes—a dynamic process — that distinguishes the craft of history from other social science disciplines, which do not always intrinsically deal with changes that occur during either short-term or long-term periods of time. In *Life and Labor* the essays have been arranged esentially in chronological order. Most of the essays deal with time periods approximately forty to sixty years long; a few treat longer time spans.

Common intellectual concerns also characterize the work of the historians in this volume. They are troubled by the processes of exploitation and alienation that have adversely affected so many American workers during the last two hundred years. They are aware that American workers never have been a totally homogeneous or monolithic group. Many of the essays explore the elements that divided, as well as those that united, workers—while they were at work and at play. A number of the essays are explicitly dialectical in their sense of historical process, examining the manner in which contradictory forces and groups mutually interact and how they are changed by the

1

resulting social and economic conflict. The contributors to this volume view class conflict as having proven essential to political, social and economic advances made by working people, but the costs—the loss of life, lost income, lost jobs—of these advances have been great. Finally, a large number of the pieces in this volume focus explicitly on the role that technology and technological change have played in influencing the work experiences of laboring people. This reflects the growing awareness of American historians, and Americans in general, of the powerful impact that technology has on the lives of human beings.

We do not believe it is particularly useful to employ here the terminology which divides labor history into "new" and "old." Basically we are reminded of Charles Tilly's critique of this type of dichotomy in his essay "the Old New Social History and the New Old Social History."[1] Labor history is a relatively new field—as distinct from labor economics or labor sociology, both of which lent labor historians significant "operating models"—and it makes little sense to talk about "schools" in labor history as one might in intellectual or political history. For the last two decades labor historians have placed much greater emphasis upon the individual as *part of* the masses. They also have paid particular attention to the way in which small, shop floor groups affected the process of production and interacted with formal union organizations. Labor historians also have focused on the way workers in their communities formed ethic and political organizations that have had a great impact on the texture of everyday life.

Compared to their predecessors, labor historians whose careers began in the late 1960s and thereafter have benefited enormously from the greater amount of primary materials available. These historians also had the benefit of hindsight: the evolution of industrial unionism in the United States since the 1930s has allowed them much more understanding of the consciousness of different groups within the American working classes. Certainly many of these historians, including the contributors to this volume, have been influenced by the creative way in which English labor historians—especially Eric J. Hobsbawm and Edward P. Thompson[2]—have approached the concept of class as a form of consciousness and action that is the product of ongoing historical processes.

The essays in this book describe and interpret the history of union organizations, strikes and boycotts, political activities, social and geographic mobility, changes in the organization of production, and the impact of new technologies. Further, they deal with life and labor together, in the understanding that neither is complete without the other. Although political scientist Ira Katznelson stated recently that "[w]hat needs to be explained is not the absence of class [elsewhere] but its limitation to the arena of work,"[3] the essays collected here illustrate that the division between work experiences and other realms of life has not been sharply defined, precisely because such realms are inseparable and are dialectically linked.

The Industrial Revolution changed human labor in three important ways: first, employers began to organize work with an increasingly extensive division of labor, separating the making of a product into simpler and simpler tasks, which could be learned more quickly and performed at higher speeds than undivided labor; second, work operations once done by the human hand (often holding a tool) now were performed by machines, which held and directed the motions of tools; third, substantial amounts of non-human power—initially water power and steam power—were applied to driving machinery, facilitating higher production speeds and increasing the weight of materials that could be moved and shaped. Third, these technological changes greatly increased the amount of control that the owner of productive equipment could exercise over the work process, both the actual physical movements that constituted work and the pace of work activity. After finishing the essays by Thomas Leary and Patricia Cooper, the reader of this volume will understand that these new production technologies did not reach all occupations at the same time and that as late as World War I there were significant pockets of nonmechanized (but very specialized) labor, even in a highly industrialized country like the United States.[4] As industrialization swept across the Western world during the nineteenth century, the average male enjoyed new political freedoms—the vote and the right to run for public office—along with unprecedented civil freedoms—of speech, travel and assembly. Ironically, for most working people industrialization increasingly created work environments which *reduced* the amount of choice workers could exercise over the actual methods of work and the speed of production.

In identifying the concurrent expansions and contractions of personal freedom that accompanied the Industrial Revolution, we do not intend to imply that a paradise existed in the millennia that preceded the last two centuries. Ever since technological changes created a significant social surplus and transformed primitive hunting and food gathering societies into "civilizations" which domesticated agriculture and significantly advanced handicraft technologies, human society has been characterized by inequitable social and economic stratification. Barbaric slave-labor systems and feudal economies that granted producers only limited (although cherished) freedoms hardly can be presented as paradigms of human emancipation and unalienated labor. As William Mulligan's essay on Lynn shoemakers demonstrates, even in artisan families, in which the handicraft process of making shoes was controlled by artisans themselves, power was not democratically apportioned: the sexual division of labor that characterized artisan production placed women in a subordinate position to men. Nevertheless, male, female and child workers enjoyed more autonomy under this less-than-perfect system of production relations than they would when mechanization forced substantial numbers of workers out of the home workshop and the farmland worked (but not necessarily owned) by family units. In a factory setting all producers were subordinate to the authority of management, although skilled workers often created significant amounts of autonomy for themselves, especially in the years before World War I.

When machine production began to supplant hand manufacture in the shoemaking trade, some skilled artisans were able to fill the factory-based hand labor jobs that still remained—especially pattern cutting and lasting—but many more shoemakers either were forced out of their trade entirely or had to become less-skilled machine operatives. Statistical studies show that by 1870 the majority of machine tenders in New England's shoe factories were female and male migrants from the farms of New Hampshire, Vermont, and Massachusetts—people who never had been artisan shoemakers.[5] An 1870 survey of shoe workers conducted by the Massachusetts Bureau of Labor Statistics found most factory laborers complaining about "machinofacture." A bootmaker noted that mechanization "has had a tendency to concentrate workmen in factories, and render them less independent of their employers. . . It seems to be a struggle for life against great odds." Another bootmaker reported that "new machinery has . . . rendered skilled labor of less value." A fellow worker noted that the "advantages of machinery have been applied wholly to the employer—it has increased production and decreased costs. It has rendered work more tedious and monotonous." Another worker, whose trade was not identified, had a similarly dim view of mechanized production: "Labor-saving machinery?" he said; "I don't know of any such machines. I have seen many labor-destroying machines."[6]

Relationships between people engaged in productive activity are influenced strongly by the resources each person or group of producers can command. Clearly, ownership of production sites—land and the structures built on it—as well as ownership of the materials and machinery used for production, gives the owner a great advantage over the people whose labor power is bought by the owner. The power of owners and their hired managers, however, is not and never has been absolute. Some workers have special skills, not widely distributed among the available work forces, that give them considerable bargaining power when they negotiate individually the terms of their employment by businessmen. Such workers always have been a small minority of the working population. Historically most workers, including workers whose skills took many years to develop, have been aware that they could benefit from associating together and negotiating, as a group, the terms of the sale of their labor power to employers. In eighteenth-century England, well before the construction of the first mechanized textile factories and the beginnings of production with machine tools, skilled artisans in different towns and cities banded together in labor unions to increase their bargaining power. By threatening and actually carrying out strikes that deprived employers of the workers' labor power, unions inflicted financial losses that served as an incentive for employers to make concessions to their employees. Some of these efforts were successful; others failed. What is important is the idea that even pre-industrial workers had that the landowners, houseowners, or contractors who employed them were, by virtue of the capital they commanded, in a superior economic position that could be confronted most effectively by collective action by the people who commanded not capital but work skills and muscle power.[7]

The new production technologies that emerged during the early phases of the Industrial Revolution did not reduce the skills of all workers. As Thomas Leary demonstrates in his study of American machinists in the years before the Civil War, many of the new machines used to shape metal were very complex, and required intelligence, physical deftness and experience in the machinists who operated them. Leary, however, also describes the emergence of special-purpose metalworking machines that created a significant division of labor in the machine shop between all-around machinists and less-skilled, more-easily-trained operatives who tended the specialized machine tools. All-around machinists who could not find jobs to match their skills protested this development. For example, in 1883

John Morrison, a veteran machinist, told a committee of the U.S. Senate that the intensified division of labor in the making of sewing machines had made

> the trade so subdivided that a man is not considered a machinist at all. Hence it is merely 'laborers' work . . . It has a very demoralizing effect upon the mind throughout . . . [the] intellect must be narrowed by it. . . In fact [the machinist] becomes almost a part of the machines.[8]

Leary's description of the progress of technology is finely drawn, and his description of the process by which the worker went "from the cocoon of artisan culture [to] the web of capitalist relations" is exceptionally clear. His story is one of a "dialectic between expiring and emerging skills." Relationships obviously changed between worker and owner/manager when machinery was introduced, yet the central point of Leary's essay is that this did not happen all at once. Instead, "manual and mechanized methods coexisted for a number of years." The balance of shop-floor control clearly began to shift toward capital but, despite the fact that new machines *began* to deskill workers, they could not be operated without those workers.

Relations of production in ante-bellum machine shops were further complicated by the practice of sub-contracting, which made some master machinists small entrepreneurs who, after negotiating the terms for making a particular part with the factory owner, then hired other machinists and less-skilled journeymen helpers. While the skilled workers who were subcontractors were able to preserve significant amounts of control over the process of production, it is clear that such skilled workers often physically intimidated their crews and drove hard bargains on wages with the people they hired (as also was true in the early iron and steel industry).

Both Leary and Patricia Cooper, in her study of women cigar workers, shed light on the complex decisions made by employers in introducing new production technologies. Leary suggests that machine-shop employers sought more than just more accurate and more precise cuts of metal when they developed or purchased new machine tools: these employers also were trying to gain more control over labor costs by reducing the skills necessary to make a particular part, which in turn lowered the amount of money that had to be paid to hire labor. Employers knew that machinery which could be operated by almost any worker with some metalworking experience would reduce interruptions in production which occurred when irreplaceable skilled workers decided that they wanted to forego additional earnings in favor of more leisure time—for resting, hunting or other recreational activity.

Cooper demonstrates that the primitive, hand-powered mechanical devices used in cigar-making before 1920 did not enable employers to determine the pace of production in the manner they desired. Even when managers manipulated piece rates to try to boost production, workers fought back by coercing high-output "rate-busters" and by developing time-savings shortcuts, which the workers kept secret, to enable them to reduce the fatigue threatened by lower piece rates because they required higher output to keep take-home pay constant. Cooper notes the attempts by cigar manufacturers after 1900 to have engineers develop machinery to eliminate the hand production of cigars. By 1920 the manufacturers had obtained the technology they sought and they used it to smash the labor organizations of cigar workers, whose numbers were reduced and whose bargaining power was limited because even the "slowest" machine operator could be replaced easily and could not—by withholding labor efficiency—appreciably lower the output of the machinery he or she tended. Since manufacturers owned the new cigar-making machinery, they could order their skilled toolsetters to prepare the machines to operate at the speeds the manufacturers wanted. Any worker whose machine(s) did not attain the output levels mandated by the manufacturer was replaced by a worker who was willing to endure the stress and fatigue to achieve the production goals set by the factory owners.

The desire of workers for some control over the scheduling of their work is not simply a phenomenon found among artisans during the transitional years of the Industrial Revolution, when workers from preindustrial backgrounds were entering factories for the first time. David Montgomery has pointed to the absenteeism and high turnover rates of unskilled and semi-skilled factory workers in the first two decades of the twentieth century, when these proletarians frequently took time off from disagreeable and exhausting jobs, resting and enjoying the control over their own time that was possible outside the bonds of the structured, supervised work environment. Workers also floated from job to job, searching for higher pay, better working conditions, or just a change, however small, from the monotony of one particular labor task. With the advent of increased job security created by trade union organization, especially in the years after World War II, absenteeism rates rose, as many American workers were less afraid to exercise control over their lives by taking time off from the world of

work when they needed a respite. In this latter period higher real
wages also cushioned the financial losses that the exercise of freedom
entailed.

Working people in the United States during the past two centuries
have had many objectives in life: to feed, clothe and shelter themselves and their families; to find meaning and pleasure in their work;
to avoid working conditions that caused damage to their bodies (including physical assaults by managers or fellow workers); to build
stable families, providing for the future happiness of their children; to
worship their god; to enjoy their leisure time; to exercise their political
rights by campaigning and voting for governmental representatives
and the officers of workers' organizations; to achieve occupational
mobility that took them out of the the ranks of the manual labor force
(becoming either the owners of business, self-employed professionals, or professionals employed by others); and to accumulate property
and other material resources, by savings and increases in earnings.
Each worker or working-class family emphasized different goals, although it is clear that basic physical survival—something never to be
taken for granted—was the primary objective of virtually all American workers. Conditions and events at the point of production had a
very strong impact on the ability of working people to pursue their life
goals.

The Industrial Revolution set into motion forces that produced contradictory results: a rising material standard of living initially for some
workers and for virtually all people in the long run was accompanied
by increased work hazards, loss of control over work processes and a
regularized work routine of daily labor, often from sunup to sun-
down, that was relieved only by unemployment or a short period of
migration to another job site. Because technological change created
many new job categories and types of economic activity, large numbers of people experienced changes in their occupations. Social scientists have coined a term, "mobility," to describe "upward" or "downward" movement on a stratified scale of occupations and income
levels. It is clear that many workers saw changes in their income,
property holdings and work experiences during the course of their
working lives. For most workers, statistics show, these changes were
gradual and moderate. But industrial growth enabled a limited number of working people to acquire large sums of money, moving from
rags to riches or, at least, to what the middle class called "respectability." In all industrial societies the dominant economic groups as the

Industrial Revolution preceeded began to believe in ideologies about social and economic mobility that implied that most people were making tremendous gains and that those who failed to so advance were morally defective or damned by god, who had consigned them to a status of inferiority and stagnation. While there was a grain of truth in these ideologies of opportunity, they created psychological frustration among those working people who accepted the ideology, yet failed to move upward rapidly.

In his essay on the Odd Fellows in Albany, New York Brian Greenberg discusses the way inter-class social organizations like the Odd Fellows influenced the ideals that skilled workers held about social mobility. Antonio Gramsci, the Italian sociologist who has influenced many twentieth-century social scientists, used the term "hegemony" to describe the effects which a society's dominant social, cultural, and educational institutions have on the thinking of the masses of people. Greenberg's essay provides a detailed view of the hegemonic process at work in fraternal orders like the Odd Fellows.

Selective recruitment of the most successful members of the working class at the top of the proletarian order often predisposed them to accept an ideology that praised them as superior, patriotic or especially godly people, which was combined with their repeated exposure to ideas that reflected the views of the middle class and elite professionals and entrepreneurs who dominated American intellectual life. Odd Fellowship in the long run was an agent of middle-class industrial culture, an organization which reflected and was dedicated to the dominant ideology of the day. This has been labeled the "free labor ideology," which posited the "inevitability" of social mobility in an open society, and claimed the existence of a "community of interest" which embraced all members within the society. This was especially important in aiding the transplantation of this initially-agrarian formation into urban, working-class America. While according to this ideology urban workers might not so often rise to be large entrepreneurs (small entrepreneurship was more common), it was considered indisputable that capital and labor still needed each other: "capital and labor are not antagonistic," said one Albany newspaper; "they are the positive and negative elements [labor undoubtedly being the "negative" element!] which complete the currents and keep the circuit of commerce and trade." Seldom was there a clearer statement of the success ethic's tie to social harmony. The effect of Odd Fellowship was profoundly conservative. It may be described best as a middle-class organization devoted to the view that America was a society without class and within which only cooperation—in this case sequential deference—was acceptable.

Charles Stephenson approaches the subject of social mobility from a different angle, noting that frequent movement from job to job, from community to community, and up and down the occupational ladder was taking place in a environment of great uncertainty with regard to continuous income, whether it came from self-employment or from working for others. But Stephenson cautions that we should not assume that the members of the "reserve army of labor" (which averaged at least ten percent of the adult population in the United States between 1880 and 1920) were ultra-alienated, nonfunctional people in the sense that sociologist Emile Durkheim meant when he coined the term "anomie." Workers "on the move" left and entered working-class communities and institutions—churches, fraternal societies, ethnic associations, labor unions, shop-level work groups, political clubs, and other voluntary organizations—which shaped their values and gave them a feeling of "belonging." Workers who resisted the inequities of capitalism did so not as isolated individuals but as members of collective bodies, which provided both emotional and financial resources to sustain working-class efforts to fight capitalists' exercise of power in the work place and in the political arena. Stephenson also interprets the strong desire of workers to achieve mobility into the ranks of small entrepreneurs and self-employed professionals—for themselves and for their children—as a reaction to the powerlessness that workers experienced when laboring in the employ of capitalists. In short, the desire of workers for autonomous work experiences, even if they could be achieved only by becoming "small capitalists," did not necessarily represent the dominance of hegemonic ideologies: rather, it represented a deeply rooted human need for freedom and control while working.

Workers also sought to achieve stability and autonomy through collective bargaining. Although American workers were told by entrepreneurs and most intellectuals that they lived in a free society, with a "free" labor market that gave them unlimited opportunity to advance, the reality was very different. Walter Licht demonstrates that the "free" market operated in a far-from-random manner in selecting members of the working class for employment on the railroads, which were one of the highest wage-paying businesses in the nation. Foremen doing hiring practiced both favoritism and extortion. This made the process of obtaining a job on the railroads dependent on personal connections, through kin associations or friendship, as well as on the possession of resources to bribe foremen (money, the bodies of wives and daughters and "donated" labor to fix the houses of foremen all were used). Licht further indicated that railroad workers experienced a great deal of unpredictable and capricious treatment from foremen and managers who acted in "arbitrary, discretionary, and often despotic ways" in the determination of pay rates, work scheduling, promotion, compensation for industrial accidents, and disciplinary actions for rule infractions. While nineteenth- and twentieth-century commentators often pictured industrial workers as anarchic and resistant to discipline and structure, Licht reveals that pressure for the regularization and bureaucratization of railroad labor policies came in large part from workers themselves.

Basically bureaucratization came about because management was convinced it had a group of "intractable workers" and because workers were concerned about the arbitrary nature of supervision. Here, as elsewhere, workers responded to their daily experiences—on the shop floor or, in this case, on the tracks—and in the case of railroaders prominent among their immediate realities was constant conflict with supervisors. The decentralization which railroad management believed enhanced overall operation also allowed—and apparently encouraged—arbitrariness. One railroad man testified that workers "were almost in a helpless condition to stand against the oppression of the petty officials." Workers attacked at this oppression in a number of ways, but the labor strike proved eventually to be the most effective. Union organizations representing railroad workers went on strike to obtain written contracts that specified rules for the management of railroad labor and created quasi-judicial grievance machinery to resolve disputes between workers and managers over the interpretation of labor regulations.

Licht posits a dialectical relationship between the actions of railroad workers and the overall patterns of railroad management established by corporate bureaucrats. The bureaucratization of basic managerial structures, necessary for effective day-to-day operation of the railroads, was not designed, in the case of labor management, with checks and balances to allow central managers to check up on the performance of managers of decentralized railroad units. Workers understood that the problem was not the existence of bureaucracy *per se*, but the lack of any mechanism to insure uniform and equitable treatment of workers. What workers sought was a bureaucracy that worked fairly—rules applied consistently and a reliable grievance system—all to be achieved through written contracts. Workers borrowed the bureaucratic techniques developed by managers but created their own synthesis to make bureaucracy serve their interests. They incorporated their own, self-governed union organizations as participants in the bureaucratic grievance structures designed to govern labor practices. The bargaining power of railroad workers was not so great that they could force management to accept all the demands labor made. But by the beginning of the twentieth century railroad workers had made great strides toward negotiating wages and work rules that improved their conditions; and many railroad workers obtained bureaucratic safeguards to guarantee that they actually would receive the benefits that had been won both through collective bargaining and bitter, often violent strikes.

Conditions and events in the work place had a very strong impact on the ability of working people to pursue their life goals. As the Industrial Revolution progressed work became more hazardous and deadly because machinery operated at a faster pace and moved greater weights than had hand work. Industrial production increasingly involved toxic substances—metals, coal and cotton dust, inorganic and organic chemicals—that created many short-run and long-term dangers for industrial workers. In the United States, until the twentieth century, industrial workers could not count on any compensation for injuries or occupational diseases; moreover, factory-inspection legislation was weak and safety laws often were not enforced effectively. In his essay in this volume Robert Asher analyzes the impact of workers' anger over unsafe working environments on their propensity to organize and to take direct action, individually and collectively, against business owners and managers whom workers held responsible for accidents and diseases. He describes the state of industrial safety in late-nineteenth and early-twentieth-century America and its influence upon labor relations. The story he relates is sobering, for it suggests that, especially in certain industries, serious and adequate safety regulation was the exception rather than the rule. It is no exaggeration to say that there was an element of terror in everyday work in such places. Risks abounded which both were unnecessary and life-threatening. Contemporaries spoke of "the daily carnage in the mines, mills, and railroads of the nation."

Using the findings of social psychologists about the relationship between aggression and violent behavior, Asher argues that the technological violence unleashed against working people often made them furious and influenced their sometimes-violent responses to a wide spectrum of grievances they held against their employers. The degradation that many workers experienced as industrial capitalism became the dominant mode of production in the United States involved both a loss of control over work processes and the physical injury and mental anguish they endured because a system of production for profit controlled by business owners did not explicitly grant workers any power to influence the safety of their work environment.

This situation existed despite government regulation. By early in this century unions and their allies had achieved the passage of safety standards and inspection by government agencies. Yet inspection staffs were inadequate and, often, the corruption of and collusion between inspectors and management effectively negated regulation. Again, it was up to the workers to deal with the situation, and they responded in several ways. However they responded, they faced long odds, for the most common response of management was to fire complaining workers, often blacklisting them as well. Asher believes this "aggression of modern technology against the lives and limbs of industrial workers" brutalized them not only physically but psychologically as well, and increased their tendency to respond to that violence with violence of their own "in all aspects of their lives."

Workers seeking better wages and labor conditions relied not only on the strike but also on the boycott, a form of "mass collective action," as Gregory Zieren puts it, that extended beyond the workplace of a particular craft into the public arena. Other workers often used their power as consumers of durable goods—like beer, clothing, newspapers and beef, and of services, especially intra-urban mass transit—to aid the workers employed by the companies that provided these products. Because boycotts involved class unity beyond the narrow confines of a particular trade or factory, they were perceived—and correctly—by middle-class and elite opinion as a more radical form of working-class action than strikes of workers in one occupation at a single work site. This accounts for the "near hysterical" response of many newspapers and politicians to the labor boycott, especially when it was combined, as it was in Toledo, Ohio—known as "the best organized city in the country" in the 1890s—with aggressive working-class political organization. Despite the extreme hostility of state courts and the federal judiciary, labor boycotting increased during the last two decades of the nineteenth century. In cities like Toledo the enhanced class consciousness created by boycotting was transformed into effective political action. Mobilized by Toledo's unions, workers pressured the city government to consult with unions on the hiring of city administrators. For more than a decade beginning in 1897 Toledo's workers elected pro-labor mayors "Golden Rule" Jones and Brand Whitlock, who favored, as did their working-class supporters, municipal ownership and the recognition of unions of city employees.

The different types of class consciousness that American workers developed were conditioned by their interactions with other workers and with members of the "higher" social classes. In his study of interclass conflict over the use of city resources for recreation in the industrial city of Worcester, Massachusetts Roy Rosenzweig shows that the explicit efforts of middle-class and elite spokesmen to monopolize public recreational space and, failing in those efforts, to exercise control over the recreational activities of lower-class people, met with significant resistance from workers. Already by the middle of the nineteenth century different middle and working class leisure styles were evident. While the latter preferred collective and participatory play and games, the former generally preferred "strolling" and contemplation. Early park designers catered to the urban middle class. There was a conflict, as it was put at the time, between "the more numerous class that frequents the park for the enjoyment of the refined and attractive features of its natural beauties" and those cruder classes which wished to . . . play ball! The first conflicts came from working-class demands for "public play space," and compromises were reached which allowed this. Using their political rights, workers selected (and elected) spokesmen who insisted that the interests of working people be respected and nurtured by government expenditures creating and maintaining appropriate recreational space.

According to Rosenzweig the changes in the relationship between the classes began with changes in the middle class itself. In the later part of the nineteenth century sport began to push aside the contemplative orientation in leisure, beginning with the upper-class "country-club set." Eventually, the middle and upper classes began to see recreation as "purposeful," "a means of self-development and self-control" rather than the "public socializing" which, to the working class, was an end in itself. Slowly the business classes began to perceive recreation's instrumental possibilities: "as a child plays," they began to believe, "so will he later work"; their goal became "to make Americans of these children." The impact of recreational specialists' involvement was severe. The development of instrumental leisure was long, slow, and complex, and had a dialectical give-and-take. In the end there were a number of tradeoffs, but finally the constraints upon the working class were firm.

While Rosenzweig describes the dialectic of inter-class conflict over the function and character of recreational space, Kathy Peiss finds a fascinating dialectical social interaction between working-class males and females. Peiss indicates that working-class men generally had more economic power than their female counterparts because most of the men received higher wages than the women with whom they were associating during their leisure hours. Working people engaged in a different type of dance from their middle-class counterparts, one which contained much more sexually-explicit forms of dancing (and contact during dancing), and over which the dancers had direct control. In the middle class, sexuality was mediated by regulating the dance and the dancer. Looking at the interaction between men and women in working-class dance halls, Peiss notes that the ritual of young men "treating" their female peers to food and drink, with women giving different degrees of "favors" in return, reflected the *economic* imbalance that existed within the working class between men and women. It is unfortunate that we do not have equally solid evidence detailing the views of working-class men and women about the *emotional* effects of the disparity in economic power between the sexes. Despite this power differential, it is clear that young laboring men and women enjoyed the freedom dance halls gave them to dance and socialize unencumbered by parental supervision. Industrialization and urbanization, by facilitating an extensive division of labor and specialization of activity, created conditions that allowed working people in cities more liberty in their time away from work, even though technology increasingly was limiting the control people had while they worked as producers to earn money for sustenance and recreation.

We have described the quest of workers for autonomy in the context both of production activity and recreational space. In her study of female cigar workers, Patricia Cooper sheds additional light on the phenomenon of on-the-job resistance to employer authority by workers. Cooper shows us that absenteeism, quitting, and sabotage were used by workers to get the space and respect they wanted. She also indicates that many cigar workers (as did male and female workers in other occupations) helped each other out by actually performing the work of sick, absent, or slow-paced fellow workers. Piece-rate workers in the cigar industry, as in other industries, also collectively sought to place restraints on the work pace of people who threatened the physical well-being and earnings of the majority of slower-working people, whose pace was determined both by physical limitations and a desire to spread out work, thereby maintaining steadier employment for everyone. Faced with gruelling work and work rules, a job often weakened because of part-time employment, and insensitive unions, the women often took matters into their own hands in courageous ways. Eventually, however, these conditions of discrimination combined with new technology in cigar-making to thwart their efforts and to push them out of the industry.

There are no statistical means available to determine how many American workers believed that the political economy of industrial work should be altered explicitly to allow workers directly to control production activity. We do know that millions of workers voted for Socialist Party candidates who were committed to workers' control over and ownership of the means of production. In 1912 the Socialist candidate for President, Eugene V. Debs, received one million votes, one of every twelve cast. Although the strength of political socialism declined after 1912, during and immediately after World War I hundreds of thousands of workers struck in support of specific demands for increased worker power to influence employment conditions—wages, hiring and promotion practices, layoffs, and safety and work speeds.[9]

During the 1920s American businessmen, aided by the Federal courts, the Presidents, and their Attorneys General, launched an anti-union offensive that left many unions in ruins. The number of organized workers declined in absolute numbers almost to the level before World War I. But employers appreciated the strength of worker demands for autonomy and representation in the decisions that governed their work experiences. Hundreds of American corporations established employee representation plans during the 1920s. If most of these plans did not give workers' representatives any real power, they helped legitimize the notion of worker representation in industrial decision making and "educated" workers to the difference between the form and the substance of representation and influence. During the 1930s employer exploitation of workers reached unprecedented levels in terms of work speed-ups and demeaning treatment of workers afraid of losing their jobs. When Congress passed legislation that recognized the principle of collective bargaining, millions of American workers enthusiastically embraced trade unionism.

Melvyn Dubofsky has studied both radical labor unions, like the revolutionary Industrial Workers of the World, and more conservative unions that attempted to use collective bargaining to achieve both higher wages and more control over work places that nonetheless were seen by capitalists to be their legitimate property. In his study of workers' consciousness in the 1930s Dubofsky suggests that most American workers, no matter how hard they fought for the right to union representation, did not lose faith in the ability of American capitalists to organize production. Dubofsky also notes that most American workers did not have any faith that socialist alternatives to capitalism would advance their interests significantly. One might add that the view of socialism available to most American workers, through news-media reporting of events in the Soviet Union, was one of a highly centralized, elite-dominated system that did not adequately provide workers institutional representation, especially in the work place.

Dubofsky also notes that union leaders who wanted to use labor organizations to expand the influence of workers over production decisions were fearful that if their demands were too radical the power of the federal government, which had shown in 1919 and 1920 how effectively it could repress union activities, would be turned from assisting the formation of labor unions to destroying them. During World War II, when rank-and-file militants of the type that Nelson Lichtenstein describes tried to advance worker control at the point of production, the National War Labor Board explicitly threatened national union leaders with the loss of union rights if they did not suppress radical activity that challenged capitalist control over the management of production technology.

Lichtenstein's account of life at the River Rouge plant of the Ford Motor Company is a detailed description and analysis of the complexity of power relationships and their relationship to the type of technology used for production; he offers us the modern-day equivalent of the Mulligan and Leary essays in focusing upon "one of the central issues of all social history: who controls the workplace?" As early as the 1920s the Ford management style had turned Draconian: the work regime, and the building superintendents and foremen responsible for it, became increasingly capricious, akin to Licht's railroad foremen. Ethnicity became a basis for discrimination, and on the shop floor the Masonic Order became influential. Lichtenstein quotes C. L. R. James' remark that "the internal work order at the Rouge came to resemble in America the closest equivalent of the labor discipline imposed by Stalinist or fascist regimes abroad." Lichtenstein demonstrates that during World War II Ford workers, led by shop stewards who were former production workers and who spent most of their time inside factories (rather than in offices as did national-level union leaders) used physical force and wildcat strikes to try to slow down the pace of production to humane levels. Ford managers were troubled by these actions, but during World War II often had great difficulty in suppressing them, since the federal government put much pressure on Ford to maintain its supply of military equipment and since the government also guaranteed the company a healthy profit, no matter how high its production costs rose. But, Lichtenstein tells us, "the counterrevolution was not long in coming." Immediately after World War II ended Ford implemented a plan of adding new production machinery and conducting time-and-motion studies to enable the company to establish precise production norms and to discipline workers who did not meet them. This policy, which was followed by other major automobile manufacturers, was successful in quelling rank-and-file militance in the workplace. But the major industrial producers who recovered some of the control over production that they had lost during the 1930s and World War II had to pay a price to organized labor for keeping unchallenged control over production: workers in highly organized industries received generous wage increases, made possible by the world-wide dominance of the American economy, and usually were guaranteed a constant level of earnings when production technologies were altered. At the same time, the post-war decade saw vicious internal "red purges" which damaged the union and bureaucratized collective bargaining. While changed in significant ways, by the early 1960s the operation of the factory at River Rouge had come full circle.

The emergence of what some economists have called dual labor markets—primary markets for well-organized workers in large, oligopolistic companies and secondary markets for other workers—was not an entirely new development. The American labor market always has been segmented. Women and minorities generally were found at the bottom of the labor market, in the jobs with the lowest pay and the least regularity of employment. Black workers, both male and female, were worse off than white workers, whether male or female. During the late 1930s radicals and progressives active within the labor movement emphasized the importance of organizing Black workers in the new industrial unions that were springing up and of promising Blacks that union power would be used to combat racial discrimination in hiring and promotion. Without the strong egalitarian, anti-racist appeals made by CIO organizers in the rubber, automobile, meat-packing and electrical industries, Black workers would have refused to join the industrial unions and it is very likely that many such organizing efforts would have failed.

Dennis Dickerson's article demonstrates that during World War II Black workers and many middle-class Black spokesmen believed that racial discrimination was so pervasive, and would be so hard to eliminate from the behavior of both employers and unions, that it was necessary to have government intervene to combat racial discrimination in employment. Detailing the operation of the Fair Employment Practices Commission, which was created in 1944, when Black leaders and white radicals threatened to organize a mass protest march in the nation's capital, Dickerson shows how it helped advance the rights of many Black steelworkers. By late 1945, however, the FEPC was under attack and by 1946 it was unfunded. Although its provisions subsequently were revived, the Reagan administration virtually destroyed the effectiveness of this legislation. Women workers also suffered from discrimination in pay, hiring and promotion. During World War II federal agencies made unprecedented efforts to eradicate such forms of discrimination. Even today, however, despite the 1972 civil rights legislation that explicitly outlawed discrimination based on gender, the earnings of women workers are considerably lower than those of men performing at the same level. Women also are disproportionately concentrated in the low-wage, high-turnover employment sectors, especially service-sector jobs, that will be feeling the brunt of technological unemployment.

Valerie Quinney's essay effectively uses oral interviews to analyze the reasons why office employment became feminized and why so many women voluntarily choose to train for careers in office work. Cooper gave us a penetrating analysis of women working in what traditionally was a man's field and in which men continued to hold all the formal authority in management and unions alike; Quinney tells us about a field which, as it grew, became almost exclusively female. She investigates the transition to a female labor force, the role of business schools, and the response of workers to their employment. The question of why office-machine work became so predominantly female has been a central one. Quinney finds not only that traditional explanations—that women were available and willing to work for cheaper wages—were accurate, but also that women sought this work because it still paid better salaries than other work open to women.

An available and eager labor force needed training, and business schools very quickly were established in response to this opportunity.

The business of business schools was to train women to operate machines and to master other office-related processes, but they also believed it their role to teach "that respect for authority, promptness, dependability, and loyalty were the characteristics which would allow them to keep their jobs." When women arrived in the office they discovered that the tyrant of Taylorism had arrived there too, and their proletarianization has continued to the present.

Interviews with office workers reveal a multiplicity of reactions to their jobs. While positive aspects of the job are important—and more often than not have to do with co-workers—the bulk of comments focus upon the workers' experience of "stress, subservience, and lack of recognition." The women interviewed convey their feelings about new computer and video display terminal (VDT) apparatus; their conclusion is that it "really creates pain." "The VDT," says Quinney, "changes the nature of the work people do."

Finally, Quinney joins the issues directly in demonstrating that machines which force workers to adapt, rather than machines constructed with workers in mind, create "inefficiency" as well as brutal working conditions. The question in dissident workers' minds, she correctly points out, is the same as it has been for more than a century of industrial production: not "shall we industrialize?" but "who shall control industrialization?"

The essays in this anthology demonstrate the complex relationship between the actions taken by workers to change their physical and economic working conditions, and the ideas people have about class, race, and sex roles. No simple generalization could summarize the diverse phenomena that constitute the real stuff of American working-peoples' history. Clearly, different groups of workers faced different circumstances and responded to them in different ways. This may be obvious to the reader who has absorbed the information presented in the essays here, but it is a lesson rarely conveyed by homogenized textbook accounts of the history of working people.

When American workers believed they were treated unfairly by employers and by governments that responded only to middle-class and elite political pressure, they frequently organized collectively to obtain redress. A historian surveying the history of class struggle in the United States properly might observe that, both in particular work locations and across the nation, there was an ebb and flow to the class struggle present in on-the-job resistance, work stoppages and political action. The absence of more frequent and overt worker protests against the exploitation that workers knew existed can be explained by divisions of skill, race, ethnicity, and gender within the labor force and, as well, by employers' skillful manipulation of them. Moreover, workers were painfully aware of the legal, physical and economic sanctions that often were applied when they challenged collectively the power of other social classes. Many historians of industrialization have been impressed by the magnitude of the risks taken (and the punishments received) by workers in the United States and other industrial nations when they took direct action to advance their interests.

The United States has experienced the impact of the Industrial Revolution for more than a century and a half, and the rate of change in work technology has accelerated constantly though this period. Technological change has been particularly rapid since 1940. Readers of this book, whatever their age, will be aware especially of the impact of computer technology on their lives. Yet despite growing incomes, more accumulated social resources and rising productivity, income distribution has not changed significantly since 1900, skill divisions have persisted, friction between workers of different sexes, races, and ethnic groups has not been eliminated (and may be intensifying in some occupations), and the gap in power between labor and management has been narrowed only slightly, still leaving most workers with much less authority than their employers. The past experiences of American workers as they tried to advance their autonomy and welfare both on the job and in their personal lives thus are relevant to the lives of Americans currently in the workforce and to those who soon will enter the world of life and labor.

From Artisan to Proletarian: The Family and the Vocational Education of Shoemakers in the Handicraft Era

WILLIAM H. MULLIGAN, JR.

The recent increase in scholarly attention to the lives of preindustrial artisans has focused very heavily on group consciousness and the challenges to the artisans' life style presented by the emergence of industrial capitalism.[1] We have a very rich sense of how craftsmen expressed their sense of heritage and group solidarity in the face of a rapidly changing economy. The rituals of craft identity have been illuminated, but the origins of that identification have been less fully explored. Why did the practictioners of a particular craft identify so closely with one another? The threat that the basic structural changes of the American economy during the early decades of the nineteenth century posed for the artisan and his world called forth the strongest possible defense of traditional mores.

Those mores, however, were not caused by that changing economy, but rather were the result of generations of shared experience. To understand the depth of artisan craft identity and its close relationship to the self-image of the individual artisan, it is useful to examine the process by which individuals became craftsmen and the extent to which the rhythms of their work lives shaped their self-image. It is also important to examine the impact that changes in the industry had on training for understanding the impact of mechanization on worker identification with their work.

The first part of this essay focuses on the experience of a particular group of artisans, the shoemakers of Lynn, Massachusetts, during the period when shoes were made by hand in that community. While the particulars of their experience may not have been universally shared by all artisan groups, the general forces at work reveal a number of useful general principles for understanding the origins of artisan craft identification and its tenacity. The essay then looks at mechanization and its impact on work and the transmission of skills.

Shoemaking has a long history in Lynn and was the single most important factor in the evolution of the community. The first shoemakers had settled there during the 1630s. The town began to emerge as a major center of the industry after 1750, and by 1800 it was the nation's leading producer of women's shoes, a speciality it continued. Lynn was also a center for innovation both in materials for shoes (morocco leather was first used in Lynn) and in machinery (nearly all the machines that transformed shoe production were invented or introduced in the town). The community remained among the industry's principal centers, until World War II.[2]

The shoemakers of Lynn have attracted substantial scholarly attention. The long period of craft production of shoes for an extended market and the development of a sophisticated putting-out system have made the shoemakers of Lynn an attractive group for studying the effects of industrialization on skilled craftsmen. The work of Alan Dawley and Paul Faler has focused on the ideology of the craft and the emergence of class consciousness among shoe workers. Neither has looked closely at the actual process of mechanization and how work was changed by the replacement of human skill and strength by machines. Both historians focus intensively on the period from 1840 to 1860 when the putting-out system was reorganized and the first machine, which affected the binding largely done by women, was introduced. Neither Dawley nor Faler follows with the same intensity the course of mechanization and the movement of work from the craftsmen's ten-by-twelve-foot shops to factories. Finally, neither is concerned with the process by which craft skills and, later, mechanical skills were learned. By focusing on the work lives and experiences of Lynn shoemakers, particularly how they learned their craft, a fuller picture of how craft identification developed and how craft consciousness differed from class consciousness will emerge.

This essay will examine the ways in which shoemakers were trained in Lynn, not only as an economic process through which skill was transferred, but also as a social process that passed values and customs to the new generation. The transmission of skill is an important part of the life of a community of artisans. It is the process that insures the survival of the group, its values, traditions, and customs. It is generally a lengthy process because more than manual skill is involved. The initiate learns a complex mix of skills and practices, but also learns to identify himself as a practitioner of the craft. He is not just someone who makes shoes; he becomes a shoemaker, someone whose identity is defined by what he does. It is the central event in the development of craft consciousness. It is very significant that training began at, or just before, puberty and ended shortly before marriage. The process of training was part of the transition to adulthood and a preparation for fully participating in the community. The shoemaker's hand skill was the essential element underlying the way of life of Lynn's skilled artisans. There were few other economic opportunities in Lynn and hardly any that offered the prestige and independence of shoemaking. Transmission of this skill was not only essential to the continuation of the town's economy but was essential to guarantee the individual's place and preserve the family's status. In examining the training of shoemakers we are also examining the process through which youths became adults.

There is a good deal of information about the training of boys to be shoemakers in several autobiographies and diaries and a large number of obituaries that have come down to us from the handicraft era. On December 22, 1817, Joseph Lye, a cordwainer in Lynn, noted in his diary, "This day I began to learn my brother Robert to make shoes."[3] Joseph was twenty-five years old and, since his father's death, the oldest male of his family.[4] It was his duty to teach his fourteen-year-old brother, just as his father had taught him. While Joseph Lye's diary is a relatively rare document of artisan life, his terse entry reveals a common pattern. Both the age at which training began and the central role of kin are repeated time after time in the career patterns of shoemakers, as recounted in their obituaries. John Bassett Alley, for example, was apprenticed at fourteen-and-a-half, and a "jour" (journeyman) at twenty. His story is similar to those of other boys, who left school to learn the shoemaker's art.[5]

These accounts are also valuable because they frequently mention in whose shop, or under whose direction, the man had learned his craft. While formal apprenticeship is occasionally mentioned, it was usually reserved for young men who were new to the community and did not have kin already in the trade.[6] Jacob Meek Lewis was, in many ways, typical of his generation. His obituary notes that he "left [Lynn Academy] to learn the trade of a shoemaker in his father's ten-by-twelve shoemaker's shop, according to the custom of those times [late 1830s]".[7] As late as the 1850s, it was still common for young boys like Luther Johnson and George A. Breed, after completing a town school education, to enter their father's "ten-footer" to learn the entire process of making a shoe by hand.[8]

If there was no kinsman to take up the training of a young man, as happened when a father died before his oldest son was ready to begin his training, the family was still an important medium of vocational guidance. In his autobiography, William Stone describes how he chose where to learn his trade. "For twenty-six years prior to 1840, my grandfather made shoes for Micajah C. Pratt, and my grandmother bound shoes for him the same length of time. . . In 1854, when I left school, it was natural that I should go into this shop and learn to make shoes."[9]

Quantitative evidence of occupational choice confirms the impression gleaned from obituaries and diaries. The 1850 census for Lynn reveals that 87.5 percent of working sons who lived at home followed their fathers' craft (see Table 1). Among no group was this relationship stronger than among cordwainers.

The first recorded occupation of those young men who were the sons of cordwainers in a sample from the 1850 census, particularly of those not yet employed that year, was taken from Lynn city directories. The occupations of nearly eighty sons were identified. The overwhelming majority (79.5 percent) of employed sons of cordwainers followed their fathers into that industry, even in the 1860s, when mechanization was beginning to change the work environment.

The three types of data examined, then, are all consistent in their emphasis. The family was a strong factor in young men's choice of a career through the 1860s. They learned their craft, in most cases, from their fathers or other male relatives. In households headed by a cordwainer, nearly every employed son was employed in that trade, or subsequently entered it as his first job.[10]

What did these young men do during the five or six years they spent as the "boy" in a ten-footer learning "the gentle craft"? Even though there are no detailed accounts of day-to-day activities, there are a number of general descriptions from which we can reconstruct both the duties of the trainee and the steps through which he learned how to make shoes. Younger boys, just beginning the long learning process, often served as errand runners. One of the boys' first responsibilities was to arrive early, especially during the winter, to start the fire in the shop stove, and to set out candles. Preparing wax for the thread used in sewing shoes was the first job related to the craft they were learning. Shoemaker's wax was made from black pitch, a quarter part rosin, and "as much oil as the season requires."[11] The mixture had to be heated in an earthen or iron pot over a slow fire and the ingredients mixed thoroughly together. The whole mass was poured into a tub of cold water (every shop had a tub which was also used to

Table 1. Occupation of Employed Sons by Occupation of Head of Household, Lynn, 1850

Occupation of Son

Occupation of Head	Professional or Proprietor (15)		Skilled Trade (6)		Cordwainer (49)		Shoe-Related (2)		Fisherman/Seaman (8)	
	No.	Percent	No.	Percent	No.	Percent	No.	Percent	No.	Percent
Professional or Proprietor	7	58.3	1	8.3	3	25.0	0	0.0	1	8.3
Skilled Trade	2	22.2	2	22.2	4	44.4	0	0.0	1	11.1
Cordwainer/ Shoemaker	3	7.5	2	5.0	35	87.5	0	0.0	0	0.0
Shoe-Related Industry	0	0.0	0	0.0	2	50.0	2	50.0	0	0.0
Fisherman/ Seaman	1	8.3	1	8.3	5	41.7	0	0.0	5	41.7
None	2	66.7	0	0.0	0	0.0	0	0.0	1	33.3

N = 80   (There were 236 sons without occupations.)

Source: Manuscript Census of Population, 1850; Lynn City Directories, 1832-1868.

Table 2. First Recorded Occupation,
Sons of Cordwainers in the Lynn 1850 Census Sample

Shoemaker	62	Fish Peddler	1
Clerk	5	Laborer	1
Printer	2	Accountant	1
Mason	1	Teamster	1
Carpenter	1	Minister	1
Bank Teller	1	U.S. Army	1

Source: Manuscript Census of Population, 1850;
Lynn City Directories, 1832-1868.

soak sole leather) and then kneaded by hand, much like taffy, until it attained the proper consistency.

Between errands, the boys watched and listened as the men worked. Gradually, they might be asked to help hold a piece of work and then to do a few stitches, or to wax a thread and attach the bristle. During the years of their apprenticeship, the boys became familiar with the tools in the shoemakers' kit—the awl, pliers, various knives and skivers, strops, and shoulder stick, learning what each could and couldn't do. He learned to last a shoe, one of the most important and difficult tasks, pulling and tacking the bound upper to a last. He learned to stitch on a sole with tight, well-spaced stitches, and to trim the soles and finish the shoe. When the crew felt he was ready, the youth made his first pair, putting together all the knowledge he had been accumulating and practicing. When he was finished, the pair would be passed around the shop with each jour examining it closely, checking the stitchwork and finally bending the sole to see how tightly it had been sewn—looking for a gap, called a "smile," the sign of poor workmanship. If the shoe held up to all this testing, the young man was ready to begin his career as a jour, with his own "berth" in a ten-footer.

This transition was generally accomplished by age twenty, although men as young as 16 are referred to as "cordwainers" in the manuscript census schedules. This raises a question about the point at which young men were considered members of the craft. If the answers they gave to the census takers are one measure of this, identification as a member of the gentle craft began some time before one had fully mastered the art. Indeed, while learning to make a shoe was part of the transition to adulthood, completing the learning process was not immediately followed by embarking on an independent life, either by leaving home or by marriage. These few years between the average age at which young men finished learning their craft and the average age at marriage are intriguing because of the close connection in Lynn between family and work. These sons almost all remained at home, living, and perhaps working, with their fathers. Unfortunately, the sources that have survived tell us little about this stage in craftsmen's lives.

His training prepared the young man to make an entire shoe by hand. This full training was considered very important, because some bosses in the 1840s were trying to break down the general level of skill by training apprentices in just one aspect of the craft, or in making only one style of shoe. *The Awl*, a short-lived newspaper published by the Mutual Benefit Society of the Journeyman Cordwainers of Lynn, attacked this practice in an editorial in its first issue: "This society intends to do away, if possible, with that injurious practice of taking apprentices for a few weeks or months, and learning them to make one kind of shoe, or what is called a shoe, and thereby multiplying poor workmen, and filling our market with miserable goods."[12]

Several career accounts suggest that this effort by Lynn artisans was largely successful. Micajah Newhall Goodridge graduated from Lynn High School in 1855, at age fifteen, and "learned the shoemaker's trade which then meant to learn whatever pertained to a shoe in all its stages."[13] According to Luther Scott Johnson's obituary, "His mastery of the cordwainer's art, which he had learned from his father, who was held in repute as [a] skilled craftsman, gave [him] the practical basis" for success.[14] Young men continued to learn the entire package of skills required to make a variety of styles of shoes until the very eve of the replacement of their skilled hands by machines, which began in 1852.

Binding—stitching together the upper parts of the shoe—was the one part of the process of making a shoe by hand that involved few males. During the formative period of the putting-out system in Lynn, between 1750 and 1800, it had become firmly established as women's work and remained so throughout the nineteenth century. Despite the important role shoe binders played in the industry work force and their large numbers in the community, very little contemporary material about their lot has come down to us. We do know, from general descriptions, that binding was one of the needle skills that young girls in Lynn learned from their mothers as they grew up.[15] Binding was the lot of a great many of Lynn's women—both while they were single and after they were married. Lucy Larcom, poet, factory girl, and briefly a shoe binder, described the binder's life in an often quoted poem, "Hannah Binding Shoes."

> Poor lone Hannah,
> Sitting at the window, binding shoes
> Faded, wrinkled
> Sitting, stitching, in a mournful muse.
> Bright-eyed beauty once was she,
> When the bloom was on the tree:
> Spring and Winter
> Hannah's at the window, binding shoes
>
> Twenty winters
> Bleach and tear the ragged shore she views.
> Twenty seasons:
> Never one has brought her any news.
> Still her dim eyes silently
> Chase the white sails o'er the sea:
> Hopeless, faithful
> Hannah's at the window, binding shoes.

Recently, Mary Blewett has uncovered the diary of a young woman who bound shoes in Beverly, Massachusetts, between 1849 and 1851.[16] Sarah Trask's experience closely paralleled that of Lucy Larcom's "Hannah." A young, unmarried woman, Trask bound shoes to eke out a living while she waited for her true love to return from a long sea voyage. More than any other source, Trask's diary reveals the day-to-day work regimen of the binder.

The diary opens on January 15, 1849, with Luther Woodberry's (Sarah's intended) departure for Boston to meet his ship. Ten days later, Sarah, after a friend showed her how to bind shoes, writes, "I will try and see what I can do, for I cannot afford to make a coat for, 33, Cts. . . if I can get anything else to do."[17] Sarah Trask was familiar with sewing as part of a pulling-out system, for her binding was an alternative way to use the same skills at, perhaps, higher wages. Interspersed in her diary with local gossip, concern for her friends at sea, and worry about her own future, are details about her binding, e.g., how many pairs she had managed to get done on a particular day. On February 20 she counted the stitches on one shoe, a size 5, and broke the total down by each part. This one shoe took 719 stitches to bind (a good day's work would be four or five *pairs*!)

Several times the diary mentions friends visiting with their work; an indication that binders could work together, rather than in isolation. More than once she records, after such a session, that "we did not [do] so much work as we ought to." Another practice referred to was a mutual assistance network through which individuals, such as Sarah, would complete batches of shoes for friends who had become ill or fallen behind. Sarah Trask abandoned both her diary and shoe binding in 1851 when she learned of Luther Woodberry's death at sea. While her experience was different in several ways from that of most shoe binders, her record shows us some important things about binding. That needle skills involved in sewing clothes could be readily adapted to binding is perhaps the most important. For many women this adaptation was not temporary, as for Sarah Trask, but continued throughout their lives.

For both young men and young women, training had taken place in a particular environment at a very important time in their lives. Learning to make or bind shoes was nearly inseparable from developing into a man or a woman. Skill was acquired from the parent of the same sex, or a close relative. It was a long process that was a natural part of growing up. Entry into the craft was the equivalent of entry into adulthood. Nearly all members of the craft had gone through the same training at the same formative time in their lives. Their adult identity and their identification with their craft were the tightly integrated base that supported the rituals of craft and fueled their resistance to changes in work customs that threatened the world they had constructed, a world in which work and family, learning and growing, were highly integrated.

The introduction of machinery and the factory system into Lynn between 1852 and 1879 had profound effects on training in the shoe industry and the role the family played in the process. The number of machines that replaced the skill of the cordwainer was impressive. Beginning with rolling machines, to prepare the various leathers, and die cutters, to cut out the pieces that would become shoes, they included stitching machines for the uppers and several types of stitchers for attaching soles. Finishing a pair of shoes also involved heel setters, edge trimmers and polishers, eyelet setters, to name only a few. By 1885, when Jan Earnst Matzelizer's lasting machine was successfully factory-tested, more than two hundred separate machines were used to make a single pair of shoes. During this relatively brief period, the nature of work and its organization changed almost completely. The time-honored skills of the cordwainer were replaced by an array of machines. The relationship of the shoemaker and the binder to their work changed, as did their ability to pass along a marketable skill to their sons and daughters.

An important but easily overlooked aspect of the process of mechanization was the centralizing role of Gordon McKay and his shoe machinery firm, The McKay Association. McKay not only controlled the key patents, but offered manufacturers a growing variety of machines, assistance in designing their factories, repair and maintenance of the machinery, and most important, instructors to train their workforce; all for a small royalty per pair. This package made the machinery attractive and affordable, and contributed to the speed with which it drove out hand labor from industrial production.

These changes affected the whole relationship between the family and work, but no aspect more completely than the transmission of skills. First, of course, the machines made hand skills totally irrelevant to the job of producing shoes. In testimony before the Massachusetts Bureau of Labor Statistics, many shoemakers and manufacturers described the process of mechanization and its destructive impact on Lynn's (and other shoe towns') way of life.[18] According to all accounts, McKay's representatives could train the entire work force of a factory in two days. The key function of training was removed from the family and taken over by the manufacturers of shoe machinery. In 1919, the Lynn Chamber of Commerce set up a trade school to train machine operatives for the city's shoe industry. The various manufacturers supported the school financially and it was free to all Lynn residents. In the space of two generations, the responsibility for training young people for full participation in the city's key industry had passed from the family to the public domain. At the same time, the nature of that training changed from initiation into a skilled craft to training in machine operation.

Lynn shoe manufacturers and the local press greeted mechanization with satisfaction. Lynn manufacturers were generally among the first in the nation to introduce new machines into production. The Lynn *Reporter* described the "wonderful revolution" that was transforming the city's largest industry in glowing terms: "This was the beginning to our flourishing city. . . [Mechanization] is the only system that can be made available for its successful application in the future. . . Old things are passing away, and all things are becoming new."[19] One of the new aspects of the trade was greater uniformity in the products. Lack of uniformity had long been a problem and seemed an unavoidable part of the hand methods of cordwainers. An

1858 shoe industry annual placed the blame squarely on the shoemakers' training.

> Most shoe manufacturers and ordinary village shoemakers learn their trades from their fathers, and the knowledge has been handed down from generation to generation, without change or improvement, and shoes are made to *fit* lasts rather than the feet which are to wear them.[20]

The binders were the first group to shift from hand work, done in the home as part of a putting-out system, to machine work done in a factory. Lynn shoe manufacturers were quick to follow the lead of John Wooldridge in introducing the machine stitcher developed by John B. Nichols in the 1850s. For a time the tradition of home work existed side by side with the emerging stitching shops, as entrepreneurs placed machines in the homes of their binders. The household budget surveys of 1875 show that some families purchased sewing machines. Thus, one budget refers to the family's sewing machine, "on which wife earned $100."[21] In 1912, Fred Gannon noted that "some men of shoe cities recall that when they were boys it was their task to turn the wheel of the sewing machine after school while mother stitched shoes on it."[22]

Home work on stitching machines, however, was never more than a small part of the shoe binding operations of the industry, and steadily gave way to work done under closer supervision in the factory. Training became the responsibility of the manufacturer and was frequently provided by the machinery maker as an inducement to install its set of machines. In 1896, two letters were published in the shoe industry periodical, *Superintendent and Foreman*, which describe two forms of training that had developed in the industry.

The first article recounts the experience of a young woman in a "school" that taught stitching:

> "Girls Taught to Stitch Boots and Shoes": Thus reads a sign on the door of a building in one of the main thoroughfares in the City of L —— . I read the sign, interviewed she who owned it, and paid five dollars with the understanding that I should be thoroughly taught all the different parts of shoemaking that come within the limits of the stitching room.[23]

Over the next two weeks, she was taught several stitching operations: stitching linings, staying, tip-stitching, topstitching, cording button holes, closing on a Wheeler & Wilson machine, and vamping. At the end of two weeks, she was "informed by Mrs. —— that that was the time a learner was supposed to remain." She had not been taught closing-on, an important stitching operation, and was then told that it was not taught. Her letter ends with the complaint that, having lost five dollars and two weeks' time, she cannot get work as an experienced stitcher because her training was so limited.[24]

This letter prompted a second in which a stitcher recounts "how I learned to stitch in the same city":

> I lived in another state and knew nothing about shoemaking. I wrote to a firm at L —— . . . I asked for a chance to learn. . . I would be given a chance. . . I was taken in charge by the foreman. I was not even used to a sewing machine, but was given some pieces of leather and set work. . . The next day I commenced front staying. . .
>
> I never gave time but that first day, and received the pay for my first case. After working at that nearly two years, in the dull time picking up other small parts, one of the firms asked me to learn vamping when I had any waiting time. I tried and had very little trouble—. . .
>
> On all these things I received the money for every case, and never gave anything to learn. I worked there ten years. If any girl wants to learn to stitch, I advise her to apply to some good firm and learn in a thorough manner. . .[25]

Within a generation, young women had lost the ability to readily transfer to binding the sewing ability they had learned as part of the general "needle skills." Many found themselves in the situation described in the second letter: "I was not even used to a sewing machine." For women, the shoe manufacturers, frequently aided by the machinery manufacturers, provided the requisite training.

The pattern of women's work after mechanization is not very different from that of other industries—the rapid adoption of a newly-developed machine that replaced a hand operation, centralization of work under more immediate supervision by the manufacturer, and finally transfer of control over access to economically-useful skills from the craft group to the manufacturers. The manufacturers came to control not only access to markets and raw materials, as they had before mechanization, but tools, the work place, and access to skill. The male cordwainers followed their less-skilled wives, daughters, and sisters into the factory within a very few years, when Gordon McKay and his associates had perfected a stitching machine for soles originally developed by Lyman Blake.

The adaptation of McKay's machine was speeded by two factors—the Civil War, which greatly increased the demand for shoes, and McKay's royalty system for marketing. The Blake and McKay stitching machine rapidly led to the introduction of a factory system with different parts of the process of making a shoe segregated into specific areas within the factory and performed by different groups of workers.

The factory was an inhospitable environment for the traditional practices of the gentle craft. It differed in many ways, some subtle and others readily apparent, from the ten-footer. The camaraderie of the old system, with its close contact with family and fellow worker, could not be reproduced among a large factory work force, divided into functional rooms, working by the clock and the rule book, and cut off from family and community during work hours.

The introduction of the factory system changed the world of work in a number of ways that had significant impact on the family. One of the most immediate was the separation of the home and the work place. The simple fact of spatial proximity had been of great importance. Because of its location near homes of workers, the ten-footer played a key part in the socialization of the children of shoemakers. Work was not something done far away from home, but was something familiar to children as they grew up. They could literally move in and out of the work place from an early age. For women, shoe work had been done in the home. Before the 1830s women generally bound the shoes made by their own men. Even after the manufacturers had broken this pattern by putting out binding, the binders still worked at home, near their many other responsibilities. When binding entered a separate building (in the 1850s a stitching shop, and in the 1860s a factory), married women were largely replaced in the work force by young unmarried women, known as "factory girls," to distinguish them from the home-work binders. The "full-time" status of factory work and its spatial separation from the other responsibilities of married women were largely responsible for their withdrawal from the work force, which was not reversed until after 1910, by which time the predominantly native-born workers of the nineteenth century had given way to immigrants.[26]

The family in Lynn did not become irrelevant following the mechanization of the city's largest industry, but its role became more circumscribed. The broad contours of this transformation are consistent with the general outlines of the model of structural differentiation developed by Talcott Parsons and applied to the British cotton textiles industry by Neil Smelser.[27] In the 1850s, husband, wife, and their children had their lives ordered by the demand and rhythms of work. Children passed into the trade as part of growing up. Learning to make a proper pair of shoes was just one part—a very important part, to be sure—of growing up in Lynn. The work practices of the hand craft were highly traditional—home-based married women and unmarried girls working in subordination to the male family head, who dealt with the outside world. As machines replaced these hand skills, this system rapidly broke down. Married women left the work force as the work place moved away from the home.

As all members of the family came to deal directly with their employers, a great variety of alternative choices about work became possible. The head of the family lost economic power because the machines that had replaced his skill diluted his role as a transmitter of craft skills. Since the employer now controlled the tools and access to them, training became his responsibility and helped cement his control over work. The family remained a key part of individuals' lives, the unit around which much of life revolved, but it was no longer as involved in all aspects of its members' lives as it once had been.

Unfortunately, it is difficult to get at the emotional aspects of family life historically. We know, for example, that Joseph Lye "learned" his younger brother Robert "to make shoes" and that at the time Joseph was head of his family. In conjunction with an array of other data, that helps us to understand both the structure and function of the artisan family in Lynn. But it tells us nothing of how either party looked on their relationship. Who decided that Robert would learn his brother's (and father's) craft? Was Joseph anxious to teach his brother, as his father had taught him, or was this an unpleasant duty that had to be done? There is no way to know, and little basis for any sort of judgment at all. Joseph's laconic style might be significant, if it were not common in his and many other diaries.

The family has proven to be a very tenacious institution. Despite periodic predictions of its imminent demise, it retains the same essential structure today that it had many hundred of years ago. In Lynn, mechanization did not alter the structure of the family in any significant way. It did, however, profoundly alter the role the family played in the lives of its members, especially in the relationship between the family and work.

This relationship was not destroyed by the introduction of the factory system. But it was changed. As work was removed from the household, the role of the father lost much of its significance. He was no longer the one who taught his sons their trade and who dealt with the merchant for the whole family. Even if he and his sons worked together in the factory, his lengthy experience was of little if any advantage and not a source of knowledge his sons might seek to draw on.

Most important, training became truncated and segregated. Boys and girls were no longer indoctrinated into the craft as part of the natural process of growing up. After the introduction of machinery and factory discipline, work was one segment of multifaceted lives. Those who seek to understand the rapid demise of craft consciousness and the very slow emergence of class consciousness among American industrial workers would do well to examine carefully the paths men and women followed to the workshops.

Industrial Ecology and the Labor Process: The Redefinition of Craft in New England Textile Machinery Shops, 1820-1860

THOMAS E. LEARY

The history of working people in the United States is inseparable from the larger history of capitalism. Studies focusing on the work place must therefore consider two issues in the development of capitalism and its specific forms of social inequality: how the products of human labor are appropriated and the quality of control over the work processes that transform the raw materials of nature into useful objects.[1]

One consequence of industrial capitalism has been a dramatic shift in the social relations of power over these issues concerning production, but that change did not proceed uniformly. Prior to the mid-eighteenth century in England, for example, the operations of merchants had been confined principally to the sphere of exchange. Even where commodities were produced through orchestrating outwork or subdividing handicrafts, it was still unusual for capitalists to exercise direct control over the details of daily work. During the decades after 1750, though, some manufacturers did begin to intervene in the actual process of production. Armed with new forms of technology and new tactics for disciplining labor, they invaded the territory of artisans and household producers, and commenced capturing producers' traditional control over work processes. The development represented a step in capital accumulation that went beyond juridical appropriation, the movement to establish legal title over the apparatus of production or the products themselves. In cotton spinning mills, the most advanced sector of early industrial capitalism, workers on both sides of the Atlantic experienced the alienated labor of the industrial revolu-

tion: production divorced from the household; manufacture centralized around inanimate power sources; work rationalized and regulated by the actions of machines; and work rules imposed by the owners
of those machines.

However, not all new forms of industrial production followed the
pattern foreshadowed by the dark, Satanic mills of England. In
branches of the metal trades many early versions of the capitalist labor
process featured a combined and uneven development of both industrial and handicraft practices.[2] In trades where the diffusion of fully-
mechanized technology and rationalized hierarchy in the work place
was slow and piecemeal, industrial capitalists were unable initially to
establish hegemony over the shop floor. Worker resistance could then
take the form of a contest over the management of production as well
as the level of wages. Rather than deskilling the labor force as a
whole, new techniques of production and work organization in metalworking allowed clusters of skilled workers to maintain some degree
of individual or collective control over aspects of the manufacturing
process. This situation was comparable in some respects to the artisanal production that had preceded industrialization, even though
skilled industrial workers did not control the sale or disposition of the
products they made.[3] Within this mosaic of uneven development,
changes in the meaning of "skill" were quite specific to particular
metal trades, and the work experiences of separate generations could
be quite distinct. Insofar as social formations and class composition
were modulated by relationships among owners, supervisors, and
workers at the point of production, empirical studies of the industrial
labor process can aid in formulating more accurate periodizing of
comparative capitalist development, as well as in understanding the
influence of everyday work routines on the actions and outlooks of
craftsmen and operatives during this transitional phase.

Around 1790 artisans—both British immigrants and native Americans—had begun constructing early U.S. textile machinery.[4] Many of
these artificers had transferred to their adopted trade from such crafts
as blacksmithing, carpentry, or clockmaking, as well as from noncom-
mercial agriculture, but the unprecedented nature of the work necessary to construct these innovations watered down the influence of
established custom. Still, this background of craft production was
likely to have included some approximation of control over both product and work process by virtue of integrated mental and manual
skills.[5] The generation of autonomous artisans and autochthonous
yeoman/mechanics recruited between 1790 and 1810 worked chiefly in

scattered shops located on the premises of the mills themselves. The workmen represented trades whose common techniques and relations of production initially were not predicated on the mechanized sequence of operations and rationalized wage labor then being introduced into the spinning factories.[6] However, the expansion of manufacturers' demand for machinery, especially between 1807 and 1815, soon tested the technical and organizational limits of handicraft practice and decentralized production.[7] Within a nascent market economy some entrepreneurially-minded mechanics began emerging from the cocoon of artisan culture and entering the web of capitalist relations. They transmuted their workshops into specialized facilities for producing textile machinery, but this metamorphosis did not occur overnight. David Wilkinson (1771-1852) of Pawtucket, Rhode Island, for example, had helped Samuel Slater make the first workable set of Arkwright machines in this country during 1790. About 1810 Wilkinson fathered a pioneer cotton machinery shop which had developed within the womb of his family's existing artisan ironworking business and still retained an umbilical link to those practices and attitudes. The shop of Nathan J. Sweetland, another Pawtucket mechanic who had begun making textile machinery, continued to undertake standard blacksmith work during the War of 1812.[8]

Out of such origins the textile-machinery industry was consolidated in several New England communities between the 1820s and the Civil War: Providence and Pawtucket, Rhode Island; Lowell, Massachusetts, and its principal clones (Chicopee and Lawrence, Massachusetts; Manchester, New Hampshire; Saco, Maine); Fall River and Taunton, Massachusetts; the woolen machinery center of Worcester, Massachusetts, as well as particular plants in locations such as Whitinsville, Newton Upper Falls, and North Andover, Massachusetts.[9] There were differences in the internal structure of this industry caused by geographical constraints (such as availability of water power), level of capitalization and form of ownership, scope of product line, and marketing arrangements, as well as the potential for individual mobility into proprietorship.

Despite these variations the larger machine shops of the period developed a common ecology of production. On the shop floor, machinists used partially-mechanized production techniques where the persistance of critical manual and mental abilities was combined with the uneven introduction of machine tools that could dilute or displace such skills. The daily routines of many workmen were determined by a complex set of internal labor markets and decentralized authority

relations known as "inside contracting," a form of industrial organization distinct from and incompatible with the managerial bureaucra-
cies through which capital would later attempt to extend its control
over the production process. Within antebellum shops, textile machinists cultivated a hierarchy of mixed skills, and their occupational
culture included a contradictory amalgam: partial autonomy reminis-
cent of artisanal production, resistant to direct capitalist control, combined with a new form of segmentation and divisions among workers
themselves. By analyzing the process of production through its intertwined components of material culture and social relations, it is possible to reconstruct the ecology of these work places and the everyday
lives of the people who once inhabited them.[10]

I

The material environment of production in a textile machinery business consisted of its buildings, power generation and transmission
systems, materials handling apparatus, machinery and small tools.
Though large workspaces had been exceptional during the first quarter of the nineteenth century, a number of plants with increasingly
standardized layouts that integrated foundry, forge, machining and
fitting operations were constructed by 1860. These complexes were
evidence of capital's growing influence upon the labor process and
graphically expressed the trend away from making textile machinery
by artisan methods in craft-oriented shops. However, the scope and
pace of change in production technology, particularly in metalworking machine tools, was insufficient to impose the kind of increasingly
uniform, mechanized labor discipline possible in vanguard textile
mills. Because of the asymmetric nature of technological change in
this particular trade, the skills of machinists formed a new hierarchy
of combined manual and operative abilities that was distinct from
handicraft practice and yet retained elements of those traditions. This
same lack of uniformity in the material conditions of production also
broke up the work force, leaving possibilities for varying degrees of
limited autonomy in the conduct of daily work routines on the one
hand, while on the other hand forming a basis for segmentation.

When Pawtucket's David Wilkinson had set up his machinery-
making business in 1810, it occupied the first floor of a cotton mill that
measured 71 feet by 34 feet, a structure not dramatically out of scale
with its environs.[11] Mill-based shops of that period could have been
considerably smaller. In 1813-14, machinery for the Troy Cotton &

Woollen Manufactory in Fall River was constructed in a workspace two stories high and 25 by 36 feet, with a 16 by 25 feet blacksmith shop.[12] Wilkinson's business expanded considerably during his first decade of operations, but his activities remained confined to a series of modest workshops along the small power canals branching off the Blackstone River. As of 1823, Wilkinson's properties included a second machine shop (irregularly-shaped, 40-42 feet x 35 feet) and two other structures (one 60 feet x 28-35 feet, the other approximately 50 feet x 25 feet).[13] The size of the workshops at Wilkinson's disposal indicates some continuity with the earlier artisan ironworking operations in Pawtucket, as well as the limited waterpower available there.

During the same year that Wilkinson was operating out of these scattered facilities, the Locks & Canals Company laid the groundwork for a central machine shop in what would become the city of Lowell. By vertically integrating machinery construction with a local energy monopoly over water power and the development of multiple mill sites, substantial Boston investors created a physical environment in which the impact of capital on the work of textile machinists was measurably greater than in the case of Wilkinson's shops. Begun in April of 1823 and completed in 1825, the Locks & Canals shop was similar in size to other first generation Lowell mills. One source gives the shop's dimensions as 154 feet x 50 feet, and an 1850 illustration indicates that the main building rose three and a half stories above the basement with a clerestory monitor in the cross-gable roof, for illuminating the half-story attic.[14] In an effort to integrate operations, a foundry for making iron castings was added to the shop in 1840, bringing molders and other workmen from that branch of the iron trades into proximity with the machinists.[15]

During the two decades preceding the Civil War, substantial additional capacity was laid out: flask shop (1841-42), 38 feet x 32 feet, two stories; No. 2 shop (1846), 172 feet x 65 feet, four stories; No. 3 shop (1846, expanded 1881), original dimensions unknown; foundry warehouse (1846), 104 feet x 53 feet, three stories; No. 4 machine and erecting shop (1851), two parallel buildings, each 160 feet x 72 feet and two stories high, connected by a one-story annex for polishing; heavy machine and turbine shop (1851), 93 feet x 60 feet, one story; pattern storage house (1856), probably 102 feet x 25 feet, two stories.[16] Space within these works had to be allocated among a number of operations besides those related to textile machinery, although the locomotive business which had been undertaken in 1834 was abandoned between 1854-55 and 1861.[17] This elaboration of specialized structures also indicated that the metalworking trades now required in capital goods industries were becoming not only larger but more diverse.

The Lowell machine shop was not the only complex to dwarf the work spaces that had once housed operations such as David Wilkinson's. During the mid-1840s, a watershed period in the industry, a variety of capitalists and master mechanics erected several shops that made use of steam as well as waterpower. Among the most notable for their size, if not their financial success, were: the Essex Company machine shop in Lawrence, with a principal building measuring 404 feet 6 inches x 64 feet 6 inches, and four and one half stories high;[18] William Mason's plant in Taunton, where the main machine shop was 315 feet x 45 feet, part of which was two and another part three stories high, plus attic;[19] John C. Whitin's shop on the Mumford River, between Providence and Worcester, whose main building was 306 feet x 102 feet—unusually wide—with two stories and a basement;[20] and the shop built by James S. Brown in Pawtucket when he vacated the congested waterpower sites such as Wilkinson had used, for which the main building was 360 feet x 60 feet with two stories and attic plus a basement running half its length.[21]

Toward the close of the antebellum period several makers of woolen machinery also invested in new plants, though not on the same scale as the cotton machinery shops. The steam-powered mill that fancy-loom manufacturer George Crompton added to his existing Worcester facilities in 1860 measured 110 feet x 50 feet with three and one-half stories.[22] In North Andover, Davis & Furber extended their 100 foot x 40 foot building on Cochichewick Brook by some thirty feet in 1854, and raised the attic to a full third story in 1857 by lowering the pitch of the roof. On the eve of the Civil War, the company also had under construction a new four-and-one-half-story machine shop, 156 feet x 50 feet.[23]

The size and configuration of these medium- and large-sized textile machinery shops were influenced by the generic limitations of contemporary building technology, with its loadbearing walls and mechanical power transmission systems that consisted of central line shafts with a leather-belt drive to each machine.[24] For these reasons the exterior of a machine shop might superficially resemble a textile mill, although the thermal processes housed in associated foundries and forges required different arrangements.[25] Nonetheless, the increasing dimensions of the plants cited above measured the growth of the industry from its early years as an appendage of the mills, and they reflected the greater role capital now played in shaping the spatial relations of production.

Inside these ever-larger cages erected by the more advanced New England textile machinery companies, common and exotic machine tools were put through their paces by men and boys whose duties called for degrees of judgment and intervention that ranged from minimal to critical. The capital equipment with which these hands worked had already eradicated some manual skills in roughing and finishing the shapes and surfaces of certain components, but most semi-automatic machine tools were not servomechanisms. Manipulating them demanded practical knowledge and physical coordination, attributes that machinists used in exercising some individual or collective control over the labor process as well as for establishing favorable economic bargaining positions.[26]

Other aspects of machinists' work essentially remained handicraft tasks: toolmaking, filing, and fitting demanded dexterity and, in many instances, mental acuity. This dialectic between expiring and emerging skills formed a crucial aspect of the redefinition of craft in the occupations of textile machinists.

During the early history of the metalworking trades, not all manufacturers felt obligated to invest in innovations that would deskill their workmen. John White, Quaker proprietor of a Philadelphia manufactory where wrought-iron screws were cut by hand (c. 1817), doubted that a "labor-saving" attachment to his usual equipment would be beneficial:

> When I hire a workman I hire his brains as well as his hands. They are naturally careless enough and if thee would save their thinking and give part of it to the machine, it would only make them more heedless, and I would be the sufferer. If I were to spend money to adopt thy gimcracks, I would still be obliged to have the man to watch them, to set the tools and keep them sharp and in order, and why not let him do the work? It is better for him than to stand with his hands in his pockets; they would soon be in mine.[27]

By contrast, British and American machine tool builders such as James Nasmyth gradually proved able to devise a series of machine tools that altered the labor process as practiced in the shops of traditionalists such as White. In his *Autobiography*, Nasmyth elucidated his rationale for developing machines with the potential to transfer power over production from labor to capital:

> The irregularity and carelessness of the workmen naturally
> proved very annoying to the employers; but it gave an in-
> creased stimulus to the demand for self-acting machine tools by
> which the untrustworthy efforts of hand-labor might be avoid-
> ed. The machines never got drunk; their hands never shook
> from excess; they were never absent from work; they did not
> strike for wages; they were unfailing in their accuracy and regu-
> larity, while producing the most delicate or ponderous portions
> of mechanical structures.[28]

Nasmyth, having little tolerance for workmen who spurned the
bridle of industrial discipline and the saddle of evangelical morality,
was an untiring propagandist for the virtues of his surrogate iron
children. He saw such offspring of the recent marriage between science and capital as instruments for reorganizing work, with "thinking" now embodied in the tool:

> So completely was the workmen [sic] in attendance on self-
> acting machines relieved from the necessity of labor that many
> of the employers, to keep the men from falling asleep, allowed
> them to attend to other machines within their power of superin-
> tendance. It kept them fully awake.[29]

In this context technological change involved more than the unfolding
of neutral engineering logic. Another dimension of this "progress"
manifested the underlying clash of contending interests at the point
of production.[30]

Nasmyth felt that the key principle in early machine tool development involved substituting the "holding of a tool by means of an iron
hand" for the unsteady hand of the workman himself.[31] This innovation formed the kernel of English tool builder Henry Maudslay's
achievements during the Napoleonic wars and a basis for subsequent
designs by other mechanical engineers. During the first half of the
nineteenth century a series of machine tools was devised to produce
the assorted shapes and surfaces of machinery components: industrial lathes which could turn true cylinders or cut accurate screw
threads; planing machines to produce truly flat plane surfaces; shap-
ers; slotters; drilling and boring machines; gear cutters; and milling
machines which used multiple-tooth rotary cutters rather than the
single-point tools of the lathe and planer to remove metal.[32] The
engineers who designed these tools sought to manufacture more
accurately shaped metal parts in larger quantities than was possible
using only manual techniques; but in doing so they linked technologi-

cal innovation more closely with private ownership of those innovations.

Machine tools were capable of uniform workmanship, but their sequential introduction did not necessarily result in a uniformly de-skilled work force. For example, Maudslay's synthesis of an industrial lathe that incorporated a slide rest eventually resulted in the decline of manual turning techniques which had depended on human eye-hand coordination to regulate the movement of the cutting tool along several axes (longitudinal traverse, cross-feed for depth of cut, elevation of the tool and the angle at which it met the work piece) with only a simple T-rest for support.[33] Hand turning required an art akin to that of a sculptor, but it was not suited to precision work in metal. The rigid grip of the "iron hand" maintained a fixed distance between the point of the cutting tool and the work piece that was better suited to coping with variations in the composition of metal (such as air holes in iron castings) than the more irregular pressure exerted by hand turning.[34]

As with Maudslay in England, David Wilkinson also saw that the hand-held tools and hand-cranked lathes he and others had used in turning the rollers and spindles for Slater's first machines of 1790 would not be adequate for more exact work in metal.[35] Adapting his patented screw-cutting machine of 1798, Wilkinson had, by 1806, built a slide lathe with a weighted three-point rest that may also have been capable of traversing the tool longitudinally without manual activation.[36] Lathes with chain-driven slide rests based on Wilkinson's designs became standard machine shop equipment by the mid-nineteenth century.[37]

Although the talents of artisan hand turners such as those in John White's shop were rendered obsolete, the machinists who now operated these general-purpose industrial lathes still performed rather complex tasks that required judgment and skill in setting up different types of work and in adjusting speeds and feeds. On the slide rest, for example, the machinist would have to turn thumb screws in order to adjust both the cross-feed and the vertical elevating screw. In an 1852 diary entry, journeyman machinist George Clark explained how he had to retract and advance the cutting tool adroitly when turning the slightly crowned surfaces on pulleys that would allow driving belts to ride without slippage:

> They are generally turned rounding by easing off the tool as it approaches the center and advancing it occasionally after pass-

ing the point, thus leaving the face of the pulley from ⅛ to ¹⁄₃₂
inch rounding.[38]

He was referring to slight cross-feed adjustments that he had to ex-
ecute at precisely the right moments.

Manual and mechanized methods for making textile machinery
parts and assembling the final product coexisted for a number of
years. After the appearance of Wilkinson's lathe, fully a generation
elapsed before machines capable of producing place surfaces came
into use.[39] However, judging by nomenclature, a number of special-
purpose tools for cutting particular metal shapes were actively used
in the larger textile machinery shops of the 1840s and 1850s.[40] For
example, even during the early days of the trade in Pawtucket, both
millwright Sylvanus Brown and English machinist-néejoiner John
Blackburn tried to improve upon the hand methods for turning and
fluting the drawing rollers used on the Arkwright-style machinery.[41]
Some of the earliest equipment acquired (c. 1814-1817) by the Waltham machine shop of the Boston Manufacturing Company was devoted to turning and fluting such drawing rollers.[42] This class of
specialized machinery marked the appearance of capital-intensive solutions to the demands of increased production; the same invest-
ments could also facilitate introduction of less-comprehensively
skilled workers to tend the machines.

By 1855 the operations on drawing rolls that had originally been
done by hand turning and filing could be parcelled out among a series
of specialized machines. The Lawrence machine shop included a "6-
inch engine lathe: double bed with 6 heads for turning top rollers and
fluted rollers for spinning frames," a "Slabbing engine: 4-foot bed for
squaring ends of fluted rollers and milling nuts," a "fluting engine:
has centers for fluting 3 rollers at once with self-acting dividing index," and a "Machine for filing fluted rollers: two heads."[43] Work on
special-purpose machines tended to be more repetitive than running
a versatile tool such as the industrial lathe. One man restricted to
tending six self-acting spindle-bushing drills in a single frame had
little opportunity to develop well-rounded competence.[44] The prolif-
eration of such equipment began to alter both the distribution of skills
in a machine shop's work force and the balance of power between
labor and capital on the shop floor, by reducing the proportion of
machinists who possessed the blend of mental and manual ability that
earlier generations of artisans had cultivated.

Even with the advent of mechanically-sophisticated capital goods, antebellum textile machinists were neither uniformly nor completely deskilled. The partially-developed logic of many semi-automatic tools continued to require some degree of interaction between operative and mechanism. As in John White's day, cutting tools still had to be sharpened and set, and in textile machinery shops toolmaking ordinarily was not centralized within an elite department. Even the cybernetically-inclined Nasmyth recognized that "the quality as well as the quantity of work producable from turning lathes and planing machines, entirely depends upon the skill of the operator in giving to his tools the proper from."[45] Since machine tools might be incapable of finishing products to exactly the required dimensions, hand skill at the workbench could remain an important ingredient in daily shop practice. Future sculptor John Rogers noted this during his tenure at the Amoskeag shop in the early 1850s. "All the finished work has to be turned in the engines, as you saw me doing, then filed and polished in the lathes, but there are nice joints to fit and a great deal of work which has to be filed in the vice."[46] For special jobs, some skillful mechanics were capable of making jigs, fixtures, and templates that would later fill the drawers of their personal tool chests.[47] Machinists usually had to be able to use gauges and measuring devices for checking the dimensions of their work. The proper use of these metrological instruments depended upon the machinist's optical faculties.[48]

Capital had molded the material environment of the mid-nineteenth century machine shop according to its own imperatives. Nevertheless, because portions of the work force possessed skills that could not readily be replaced, they retained a significant role in determining how they carried out their daily work. Workers' control over daily output could, in turn, hamstring the rate of capital accumulation in textile machinery companies. Proprietors who sought to enlist technological innovation as an instrument of work-place control often found that its very nature preserved partial autonomy along with fostering segmentation by skill level. As master mechanic and journeyman became capitalist and laborer, the tenuous balance of power among maturing interests in this industry also grew, in part out of the complex organization of production in these shops, a topic which we shall now trace.

II

No aspect of the labor process in New England textile machinery shops has occasioned more comment from historians than "inside contracting" and the related phenomenon of "job work."[49] These peculiar institutions melded fragmented intramural bargaining relationships with a decentralized structure of authority over production, and they touched aspects of contemporary class dynamics as well. E.J. Hobsbawm has pointed out that early industrial capitalism did not expand solely by subordinating larger aggregations of workers directly under factory masters.[50] The burgeoning capital goods metalworking industries manufactured a range of complex products that required the input of skilled workmen, but the market for their commodities fluctuated sharply.[51] To avoid carrying high overhead costs or scratching up large amounts of circulating capital, proprietors often delegated the responsibility for mobilizing a labor force and organizing the details of production to an intermediate layer of their skilled craftsmen. This expedient sometimes gave a segment of workers the equivalent of an entrepreneurial profit motive in their transactions with other hands. Filtering production through a stratum of privileged operatives gave them directorial control over substantial portions of the labor process in their own baliwicks. Although not all work in any given shop was put out under contract, such arrangements flourished in the antebellum metalworking and machinery shops of the Atlantic states, including those hothouses of mass production methods, the federal armories.[52]

Inside contracting and job work were not synonomous. Journeyman machinist George Clark recorded a typical example of an inside contract in one of his diary entries:

> Luther commenced working by the job Jan. 1st. . . His job consists of two 14-foot gear wheels made in ten segments each, one 20-foot gear in 12 segments, and 8 roll stands with nuts and screws complete. The job is to be completed by the first of April and the price is to be $1,000. Evens, Doolittle Weaver, a boy, and one or two Irishmen are employed by Jim on his job.[53]

In this instance, Luther, the contractor, was a shop workman who had reached an agreement with the proprietor to make this batch of products for a stipulated price that included his own daily rate of pay, the wages of his several helpers, and (theoretically) a surplus over whatever costs he incurred that would represent his "profit" on the job. Contractors enjoyed substantial latitude in planning and directing how work would be carried out on their jobs; they likewise wielded disciplinary authority over the assorted journeymen, apprentices, and laborers who comprised their task forces, an authority which may have been tempered by interpersonal relationships within the relatively small work groups.

Job work resembled inside contracting in that both were based on payment for commodities produced rather than for length of time worked. However, not all job work involved the complex bargaining and authority relationships that were part of contracting. A month after describing Luther's contract, Clark recorded that he himself

> took a job of 6 car wheel chills to turn and to fit up the flask, which is of cast iron pinned upon the chill on one side and to be fastened with four ⅝ screws on the other, subsequently 2 more chills have been added to the lot, for all of which I am to receive $25.33.[54]

Since he was able to complete the chills in five and one half days, Clark earned the equivalent of $4.60 per day—considerably in excess of the $2.00 he ordinarily was paid on his straight daily time rate.[55] This "job" was much smaller than Luther's in terms of its dollar value, and Clark handled the work without paying or supervising assistants. On these smaller jobs a journeyman such as Clark would have retained a degree of discretion in his approach to the machining and fitting tasks at hand that would not have been present in subdivided repetitive work. The daily labor process in larger shops making textile machinery and other products was a labyrinth of these typical forms of hierarchical inside contracting and autonomous job work, as well as the more regimented repetition work and common labor also associated with nineteenth-century factory organization.

Inside contracting reflected the weakness—and, in some respects, the absence—of the centralized controls over production that capitalists would later consolidate by conscripting cost accountants and professional engineers into their service, and by borrowing such authoritarian tactics as line-and-staff management from the military bureaucracy.[56] The origins of contracting in textile machinery lay in the formative years, when skilled mechanics had equipped early textile factories out of mill-based or independent machine shops, organizing and executing the manufacture of textile machinery on the basis of their familiarity with the details of the entire process, and making use of whatever physical facilities and helpers were available or necessary.[57] When these *ad hoc* arrangements were transplanted into larger works, they tended to become more specialized and routinized into quasi-departmental functions where contractors or jobbers still retained practical power in the production process. In the large Lowell shop of the 1820s, a period when "much of the work was given out to the most skillful and reliable machinist," some men continued to be responsible for the production of entire machines, while others performed more specialized tasks on components such as loom woodwork or gearing.[58] On both divided and undivided jobs, control over the work process remained lodged in the heads and hands of particular machinists.

The practice of inside contracting remained in vogue because it synchronized the material interests of entrepreneurs and certain workmen. First, it permitted textile machinery companies to establish their direct labor costs before quoting customer prices on finished products, a rudimentary form of cost accounting to guide entrepreneurs in anticipating their profit margins.[59] Second, the conventional wisdom of the time held that contracting elicited latent innovative impulses.[60] Should a contractor devise improved machinery or methods that raised output or lowered unit costs on his particular jobs, then the difference between the money saved and the stipulated contract price would benefit the contractor, not the company. However, this situation was also fraught with potential for the contractor to profit in an entrepreneurial sense through exploiting the other members of his work group by manipulating the wages paid for their labor. The trade unions formed by both British and American machinists eventually opposed such arrangements because they appealed to individual accumulation at the expense of craft solidarity.[61]

The inside contractor was the platypus of Victorian industry: part skilled craftsman, part project manager, part entrepreneur. He can be seen as a comprador poised between a shop's actual proprietors and a particular group of workers, as the direct purchaser of their labor power; he was also a bulwark against proprietors' efforts to intervene more actively in the affairs of his particular fiefdom. The cleavage along economic lines is best seen through income differentials. Because of gradations in age and skill as well as the potential for coexploitation, contractor's earnings often substantially exceeded those of other machinists, although the discrepancies may not have been as large as Kirk Boott indicated when he remarked that at the Lowell machine shop of the 1830s daily wages averaged about ninety cents, "but as a large portion of the work is by contract, and done by the apprentices, many [contractors] earn $4-6 per day."[62] In another more representative case, during the year 1851 Nathaniel W. Everett performed $848.18's worth of both job and day work covering 230 and three-quarters days for the Pettee textile machinery shop in Newton

Upper Falls, which was the equivalent of $3.68 per day. He paid the three hands who worked with him during the year a total of $175.51 for 163 and three-eighths days' labor, at rates between 78¢ and $1.50 per day. If their wages were deducted from Everett's total earnings, then he earned the equivalent of $2.92 per day.[63].

Alongside these income differentials, however, a version of artisan craft control traditions still persisted on the shop floor where decentralization of authority was endemic. Skilled craftsmen working with journeymen and apprentices of their choosing organized the daily routines of production and exercised a degree of self-management by virtue of their knowledge of complex machine tools and production techniques. The contradictory nature of inside contracting in effect allowed some machinists to purvey the products of their labor rather than selling only their labor power, even as contracting also introduced market relationships into the intramural transactions between two different categories of workers.

On the eve of the Civil War capitalist intervention to facilitate accumulation and control over production was increasing, but remained incomplete. At the Davis & Furber woolen machinery shop in North Andover, a series of labor cost calculations made during 1860-61 revealed the extent to which the operations necessary to produce particular machines had been subdivided and evaluated by a company whose major proprietor was striving to implement more centralized methods of works management.[64] In the room that made carding machinery, for example, three machinists executed job work in wood, covering six distinct operations; four hands took five jobs involving iron work. A total of twenty six "prices" for iron work on cards also were recorded: The amounts listed for these various job prices ranged from the $6.00 that Thomas Ivory II, an Irishman, earned for turning each set of shafting on cards with iron strippers, down to the two cents per item for simple tasks, such as "polishing shafts" and "regulating screws," which were rated at two cents per item. The majority of these listed prices were under one dollar. The preponderance of prices at the lower end of the range indicates that as the company's output expanded, work had become increasingly specialized. Fewer machinists were in positions where they could acquire comprehensive skills. However, the situation was not without ambiguity. Several hands continued to perform relatively complex jobs with higher prices per unit, or demonstrated versatility by being responsible for a number of small jobs.

By contrast, the highly skilled Horatio Dennett (1814-1898) headed a smaller department where he fashioned the woodwork for looms and finishing machinery. His job prices were uniformly higher, ranging up to twenty dollars, in addition to an exceptional day rate of four dollars. In this department skills and practices linked to artisan production continued to survive against the encroachment of capital.

Note, too, that the vocabulary of all these transactions retained archaic elements. Though the company conceptualized these figures as "costs," their workmen apparently preferred perceiving their pay as "prices" received for components produced rather than "wages"for their labor. Job work in this machine shop may still have evoked a complex of attitudes comparable to those held by earlier generations of independent artisans antipathetic to wage labor, although the categories of political economy with which Davis & Furber's hands operated must remain a matter for speculation.

The internal organization of textile machinery shops placed a particular stamp on apprenticeship whose ramifications extended to the patterns of skill distribution in the overall work force. The vocational education of young machinists was carried on primarily by senior men via oral tradition, work-place socialization, and hands-on experience. However, the quality of training varied with the extent to which capitalist rationalization had penetrated the work place, narrowing the options available to the senior machinists who trained the younger hands. In large shops where, due to diversified production, work had become highly specialized, apprenticeship training was likely to be pushed in the direction of skill dilution. Conversely, in smaller shops, with a less extensive division of labor, craft training persisted in providing all-around skills. The contrast can be glimpsed in the policies adopted by the Lowell and the Whitin shops. At Lowell during the 1820s boys were apprenticed to the contractors under the aegis of the Middlesex Mechanics Association.[65] Four decades later, at the more casual Whitin shop, apprentices were placed directly under the eye of the shop superintendent.[66] Although the latter situation might seem more indicative of direct control over the content of training by the company itself, with a greater potential for rationalization, during that period it could also lead to learning more comprehensive skills. By circulating apprentices through a number of departments, the boys would gain familiarity with a wider variety of Whitin's operations than would be possible if they were restricted to repetitve work under a contractor whose own job had become specialized, although not all work done in the Lowell shop fell into such restricted categories.[67]

O.H. Moulton recalled entering the Saco shop in 1843 at the age of fourteen:

> In that, as in most similar establishments, much of the work was done by contract, experienced machinists taking certain parts of a machine to do by the job, and employing cheap help, many of them boys, to do constantly the same thing. In this way, even boys would soon become so adept in a single process as to be quite profitable to the contractors employing them, yet would obtain but little real knowledge of the machinist's trade in its various operations.[68]

Young men with such limited all-around training were prime candidates for tending those special-purpose machines that were altering the character of manual and mechanized operations in leading textile machinery shops. The following year, Mouton transferred to a different environment, the machine shop of the nearby York Manufacturing Company's cotton mills.

> This shop was mainly for making repairs on the machinery of the mills, and afforded opportunity for a great variety of work. Having spent 5 years in this establishment he was, at 20 years of age, an expert machinist.[69]

In 1855 an Alfred C. Manning of Boston (using a standard printed form) took one John H. McGarrigle as an apprentice, covenanting— no less—that, if the youth foreswore vice and insubordination, he would "teach and instruct, or cause the said Apprentice to be instructed, in the art, trade or calling of a Machinist by the best way or means that he may or can (if said Apprentice be capable to learn)." The format of this agreement harkened back to earlier forms of indenture (including Samuel Slater's 1783 agreement with Jedediah Strutt), and young McGarrigle might have concluded upon inspecting this document that he would eventually graduate into a "calling" that represented more than the sum of its marketable skills.[70] On the other hand, while agent of the large Amoskeag shop in 1844, William Burke wrote curtly that in the case of a particular apprentice, "We think that the Foundry will be the best place for him."[71] He routinely discussed the wage rates that the youth would receive during his four-year term of indenture, but refrained from cataloguing any behavioral norms or indulging in rhetoric about arts, trades, or callings, since the relationship appeared to be restricted to a cash nexus. Clearly the status of apprenticeship as a vehicle for acquiring and transmitting the skills and culture of the machinist's trade was also a weathervane, shifting according to the nature of the conflicts and accommodations between shop owners and senior workmen.

As an important cog in the internal administration of the machine shop, the inside contract system regulated the division of labor and allocation of authority to a significant degree, but it did not cover all shop workers. At the Saco machine shop in 1850, 130 men and boys worked under sixteen contractors; an unknown number of other hands were employed directly by the company.[72] Along another dimension, by this period both contractors and textile machinery companies had instituted two parallel systems of wage payments—by the day and by the job or piece. The outcome of these administrative practices may be construed as a four-fold typology in which any worker could be confronted by different forms of both supervision and remuneration. These permutations resulted in a variegated labor force where one worker's relations to capital, supervisors, and one another differed enormously. To take only one example, overlapping systems of time and job or piece rates meant that hands working alongside each other might have significant differences in their levels of income, as well as in their attitudes toward limitations on output, the informal quotas that became key tenets of trade union responses to the anarchy of capitalist production and the gyrations of the business cycle. Various forms of payment-by-results tended to undermine the enforcement of quotas, although George Clark saw nothing amiss in running two lathes at once (a practice discouraged in some British shops) even though he was paid primarily by the day.[73] Given this maze of bargaining situations and authority relationships among textile machinists themselves and vis-à-vis shop proprietors, conflicts within the occupational culture should not be surprising.

The daily round of work in one large textile machinery shop was described in some detail by John Rogers, who entered the Amoskeag shop in 1850 after difficulty with his eyesight had forced him to abandon bookkeeping. Although not necessarily representative, his letters still provide a good bit of information about shop conditions and operations. During his first summer he worked six days a week, twelve and a half hours per day, from 5 a.m. to 7 p.m., with a total of ninety minutes for meals. This schedule exhausted him to the point where he was compelled to retire soon after the evening meal to get some sleep before the summons of the first bell at 4:30 a.m.[74] In the fall, it became necessary to illuminate the shops in the early evening. Work then began after breakfast at 7 a.m. and concluded at 7:30 p.m., except on Saturday when the shop shut down at dark. "The time we are lighted up seems as long as all the rest of the afternoon. . . ."[75] Around the vernal equinox, "The long-wished-for-time arrived last week for blowing out the lights, as the 20th of March is the last day we light up and now we get out at dark," a temporary shortening of the work day.[76] In 1853 the hours of labor were reduced to eleven in the wake of renewed agitation by the Ten-Hour Movement.[77] Rogers made no mention of provisions for overtime pay. There were occupational safety and health hazards: he burned his tongue when a lathe threw a hot iron chip into his mouth; he saw a shopmate's thumb torn off.[78] His personal opinion of his fellow workers was mixed. "Nearly all the workmen in the shop are between twenty and thirty and a good many are low sort of fellows, but there are many of a different stamp and some at work at my bench are fortunately of the latter kind."[79]

Rogers proved to be adept at his work and occasionally seems to have found his experience stimulating: "Our foreman has already advanced me to some much finer work than what I commenced with and the time passes quickly as I get interested in it. . . . My work varies constantly so I rarely have a job last over a day or two which makes it less monotonous."[80] He got on well with his foreman. "Our *Boss* gave me a drawer full of tools the other day which I keep locked for my own use. . . . Mr. Buxton said I did my work as well as hands he had that had been with him a year or two."[81] This aptitude, or favoritism, may have colored his relations with other workmen. "A man who entered the same day that I did grumbles a good deal about my promotion beyond him. . . . "[82]

The mode of production that began to take shape during early industrialization increased capital's ability to appropriate the products of labor, but formal ownership did not automatically confer unilateral capitalist control over the labor process in all the new factories. In antebellum textile machinery shops the nature of the labor process also reflected workers' real power over certain details of daily production, as well as the internal divisions within their own occupations. It has not been my intention to argue that textile machinists' actions and attitudes concerning their jobs were determined exclusively by their experiences in the work place. The accommodation and the militance of the first generations who followed this trade, topics that lie beyond the scope of this essay, had complex causes, including the interaction of politics and culture in crystallizing class structure. Nevertheless, in this industry an ecology of manufacture that was developed in the interests of capital accumulation still contained a reconstituted form of craft control over the planning and execution of work and, indirectly, over the process of capital formation itself. Within the early machine shop environment a new skill hierarchy and potential relations of coexploitation among workers themselves also came into existence as part of the redefined craft system.

We conclude with the words of two machinists from the Davis & Furber shop that convey a sense of these contradictory qualities in their lives and work. In 1853 the local newspaper carried a fictional piece combining conventional pieties with the thinly disguised experiences of William Chase, then an apprentice in the forge. Judging by his fictional counterpart's attitude, the radical disjuncture between an artisan blend of mental and manual work of which Harry Braverman and others have written was not yet fully manifested at the shop where Chase worked:

> We are machinists, causing gross material substances to assume shapes of beauty and fitness, under the mysterious supremacy of our will. Some call this a low, a common business, a mechanical operation, but it is not so. There is a mental power to which matter must bow, and there is nothing higher than to elevate and ennoble our conceptions so as to make the plastic matter subservient to the best interests of man.[83]

Against this relatively sanguine picture we may juxtapose the words of an older man who lived to see dramatic changes as Davis & Furber grew from a craft-based job shop into a capitalist factory during and after the Civil War. Samuel Henry Furber (no relation to the proprietors) spent four decades in the Davis & Furber mule room and wrote the following lines on the title page of an old exercise book, perhaps as an epitaph for his own career:

> Oh luckless hour when Henry Furber left his Father's roof and commenced the trials and discouragements of the machinists [sic] trade.[84]

CHAPTER 4

Worker and Community: Fraternal Orders in Albany, New York 1845-1885

BRIAN GREENBERG

Recent studies of nineteenth-century American society emplasize the impact of geographic mobility. Workers in these interpretations are a surging, isolated mass, alienated from and impotent in dealing with the existing social order. These "men in motion" are assumed to have lacked all traditional ties to particular communities, to have formed a "floating proletariat" never quite able to sink roots.[1] Certain speculative essays, however, particularly those by Eric McKitrick and Stanley Elkins and by Rowland Berthoff, indicate that a network of voluntary institutions existed in nineteenth-century American society whose "portability" reflected an adaptation to extensive mobility. Americans on the move needed and found connections in new places, and, in their new communities, they reached out to voluntary associations similar to those that they had left behind.[2]

Voluntary associations were an essential part of nineteenth-century American society. When the need arose to accomplish some project of general importance in the nineteenth century, Americans most likely formed an association rather than assign responsibility to government. This feature of "civil life" in America attracted the attention of Alexis de Tocqueville as he traveled through the United States in the 1830s. "Americans," he observed

> make associations to give entertainments, to found seminaries, to build inns, to construct churches, to diffuse books, to send missionaries to the antipodes; in this manner they found hospitals, prisons, and schools. If it is proposed to inculcate some truth or foster some feeling by the encouragement of a great example, they form a society.[3]

Ethnic and religious groups of all kinds formed voluntary associations and counted among their members people from all social classes. The fraternal order was a particularly popular form of voluntary associ- ation that flourished in the nineteenth century. Primarily social and recreational organizations, these societies also served benevolent, philanthropic, reform, and other purposes.

As industrialization proceeded during the nineteenth century, workers' consciousness—their perception of the social order—was formed by their interactions not only with fellow workers in the work place but also with members of other social classes, often in fraternal societies. Within this context the fraternal order acted as a "mediator," as an agency which acquainted workers with the viewpoints of other groups in the city and gave them a sense of participation in the community. In this way, fraternal societies mitigated the possible alienation of workers from the social order.

Fraternal orders also functioned in other ways important to the community. Industrial capitalism challenged workers' traditional way of life and attempted to instill more rigid work rules and habits. Current research on early American industrialization emphasizes the importance of the way workers were socialized, insuring their accep- tance of the new work ethic.[4] The fraternal society exemplifies one way in which the community "taught" workers the moral obligations of a "worldly asceticism," characterized by diligence, sobriety, hones- ty, industriousness, and frugality.[5] As agencies of morality, these soci- eties helped preserve the existing social order.

Tocqueville also indicated that voluntary societies were intended to be educational in that they transmitted dominant social values. In mid-nineteenth-century America, faith in the superiority of the "free labor system" formed the basis of the dominant ideology. Proponents of the free labor system celebrated the North's dynamic capitalist economy and the opportunity and dignity it was said to offer to the workingman. Ideally, class divisions should not be allowed to become permanent, because society's well-being required that individual am- bition and industriousness be rewarded. Since all members of society presumably would benefit from economic expansion, a mutuality of interest in maximizing output and efficiency prevailed among them. When they acted in concert, capital and labor were thought to be part of an economic process that produced prosperity for all.[6]

The fraternal society functioned as one portable institution by which continuity, stability, and control were maintained in the nine- teenth century. This process will be examined here in terms of one specific community: Albany, New York, between 1845 and 1885. Never a major industrial center, Albany is typical of an earlier period of American economic development, a transitional phase in which an older, more personal social order was confronted by the modernizing effects of industrialization. The Independent Order of Odd Fellows (IOOF) was particularly active in Albany during these years and illustrates the social and cultural significance of fraternal orders.[7]

Men from all occupations in Albany joined local Odd Fellow lodges, and members from the city's working and middle classes mixed within the ranks of Odd Fellowship. In this way, the IOOF exemplified the free labor ideal of an open-class, harmonious social order. Further, the symbolic "lessons" of Odd Fellowship's ritual served to teach all of its members those qualities essential to an industrial work ethic. By promoting these values, Odd Fellowship particularly effected the socialization of the workers who joined the order. Moreover, by mediating class relations, the IOOF helped shape Albany workers' perception of the changing social order.

Only a few thousand men belonged to American fraternal organizations at the beginning of the nineteenth century, primarily as members of the Free and Accepted Masons. But by the end of the century some seventy-eight fraternal orders existed, with over six million members. One study of fraternal societies in the United States claims that lodges outnumbered churches in all the large cities.[8]

Although they differ over the specifics, the order's official historians agree that Odd Fellowship originated in England in the eighteenth century. English workingmen are said to have organized the society for social purposes and to aid the brethren and to help unemployed brothers find work. The formal organization of the Manchester Unity in 1814 officially launched the Independent Order of Odd Fellows as a social, or "convivial," society. In March 1819 at a meeting over a Baltimore tavern, a recent emigrant from England, Thomas Wildey, established the first Odd Fellow lodge in the United States.[9]

During its early years, American Odd Fellowship spread slowly as lodges were concentrated in the port cities of Boston, New York City, and Philadelphia. By 1830, however, some one hundred lodges had been chartered, with 6,743 members. Of the seven Odd Fellow lodges in New York State at this time, six were in Albany; the first, Hope Lodge No. 3, dated from 1826. Firmly established in four states and the District of Columbia by 1830, Odd Fellowship had "passed the period of probation. . . . Already an army has been enlisted in the service of the cause of Friendship, Love and Truth."[10]

The order structured its government as a "fraternal republican Union." Control over the IOOF resided with the national body, the Sovereign Grand Lodge (SGL). Each state had a State Grand Lodge; subordinate local lodges carried on the work of the order in the cities and towns.

The SGL maintained "supreme jurisdiction in the general laws and usages of the Order, the lectures, charges and unwritten work, and [was] a court of final appeal, and . . . the National legislature of the Order."[11] The Sovereign Grand Lodge furnished the IOOF's "written" (nonsecret) work to the state and subordinate lodges; only the grand secretary of the SGL had access to the order's "unwritten" rituals and symbols, which were in secret journals.[12] Odd Fellowship expected all state and local bodies to enforce strict adherence to its ritual. It explicitly enjoined them to "neither adopt nor use, or suffer to be adopted or used, any Charges, Lectures of Ceremonies, Forms of Installation or Regalia [other] than those prescribed by the S.G.L." Thus the national body mandated and controlled the symbolic language and rituals of Odd Fellowship. As the Odd Fellows' manual stated, "The Signs, Grips and Passwords of the order are designed to speak one universal language to the initiated of every nationality the world over."[13]

The order expected the subordinate lodge to formulate bylaws and rules of conduct that would regulate the work of local Odd Fellowship. The local lodge elected its own officers and maintained the order's benficial relief features.[14] In addition, the subordinate lodge governed the process of becoming an Odd Fellow, which involved a series of four steps, known as degrees, each having appropriate emblems, regalia, and lessons. Within the lodge the "Priestly Order" was the highest, or Scarlet, degree.[15]

The most important function of the subordinate lodge was to perpetuate and extend Odd Fellowship through the initiation of new members. The order restricted membership to white males over twenty-one, who believed in the Supreme Being and were of good health and moral character.[16] Although the specific procedures governing initiation were left to the subordinate lodge, the order urged them to test the honesty and sincerity of proposed new members "at the threshold."[17]

Descriptions of the social composition of Odd Fellow membership during the nineteenth century vary. One of the order's historians, Theodore Ross, claimed that it was composed of the "great middle, industrial classes almost exclusively." Wildey described the members of the Grand Lodge of New York in 1830 as mainly English and Scottish mechanics and tavernkeepers. But by 1840, according to another official historian of Odd Fellowship, the order had extended its reach to include members from every "department of business, . . . men of every sphere of life, . . . men of character, influence and power."[18]

Only a few records for Albany's Odd Fellow lodges have survived, particularly a list of all members in 1845 and membership lists for certain lodges in 1850, 1872, and 1882. Nevertheless, from the names on these records and the names on lists constructed from the records of the New York State Grand Lodge, some general conclusions about who became an Odd Fellow in Albany in the nineteenth century are possible.[19]

Was Odd Fellowship membership representative of Albany's social composition, and did it function as mediator between workers and the rest of the community? That workers became Odd Fellows is easily confirmed. A check of the 1845 list of Odd Fellows in Albany for occupation in the city directory reveals that many members in each lodge could be classified as workers. In addition, membership lists were divided by degree attained, and in every Albany lodge workers are present in each degree, including the Scarlet, and among the Past Grands. Most of these individuals were skilled workers—carpenters, printers, stonecutters, coachmakers, painters, and masons are most commonly noted. The directories identify only a few members as ordinary laborers.[20]

Every lodge had members with diverse occupations. Among professionals who joined, attorneys were the most prominent. Many of these men were important civic leaders in Albany. Most attorneys had joined the city's oldest lodge, Hope Lodge No. 3.[21] But in every lodge it was men involved in commerce who comprised the largest group of members. Wholesalers, retailers, and owners of dry goods stores, as well as greengrocers and other small businessmen and peddlers, joined Albany's Odd Fellow lodges. In each lodge, as with its working-class members, men with both large and small business interests can be found in all the different levels of Odd Fellow degrees.

Another way of analyzing Albany's Odd Fellow membership is to determine its religious and ethnic makeup. Judging from the names on the 1845 list, the city's Odd Fellows were predominantly Protestant, or at least not Irish Catholic. Many Dutch names appear, but German names appear more frequently and in larger proportion than the German population in Albany. Although German names can be found on the lists for all lodges, the greatest number, as would be expected, belonged to German Colonial Lodge No. 16. But this was not an exclusively German lodge.

In 1845, Odd Fellowship was representative of the socioeconomic and ethnic mix of at least the Protestant segment of Albany. Primarily a commercial city, Albany's economy depended heavily on the advantages afforded first by the Erie Canal and later by the development of the railroad. The city's small-scale industries still relied on such skilled trades as brewing, stove and ironware molding, boot and shoemaking, cigar making, and printing. Looking at Albany's ethnic makeup the majority of Albany's population in the mid-1840s consisted of the descendants of early Dutch immigrants, Protestant Yankee emigrants from Connecticut, Massachusetts, and Rhode Island, and more recent German immigrants. Albany also had a large Irish-Catholic population at this time, and after the famine migrations of the late 1840s, the Irish Catholics became the majority group. But few Irish had joined the Odd Fellows by 1845.[22]

Later membership lists, for Mountaineer Lodge No. 321 in 1872 and American Lodge No. 32 in 1882, continue to reflect Albany's socioeconomic structure.[23] After 1845 workers still joined the Odd Fellows, if anything in greater numbers, and still achieved all degrees within the lodges. Examining these two lodges, the growing impact of the railroad on Albany is also clear. Many railroad workers, including engineers, conductors, brakemen, and firemen, now belonged. Machinists, blacksmiths, and carpenters, many of whom probably worked at the shops built by the New York Central Railroad in West Albany, also became members. Molders and other skilled workers continued to join, as did a number of individuals that the city directories identify as foremen.[24] There were still relataively few members who can be identified specifically as laborers.

With the increase in the number of skilled workers among Albany's Odd Fellows came a relative decrease in the number of men following commercial pursuits, either large- or small-scale. Also, almost no attorneys are listed as members of Mountaineer Lodge No 321 in 1872 or American Lodge No. 32 in 1882. On the other hand, individuals connected with insurance now appear. As was true for members on the earlier lists, middle-class or professional members of the community can be found in all of the degrees within the lodges.

Albany Odd Fellows in the 1870s and '80s continued to be largely Protestant, although Irish names do appear on the later membership lists more often than before.[25] German names remain well represented among the membership. German Colonial Lodge No. 16 was still in existence, as was Albany City Lodge No. 385, which has been referred to as a German lodge.

A census of Albany's Odd Fellow elite, constructed from records of the Annual Proceedings of the State Grand Lodge for selected years between 1846 and 1889, and two small lists of the members of the Grand Encampment for 1867 and Albany Patriarchs' Lodge No. 1 in 1846, confirms that many workers rose to prominent positions within Odd Fellowship. Again, members with other occupations were also part of the elite, reinforcing the idea that all elements of the community participated in Odd Fellowship.

Thus, Ross's contention that Odd Fellowship consisted of the "great middle industrial classes" seems a fair assessment of the membership of Albany's Odd Fellows, particularly in the later years of the nineteenth century. Albany workers, especially skilled workers in the city's dominant trades, did participate in Odd Fellowship. The IOOF in Albany was clearly one community institution where workers came in contact with members of other social classes and formed relationships that went beyond those of the work place. The significance of this contact, however, lies within the context of the ideological role of Odd Fellowship.

American fraternal orders developed theories and legends explaining their origins. The Masons traced their ancient mysteries back to the building of King Solomon's Temple, and the Knights of Pythias to the legend of Damon and Pythias. The orders believed that the prestige and stability of their fraternity, as well as the personal status of individual members, were somehow enhanced if it had roots in antiquity.[26]

American Odd Fellowship, in its early years, traced its origins to the Roman legions in Britain and Gaul. But the order soon abandoned this legend and proclaimed that its real genesis lay in the "enlightened civilization" of the "greatest republic," the United States. As one of its leaders declared, "Odd Fellowship, as we know it, is an institution of modern times, grown in *our* midst and fashioned by *our* hands."[27] To adapt Odd Fellowship to American conditions and needs, the order made certain reforms in its practices. Because nineteenth-century Americans tended to move about the country, the IOOF, in one of its earliest changes, provided members with "traveling cards." These cards certified that the bearer was an Odd Fellow and recommended that he be afforded the "friendship and protection" of all lodges. In another reform, one aimed at making American Odd Fellowship more respectable than its British counterpart, the order banned intoxicating beverages and tobacco from its meeting rooms. One official historian of the Odd Fellows celebrated the "abolition of all social and convivial practices at Lodge meetings" as "among the first improvements to the Order in America required by duty and a decent respect for the opinions of mankind." Since then, he added, Odd Fellowship has gained "the respect and esteem of the virtuous of all classes" and consequently increased its membership greatly.[28]

As it evolved in the United States, Odd Fellowship introduced other reforms to give the American ritual a deeper, more moral, significance. These adaptations reflected a new view of the role of the IOOF's essential function, which the fraternity formalized in the 1840s, years of phenomenal growth for the order and a period of significant reform in American institutions. During this decade, the American Order formally withdrew from the Manchester Unity, the Supreme English Odd Fellow society, and developed its own distinctive ritual.[29] James D. Ridgely, often called the father of modern, ethical Odd Fellowship, led this movement. At the Sovereign Grand Lodge session of 1844, Ridgely described the prevailing mood as a call for change: "There came . . . a demand, general, earnest, irresistible, for an improved work, a moral more distinctive and didactic, a sentiment more elevated and inspiring, a principle of deeper significance, a purer and truer tone, and the embodiment of all these in a literature worthy of a cause so noble and a work so great."[30]

By breaking with England, American Odd Fellows sought to establish the order as a major moral reform institution. The new ritual, adopted by the national organization in 1845, remained virtually unchanged to 1880. An official history of the order referred to this period as Odd Fellowship's "Golden Years." Odd Fellows identified the order's role in society as encompassing a more exalted function.[31] As Cornelius Glen, an Albany Odd Fellow who in 1858 rose to Most Worshipful Grand Master, stated: "Our lodges were instituted for higher and holier objects than those of pecuniary gain—we seek to improve and elevate the character of man, and imbue him with proper conceptions of his fellow man."[32]

Odd Fellowship sought to accomplish these higher and more noble objectives by teaching Americans those lessons of morality that formed a "proper education." A leading Odd Fellow in Ohio described how the order went about this task: "In the Lodge-room under the stimulus and magnetism of numbers, exciting the brain to highest activity, these great fundamental principles of our Order, and of society, are evolved and pressed weekly upon the minds of members."[33] The experience of being an Odd Fellow was itself educational: "Lessons taught by example are more thrilling than those gathered from the history of past events. There is no school so good as that of self-experience."[34] The lessons that Odd Fellows needed to learn were embodied in the structure and regualtions of the order and the form and substance of the degrees. These lessons emphasized the moral obligations of the industrial work ethic and the dominant free labor social views.

The order infused its lectures and charges with moral and religious instruction designed to instill in members a religious spirit, temperance, industriousness, and self-discipline.[35] In order to become members, as noted earlier, all Odd Fellows had to affirm their belief in the Supreme Being. At least one Albany lodge opened each meeting with a prayer. Albany Union Lodge No. 8 maintained that, as Odd Fellows, members were protected from the evils of the world "by the shield of Omnipotence. . . . We are as if all Christians were united in one sect, assisted and assisting—a band of brothers!"[36] In the lecture of initiation, the All-Seeing Eye reminded the Odd Fellow that "the omniscience of God pierces into every secret to the heart. . . . Let us, therefore, so regulate our conduct that we may not fear the scrutinizing eye of anyone."[37]

Part of Odd Fellowship's religious instruction was the moral dictum of temperance. As already noted, early in its existence in the United States, the Odd Fellowship adopted regulations banning liquor from the lodge rooms. According to A.B. Grosh in the *Odd Fellow's Improved Manual*, "Our laws teach us respect for ourselves, temperance in our desires, chastity of person, and purity in heart and mind. Drunkenness is a worse than beastly vice."[38] The lectures of the first degree of Odd Fellowship required initiates to pronounce drunkenness "the vilest and most pernicious of all vices." Subordinate lodges provided for the expulsion or suspension of members found guilty of repeated intoxication.[39]

Odd Fellowship instructed a member not only to be temperate but to "keep free from all excess and pollution."[40] One Albany lodge specified that a prospective member "be of good moral character, of industrious habits, and exempt from all infirmaties which may prevent him from gaining a livelihood for himself and family."[41] Lodge regulations governing relief benefits for illness stipulated that they be given only if the prospective recipient's "sickness or disability does not proceed from immoral conduct."[42]

Odd Fellows believed that the relief benefits made the order a practical reform, whose advantages "worthy men of all capacities may enjoy, and in which all can assist in practical benevolence." A lodge member in distress was to be relieved with "cheerful alacrity," and "this is done, too, as the duty of his brothers, and without taking away from his independence."[43] Odd Fellowship desired to enhance, not diminish, a member's self-reliance.

The procedures, lectures, and degrees illustrate the character-forming feature of Odd Fellowship. The system of graduated admission assured the order continued control over a member's behavior. At one point in the rules, initiates were told that "the solenmities may be novel, even startling by their novelty, but they are perfectly chaste, dignified, and serious as the lessons they are designed to teach. . . . Give yourself, then, passively to your guides, to lead you withersoever they will."[44] The attainment of higher degrees was equated with both "receiving the unqualified blessings of society and recognition of the individual's fraternal worthiness."[45] According to Ridgely, the degrees aimed by successive steps "to form a workman, and to put him to appropriate labor. The treatment is pictorial, by example, and didactic."[46]

Each degree had its own series of emblems and symbols revealing the lessons of that degree and of Odd Fellowship in general. Within the different degrees, symbols of united effort, mortality, and religion reinforced the order's moral nature. Above all, the emblems reiterated the necessity of industriousness and self-discipline. They warned an Odd Fellow not to waste time, to use his time wisely. The Hour Glass, an emblem of the third degree, reminded the Odd Fellow that " 'procrastination is the thief of time' and that constant and persistent labors are bound to result in deserved and merited success." The symbol of the Arrows directed "that we shall pursue our daily tasks and perform our bounden obligations in the straight, direct and narrow path of duty."[47]

In sum, the structure and literature of Odd Fellowship stressed certain moral precepts endorsed by middle-class society at large. Odd Fellowship sought to inculcate in its members a religious spirit, self-discipline, industriousness, and temperance in all things. As written in the introduction to the bylaws of Albany Union Lodge No. 8, "The only and sole object of the Independent Order of Odd Fellows, is to

carry into effect social and benevolent purposes, to inculcate principles of faithful intercourse with all men, charity, and useful moral
precepts."[48] In promoting what are often called "bourgeois habits,"
Odd Fellowship acted as a moral policing institution within the community.

By emphasizing the moral values accepted by the community at
large, fraternal societies became "bulwarks of the *status quo*, conserv-
ers of traditional morality, transmitters of existing social values."[49] In
Albany, in the mid-nineteenth century, the "free labor" ideology best
describes this dominant consciousness. Adherents of free labor ideas
defined American society in optimistic terms, as progressive and dynamic, as providing the means for workers to advance upward on the
social scale. Although they recognized differences among individuals
and groups, they anticipated that these differences would not become
fixed as class relationships. In free labor terms all that was thought
necessary for society's well-being was for both capital and labor to
acknowledge their shared interests.[50] In its symbols and regulations,
Odd Fellowship reflected such free labor values.

That the free labor ideology characterized Albany's social consciousness is illustrated in the comments of two leading newspapers
in the city on the issue of establishing by law the eight-hour workday
in New York State. Accepting the key free labor concept of mutuality,
both newspapers condemned workers' demand for an eight-hour
working day as a "class position." The *Argus* recommended to workers that they recognize that "the army of Labor and Capital in hostility
is war, and war is always destructive to both parties. The combination
of capital with labor is peace and in its train follows plenty."[51] Similarly, the *Albany Evening Journal* maintained that "capital and labor are
not antagonistic. They are the positive and negative elements which
complete the currents and help the circuit of commerce and trade.
Neither can exist without the other, and both have claims to consideration."[52] Both newspapers tried to promote what they saw as the
natural harmony of interests that should exist between all members of
the community.

Committed to a fluid social structure, free labor adherents still
emphasized the importance of hierarchy and place as well as mobility.
Based on his standing within the order, each member was assigned a
particular place during such lodge room ceremonies as initiation. In
public processions, each member had a proper position according to
his rank in the lodge. All Albany lodges had rules governing the
asking of questions during meetings and assessed penalties for im-

proper language or use of disrespectful expressions towards officers or other members.[53]

Odd Fellowship accorded status to its members in relation to the degrees they had attained. Certain regulations reinforced these status distinctions among members. The most important work of a lodge took place in the Scarlet Degree, and only members of this degree could hold elective offices. Procedures to regulate the use of traveling cards also recognized these distinctions. To insure that a brother was accorded the honors to which he was entitled, all traveling cards had to state the member's rank and degree. A lodge could bar a traveling brother if it was holding a meeting in a degree higher than his.[54]

Each degree had appropriate regalia as well, and Odd Fellow regulations mandated the wearing of these costumes. The members of one Albany lodge resolved in their bylaws that "no member shall be permitted to enter the Lodge unless he was clothed in suitable regalia; nor shall he be allowed to speak or vote on any question, unless clothed in the regalia appropriate to his rank or degree."[55] Thus, the regalia became "criterion of social distance not only between members and nonmembers but among the members themselves."[56]

In their study of working-class culture during the American industrial revolution, Alan Dawley and Paul Faler argue that the newer industrial values "were constructed out of older materials. . . . In preindustrial times, individual initiative was fused with deference to social superiors, while in the new setting individualism was alloyed with a belief in equality of opportunity."[57] Equality of opportunity, as will be shown, was a notable theme in the ideology of Odd Fellowship, but this did not preclude deference to those who had made the most of their opportunities.

Recognizing social distinctions, in common with the larger society, Odd Fellowship emplasized the value of mobility and the success ethic. In the United States the success ethic meant, in the dominant middle-class view, freedom of opportunity—an open path upward for men of talent and energy. Yet to free labor adherents equality did not denote a leveling process but rather an equal chance in the race for wealth.[58]

The leaders of the IOOF in the United States dedicated the order to functioning as an open-class society. The central symbol of Odd Fellowship was the Three-Link Chain, symbolizing Friendship, Love, and Truth. The order defined "love" as that which bound Odd Fellows together "without reference to those artificial distinctions which exist among mankind, and separate them into a diversity of grades and of classes, each laying peculiar claim to notice."[59] As should be true in the larger society, worthy individuals from varied social backgrounds moved up in the order to achieve the highest degree. An Odd Fellow earned the right to advance by exhibiting the proper habits of good citizenship, truthfulness, temperance, religious feeling, and industriousness, and by learning the ritual of each higher degree. As Ridgely observed, Odd Fellow degrees were not open to the multitude but were earned by the worthy and well qualified.[60]

In order to expand its scope and significance, American Odd Fellowship, in its earliest years, added a higher degree, the patriarchal, which brought Odd Fellows together into Encampments formed outside the subordinate lodges. Each separate lodge was thought to unite Odd Fellows into a single family; the mission of the Patriarchs was to unite Odd Fellowship with the world.[61] By joining an Encampment, an Odd Fellow could rise to an even higher station than he could achieve in the subordinate lodge. Believing that American society depended on giving "free scope to ability, perseverance, courage and ambition," Odd Fellowship had instituted "a higher summit" through the patriarchal degree.[62] By creating a structure that encouraged mobility, Odd Fellowship exemplified a society that provided upward movement for men of talent and energy.[63]

In promoting the fraternal relations that should exist among "brothers," Odd Fellowship symbolized the free labor principle inherent mutuality of interests between labor and capital. In Odd Fellowship the spirit of fraternity was "inspired by our cardinal idea of tolerance, [and] the mutuality of human obligations and sympathies, elaborately embodied as generic truths in our codes."[64] The authors of *The Odd Fellows' Pocket Companion* observed that "the sentiment upon which our institution depends most for support and existence, is the sentiment of *true brotherhood*; that mutual principle which should prompt [us] to lay aside all personal differences and sacrifice all party considerations for the benefit of the general weal."[65] In the term "united effort," Odd Fellowship expressed the concept of mutuality. For example, the emblem known as the Tee Square and Sword reminded the Odd Fellow "that justice and mercy should be administered without reference to the refined and subtle distinctions of men. Let us weigh well our conduct, and do unto others according to the injunction of the Golden Rule."[66]

The beneficial features of the order provided a means for members to acknowledge their mutual obligations. In Odd Fellowship, "the bonds of fraternity draw us together in our lodges; they induce us to feel and relieve each other's distresses; they lead us to console the afflicted . . . [as] a family of brothers."[67] The order did not see beneficial obligations as charity; rather, whatever his "circumstances of life," a fraternal brother was to receive the aid, the counsel, and the protection of his fellow members, *not as a favor merely, but as a right.*"[68]

At a time when government provided few social services, when unemployment insurance and workmen's compensation were unknown, these beneficial features were significant. Between 1824 and 1886 the New York State Grand Lodge spent $4,500,000 on relief programs. In Albany County alone, the Order spent over $150,000 by 1886. Nor was an Odd Fellow barred from receiving these benefits by distance from his lodge. In fact, in 1870 Albany's lodges jointly inaugurated an Odd Fellow Board of Relief and specifically charged it with responsibility for assisting "the distressed traveling members" of the order. In times of particular need, such as the depression of the 1870s, Odd Fellows in New York and Albany increased substantially the amount they expended on relief.[69]

The concept of mutuality was inherent in the ideals of brotherhood expressed by Odd Fellowship. As one Odd Fellow noted:

> The conflicting and discordant elements of society can find repose and safety, only in the conservative spirit of philanthropic institutions . . . whose mission is to teach us that 'no one liveth to himself,' but that we are created and placed here to labor for our fellow-men, to improve our social condition.[70]

Ridgely wrote that the remedy for the evils that exist in the world was revealed in the degrees of Odd Fellowship: "That remedy is FRATERNITY. It has but one form: *association*; but one principle, *benevolence*; but one doctrine, *toleration*; but one order, *equality*. Thus all the workmen are one, and the work itself is unity. It follows that the end is to unite all mankind into a vast and loving brotherhood."[71] Viewing society as an organic whole, believers in the free labor ideology assigned to each part duties and responsibilities, the whole being dependent on the contributions that each part made. It is this conception of the social order that Odd Fellowship most exemplified.

The leaders of nineteenth-century American Odd Fellowship assumed that moral and social reform were inextricably related and that the Order, through the agency of its moral lessons, would help insure social stability and cohesion. Looking back over more than thirty years of the American ritual, Ridgely concluded:

It is the experience of the world, and the teaching of history supplemented by careful observation, that of all the powers that exert a controlling influence upon society, none exceeds 'moral power.' It gives to citizenship the highest incentive to character, which forms the basis and bulwark of society, and supplies the general virtue and intelligence upon which the State relies.

He further observed that Odd Fellowship constituted "an important organization, not only in controlling the general sentiment but in educating the popular feeling. . . . Society is enlightened and trained under a proper education, the people become happy, industrious, thrifty, and liberty restrained by law is supremely triumphant."[72]

During the nineteenth century workers formed relationships among themselves in their taverns, unions, and social clubs, and with members of other classes in community social institutions. Odd Fellowship was just one such community institution that helped shape workers' perception of industrialization in nineteenth-century Albany. By participating in noneconomic voluntary societies such as the IOOF, Albany workers met as brothers with individuals from all classes in the community. Further, as Odd Fellows, they were instructed in conventional habits, including self-discipline, temperance, and industriousness. In so educating its members, Odd Fellowship contributed to the general acceptance of those personal habits felt essential to an industrial work ethic.

Community institutions such as Odd Fellowship transmitted the dominant social values. In Albany, during the period of its industrialization, these values included a belief in hierarchy, place, the success ethic, social mobility, and, fundamentally, the mutuality of interests among all groups in the community. These values were both symbolized and realized in the regulations, literature, and benefits of Odd Fellowship.

CHAPTER 5

"There's Plenty Waitin' at the Gates": Mobility, Opportunity and the American Worker

CHARLES STEPHENSON

Of toil and sweat, and sweat and toil
The worker has no lack
Weary when the season's "busy"
Hungry when it's "slack."

The entrepreneur is King in America, we are told, yet the ranks of small business, at least, are the most unstable in the American economy. Why do so many people seek to enter those ranks—or, more particularly, why do so many members of the working class seek to start their own small business? Because, the answer usually goes, they want to escape from the ranks of labor, where it is almost a sign of defeat to remain, and to experience that most American of all economic achievements: social mobility.

The lot of the American worker never has been easy, to be sure, and laborers have responded to their situations in multifaceted ways. Yet the explanation above is at once too grounded in middle-class expectations and too little cognizant of the actual motivation of the many workers who sought to enter—not, as I shall suggest, rise to—the ranks of small business owners. In this essay I shall address a number of questions central to working-class life and labor in nineteenth- and twentieth-century America, including two issues related in intriguing ways—social mobility and steady employment—and I shall suggest new ways in which to view those issues. I will look in particular at much of the recent literature which has dealt with these and other pertinent issues, and finally suggest a new synthesis of them. The business of America may be business, to be sure, but perhaps not always for the reasons expected.

Since its articulation by sociologist Pitirim Sorokin in *Social Mobility* (1927) the concept of social mobility has led social scientists to investigate a phenomenon which always had been central to the way Americans thought about their lives.[1] The objective concept itself—which addresses the movement of individuals upward or downward on an occupational ladder—is entirely valid: what happens to a country in the process of industrialization? How do social structures change? Changes in social structures—that is, individual movement within a broadly defined social system—influence and indeed can be used to predict other changes—for example, in cultural, political, and social orientations. Historians, especially during the 1930s, began to use social mobility to answer other questions—especially, "why is there no socialism in America?" The answer often was "because of the general belief in and availability of social mobility." Whether this condition is said to foster false consciousness, or to offer an alternative to proletarianization, it has been perceived as a barrier to a state based on principles of equitable production and distribution. Yet at the same time the assumption that social mobility was an instrinsically desirable goal—an ideological assumption at its base—too often has gone unexamined.

The historical investigation of urban social mobility in America essentially began in Stephan Thernstrom's *Poverty and Progress*, a seminal study of the working class in Newburyport, Massachusetts. Thernstrom was critical of sociologist Lloyd Warner who, in his "Yankee City" series, had used Newburyport to develop generalizable hypotheses about mobility and culture in American life. Thernstrom criticized Warner both for his lack of historical perspective and for his "impatience with objective measures of class . . . his inability to deal with social mobility satisfactorily."[2] Thernstrom also addressed himself to the apparent lack of radical tendencies among American workers both implicitly in *Poverty and Progress* and explicitly in other essays. His discoveries in Newburyport excited and have attracted the attention of historians for two decades so far (and undoubtedly will continue to do so).

Based upon U.S. Census manuscripts and other such lists, and utilizing elementary statistical techniques, Thernstrom measured both geographic and social mobility over three decades in Newburyport. He hypothesized that his failure to link a large number of names between censuses could only be due to those people having moved

away from the city.[3] Of those who stayed—whom he had linked—
however, few were "successful" in terms of moving up the social or
occupational ladder. On the contrary, most workers who "stayed" in
Newburyport spent their lives near the bottom of virtually every
social scale. Yet there was a distinctive characteristic of those Irish:
they may not have risen on an "objective" social scale, but they did
make enormous sacrifices in order to gain security by buying homes.[3]
On the basis of these discoveries Thernstrom concluded that social
mobility was not so widespread as earlier commentators had claimed:

> In the United States today the climb upward from the bottom
> rungs of the social ladder is not often rapid or easy, but it never
> was, if the experiences of the working class families of nine-
> teenth century Newburyport are at all representative. Few of
> these men and few of their children rose very far on the social
> scale; most of the upward occupational shifts they made left
> them manual workmen still, and their property mobility,
> though strikingly widespread, rarely involved the accumulation
> of anything approaching real wealth.

He called these "petty success stories," but at the same time doubted
that "the presence of opportunity of this kind is a sufficient test of the
good society."[4]

The points that Thernstrom developed further in his writings were
these: first, what he perceived as widespread geographic migration
was detrimental to the formation or preservation of community or of
class consciousness. He characterized those he had not recovered in
his record linkages as "floaters" who "were not 'members of the
community'."[5] "The bottom layer of the social order in the nineteenth
century American city was . . . a group of families who appear to have
been permanent transients, buffeted about from place to place . . . ",
"tossed helplessly about from city to city, from state to state, alienated
but invisible and impotent." Second, while social mobility, in terms of
a significant, measurable rise in social status, itself was more illusory
than real, working-class attemps to alleviate insecurity—that is, pursuing property mobility—did consume energy and absorbed the explosive aspects of frustration and dissent. Thus one explanation of
what Thernstrom saw as "the relative absence of collective working-
class protest aimed at reshaping capitalist society" was that "the
American working class was drawn into the new society by a process
that encouraged accommodation and rendered disciplined protest
difficult," that is, by the lure of social mobility and as a result of the
helplessness of being numbered among that "floating proletariat."[6]

The professional reaction to *Poverty and Progress* was an almost overwhelming excitement. Literally scores of emulators have tested and retested Thernstrom's hypotheses. Thernstrom himself subsequently investigated Boston and decided that, while his conclusions concerning population mobility were accurate—"in *no* American city," he said, "has there been a large lower-class with continuity of membership"[7]—his conclusions about social mobility had tended to *understate* it and that opportunity, therefore, was more prevalent than his previous data suggested.[8]

This also represents the thrust of those who have followed Thernstrom. In what is perhaps the most-fully developed statement of that tradition Michael Katz has said that transiency and inequality are "the two great themes of nineteenth-century urban history." Katz characterized migrants as "failures," a "swirl[ing]" mass, "rootless . . . detach[ed] from community," "isolated," "restless, driven" people.[9] He said that:

> two social structures [coexisted] within nineteenth century society: one relatively fixed, consisting of people successful at their work, even if that work was laboring; the other a floating social structure composed of failures, people poorer and less successful at their work, even if that work was professional, drifting from place to place in search of success.[10]

Katz's earlier research on Hamilton suggested migration levels which reached proportions unheard of elsewhere—with a loss in three months of a quarter of the population. "The continual circulation of population," Katz believed, "prevented the formation of stable and closely integrated communities within nineteenth century communities" and, he concluded, "the facts of transiency destroy any further illusions about community; the population simply changed too rapidly."[11] In this he agreed with David Gagan's assessment of an area not far from Hamilton. "For those people who dwelt only fleetingly in Peel County, as they must have done in other communities, 'community' could have no more meaning than simply the next place they came to as replacements for those who had just left."[12]

At the same time Katz found a highly stratified social system, and he proposed that "the central intellectual task for the student of past societies is to find a satisfactory way of interrelating structural rigidity and personal transiency." The interpretation which others have offered of this interrelationship is that, in a sea of change and flux, conceptually a combination of Robert Wiebe's "island communities" and Thernstrom's "eternally sifting mass," "responsible" groups had to emerge in order to offer to the community a stability which it otherwise would not have had. "Chaos and order could exist," it was said, "with chaos actually enhancing order and stability."[13]

Katz agrees with Peter Laslett's suggestion that "an unchanging, *unchangeable* social structure may well be essential to a swiftly changing population;" apparently Katz believes that the Slavic immigrant whom Wiebe quoted as saying "my people do not live in America, they live underneath America" was at least for the time being in the proper place for the necessary preservation of stability.[14] Thus we are left with a virtually closed structure in which the majority of people roam about the land looking for success (ordinarily economic), while at the same time a privileged and largely "stable" few preserve a system of rigid social and economic inequality not only for the good of the "community" but also for the good of the migrants themselves!

Migration has been blamed for just about everything in modern American history, from cultural breakdown and the absence of socialism in the United States to, most recently, high rates of suicide. Vance Packard popularized the view of migration as a destructive act in *A Nation of Strangers*, in which he spoke of "a society of torn roots." A description of the book claimed that "such constant uprooting robs the individual of his sense of identity. It leads to gnawing loneliness and moral bankruptcy."[15] More recently, in a highly speculative essay, Howard I. Kushner has said that "the suicide rate seems to mirror migration. . . . where ever the in-migration is the greatest as a percentage of the ʊtal population [notably the American west], so is the overall suicide rate." Kushner suggests that

> migration itself may be a strategy of risk-taking pursued by some who feel particularly self-destructive. Migrants tended and tend to be people in search of self-transformation [who often experience] guilt for having rejected past values and rituals.

He concludes: "those migrants who killed themselves experienced severe object loss which they proved unable to ritualize."[16]

We have ample evidence with which to question these hypotheses. Samuel Hays has correctly attacked what he calls the "simplistic reasoning" which leads "from data about high levels of migration to conclusions about either social atomism or social disorganization."[17] There is a growing body of research in social history dealing with the cultures of the working class and of ethnic communities which tells us clearly that those cultures were decidedly too robust to be destroyed by continuing movement.[18] In additon to that, recent research also has called into question the entire hypothesis of the "headlong movement" so widely accepted. My own study of the period between 1875 and 1905, also based upon censuses but in this case with statewide information and utilizing a successful tracing procedure, for example, suggests conclusively that migration did *not* reach such dizzying levels, and indeed was far below the levels posited by earlier investigators.[19] Thernstrom himself foresaw the criticism of his estimates: "the Newburyport laboring population," he said, "was not nearly volatile enough to account for all [the untraced families]. It is clear that the compiler of the directories either did not know about or did not choose to include many working class families in his volumes."[20] Nonetheless, previous investigators of migration patterns formulated and came to accept the hypothesis that *all* of those who were not recovered—who could not traced from one record to another—had migrated. This conclusion is not valid; migration rates simply were not that high, nor was migration so damaging to community as has been proposed.

Subsequent historians have been somewhat more ambivalent about *social* mobility. Since they rarely were able to any significant degree to trace migrants, most mobility analyses dealt only with the "linked," and the concentration upon social and occupational mobility has proceeded in two directions. In one, historians seem to have accepted the definition of social mobility both as desirable and as being a sign of an "open," and therefore a "just," social and economic order. Howard Gitleman went so far as to say that "when compared with other realities, Waltham [Massachusetts] was the scene of a human victory,"[21] because of the possibility of social mobility there.

A concentration upon methodology characterizes the second direction and appears sometimes to have preempted concern with the conceptual impact of the findings (supporting Albert Einstein's observation that "a perfection of means and a confusion of ends seem to characterize our age"). Recently we have gotten more and more finely-graded tables of occupational and status rankings and prestige. In attempting to answer certain questions about the "objective" processes of industrialization the more finely tuned the instrument of measurement the better. Still, it is clear that in our effort to deal more effectively with "objective measures of class," we have begun to lose our grip on the meaningful questions with which we started. As James Henretta has said, more recent studies "have used flawed ideological description as a methodological premise; and the quest for technical exactness and statistical finesse has become more important than an understanding of the lives and cultural values of the historical actors themselves."[22] Again, Katz has provided what may be the logical conclusion of this direction of thought, when he suggests that "the degree of class *cleavage* as well as class *consciousness* follows from the crystallization of tangible components of stratification. . . ."[23]

Recently, however, searching critiques of this social mobility literature have begun to appear. Samuel Hays, for example, has commented that "vertical mobility studies have not been able to generate much historical vision . . . and their contribution to the conceptual recasting of history has been very thin."[24] David Montgomery has charged that the pervasive emphasis upon social mobility in these studies "contains an inherently self-confirming bias." By concentrating solely upon changes in occupation, Montgomery says, "the social life of the working class has been ignored in favor of an interpretation which emphasize[s] middle class attitudes toward work and social values." In his view, the "elaborate patterns of economic and social differentiation produced by the working class [go] unrecognized."[25]

Both Henretta and Margo Conk share this dissatisfaction with the emphasis upon social mobility in work-class life and experience. Conk has challenged the occupational-ranking system used in compiling census statistics, finding bias inherent in the system itself. She charges, first, that the structure of those rankings reflects the census director's own ideological bias. "the *technical* definition of skill," she notes, "gives way to a *cultural* definition when the technical information is ambiguous." For example, Alba M. Edwards of the U.S. Census Bureau arbitraily decided "to divide the manual workforce, some 45 to 50 per cent of the working population, into three groups, each roughly 15 per cent, implying that the United States did not have a large homogeneous 'working class' that was internally coherent and capable of political activity." Conk believes that "the assumption that consciousness may be extrapolated from 'structure' can be traced to the writings of statisticians who used occupation statistics for policy purposes during the late nineteenth and early twentieth centuries." Essentially then, Conk says, "statisticians and economists devised the 'social-economic' status hierarchy scale to analyze the growth of a militant working class, a threatening immigrant population, and an urban society plagued with poverty and political unrest;" the "middle-class principles" so applied "were designed to redefine and reorder the essential social-economic relationships that changed with urbanization and industrialization."[26]

Henretta labels the emphasis on social mobility an "unexamined

legacy of 'consensus' historiography to the first generation of quanti-
tatively-oriented social historians . . . ," and attacks its ideological
assumptions which, he says, not only stem from cold-warrior origins
but are "predicated upon the universality of the values and goals of
the white, upwardly-mobile, Quaker or Protestant middle class."
Thus he agrees with Montgomery that an emphasis upon social mobility "distorts the meaning of the life-experience of other ethnic,
racial, or class groups." Henretta believes that Thernstrom's Newburyport Irish, like William Sewell's workers in nineteenth-century Mar-
seilles who refused occupational "advancement" in order to remain in
their close-knit community, showed "little evidence that either behavior or goals were shaped by the ideology of individual social mobility."
Although Henretta notes that "participation in a capitalist economy
did not necessarily imply an acceptance of the ruling ideology,"
Sewell knows that "they were inevitably drawn into this economic
network." The thrust of their involvement, however, was "a quest for
'security and dignity,'" "rather than an acceptance of the middle class
ideology of occupational advancement." Ultimately Henretta laments
the fact that the countless hours invested in gathering and analyzing
statistical information "might have been spent in reading diaries,
newspapers, or letters—in discovering the felt *meaning* of the lives
and cultural values of the historical actors. . . ." Here (despite his
overreaction against the utility of statistical information) Henretta has
offered us the insight required to begin to "conceptually recast" the
structure of some of these questions. At the same time, both Henretta
and Sewell suggest that workers might have been engaged in what
generally has been labeled "conservative" activities for reasons quite
different from those which may be "obvious" to middle-class ana-
lysts.[27]

The tendency to emphasize "close-to-home" questions in some
areas of social history to the virtual exclusion of the larger community
also is manifest in much of the writing in the field, perhaps no place
more pronounced than in John Bodnar's work. Bodnar has suggested
that the drive for security was such that what happened outside the
home and the family had little, if any, influence on them. While not
entirely ruling out its influence, Bodnar is highly critical of historians'
emphases on the work-place experience as a primary motivating factor in workers' lives. "Rarely acknowledged in discussions of workers'
thoughts and actions," he says, "is the fact that deeply conservative
tendencies pervaded the American working class well before the labor
movement of the 1930s." This conservatism stemmed from the quest

for security, and "the rise of a family-centered world," and apparently obviated any independent action on the shop floor. "Clearly," he says, "family obligations dominated working-class predilections and exerted a moderating influence on individual expectations and the formulation of social and economic goals." This is evidence, Bodnar asserts, of "the predominance of family interests over personal ones." "[F]or most workers and their families," he concluded, most of their activities, certainly including labor protest, "represented an affirmation of a pragmatic world view that included the valuation of job security and a steady wage as the means to family stability." "Regular employment remained the foundation of the enclave itself"; other factors were present but "ancillary." "It was to this larger world" outside the workplace, Bodnar seems to say, "that the worker's consciousness and behavior were tied."[28]

The importance of family and everyday life outside the factory will surprise few. There is, however, another way to view these factors. Certainly we can correlate strikes and other forms of job action generally with periods of economic upturn,[29] but that is far from saying that in the constant cycle of changing employment individual workers were so frightened as to submerge themselves into "a faceless mass." Resistance to the inequities of industrialization as it was organized by corporate capitalists was forthright and constant, making American labor relations perhaps the most violent in the advanced industrial nations. Those who were caught in the employment cycle—that is, most workers—were participants in resistance, too. The existence of "multiple consciousnesses"—different levels of priorities—was a reality among these workers as it is among all groups.[30] The depth of defensiveness Bodnar envisions was not the norm; instead it is a conservative reconstruction.

Much of the discussion, pro and con, over the belief in and the reality of social and occupational mobility in American life largely has ignored the concept which has come to be called "the free labor ideology." As formulated by Eric Foner, the free labor ideology summarized not only the political philosophy of the Republican Party prior to the Civil War, but also contained essential elements of a more-broadly-based middle-class world view. It included "the ideal of equal opportunity for social mobility and economic independence" within a structure which emphasized a community of interest among different levels in the process of production. Fundamental to the ideology was a view of classlessness—the belief that any class divisions which did exist were not permanently confining—combined with a respect for "traditional concepts of social hierarchy." As such, as one historian tells us, free labor "assisted in the transitional processes of industrialization."[31] It emphasized "the dignity of labor" at the same time as it promised "an escape from labor."[32] "There is no permanent class of hired laborers among us," claimed Abraham Lincoln:

> "Twenty-five years ago I was a hired laborer. The hired laborer of yesterday labors on his own today, and will hire others to labor for him tomorrow. Advancement—improvement in condition—is the order of things in a society of equals."[33] "If any continue through life in the condition of the hired laborer, it is not the fault of the system, but because of either a dependent nature which prefers it, or improvidence, folly, or singular misfortune."[34]

As the *New York Times* put it, "our paupers today, thanks to free labor, are our yeomen and merchants of tomorrow." To Republicans "free labor meant . . . the opportunity to quit the wage-earning class." Still, we must remember that "the line between capitalist and worker was to a large extent blurred in the ante-bellum northern economy, which centered on the independent farm and small shop." According to Foner, however, ultimately "the aspirations of the free labor ideology were . . . thoroughly middle class" in the quest for self-employment and ownership of "a business, farm, or shop."[35]

Free labor was a middle-class ideology, but one which contained significant elements attractive to many segments of the working class. We know that, in the face of the "nation in frantic pursuit of wealth" many American workers challenged the growing business structure by seeking to go "beyond equality."[36] Still, perhaps this was not so fully a rejection of the basis of the free labor ideology as an effort to defend its fundamental features, now being shunted aside by the developing industrial capitalist economic structure. In the latter part of the nineteenth century the "gospel of success" reached its zenith. All segments of American society, workers as much as the middle class, were assailed by its imagery. Post-bellum versions of the gospel of success were much crasser in form than Lincoln's belief had been, but it expressed not only the crude beliefs of an acquisitive society; it also posited the virtues of application and achievement. Over that period the belief in "free labor" itself, though increasingly strained and more and more rejecting the harsh appeals of acquisitive individualism, did not fade away. In his study of the working class in Albany, New York between 1845 and 1885, Brian Greenberg tells us that the

free labor ideology was not so quickly jettisoned by American workers
who had adopted it earlier. Certainly it was changed, as Greenberg
says: "for workers in Albany during the transitional years, a dialectic
evolved between the dominant, middle-class community consciousness characterized by free labor social values and workers' class consciousness."[37] Fundamental aspects of the ideology continued to influence important segments of the American working class in the
latter ninteenth century, and those segments often were among the
more influential in charting the direction of working-class thought.

We have more than sufficient evidence to show concerted resistance
on the part of much of the working class to the doctrine of "acquisitive
individualism" which characterized American industrialization.[38] Yet,
at the same time we know that, despite the committed and often
violent resistance to capitalist-directed industrialization, and despite
the widespread disaffection, dissatisfaction, and frustration with
which many workers labored, not only was that resistance ultimately
unsuccessful, but capitalist hegemony ultimately was achieved. Perception, even as opposed to reality, is of critical importance in terms
of what people believe and the ways in which they behave. Their
perceptions were critical in this instance because, after all the methodological issues are resolved, the social mobility statistics are real, and
there was ample evidence of individual advancement to appeal to
those willing to believe. Herbert Gutman, for example, has told us of
some of the more notable examples:

> what matters [in evaluating social mobility] is the fact that the
> rags-to-riches promise was not a mere myth in Paterson, New
> Jersey, between 1830 and 1880. So many successful manufactur-
> ers who had begun as workers walked the streets of that city
> that it is not hard to believe that others less successful or just
> starting out on the lower rungs of the occupational mobility lad-
> der could be convinced by personal knowledge that "hard
> work" resulted in spectacular material and social improve-
> ment.[39]

Social mobility occurred often enough for its possibility to be taken
seriously by many workers, if they desired it.

Historians long have recognized one of the constant components of
working-class life: the threat of unemployment. As Bruce Laurie has
pointed out, historians are more apt to pay attention to workers when
they protest against *over*work than when they talk about the *lack* of
work. This may produce more scintillating reading, but "it encour-

age[s] a narrow view of the working class experience." Unemployment and underemployment—the line between them often was very thin—were endemic to working-class life (as to some degree they remain so today). E.P. Thompson has noted in a different context that "the very notion of the regularity of employment is an anachronistic notion, imposed by twentieth century experience upon nineteenth century realities." "Habitual uncertainty of employment," he declared, "was the problem in most industries and in urban experience generally" in the earlier period. Irwin Yellowitz reported that working-class "idleness" was "a basic feature of the American economy" during industrialization.[40]

Irregularity of employment stemmed from several causes. Seasonality of industry itself is the most obvious: an inability, for example, for outdoor workers to work during the winter months. Not only did the weather prevent such work, but winter often closed down transportation systems, especially waterways. Thernstrom reported that the common laborer in late-nineteenth-century Massachusetts averaged no more than about 230 days of work per year and was in danger of losing his job at any time. Virginia Yans-McLaughlin has told us that unskilled seasonal workers around Buffalo and the rest of western New York often were without work for six or seven months of the year. Some families there would work intensely, involving all able-bodied members, through and beyond the summer, often violating compulsory school attendance laws to keep their children at work, and sometimes were able to save enough to carry them through a winter without work. Some industries simply were seasonal in their production patterns, or responded to demand rather than stockpiling materials. In the railroad industry, one observer reported, that "irregularity is constant; it is impossible to tell on Monday morning where one will be on Wednesday." Cloakworkers and garment workers also generally had only seasonal work. Helpers, for example, ordinarily worked (often were overworked) for six or seven months a year, with a layoff from the middle of November to the middle of January. O.J. Abell observed that the seasonality of automobile factories "contributed its interest to the general unrest."[41]

Economist R.M. MacIver observed in 1919 that "the standing menace of unemployment acts as a pernicious influence over the whole field of industry," and it was central in the minds of workers. Abraham Karp recounts the experience of Morris R. Cohen's father, who had been out of work and discriminated against to the point that he was "more or less reconciled to the fact of unemployment." Jacob Riis observed women from the sweatshops: "her own and her husband's work brings the family earnings of up to $25 a week, when they have work all the time. But often the time is put in looking for it . . . six months of the year the cloakmaker is idle, or nearly so. . . ." A letter from immigrant Yonah Medinkoff laments: "because the work at our place is at an end, and I may have to be without work . . . I do not know what to do." Daniel Rodgers has said that "for the potential greenhorn the *governing* experience was the irregularity of work—the initial, painful shock of unemployment which led in turn to entrapment in a brutal round of temporary jobs," and John Cumbler has noted the irregularity of employment in the Massachusetts shoe industry in the later-nineteenth and the early part of the twentieth centuries: "not more than one-half" of the workers "would have more than eight months of full work. . . ." In short, as labor economist W.M. Leiserson said in 1916, "unemployment is a constant and inevitable risk for almost all working people. . . ."[42] Even when work was plentiful its tenuousness seemed to be recognized constantly: "the feeling of plenty of work for myself and others in the machine shop," said one machinist, "seems the biggest thing in my mind today, [there seems] no danger of being laid off."[43]

Because industrial employment was endemically seasonal and industrial development geographically widespread, migration, too, was a fact of life. The rates of movement were nowhere near as high as have been suggested previously, and there was no great, permanent, helpless floating proletariat, but industrial development was geographically diverse, and intricate patterns of migration developed. One primary pattern was temporary movement. This included the long-term experience of the many thousands of European immigrants who saw their presence in America as a temporary expedient designed to raise money as well as the short-range movement of the worker who, while settled in one locale, followed a circuit over which he traveled for work and returned home regularly.[44] Cumbler relates that the "floating population" of Lynn was composed especially of young workers who traveled regionally in search of work during the off-season. When work was available in Lynn they would return, and "eventually they would settle down in the city and become permanent residents."[45] Patricia Cooper characterizes young cigar makers' travels as "footloose," but well defined.[46]

There *was* a "reserve army of labor," but a reserve army and a group of helpless, alienated floaters are not the same thing. Marx's formulation was more accurate: "Modern industry's whole form of motion depends on the constant transformation of a part of the working population into unemployed or semi-employed hands," he said, because "there must be the possibility of suddenly throwing great masses of men into the decisive areas without doing any damage to the scale of production in other spheres." The nineteenth-century American worker surely would have agreed with Marx that "an accumulation of misery [is] a necessary condition, corresponding to the accumulation of wealth" but, perhaps over the long range, in the aggregate rather than permanently for each family. Marx's further formulation also is borne out: the developmental cycles of modern industry depend "on the constant *formation*, the greater or less *absorption*, and the *reformation* of the industrial reserve army or surplus population."[47] Thus, while there is a reserve labor supply available, it is not necessarily always composed of the same individuals—as Leiserson said, "the personnel of the 'army' is constantly changing."[48] Nor was it necessarily an unskilled work force, considering the changing demands of differential industrial development. A proportion of the working class was endemically unemployed, but the patterns of development, employment, and response were sufficiently intricate and complex to insure that it was the composition of the "floating population" that was "constantly shifting."

What we see here is that the irregularity of work certainly engendered a constant insecurity among many workers, and this did not characterize the experience of only a small part of the working class. The irregularity of employment was the reality for all, and insecurity was a constant. Workers felt the cycles of unemployment very deeply. Whiting Williams was one of a number of white-collar workers who spent time laboring with the working class, and he had been viewed as a generally perceptive and accurate observer. To Williams it became clear that "the job's the thing . . . the job is the axis on which the whole world turns for the working man," and that the objective irregularity of employment became for each individual "the terror of joblessness. . . ," the "hopelessness, the foreboding disastrousness of joblessness." "It does seem almost impossible to over-estimate the all-importance of the job to the worker." Even a few days of "failure [to find work] burns deep into their souls." One unemployed steel worker told Williams that he liked to frequent a bar on Saturday afternoon and drink a little. " 'How much?' Oh, only enough to make me feel as though I had my old position back . . . you know."[49]

Williams described the scene at the factory gates when job-hunters stood hoping to be chosen for work on that day. "Men don't seem to

chat or make friends then because each feels the other his competi-
tor—so we all stood shivering, silent, and intent. . . . " "The gulf
there is between men at such a time! Between those who . . . [feel]
themselves members of the privileged class of job-holders, and us who
looked on in envy. The only bigger gulf I can imagine to-night is
between such as us and . . . the plant policeman."[50]

Many immigrants, especially those who sent money home and
intended to return themselves to their native land, were not much
concerned with buying a home, but they were concerned about regular employment. "The one essential" for them, says David Brody, was
"employment itself," and he quotes one immigrant steelworker as
saying "when there is [no job] . . . America is worth nothing." Steelworkers, in particular, were caught in a cycle between overwork and
chronic idleness. Brody notes that the Immigation Commission in
1908 found that "thirty per cent of the immigrant steelworkers . . .
worked less than six months, almost two-thirds under nine months"
of the year." "The Slavic steelworker found entirely acceptable the
terms of work imposed by the system of economy," Brody says; "only
unemployment was impossible to accommodate within the immigrant's purpose." For some caught in the cycle—even the employed,
Williams believed—"there is so wide-spread and so deep-set a conviction that for them there is no chance to break thru" their situation—
Gompers had said of immigrants that they "are caught in the clutches
of a struggle for existence so exigent that it leaves neither opportunity
nor strength for betterment."[51]

The possibility of advancement still was believed to be real, indeed
was to be expected as one grew older and spent more time in a craft,
and on a job, even if in this irregular and intermittent fashion. One
way in which to adapt to changing economic developments, and to
seek some small degree of advancement, was through changing jobs,
and there was an extraordinary amount of job changing. My own
studies of migration and economic development in the United States
reveal an intensity of job shifting that is nothing short of startling, but
it only confirms the observations of other investigators. Daniel Rodgers reports finding "an astonishingly restless and mobile labor force
. . . a constant shuffling of men" in and out of plants:[52]

> To keep a work force of about 8,000 employees, for example, Ar-
> mour in Chicago hired 8,000 workers during the course of 1914,
> and the pattern was repeated over and again in the early-twen-
> tieth-century factories. Larger turnover surveys concluded that

about one-third of the employees of a typical factory held on to
their jobs a year or less, and, because they moved so often, annual factory turnover in normal times was at least as high as
the 100 percent reported at Armour. Turnover in the wool industry between 1907 and 1910 varied between 113 and 163 per
cent; in 1913-1914 a Bureau of Labor Statistics survey of sixty-
eight manufacturing plants found an average yearly turnover of
115 per cent, despite the current economic slump. At casually
managed plants or regions troubled by labor shortages, the
turnover rate ran still higher. It reached 176 per cent in the
Southern textile industry in 1907, 252 per cent in a sample of
Detroit factories in 1916, and the bewildering rate of 370 per
cent at Ford in 1913.

Stephen Meyer noted that the high rates of labor turnover—training
replacements and so forth—in 1913 cost Ford about $2 million. "They
are conducting a continuous, unorganized strike," said John R. Commons. Job turnover also was a response to be being laid off for union
activity, because of accidents, for strikes or other job actions—for a
myriad of other causes. Men often quit, company spokesman Boyd
Fischer claimed, because they "are often ignorant, narrow, highly
sensitive to trivial wrongs or fancied oppression by 'capital.' " "All
the workmen I have known individually," he said, "have gone to new
jobs dead broke."[53] His conclusions were prejudiced by his position,
but his understanding of the level of job turnover certainly was correct.

Yet job changing is not by any means the same thing as migration.
Even geographically-stable workers were highly likely to change jobs.
Automobile workers, noted Myron S. Watkins, "are continually on
the alert for 'better pay,' and a difference of five cents per hour in
favor of a new job will lead them to 'throw up' an old job without
delay." A number of other reasons—from seeking more overtime to
attempting to 'steal a trade' also are mentioned. The point is that
workers engaged in *rational* movement; by and large most workers
changing jobs were circulating among jobs and factories in local areas
and not simply leaving the area. Most accounts do not reckon with the
employment cycle in figuring the rates of job changing, but certainly
this must have been a major component in the process.[54]

Still there remained in many quarters, among many workers, the
belief that advancement in their positions *was* a possibility, and a
feeling as well that such advancement should be sought. Although,
for example, one of the workers at the Lowell textile mills in 1844 said

that "I won't stay here and be a white slave," another reasoned that "we must not forget that there are advantages, as well as disadvantages, in this employment, as in every other. If we expect to find all sunshine and flowers in any station in life we shall most surely be disappointed. . . ."[55] Immigrants shared this ambivalence. Mary Antin recalled that "being set down in the garden of America. . . . I am bound to make my days a triumphal march toward my goal," and see "my grievances melted away."[56] Jacob Riis helped perpetuate this view: "the poorest immigrant comes here with the purpose and ambition to better himself and, given half a chance, might be reasonably expected to make the most of it." "This sweater's family . . . in a few years will own a tenement somewhere and profit by the example set by the example set by their landlord in rent-collecting."[57]

Given the reality of irregular employment, the constant fear of unemployment, and the ever-present insecurity engendered by these employment cycles, it might indeed be supposed that workers became "invisible," "alienated," and "helpless," buffeted about by objective economic forces. Both middle-class commentators and working-class radical organizers supposed it was so; it would seem to have been so. Even when there were jobs the whims of employers and foremen introduced insecurity; the black list was a reality; usually there were plenty of others waiting—"plenty waitin' at the gates," they said—to take the place of anyone who displeased his superiors. It was said that men with families were particularly vulnerable, and that the spectre of unemployment and insecurity so traumatized them that it made them plastic, acquiescent to the demands of employers because they feared for their jobs.[58]

At the same time we have account after account of the desire of large portions of the working class to achieve just what the free labor ideology had promised—entrepreneurship, self-employment. Today's pattern reflects yesterday's: Rodgers notes that

> in surprising numbers [industrial] workers harbor entrepreneurial hopes of their own. . . . Bendix and Lipset's study of Oakland, California in 1949-1950 found that *two-thirds* of the blue-collar heads of families had at one time thought of going into business for themselves . . . studies of the automobile industry in the 1940s and early 1950s seemed to confirm their findings.[59]

John Briggs discovered an orientation toward proprietorship among many Italian immigrant wage earners he studied; Michael Katz tells us that workers wanted the same thing in nineteenth-century Hamilton, and my own studies reveal an enormous amount of movement back and forth between manual occupationals and lower-white collar jobs, and self employment. One worker put in his diary what many others thought: "I can't help feeling a little insecure and sort of wonder if I could not start in some business for myself." This was a constant theme expressed by many workers.[60]

What this illustrates is that the working class was motivated in large part by the fear and insecurity engendered by the endemic irregularity of employment, and constantly made efforts to confront and to solve this situation and to achieve a resolution. There were two clear solutions: one, to rise in the working-class ranks to the higher levels of skilled work—still vulnerable but less seldom laid off—or, second, to escape altogether from the ranks of manual employment into self-employment, perceived as offering more secure or more satisfying possibilities for the individual. The tendency that Thernstrom and others have noted for many workers to sacrifice mightily to purchase their own homes may have been another route[61]—at least then there was a stable homestead—but workers knew there was at least some possibility of a more amenable job stituation in other ranks.

The immigrant Louis Adamic and many of his fellows knew that "in America there was no stability," that "America the jungle swallows many people who go there to work. She squeezes the work out of them"; "more are swept under than rise." He had been warned by a friend who said simply "I was there too long. I worked too hard." Adamic's friend Yanko Radin expressed a characteristic outlook of many workers, immigrant and nonimmigrant alike: "for many people," he said, "I don't doubt, America is a bad place, but," he added, "I am not afraid. . . ."[62] Workers knew first hand the vicissitudes of their lives and employment situations but, despite the terror of joblessness, their will was indomitable and their confidence strong: they believed they could succeed, as part of a working-class community, despite the hardships they knew they would encounter.

The absolute dichotomy that has arisen between pro-/anti- middle class is a false one, and to label workers who sought self-employment and small business automatically as "bourgeois" misses the point. The quest for self-employment for them was not always an effort to flee from good and honest hard work—this they valued—and they knew the life of the lower middle class was hard in its own right. It was instead a quest for *dignity*—an effort to flee from the arbitrariness of the capitalist employer. Nor did it mean they turned their backs on their friends and fellow workers.

The inappropriateness of such supposition to the contrary can be seen in the account Cumbler offers of Fall River, Massachusetts, which was known as "the center of militant unionism." In Fall River the textile union, which continually sought a number of alternatives to capitalist organization of industrial production, developed a special program to aid union members who not only had been laid off but blacklisted as well: grants *to open a small business.* "Men who have been discharged from one mill and are unable to obtain work in any other," said a Fall River union official, "have to go into some business. It was only the other day we gave a spinner one hundred dollars to go into another business, and he will probably open a liquor store" or, like many other discharged operatives, a tavern. We also learn of "penny capitalists" in ninteenth-century England, what John Benson calls "working-class entrepreneurs," workers and working-class families who constantly "branched out" into small-business enterprises in order to make ends meet. For whatever reasons they did this, it was not in simple emulation of the middle class. Clyde and Sally Griffen found worker-small business links in Poughkeepsie: "For manual workers," they report, "self-employment at the least offered the pos-sibility of economic security in old age. That motive," they add, "re-mained potent long after hopes of achieving any prominence in Poughkeepsie diminished." Herbert Gutman furnishes information that confirms this interpretation when he describes his discovery of the support small shopkeepers in younger industrial cities offered to striking workers. Not only did they support those who shopped at their stores; in many cases they also supported those at whose side they had worked and well might work again.[63]

Small shopkeepers had their own problems and, in all probability, the longer they wrestled with the concerns of entrepreneurship and survival the more those concerns came to consume their attention. They were constantly aware of the insecurity of small business, and would not find it easy to accept failure. Small shopkeepers who rose from the ranks of the ethnic working class in Bayonne, New Jersey, for example, identified strongly with the middle class,[64] and this was true elsewhere. It is well to remember Jefferson's dictum that "merchants have no country," but just as well to remember that, at least initially, for many small business owners their class position was ambivalent.

It is not realistic to deny the existence of the desire to achieve and to advance among nineteenth- and twentieth-century workers. It was present, and for many of them hard work was not directed only toward generation of savings and home buying; it also was aimed at advancement and savings, often toward investment in one's own business. It almost would appear that the American worker was responding to the middle-class success ethic. It seems apparent that this, however, was not always the case. Large numbers of American workers sought social mobility. For many of them, however, it was not simply a matter of advances in status or wealth, but a quest for the security necessary to feed a family, even, at worst, to avoid a pauper's burial. A worker moved toward a situation in which he could provide his *own* steady work, or toward a position more likely to guarantee it, and to escape not so much from labor as from domination; it was not the *work* which was onerous, though hard it was—it was the capriciousness of *control*. Even though class perspectives might seem to have merged here, they merely coincided. To the worker seeking security for his family, the desire to provide that security was not a repudiation of his class nor of his culture—rather, it as easily was an affirmation of them. The solutions to insecurity were those made available by a capitalist economy, but their formulation in this case was indigenous to the working class. They interpreted in their own fashion the dignity that the free labor ideology offered. Perhaps it was inescapable in the end that the pervasive and pernicious nature of the capitalist economy would offer only a small range of solutions, and that they in turn would induce a form of acceptance of that structure in the process of struggling to survive within it.[65] But at least American workers sought "success" for their own reasons and on their own terms.

Chapter 6

The Dialectics of Bureaucratization: The Case of Nineteenth-Century American Railway Workers

WALTER LICHT

In May of 1877, top executives of the Illinois Central Railroad (IC) received word of a potentially explosive situation on the line. In the shop town of Waterloo, Iowa, local officials allegedly had purchased sizable parcels of land which they had subdivided and were now compelling IC shopmen to buy at high prices as a guarantee of continued employment. A further accusation was lodged that one foreman had opened a boardinghouse and a general store, which families of railroad employees were coerced into patronizing. President William Ackerman of the IC ordered an investigation of the charges and eventually a number of the accused were censured, although the allegations were never fully substantiated.[1] The case, whatever its particulars, illustrates the conditions under which the first two generations of American railwaymen worked.

The operating railroad workers of America's pioneer railroads entered large-scale organizations which were bureaucratically shaped by a remarkable group of innovative and sophisticated corporate business managers.[2] Early railroad executives devised organizational structures and bureaucratic principles and techniques of management to bring order to the vast networks of men and machines over which they presided. The systems they developed in turn served as models for complex vertically- and horizontally-integrated industrial and commercial firms that began to dominate the country's economic landscape in the late nineteenth and early twentieth centuries.

The events in Waterloo, Iowa, in 1877, however, suggest that formal plans, guidelines, and official pronouncements provide a poor measure of the real world of daily work. A look behind the tables of organization and published reports reveals that pioneer railwaymen entered new work organizations fabricated by inventive railroad leaders only to find their work experiences determined by personal relations with supervisors and foremen. In the early years, local officials handled recruitment, discipline, compensation, job assignments, work loads, promotions, and injury and death benefit awards, among other aspects of work, in arbitrary, discretionary, and often despotic ways, despite rules and regulations and strict hierarchies of authority and accountability established from on high.

In the late nineteenth century, American railroad workers would organize and protest against the uncertain conditions of their employment. In the name of fairness, justice and security, they would demand stricter bureaucratic procedures and standards to collectively control as much of the work experience as possible—in effect, demand to have the bureaucracy function on their behalf. But the nation's first railwaymen labored under different, less ordered and equitable circumstances, and their history sheds light on bureaucratization, the labor process, and work in industrializing America.[3]

The earliest glimpse of the administration of America's pioneer railroads is provided in a report prepared in 1838 by Jonathan Knight and Benjamin Latrobe, two civil engineers in the employ of the Baltimore & Ohio Railroad.[4] Knight and Latrobe surveyed the operations of four rail lines. On the twenty-seven-mile-long, two-engine, three-trips-per-day Long Island Railroad, they found one manager supervising a fifty-odd-man task force of ticket masters, conductors, enginemen, brakemen, machinists, carpenters, and track, yard and station laborers. Authority was slightly more decentralized on the Boston & Worcester Railroad. There, Knight and Latrobe noted that a general superintendent had delegated power to depot masters at the ends of the line who shared responsibility for the supervision of all employees. On two other lines, the Boston & Providence and the Boston & Lowell Railroads, the two engineers also discerned primitive decentralized management structures, but these two companies added a new wrinkle. The superintendents of each had appointed master enginemen to oversee the machine shops and the activities of the locomotive drivers and firemen, thus dispensing power not only geographically but functionally as well. The simple administrative arrangements of these early railroads obviously reflected the small-scale nature of operations at the time.

As the operations of railroad companies expanded in size and complexity in the 1840s and 1850s, the problems of managing large numbers of employees became more pressing. The first railroad seriously to be affected was the Western Rail Road of Massachusetts. When that line had opened in 1839, the company adopted a loose regionalized and departmentalized structure, with two depot masters, a master mechanic, and a road master placed in charge of operations.[5] In 1840, after a series of accidents, including a spectacular head-on collision near Westfield, Massachusetts, and a subsequent state investigation of the road's management, the board of directors of the Western was forced to reorganize the company's administrative procedures.[6] The directors then agreed on a new regional approach in which the road was divided into three sections.[7] A general superintendent appointed masters of transportation and roadmasters to oversee activities within each region. One master mechanic was placed in charge of the Western's repair shops. This divisional approach thus localized authority and served to create in effect three small operating units within the one company. In addition to the structural changes, the board of directors issued a manual of regulations strictly delineating the tasks and responsibilities of each manager and operating employee. The regulations established a clear chain of command with rules to guide the actions of each level of the network.

In 1847 the managers of the Baltimore & Ohio Railroad took the next important initiatives in developing new administrative practices.[8] Working with a committee of board members, Benjamin Latrobe, now chief engineer for the firm, devised an organizational plan for the road. This was the first to create an office of treasurer, responsible for handling all external financial matters and for supervising the secretary and the chief clerk of the company, who were placed in charge of controlling and checking the internal flow of revenues. The report provided detailed new procedures for collecting fares, receiving and receipting freight, and transmitting funds. It also established a general superintendent to oversee "The Working of the Road." Under his direct command were three departmental heads: a master of the road, who appointed local supervisors to see to the upkeep of the track, depots, bridges, and other physical structures not connected with the machine shops; a master of machinery, who delegated authority and assignments to machine- and repair-shop foremen; and the most important functional official, the master of transportation, whose duties "embrace[d] all such as belong specially to the forwarding of passengers and tonnage of the road."[9] In his charge were engineers, firemen, conductors, fuel, lumber and depot agents, and stationmasters—the latter in turn overseeing the work of station help. The B & O plan clearly set forth the responsibilities of managers and subordinates. The plan further provided for a system of monthly reports that each administrative level was expected to present to those immediately above. The plan was noteworthy for its highly-developed departmental approach to business management.

A crucial modification of the B & O Railroad structure was effected in the 1850s on the New York & Erie Railroad. When the line's operations began in 1851, it was by far the largest railroad in the country; by the mid-1850s, it employed more than four thousand men. High costs, great inefficiencies, and waste plagued the Erie in its early years and there was a pressing need for systematized management.[10]

Daniel McCallum, general superintendent of the Erie, seized the opportunity. He first divided the line into four geographical regions and appointed divisional superintendents who were made responsible for the day-to-day movement of trains and traffic and the upkeep of roadbeds and buildings within their domains.[11] McCallum also created departmental offices to conduct functional activities—the purchase of fuel, the general handling of freight and passenger business, the building and repair of machinery, and the operations of the telegraph system. A mixed departmental-divisional structure was thus created. McCallum further established a system of detailed hourly, daily, and monthly reports. He ordered Erie employees to wear prescribed grade-specific uniforms. The notion of systematized administrative hierarchy was so important to him that he released to the public an organizational chart of the Erie's operations, probably the first of its kind for an American business enterprise.[12]

McCallum, however, never solved a critical problem on the Erie— the unclear relationships between departmental and divisional officers—whether, for instance, a stationmaster was directly subordinate to the general freight agent, the general ticket agent, or his divisional superintendent. It remained for executives on the Pennsylvania Railroad to fully develop McCallum's innovations. In the 1880s, the Pennsylvania emerged as the nation's largest carrier, with over five thousand miles of track and 50,000 employees. The basic administrative structure, improving on McCallum's work, was actually conceived in the late 1850s when the line was half the size of the Erie.[13]

The Pennsylvania plan was devised in 1858 by J. Edgar Thomson, president of the road during its formative years. Thomson followed McCallum's model in establishing an office of general superintendent to oversee the performance of functional department heads and divisional officials. Thomson's crucial refinement involved the delegation to regional officers of direct and definitive charge of all operations within their domains, including the daily movement of traffic, maintenance of the roadbed, and the work of the shops.[14] Under Thomson's scheme, departmental heads at central headquarters received authority to develop plans and overall strategies, set standards and procedures, make inspections, and advise divisional officers, but were afforded no direct role in the daily supervision of operations and employees.

The Pennsylvania plan thus established a clear differentiation between the functions of line and staff officers, between operational and entrepreneurial decision makers. In its unique combination of the divisional and departmental approaches of the Western and B & O plans, the Pennsylvania scheme eliminated the ambiguities of the Erie system. In decentralizing authority and the supervision of activities, the Pennsylvania design also created small, relatively independent units, in effect local fiefdoms, within the one mammoth enterprise.

With minor variations, other major trunk lines in the United States during the last half of the nineteenth century adopted the Pennsylvania's line and staff differentiation in their administrative plans.[15] Mid-nineteenth century railwaymen thus worked in enterprises where ownership and management evolved as separate domains; where chains of salaried officials, whose sole function was that of managing, supervised tasks; where a multiplicity of assignments existed, each defined specifically; where authority was delegated and functions performed according to stated guidelines; and where the work was compartmentalized into separate, often geographically dispersed units—work situations, in other words, in which each person occupied a small place in a large complex setting. The railroads were the first American enterprises to introduce bureaucratic principles and techniques of management. And their laboring forces were the first American workers to enter such kinds of employment structures.[16]

For various reasons, actual railroad operations in the early years rarely corresponded to formal administrative designs or prescriptions. Pioneer railroad executives carefully and deliberately divised bureaucratic structures to manage the performance of work; yet, once the administrative charts were drawn and in place, the manner and spirit in which the work was supervised was left to individuals and circumstance. The first generation of managers in fact devoted little formal attention to labor-related matters and held few views in common on the subject. Labor loomed as an area of interest inasmuch as labor costs represented a major component of railway operating expenses, but personnel problems and industrial relations did not emerge as a particular conscious conern.[17] In the last quarter of the nineteenth century, violent confrontations between railroad management and labor would force subsequent generations of executives in the industry to treat labor matters with due care and consideration.

Bureaucratic decentralization also bred arbitrariness. As power was dispensed and dispersed by plan, official rules became less sanctified and obeyed at local levels. Because railroad operations and services were so irregular in the first fifty years of rail transport development—a reflection of the instability of commercial activity in general—formal guidelines quickly lost meaning and force in what invariably were contingent situations. This can be seen at all stages of the work experience; a good place to begin is with the whole question of recruitment at the point of hire.

American railroad companies through the 1860s faced the enormously difficult task of recruiting large new labor forces into all branches of the trade. Not surprisingly, early railroad managers recruited each class of railway labor from occupations and pursuits where skills were roughly analogous and transferable. The first conductors, for example, came from existing transportation concerns and were men familiar with the needs and demands of the traveling public. P. C. Hale and James Potter, the first conductors on the Eastern Railroad, and S. A. Lawrence and Humphrey Cozzens, pioneer conductors on the Atlantic & St. Lawrence, were former stagecoach drivers.[18] The first group of conductors on the Chicago & Rock Island Railroad in the 1850s were former captains of packet ships on the Great Lakes.[19] Stationmasters similarly were drawn from commercial enterprises specializing in transportation services—mercantile firms, overseas shipping companies, and stagecoach and freight wagon lines, while the clerks who assisted them in receipting and bookkeeping tasks were recruited from business and government offices where they had developed what one early applicant for a railroad clerkship called a "handsome hand" and an ability to keep orderly ledger books.[20]

In a similar manner, the small but growing iron, machine, and building trades provided the blacksmiths, machinists, and carpenters who manned the repair and construction facilities of the early railroads. From those machine shops where the first locomotives were built also came the nation's pioneer corps of engine drivers and firemen. When the South Carolina Canal & Rail Road Company became the first line to commence scheduled steam locomotive service in

1831, at the throttle of the company's engine was Nicholas W. Darrell. He had been a machinist's apprentice in the West Point Foundry in New York, where the engine parts were forged. Darrell traveled south with the finished components of the engine, directed its assemblage, was hired by the line to be its sole locomotive driver, and eventually became the firm's first superintendent of machinery.[21] Pioneer railroad companies thus drew their engineers and, in most cases, firemen from the machine shops where the pioneer locomotives were built. These men generally were machinists or machinists' apprentices by training and trade; many actually had been involved in the construction of the engines which they eventually drove, and they came to the railroads with a good deal of mechanical expertise.[22]

Finally, early railroad companies had on hand a general pool of casual day laborers to fill unskilled positions such as station and yard hands, track maintenance workers, and brakemen. In the North, the growing immigrant population served as an important source of unskilled labor; in the South, the pioneer railroads relied heavily on readily available supplies of hired and purchased slaves.[23]

The early railroads thus tapped outside sources to fill their labor supply needs; in later years, they would develop internal promotion schemes and practices to facilitate recruitment of upper-grade workers. In general, the nation's first railroads experienced little difficulty attracting a large and adequately skilled work force. Letters in corporate archives reveal that potential recruits deluged companies with applications.[24]

But while their hiring needs were met adequately, the early railroads encountered severe problems in labor retention. Turnover remained extremely high throughout the period from 1830 to 1880; payroll analysis of six mid-nineteenth-century railroads reveals that upwards of fifty percent of the men engaged at any given moment remained with their respective companies for a maximum of six months.[25] Seasonal factors, the irregular labor needs of the carriers, disciplinary discharges, accidental injuries and fatalities, and frequent job-hopping between firms all contributed to high rates of employee turnover.

Initially, hiring was a highly formalized process, with boards of directors examining applications and credentials and electing railwaymen to their posts. Surviving minute books of the Boston & Worcester Railroad show that in 1834 the directors of the line voted "that J. Leach be employed by the superintendent as Engineer to take charge of the Locomotive, called the Meteor, at the rate of two dollars per day." Similar entries report the approval or rejection of requests for employment as station agents and clerks, conductors, firemen, carpenters, and even maintenance-of-the-way men.[26]

As rail lines increased the size and scope of their operations, and as their administrative structures became more multi-layered and complex, recruitment became less formalized. The power to hire gradually came to rest with local departmental and divisional officials and supervisors.[27] This eliminated lengthy and involved approval procedures, but also opened the entire process to various forms of discriminatory favoritism.

Family connections became a very important asset in securing employment. In his reminiscences, *Railroadman*, Harry French explained that he obtained his first job with the aid of his older brother's influence with a local supervisor. French later provided the same kind of help for his younger brother.[28] Similar stories are told in the autobiographies of other pioneer railwaymen.[29] Additional evidence of the importance of family connections can be found in surviving payroll records, where groups of similarly surnamed employees abound; in letters of application, where frequent reference is made to relatives in the trade, and, finally, in corporate memoranda, where the reality of familial interventions was both recognized and partially encouraged as a means of engendering loyalty and discipline.[30]

The exact extent to which family connections were important in obtaining work in the railroad industry a century ago is difficult to ascertain. Two sources indicate, however, that as many as half of the men in the trade may have had kin working alongside them. In 1900 the Illinois Central Railroad gathered biographical information on several thousand of its employees for a celebratory company history. Of the 155 workers born before 1850 (they were among the first to be employed on the line), fifty percent reported having at least one close relative in the trade, most of whom worked for the Illinois Central.[31] A recently finished study of employment patterns on the Atchinson, Topeka & Santa Fe Railroad in the late nineteenth century similarly found that as many as half the men on that line had relatives working for the company.[32] Whether it was a result of nepotism or of workers hearing of vacancies and beseeching local foremen to hire their brothers and sons, the available evidence indicates that direct family connections played a significant role in nineteenth-century railroad recruitment practices.[33]

Other personal and political associations also represented valuable assets in securing railway employment. Close friends could be as helpful as relatives in obtaining jobs. Letters of recommendation from clergymen, former employers, railroad company stockholders, prominent members of the community, and political figures served to enhance the chances of recruits. When Alvah Hersey applied for a job as a depot master in 1849 to the Atlantic & St. Lawrence Railroad, he included in his application a testimonial to his moral worth and general abilities that was signed by stockholders of the road.[34] Herbert Hamblen, in his reminiscences, *The General Manager's Story*, related the experiences of a veteran engineer named Pop, who was a machinist by trade. Pop apparently never fired an engine a day in his life and stepped right into a locomotiveman's position. As he explained; "When the road opened, I had a letter from a big man. I asked for a job and was given an engine at once."[35]

Familial and nonfamilial connections, of course, could be as crucial in second and third attempts at securing employment as in inital hiring. A clear pattern emerges in surviving reminiscences. Veteran railwaymen, privy to job information carried by the rumor mill of the rails, frequently hopped about the country in search of better opportunities, often to find relatives, old friends, fellow employees, and former superivsors—a veritable nationwide network of contacts—to assist them in obtaining new employment. A common practice was for superintendents and foremen to take their favorite employees with them in their frequent moves between companies.[36] A free-floating market of anonymous applicants who would be judged purely on grounds of merit and achievement-oriented priorities—a model suggested by classical labor economic theory and inferred in recent studies of geographical mobility—thus did not exist for the nation's first two generations of railwaymen.

If family or personal connections failed, bribery loomed as another means of obtaining employment. The outright selling and purchasing of jobs was a common practice in the railroad industry in the nineteenth century. Investigators on the Baltimore & Ohio Railroad in the 1860s discovered that shop foremen on that line were extorting an average of five dollars per month from new employees.[37] Similar probes on the Chicago, Burlington & Quincy in the 1870s revealed that one divisional superintendent required all men under his charge to buy insurance policies from him as a prerequisite for employment, and that the practice of offering gifts and money to foremen and supervisors as payment for jobs and continued work affected all branches of the line. President Harris of the C B & Q ordered a stop to such practices. "Let us keep Satan out as much as possible," he beseeched, but the demanding and giving of gifts continued to haunt the road.[38] Evidence from arbitration proceedings in the early twentieth century indicates that such practices had been established as customary throughout the industry in the early years and were a bone of contention between management and employees.[39]

Once workers were hired, railroad managers faced the task of molding their employees into a diligent and disciplined work force. Dividing labor and supervision into clearly defined, limited spheres and hiring family-based teams of workers helped to accomplish this end. America's pioneer railroad managers also tried to restructure the behavior of their employees more directly and deliberately, using rule books and disciplinary proceedings.

In the first decades of the development of rail transport, railwaymen were handed single sheets of paper listing timetables and company regulations. By the 1870s, rules governing the performance of duties had multiplied to the point where employees were given rule books often one hundred pages long. New employees had to pledge to read the rules thoroughly and to carry them on the job at all times. Companies informed workers of additions and amendments to existing standards through a steady stream of printed circulars.

The rule books demarcated lines of authority, gave precise instructions for the exercise of tasks, and established prescriptions for personal behavior. Railwaymen learned to whom they were accountable and the exact responsibilities of each position. The rule books formally demanded of them compliance, diligence, propriety in manners and appearance, and strict foreswearing of smoke and drink. Some railroad regulations even called upon employees to spy on their work mates and report any infractions of company edicts.[40]

Company rules and regulations, however, rarely had much meaning in actual practice. No matter how detailed and precise the regulations were, there was still a great deal of indeterminacy and contingency in railroad work during the early years. Foremen and supervisors presented workers with barrages of impromptu assignments to be assumed without extra compensation.[41] Herbert Hamblen in his reminiscences describes how, in addition to his normal responsibilities as a pioneer brakeman, he served as the engineer's flagman, opened and closed switches, coupled and uncoupled cars, watched for the caboose on curves and over hills, took water into the tender, shovelled coal down to the fireman, rang the bell at crossings, turned off the blower, oiled the valves, and lit the driver's cigar.[42] Tales like this can be told of railway workers in every grade of employment.

For pioneer railwaymen, a normal day's work rarely proceeded according to official guidelines. In the late nineteenth century, American railroadmen would collectively demand protection from and compensation for work performed above and beyond duties which were by then to be defined in rules that union and management had agreed upon.

Company regulations also had little meaning in practice because they were constantly forgotten, ignored, or consciously defied. Undisciplined worker behavior bedeviled early railroad managers. Worker intractability took many forms: pilferage, embezzlement of revenues—Allen Pinkerton estimated that pioneer conductors kept on an average one-third of the fares they collected—insubordination, negligence, carelessness, rowdiness, gambling, immorality, incivility toward passengers, union activism, and last but not least, pandemic alcoholism.[43] Pioneer railwayment proved to be a rough lot, who worked on and ran the trains according to their own timetables, both figuratively and literally, as many an early manager complained.

In the early years, labor discipline was usually handled formally by boards of directors and top officials. Later, as the power of appointment was localized, so too was authority over discipline. Typically, few guidelines were established, and the process became less and less systematized. Decentralization without formal grievance procedures bred arbitrariness. Surviving discharge records of the Erie and of the Chicago, Burlington & Quincy Railroads include infractions such as "bad reputation," "bad company," "family troubles," "dead beat," "too independent," "worthless," and "treacherous." Inconsistencies between the two records further suggest that there was a wide latitude in interpreting misdeeds. The significantly greater percentage of discharges for drunkenness on the C B & Q, indicates that either alcoholism was more chronic on that line or less tolerated.[44]

If the reasons for disciplinary actions were often arbitrary, the penalties imposed were even more so. It was left to local supervisors to determine whether a worker either would be informally warned, officially reprimanded, fined, demoted, temporarily suspended, dismissed with the possibility of reinstatement, or permanently discharged. In the absence of clear-cut standards and procedures, subjective factors came to influence the decision-making process. Jesse Dungan, a habitual drunkard who worked in the machine shops of the Baltimore & Ohio Railroad in the 1860s, maintained his position despite constant violations of company rules because, as his foreman noted, "he was an old employee and in bad circumstances."[45] Veteran status obviously helped. So, too, could family and personal connections. Edgar Custer, an early locomotiveman, recalled in his reminiscences, *No Royal Road*, being summoned into the office of his division superintendent to answer charges of running his engine at excessive speeds. "He was an old friend of my family," Custer remembered. "I felt rather hopeful." Custer's optimism was justified. He was only suspended for two weeks for an infraction which normally warranted automatic discharge.[46]

The disposition of cases could also be influenced by economic conditions. During busy periods, when labor was short and in demand, supervisors had to overlook certain pecadillos. Finally, the personality of each foreman was a crucial factor. There were both unforgiving tyrants and compassionate father-figures in the industry, each type dispensing justice in his own way.[47] Given the artbitrary nature of the whole process, it is not surprising that, once organized, railwaymen would petition for the institution of formal disciplinary and grievance procedures.

Pioneer railway managers also relied heavily upon positive incentives as well as negative sanctions to instill loyalty and discipline. The work had many rewards. Railwaymen in the early years received compensation that was as good or better than workers in other endeavors, and, with few exceptions, continually experienced gains in real income. Moreover, their wages tended to rise at greater rates during good times and fall to a lesser extent during deflationary periods than wages of other American workingmen.[48]

Railway workers also had available diverse legal and illegal means of supplementing their incomes—bonuses, premiums, overtime payments, and opportunities to pilfer, embezzle, and engage in their own transport-related sidelines—as well as a variety of informal and formal fringe benefits, such as tips, housing, free passes, shipping privileges, and even paid vacations.[49] The promise of future promotions was a strong work incentive, too. During the early years, with the rapid expansion of the industry—railway employment mushroomed from five thousand in 1840 to more than four hundred thousand by 1880—significant opportunities for advancement existed. Finally, the work offered intrinsic rewards, in terms of newness, adventure, and camaraderie, which also functioned to encourage diligence and attention to duty.

Monetary and other material rewards, however, were dispensed rather unsystematically. During periods of financial difficulty or currency shortages, for instance, railwaymen frequently went without pay for lengthy intervals or else were reimbursed in kind or in worth-less notes. Workers on the state-owned and -operated Philadelphia & Columbia Railroad waited four months to be paid in 1851, when the state legislature failed to pass a funding bill.[50] In the 1850s employees on the Chicago, St. Paul & Fond du Lac Railroad often went for five and six months without compensation, while Harvey Reed, in his reminiscences, *Forty Years A Locomotive Engineer*, even recalled work-ing for the much besieged Illinois-Midland Railroad for two years without receiving direct reimbursement.[51] Workers on the bankrupt Norfolk & Western Railroad after the Civil War had it slightly better. They were compensated in cornmeal, salt pork, shelter, and a prom-ise of future pay.[52]

Even in normal circumstances, compensation was an ambiguous matter. Railroads experimented with different methods of computing worker's earnings; from one month to the next, railwaymen rarely knew what to expect in their pay vouchers. Under time-rate pay-ments, further confusion arose as to what exactly constituted a stan-dard and accepted hour's, day's, or month's work; under piece rates, men received pay for work only when called, and fluctuations in the time taken to complete tasks seldom were taken into account.[53]

Local foremen also used their own discretion in paying men under their charge, even when top managers issued official wage schedules. Clerks and station laborers employed under the supervision of Agent C.W. Perviel, for instance, were found by Baltimore & Ohio Railroad executives in 1859 to be receiving frequent raises and to be paid in what was described as a completely liberal, "loose and unauthorized manner."[54] A group of track workers on the Illinois Central in the 1850s, however, were not as fortunate. An investigation by IC officials discovered that, among other indiscretions, their supervisor em-ployed and paid them at less than the suggested rate, and pocketed the difference.[55]

More important, by controlling work loads local supervisors indi-rectly controlled the actual earnings of nineteenth-century railway-men. Employment, especially in the early years, was highly irregular, largely due to the seasons. Men worked twenty-six or more days one month and ten the next. The first full-scale study of the steadiness of railway employment, in fact, completed by the Federal Bureau of Labor in 1889, revealed that close to fifty percent of the men in the industry worked less than one hundred days a year.[56] The ability of local supervisors to determine the very livelihoods of railway workers emerged as a festering grievance. Once organized, railwaymen would press for standardized union contracts, which established guaranteed incomes based on minimum time and task requirements with strict provisions for overtime and extra-work compensation.

The dispensation of many fringe benefits also remained a discretionary prerogative of local authorities. Whether men could supplement their incomes with bonuses and premiums, have access to company housing, and receive paid vacations depended on how well they stayed in the good graces of their foremen. On the last point, surviving memoranda in the archives of the Chicago, Burlington & Quincy Railroad offer some telling insights. Top executives of the line, like Charles Eliot Perkins, recognized that lower-level officials, acting on their own authority, frequently granted paid leaves to their men as reward for good service. Perkins decided to give formal approval to the   , but expressly instructed that it remain a secret preroga-
  .e of local supervisors.[57] Finally, like hiring and firing, the power to
  promote which in the early years was handled formally by boards of
directors, also eventually passed to local authorities. Promotion was a basic part of railroad work; it served both as means of filling upper-grade posts and as a form of work incentive. By the 1860s, American railroads had developed fairly well-defined career ladders for each branch of the trade.[58] With bureaucratic decentralization, however, the question of who received promotions, the criteria applied, and the timing of advancements rested in the hands of local officials.

Once again family, personal, and political connections helped. A federal commission investigating the railroad industry during the First World War found that nepotism was rampant in the early years of development. A "master mechanic might have a favorite nephew," the commission reported, "who, after firing an engine for six months, might be given the best passenger run on the road."[59] Letters in corporate archives similarly reveal that prominent stockholders and polititicians intervened to secure promotions for relatives and friends.[60]

Better positions, not surprisingly, were also bought and sold. Eugene Mahoney, a pioneer engineer on the Jersy Central, recalled that promotion on that line depended on two to fifteen years of service, and the "price was gold watch chains, rocking chairs, bottles of wine, poultry, quails and cigars." "The Master at Jersey City had so many cigars on hand at one time," Mahoney added, "that he placed them on sale in a cigar store on Communipaw Avenue."[61] As Robert Harris, president of the Chicago, Burlington & Quincy, sadly concluded in a letter discussing the process of promotion: "Personal preference, from one cause or another, more generally determines the selection."[62] Once organized, railwaymen would demand that promotion procedures become routinized and less arbitrary.

Accident and death benefit awards represent a final, but most critical, aspect of the work experience left open to discriminatory decision making. Before the inception of automatic coupling and braking systems railwaymen led unusually precarious lives. The nature of their work cannot be understood fully without grasping completely the ever-present threat of accidental injury and death.

A precise count of the number injured and killed in rail service before 1889 is impossible. In that year, the newly established Interstate Commerce Commission began to collect data on accidents from all railroad companies in the country. For the year ending June 30, 1889, the ICC reported that 1,972 railroadmen had been killed on the job and 20,028 injured; with a total work force of 704,443, that meant that in that year one out of every 357 employees was killed in service, and one out of every thirty-five injured.[63] Information provided by state and company reports for the pre-1889 period, although scattered and incomplete, generally conforms to the picture presented by the ICC data for 1889. The rates for men killed and injured also tended to increase over time, implying a worsening situation.[64] As the railroads expanded their operations, as passengers, freight, and traffic multiplied, the demands on workers apparently increased proportionately. So, too, did the chances for mishaps and casualties.

Aggregate figures, however, obscure differentials among grades of railwaymen. Trainmen—engineers, firemen, conductors, and brakemen—led the most precarious lives by far. In 1889, for every 117 trainmen employed, one was killed; for every twelve, one was injured.[65] The plight of pioneer brakemen especially deserves mention; whether in coupling cars or braking, the perils of their labor were staggering. Their job was so hazardous that "old time" brakemen often were recognized by missing fingers or crippled hands. When applying for new employment, they carried vivid proof of their experience, and foremen looking for veteran workers were known to consider missing fingers an apt qualification for employment.[66] At times the pressure of the work could become unbearable, and suicide loomed as a desirable alternative. A reporter for a Baltimore newspaper filed the following report after interviewing a group of B & O brakemen in the summer of 1877:

> In two instances, it is said, brakemen after the loss of rest and under the depression of reduced wages, etc., have purposely

thrown themselves under the wheels. Nearly all the men talked with said at one time and another when melancholy, they had meditated about stepping over the bumpers and meeting instant death.[67]

Workers disabled in accidents and the widows and families of deceased railwaymen faced a grim and uncertain future. In making claims for compensation for their losses they found that the legal system offered little or no relief. Judges generally applied the common-law principle of implied contract in assessing the merits of the claims. Under implied contract, the courts held that employees, in engaging to serve a master, accepted all conditions of such service, including all the ordinary risks incident to their employment. The courts also held that the railroads could not be held liable when the negligence of one worker led to injury another worker. The companies were quick to warn workers in printed rule books and circulars that management would not be held liable to claims resulting from the carelessness of non-supervisory employees.[68]

On an informal, discretionary, and completely voluntary basis, American railroad companies in the nineteenth century did offer limited relief to employees involved in accidents. Carriers frequently paid the medical expenses of injured men or awarded them flat charitable grants. While recuperating, fully disabled men also were often kept on the payroll while at home or, if possible, employed in less demanding tasks. Injured trainmen on the New York & Erie Railroad in the 1850s were placed in clerical or depot positions; officials on the Illinois Central similarly made a practice of allowing disabled brakemen and others to occupy spots as flagmen and watchmen; while on the Chicago, Burlington & Quincy, the Chariton branch of the road, where there was only limited freight service, was reserved for old and crippled engineers and firemen.[69]

Railroad companies also extended relief to widows and the families of railwaymen killed while in service. Carriers sometimes paid medical fees, donated burial expenses, granted direct monetary awards, or even offered to hire children of fatally injured men. In extending relief, it should be noted, the motives of nineteenth-century railroad managers were hardly benevolent. Furnishing awards provided the roads with a clear and facile avenue for avoilding legal liablity, for families receiving company-offered relief normally signed waivers agreeing not to bring suit against their employers.[70]

The process of dispensing benefits was clearly arbitrary. An employee's previous standing in the firm, rather than his or his family's actual needs, played an important role in making decisions. A memorandum in the archives of the Baltimore & Ohio Railroad, for example, indicates that officials were advised to judge the merits of a claim on "what the conduct of the party has been in reference to providence, ability displayed, courage and assertions for the interest of the Company."[71] The grade of the employee also figured in the size of the award. If a brakeman and a locomotive driver were both injured in an accident, it was not unusual for the engine driver to receive a substantially larger gift.[72]

American railway companies continued to dispense relief in an *ad hoc* discretionary fashion through the 1870s. While European railroads began instituting structured, inclusive insurance programs as early as mid-century, interest in and acceptance of such proposals came very slowly in the American industry. Following the railroad strikes of 1877, however, several major trunk lines moved to establish insurance plans both as a means to avoid liability suits and as part of conscious efforts to regain the loyalty of their men.[73] For their part, railwaymen, once organized, established their own union-run programs. Railwaymen also continued the custom established early of collecting contributions from among themselves for the sick, the disabled, or the families of killed comrades. As Harry French recalled, "Reckless indeed was the worker who 'passed up the hat' when it was offered; one never knew when it would be going around for him or his widow."[74]

The world of work for the first two generations of American railwaymen was a world of insecurity and uncertainty. Local officials handled critical aspects of the work situation in arbitrary and discriminatory ways. Before 1870, when railroad workers protested against the conditions of their employment in daily confrontations with supervisors and foremen, they usually complained as individuals; evidence of trade-union organizing and strike activity exists but on an intermittent and unsustained basis. It remained for the third and fourth generations of American railroad workers (1880-1920) to change the circumstances under which men labored in the trade. The history of America's pioneer railwaymen, however, adds an important perspective to their struggles.

In the last quarter of the nineteenth and the first quarter of the twentieth centuries, the nation witnessed a succession of dramatic and often violent confrontations between railroad management and labor. The spontaneous nationwide strikes of July 1877, the Gould strikes of the mid-1880s, the Burlington strike of 1888, the momentous Pullman strike and boycott of 1894, the bloody Harriman strike of

1911-1914, the threatened walkout of trainmen in 1916 which forced Congress to pass the Adamson Act (imposing the eight-hour day on the industry), and the railway shopmen's strike of 1922, which engaged more than four hundred thousand workers, are the better known and documented incidents of rail labor strife.[75] A complete listing of disputes after 1877 would include countless other less dramatic but no less intense job actions.[76]

Traditionally, the strikes of the modern era have been interpreted as straightforward reactions by railroad workers to announced wage cuts and generalized economic distress; more recently, historians following the lead of Herbert Gutman have pictured the great battles of the post-1877 period as local community responses to the growing, encroaching political and economic power of concentrated capital, a power destructive of cherished republican ideals and a power best symbolized by the the nation's first and largest corporations—the railroads.[77] Both views tell important parts of the story, as much as a single story can be written. However, a significant component is left out.

Years of accumulated grievances also motivated railwaymen in their dramatic confrontations with railroad management. The arbitrary handling of recruitment, discipline, wage payments, work assignments, benefits, promotions, and gratuities by supervisors, as well as the inescapable perils of the trade, engendered deep frustration and bitterness. An article in the *Locomotive Engineers' Journal* in December 1875 conveyed workers' feelings and the problem:

> In the majority of cases a man's employment depends not alone upon his good behavior, ability and trustworthiness, but upon the whim of his superior; he is hired for no specific time, holds no contract with his company that serves him employment, and is liable to be discharged at any moment without warning.[78]

During the great confrontations of the late nineteenth and early twentieth centuries, railwaymen voiced constant, although not always newsworthy, complaints against the capricious rule of local supervisors and foremen. In accounting for the violence of July 1877, one anonymous correspondent to the *Locomotive Engineers' Journal* explained:

> The uprising was the natural result of arbitrary rules and unjust discrimination allowed officers and operations, a culmination of stupid mismanagement and the fruits of unwise policies, and

the explosion was as unexpected as would would be a thunder-bolt from a cloudless sky.[79]

Perhaps the clearest statements come from the Pullman strike and boycott of 1894, where the arbitrary power of supervisors was the common denominator of complaint. An official demand of the strikers was an end to the "constant harassment of foremen."[80] A federal commission established to investigate the disorders later collected testimony; it was inundated by tales of favoritism and nepotism and the despotic character, violent tempers,and often brutal acts of fore-men.[81] The revelations came as something of a surprise, since the investigators had expected wages and hours of work to be the only grievances of note. The following interview with Franklin Mills, a discharged Baltimore & Ohio employee, is instructive:

> *Commissioner Kernan*: What was the feeling among the employ-ees on the Baltimore & Ohio with regard to striking prior to the time they struck?
> *Mills*: It was not favorable.
> *Commissioner Kernan*: Had there been any cuts in wages about which they were dissatisfied?
> *Mills*: Not lately, the most of the difficulty on the Baltimore & Ohio was favoritism, pets and maladministration of some of the petty officers.[82]

The U.S. Strike Commission of 1895 also heard from Charles Naylor, a local officer of the American Railway Union and a fireman on the Pittsburgh, Fort Wayne & Chicago Railroad. Naylor placed the disruptions of the year before in the clearest perspective:

> In a large number of roads there was a feeling among the em-ployees that they were almost in a helpless condition to stand against the oppression of the petty officials, and the petty offi-cials took advantage of that feeling and deviled the men, just as their particular temperament at the moment led them to do.[83]

Between 1877 and 1922, American railwaymen outwardly protested against the conditions of their labor in a series of headline-capturing confrontations. At the same time, they engaged in intense behind-the-scenes union organizing to secure collective contracts to make their work more secure and controlled. By 1901, fifteen separate rail-road craft brotherhoods had entered the field and enrolled upwards of eighty percent of the men in their respective jurisdictions.[84] Their success was due in no small part to the more disorderly strike activity that they engaged in at the same time, actions which convinced many railroad executives of the need and wisdom of developing new personnel policies.

The turbulence of the period both surprised and frightened railroad managers. In a letter to John Forbes, a director of the Chicago, Burington & Quincy Railroad, Charles Eliot Perkins, vice-president of the railroad, described his reactions to the events of the summer of 1877: "The strike was inaugurated [on the C B & Q] on Wednesday, July 25. I confess that I felt like a Doctor dealing with a new and unknown malady."[85]

The strikes of July 1877, and those that periodically followed, forced railroad executives into an almost frantic search for explanations and answers. Some took a hard line and called for deliberate and definitive actions to suppress union activity; others sought to regain the loyalty of their employees through exhortation. Concrete positive approaches, however, gradually gained wide acceptance. Company-established and -administered accident and death benefit insurance programs proved to be the most popular solution to labor unrest. New premium systems, high wages, profit sharing, savings and pension plans, and railwaymen's hospitals were other reforms which were discussed and received support.[86]

More important, the disruptions of the post-1877 period brought to the attention of high central executives the problem of the pervasive and onerous power of local railroad officials. As Robert Harris, president of the Chicago, Burlington & Quincy Railroad, wrote to his board of directors, companies could not expect to "stimulate enthusiasm" among employees if they remained under the arbitrary rule and supervision of local foremen.[87] While some executives called for more detailed and standardized regulations and disciplinary procedures to solve the problem, Harris argued strongly for the institution of written contracts which would clearly stipulate fixed ground rules for compensation, promotion, dismissal, grievance hearings, and seniority rights. Harris failed to persuade executives of his own company of the importance of this new approach to industrial relations. Other railroad leaders in the 1880s began to recognize not only the value of written contracts but also the value of contracts mutually negotiated by union officials and management. The despotic sway of local company officials—who were as much a thorn to staff executives as to workers on the line—could thus be curbed, and, it was hoped, labor unrest would be prevented through new contractural procedures.[88]

Through organization, strike pressure, the threat of general disorder, and the desire of some top railroad officials to stabilize their operations, railwaymen in the late nineteenth century began to achieve meaningful protection at the work place through written contracts. Typical was a contract negotiated by the Brotherhood of Maintenance of Way Employees in 1902 with the East St. Louis & Suburban Railway Company. It gave trackmen the right to a speedy, fair, and impartial company trial in the event of disciplinary charges; the right to appeal to the general manager; pay for time lost because of improper discharges; a nine-hour day, pro rata pay for the tenth hour of service, and time-and-a-half pay for work performed after the tenth hour on Sundays; promotion based on seniority; the recognition of seniority during reductions in employment; and free passage on the line after six months of service. The contract also established set wage schedules, fixed pay periods, and joint management-union procedures to handle grievances and ambiguous situations during the life of the agreement.[89]

The third and fourth generations of American railwaymen thus fought and bargained to bring order to their working lives, an order which their forebears had never had the good fortune to know. The effort of railroad workers in the post-1877 period to secure written contracts takes on new meaning in light of the history of America's pioneer railwaymen. In the name of fairness, justice, and security, later generations of railroad workers joined together to be a party to rule making and to demand further bureaucratic standards and procedures to control as much of the work experience as possible. They both lost and gained in the process. Workers who had achieved special privileges through personal connections had to sacrifice their advantages to the common good. A certain amount of the romance, adventure, and spontaneity of the work was also forfeited. The renaissance men of the trade—for instance, the locomotive drivers—no longer fiddled, jiggled, pampered, and tuned their engines. That now belonged strictly in the domain of shop work, and the drivers were to be paid only for the work stipulated in their contract. By the turn of the century, railwaymen, as one veteran engine driver, William Lynch, noted, had become both sobered and sober.[90] By fighting the arbitrary rule of supervisors and demanding more formal standards, railroad workers contributed to the bureaucratization and routinization of their own work.[91]

Yet, at the same time, they also gained substantial control over the work situation and how they were to be treated as men and as employees. This was not, to be sure, workers' control in the pure sense of worker seizure of the ownership and management of the means and processes of production (nor, obviously, were railwaymen ever able to act unilaterally, since all settlements were negotiated with managers and owners). Rather, workers attempted to maximize their control over the work experience, control over even seemingly trivial aspects of work which made their lives more secure, if not more autonomous.[92] As railroad corporations in the same period organized privately through pooling agreements and mergers to undo ruinous competition within the industry, so railway workers organized to undo competition among themselves in order to create conditions of stability. No one wanted an unfettered or uncontrollable market place, despite the rhetoric and public worship of individualism and free enterprise.

The role played by workers in demanding stricter standards and procedures also adds a new perspective to the whole question of bureaucratization. Pioneer railway managers imposed bureaucratic structures on the work situation, which proved to be dysfunctional in day-to-day relations. Conflicts stemming from worker frustration with arbitrary local supervision produced pressure from below for greater standardization. Bureaucratization thus represented both a structure and a process, a process which was dialectical in nature. Bureaucratic work organizations developed not solely as the handiwork of farsighted businessmen—as entrepreneurial or Great-Man theorists would have us believe; nor were they the results of some natural, inevitable, and uniform movement toward greater degrees of rationality and organization—as glib modernization theories imply. Rather, they emerged as part of a complex unfolding process that involved people and their conscious decision making, personal interest, and human conflict.

The case of mid-nineteenth-century American railwaymen also offers some suggestions, if not conclusions, about work and laboring people in the United States. America's pioneer railroad workers were part of a worldwide economic revolution, yet the nature of their work experiences was shaped in many important respects by peculiar American circumstances. They labored in a country with a federal system of government. American railway managers as a result could not easily or certainly secure legislation that would have facilitated the disciplining of their labor forces. Railway executives lobbied—in vain—to have state laws passed to make violations of company rules offenses punishable in civil courts. Their efforts were modeled after the British Railway Act of 1840. In securing favorable legislation,

English railroad executives had but one body to appeal to—Parliament—while American managers were forced to deal with various, often hostile state legislatures.[93]

American railway workers and their supporters also possessed full citizenship and the vote; they wielded significant political power, which was often manifest in opposition to railroad corporations at the level of local and state governments. Railway labor strikes thus became community uprisings as well. James Clarke, president of the Illinois Central Railroad, recognizing local support for railwaymen, even insisted that legislation to discipline workers would be futile since community sentiment would make it difficult for railroads to procure indictment and conviction of their workers.[94] Local juries, in fact, were reluctant to prosecute railroad employees charged with causing accidental injuries or deaths to passengers through their alleged negligence or malfeasance.[95]

Finally, American railwaymen worked in a country that did not have a highly fixed system of class distinctions, where a democratic republican ideology prevailed. In Britain, railway managers were able to superimpose the British class system on authority relations within the firm; class sanctions thus encouraged labor control.[96] In the United States, foremen, supervisors, and even high-level executives who had risen from the bottom, found the authority they possessed to be less sanctified.[97] It is both symbolic and characteristic that, when grade-specific uniforms were first proposed by railway managers, the idea met with bitter derision and opposition. The wearing of uniforms and insignia by civilian workers was deemed degrading in a democratic society.[98] Democratic ideals, in this way, offer one possible explanation why American railwaymen and their supporters in the post-1877 period were highly militant, but at the same time not politically radical as a group. As free-born citizens of the republic, they refused to countenance unjust and unfair treatment and they resorted to violent means to protest their circumstances.[99] Yet, the same egalitarian ideology promised opportunity and freedom for every toiling American. In the eyes of railway workers, the system—especially if they could exert some control over the work experience—needed no revolution.

CHAPTER 7

Industrial Safety and Labor Relations in the United States, 1865-1917

ROBERT ASHER

Ev'ry morning at seven o'clock,
There's twenty tarriers a-working at the rock,
And the boss comes along and he says, "Kape still,
And come down heavy on the cast-iron drill!"

Now our new foreman was Gene MaCann,
By God, he was a blamey [blamed mean] man
Last week a premature blast went off,
And a mile in the air went big Jim Goff.

Next time pay day comes around,
Jim Goff a dollar short was found;
When asked what for, came this reply,
"You're docked for the time you was up in the sky!"[1]

I

Industrial workers have been victimized by low wages, company stores, blacklisting, arbitrary dismissals, forced overtime, sexual exploitation, company spies, police brutality, and a host of other ills. These problems are abundantly documented in the historical literature. But historians have not yet intensively studied the effects of one of the major hardships faced by industrial laborers—the accidents and the slower, but no less deadly, physical degeneration produced by exhausting labor in hot environments where the air was often filled with particles and toxic gases. This essay will analyze the emotional tone and behavioral aspects of worker reactions to the hazards of industrial work in the United States in the late nineteenth- and early twentieth-century. We shall describe the dehumanization that work-

ers experienced when employers ignored the needs of their employees for physical security. The essay will demonstrate that the extent of
worker resentment and protest action against work hazards and the
treatment of injured and diseased workers was masked by official
government statistics that invariably understated the influence of
safety concerns on the decision to strike. Finally, we will analyze the
positive relationship between worker anger about unsafe working
conditions and the level of labor violence in different industries.

II

Industrialization altered traditional production techniques by re-
placing human power with machine power. As industrial technology
advanced, new machines ran at faster speeds and exerted more power
than their predecessors. Toxic chemicals increasingly found their way
into manufacturing processes. Technological progress enabled men to
go further under the ground to extract raw materials from the earth
and higher above the ground to erect structures of unprecedented
size. All these advances increased the risks faced by the industrial
worker. The new industrial technology was both a blessing and a
curse for society. It was immensely productive, but it was also deadly.
Especially in the United States, which before World War I had the
highest industrial accident rates among the leading industrial powers
of the world,[2] industrialization produced an ever-expanding number
of dead and maimed workers.

To understand the impact on industrial labor relations of accidents
and unsafe working conditions, it is first necessary to examine the
character of the gross negligence and systematic indifference towards
the safety of the worker that was so widespread in American industry
in the years before World War I. Intense inter-state competition, igno-
rance of the financial costs of accidents, the American propensity for
speed in construction and operation, a highly politicized civil service,
and the desire for profits made American industries, in the pre-work-
men's compensation era, the most dangerous in the western world.
Workers in transportation, the extractive industries, and manufacturing complained bitterly about management policies that produced
accidents which workers believed were avoidable.

Workers in virtually all industrial occupations encountered safety
hazards that appeared avoidable, if only management would use its
power over the work environment to correct them. Railroad workers
knew that their employers often did not hire enough car inspectors.

Consequently, unsafe rolling stock was regularly placed in service. Poor inspection of boilers, tracks, and bridges was also common. Some railroads improperly repaired rotted boilers, forcing engineers to put bran in their boilers to prevent leaks. When short of freight cars, railroads often overloaded the available equipment.[3] Railroad workers protested against being forced to operate faulty equipment and being ordered to work without sufficient rest between runs. A railroad worker who participated in the 1894 Pullman boycott told congressional investigators that on his line, an engineer who refused to work on the grounds of fatigue was suspended for fifteen to thirty days for his first act of insuborordination and was fired for his second refusal to obey an order. Overworked railroad men were often forced to work for as long as thirty-six consecutive hours. An Iowa engineer protested against such practices: "We have frequently pleaded for, and have had numerous promises for relief, but the greed for gain is too great to permit this when it means dollars and cents to a corporation."[4]

Poorly ventilated shops in the New York clothing industry gave rise to the common saying, "When a cutter sneezed, he blew a garment through his nose." Crowded machinery placement in loft manufacturing establishments (the result, in part, of high rents) increased the chance of accidents. Drive belts were often replaced on machinery without stopping the equipment. The failure to countersink small set screws often led to mangled hands and arms. High tension wires that were not color coded made the work of electrical linemen more hazardous than it had to be. Electrical companies striving for maximum productivity also endangered their employees by refusing to use a signal system to order a current switched back on after repairs had been made. Instead, the men at the switch were simply told to put the current on after a wait of five or ten minutes, a very risky procedure.[5]

Miners frequently complained of the "neglect of bosses and managers of mines to keep mines in order." "Mismanagement and faulty working cause these casualties," wrote a Colorado quartz miner in 1888. Inadequate ventilation, poor timbering, lax inspection by management personnel, dangerous procedures ordered by callous or poorly trained foremen and superintendents, and the failure to provide for effective escape in the event of fire, explosion, or cave-in all contributed to the hostility miners felt toward their employers. The tendency of mine owners and many state mine inspectors to blame the carelessness of miners for the high accident rates in American mines enraged the men who risked their lives underground each day.

They knew that low pay and the frequent attempts of management to cheat them out of the full value of their labor by faulty grading and weighing of the mineral being mined forced many workers to rush, cutting corners to earn enough to support their families. Miners also knew that many accidents could be avoided if mine owners made a genuine effort to make their mines safer.[6]

Construction workers noted that employers frequently erected unsafe scaffolding. Sometimes the problem resulted from the use of defective materials supplied by the contractor. Poorly trained common laborers were often used to build the scaffolding upon which skilled tradesmen worked. And, as a Milwaukee bricklayer noted in 1887, scaffolding hazards and accidents were often the result of "the fact that in many instances contractors do not allow sufficient time for such work."[7]

American workers knew that their employers often violated safety laws with impunity. Electricians, structural ironworkers, iron molders, and coal miners all complained about infractions of state safety codes that went unpunished because of infrequent visits by state factory and mine inspectors, who in any case were often biased in favor of the employer. Coal miners were especially aroused over the appointment, in their view, of incompetent and insincere mine inspectors. They believed the only remedy for this problem was to have the mine inspectors chosen by public election.[8]

Complaining to foremen and managers about hazards was not easy for most workers. Many employers simply fired workers who made frequent objections about safety conditions. Workers who protested about job hazards were sometimes blacklisted as complainers. Electrical linemen in Massachusetts and New York told investigators that their foremen forbade them, on pain of dismissal, from inspecting the poles that supported high wires before the men began their ascent. Construction workers who objected to dangerous scaffolding or unsafe tools were often fired on the spot. Similarly, a Colorado coal miner reported that, "If a man makes the least kick against bad air or gas, he is immediately discharged."[9] Railroad workers dared not complain about faulty equipment kept in service. An Iowa brakeman noted that when air brake systems failed, "trainmen are compelled to take trains over the road by hand . . . which is very dangerous, but one must do it or lose his job." An Ohio switchman told a story that illustrated the futility of complaining. In 1910 a yard crew told their foreman that they would not work again with a faulty engine that lacked handholds, a footboard, and a headlight on the hind end of the tank. The next night the men were furious because they were given the same engine, even though they had pointed out to their foreman that another engine was available.[10]

Once an accident occurred, injured workers were often treated with great insensitivity. In one Minnesota iron mine, injured workers were not brought to the surface immediatlely but were forced to wait until the end of the workshift before they were taken out of the mine.[11] Hospital care and transportation to the hospital were often withheld until the injured worker signed a liability release.[12] In northern Washington a foreman refused to call an ambulance to carry off a logger who had just been killed when a flying choker block smashed his head. The foremen, who simply "dragged the body off to one side and threw his coat over it," told a worker who protested that, "the ambulance won't do the kid any good now. Get back to work." But the foreman was compelled to call an ambulance when the men refused to work "until you take the stiff out of the woods." A veteran logger told off the foreman:

> Anybody's likely to get his leg, or arm, or neck broken at any minute. They take their chances on that, but we want to be treated like human beings, not like cattle.[13]

But maimed workers were frequently treated like animals.

Loggers throughout the nation were accustomed to a monthly deduction of one dollar from their wages to provide "hospital insurance" in the event of injury. Loggers also knew that this payment frequently bought them mediocre medical care. On occasion it bought them no treatment at all.[14] Consider the remark of an IWW organizer who in 1917 had been working in the logging industry in northern Minnesota:

> A man who gets badly hurt in that camp bleeds to death before any assistance. I wish to inform you of the fact that they ought to have a little something to help a man.

The organizer's own experience after he cut himself with a double-bladed axe was instructive. Although he had paid a hospital fee, the foreman was reluctant to provide help:

> Luckily I didn't hurt myself very deep. . . . I asked for peroxide to wash it out and keep it clean. . . . he had no peroxide. I said you are supposed to have some; get some bandages and peroxide. He promised to get it; but didn't. So I took some water. That water is diseased. . . . I got some lard from the cook and

bandaged it up as good as I could with some old cloths. It started healing up nicely, but these germs that were in the water
must have infected it, and the pain went up over the leg, and I
couldn't stand it no more. So I told him. He wasn't very eager
to get me out of the camp to the hospital. I said, "You get me to
the hospital now." He told me "You go up there to Duluth to
Dr. Dodge, and tell him I sent you." I said, "That won't work
with me, give me an order on the doctor." He said,"I got no order." "Well," I said, "write, give me a letter." And finally he
signed a letter. Then he told me we should report the case to
the company, and that Mr. Bristol will come to see me in a couple of days. He never showed up.[15]

Fear of adverse publicity and accident suits caused many businesses
to go to great lengths to hide accidents. Injured workers were often
transported to hospitals in carriages or other conveyances because the
use of ambulances would indicate that an accident had occurred.[16] A
Wisconsin sawyer complained that the existence of accidents was
obscured by the efforts of employers to avoid publicity: "This is about
all the news we hear; 'Somebody cut himself,' " he told state investigators in 1887. And many firms must have followed the practice of the
Lowell, Massachusetts, textile mills managers who refused to allow
any outsiders into the factories to view the scene of accidents.[17]

To prevent injured workers from bringing suit, employers often
used stealth and coercion. A Milwaukee, Wisconsin, laborer complained that a man recently killed in an accident at the International
Harvester plant "was buried as quickly as possible without the formal-
ity of an inquest, probably for the purpose of preventing the blame
being attached to the employers." In Minnesota, about 1909, a brakeman was run over by a train when his foot caught in an unprotected
switch frog. According to the Minnesota Bureau of Labor, "The next
morning the crew were at work 'repairing track' about the frog and
the whole face of things was changed." The incident was an example,
the Bureau of Labor reported, of "numerous cases of this sort of
injustice to the injured."[18]

In 1912 the Secretary-Treasurer of the Minnesota State Federation of
Labor described the manner in which a Duluth railroad tried to dis-
credit the testimony of a switchman who had witnessed the death of a
fellow switchman. A railroad detective got the man liquored up and
then enticed him into robbing the railroad's own freight depot. The
man was arrested and convicted for theft. When he appeared to
testify in the lawsuit brought against the railroad by the dead worker's

widow, the defense attorney made him admit that he was a convicted burglar. Fortunately, the district attorney smelled a rat, investigated, and initiated action that corrected the injustice to both workers. This was an extreme but not a unique case. It was common for railroads to "expressly forbid employees from giving information concerning accidents, even to an injured fellow workman, or his widow, unless legally required." Likewise, an Ohio structural ironworker who witnessed the injury of a fellow worker was told by his foreman that, "if I knew where that man lived, and I told it, I was discharged." To make matters worse, the witness related, the "injured man lay on a stretcher for ten hours waiting for a train to pass. He died in the office, on account of lack of doctor's care."[19]

Injured workers who threatened to sue or actually did sue their employers for damages were often punished for their temerity. Charles B. St. Clair, a switchman on the Chicago, Burlington & Quincy Railroad, became embroiled in a dispute with his company after breaking his ankle in 1892. For four months he received benefits from the Burlington Relief Fund. Then the company offered him a job attending a street crossing. St. Clair refused the job because he had not fully recovered from his injury, and taking the job would have interfered with his medical treatments. At this point, the railroad cut off his pension. Twenty months later St. Clair's ankle had healed. But when he applied for work with the Burlington, his superintendent "said that he would give me employment if I would release my back pension; that if I was going to sue them for the back benefits they would not give me employment." St. Clair refused to sign, and sued. The Burlington blacklisted him. Thereafter, St. Clair found it impossible to secure employment with any of the railroads running through Chicago. He was forced to work at other jobs that did not pay as well as railroading.[20]

Injured workers frequently sued their employers for damages when they did not receive an offer of compensation or if they felt that the settlement proposed by their employers was insufficient. Although there are no statistics on the subject, contemporary observers testified that large numbers of injured workers who sued their employers were dismissed, either before or after the suit was adjudicated.[21] Such firings undoubtedly embittered workers who were already angry because they felt that employer negligence had caused their injuries.

Many industrial workers echoed the demand of the Washington logger who insisted that injured workers be treated like human beings. They resented the fact that their employers denied them humane treatment, and said so: "Corporations need to be impressed with the fact that there is some humanity in the workingmen," noted an Iowa engineer who had just finished complaining about double-header freights. And the Ohio structural ironworker who told of the suppression of news about the accident he witnessed commented, "It was the employers that caused us to organize, to show them that we were human."[22]

There can be no doubt that in the years before World War I, industrial workers in the United States were very bitter about the safety and accident compensation practices of many employers. Objective analysis tells us that many of these practices were not the result of greed but reflected the pressure of the competitive industrial marketplace and the intrinsic hazards of industrial technology. But working men and women were rarely interested in scientific explanations for the degradation they were forced to endure. Personification of evil was a more natural response to the accidents they witnessed than was acceptance of explanations emphasizing nonhuman forces and processes. Furthermore, there was enough evidence of employer insensitivity and ruthlessness in allowing and causing accidents and in treating injured workers to convince workers that they were justified in blaming the visible industrialist and his managerial lieutenants for the daily carnage in the mines, mills, and railroads of the nation.

III

When industrial workers joined labor unions to increase their bargaining power and when unionized or unorganized workers went on strike, there is no question that eliminating unsafe working conditions was an important motivating factor. Unfortunately, government strike statistics invariably have understated the influence of safety concerns on worker strike activity. Federal statistics for 1881-1886 indicate five strikes for better ventilation and three strikes in protest against work hazards that might cause accidents. (Two were on railroads and a third was a strike of miners.) The next set of statistics on strikes, for 1881-1905, published by the United States Commissioner of Labor, did not categorize a single strike as safety-related or caused by an accident. Undoubtedly such strikes were indiscriminately lumped together under the classifications "Concerning working conditions and rules," "Concerning working conditions and rules combined with various causes," "Other causes," and "Other causes combined with various above specified causes."[23]

The Federal statistics classified the strike of anthracite coal miners in 1902 as one "for increase of wages and reduction of hours, and concerning recognition of union and union rules."[24] This classification obscured the influence safety grievances had on the stated demands the miners made for higher wages and union recognition. Workers frequently asked for higher wages to secure remuneration for the hazards of their jobs. When workers could not gain protection against and compensation for accidents through contracts or legislation, agitation for wage increases was the only recourse they had. In its *Consitition and By-Laws*, the Western Federation of Miners specifically related the "hazardous and unhealthful aspects of mining" to demands for fair pay. In 1902, the striking anthracite miners stated that "The rate of wages . . . is insufficient to compensate the mine workers in view of the dangerous character of the occupation."[25] Because the relationship between higher wages and occupational hazards was so obvious to workers, they rarely felt compelled to make an explicit connection between them for the benefit of journalists, government statisticians, or historians.

The demand of the anthracite miners for recognition of their union also had a strong safety component in it. The United Mine Workers of America frequently made safety an issue when it negotiated state and district contracts. The work rules set by the UMWA included many safety provisions. Locals of the UMWA often went out on wildcat strikes to protest safety violations. And the state and national miner organizations lobbied assiduously for stricter mine safety codes and for workmen's compensation legislation.[26]

Industrial workers also explicitly related requests for shorter hours to reduced fatigue and fewer accidents. As early as 1867, gold miners in Comstock Nevada, put a provision in their bylaws that set eight hours as the maximum that should be permitted for underground labor. The main reason for this demand was clear. The heat of the Comstock mines was so intense that in some places " 'miners could work for a few minutes only at a time, and sweat filled their loose shoes' until it ran over the tops."[27] In a landmark 1896 decision upholding Utah's eight-hour law for mine workers and smelters, the state's Supreme Court justified the piece of "class legislation" on the grounds of health. After describing the "poisonous gases, dust and impalpable substances" in the air of mines and processing factories, the court concluded that "there can be no doubt that prolonged effort day after day, subject to such conditions and agencies, will produce morbid, noxious and often deadly effects in the human system." If labor had to be performed in such an environment "the period of labor each day should be of reasonable length. . . . "[28]

Workers in other occupations frequently complained that long hours produced fatigue, making them less alert and more likely to make mistakes that caused accidents. In 1914 a railroad towerman in Texas told investigators that an eight-hour day, instead of the prevailing twelve- and fourteen-hour shifts, would help prevent the accidents that "may occur through towermen being tired out and not giving proper attention to duties." As an Iowa trainman similarly insisted, "Eight hours is long enough to work at this strenuous and dangerous business." And a group of craftsmen in the shipyards of West Bay City, Michigan, who struck for a reduction of hours in July 1903, explained that it was "physically impossible to maintain their health and strength permanently under the strain involved in ten hours work during the warm season."[29] Men who were engaged in hard, dangerous physical labor clearly understood that shorter hours would make their jobs safer.

Several states published data on the causes of strikes that were only marginally more informative on the accident problem than the figures from the federal government. An Illinois survey of strike causes between 1881 and 1900 reported two strikes by workers who objected to being forced to sign contracts releasing their employers from liability in the event of injury to the worker, and five strikes for an assortment of reasons: more compressed air, better ventilation and the repair of machinery, better safety, and a better workroom.[30] The Minnesota Bureau of Labor reported one strike between 1881 and 1900 by laborers who refused to sign a liability release. A 1911 strike at an iron mine in Biwabik, Minnesota, demonstrated the great sensitivity of the miners to the safety and compensation question:

> One hundred and thirty men, employees of the Bangor Mining Company, operators of the Bangor Mine at Biwabik, Minnesota, struck on October 18, 1911, upon being requested by the company to sign certain papers. The company had issued a book of rules to prevent accidents; the men were required to sign a document saying they had read the rules; that they would obey the rules and warn fellow workmen to be careful; and at the termination of their employment return the book of rules or forfeit fifty cents of their pay. The men thought that the papers contained a waiver of all personal injury claims and refused to sign it. The men then consulted an attorney who advised them that

there was no danger to them in signing the document, and after being out five days returned to work.[31]

Wildcat strikes like the one conducted by the Biwabik miners have always been a vital weapon for workers concerned about occupational hazards. In the early twentieth century, building trade unions in Milwaukee were "time and again . . . forced to a cessation of work . . . to compel the contractors to provide at least some protection to the workmen. . . . "[32] Structural iron workers in Chicago also repeatedly walked out in the era before workmen's compensation, to compel employers to observe local safety ordinances.[33] In the logging industry there was a working class tradition of shutting down lumbering and processing operations for the remainder of the day in which a serious accident took place.[34] And when the heat in early iron factories became unbearable the workers sometimes simply packed up their tools and went home.[35]

Safety issues often led to wildcat strikes by miners. Miners in Braidwood, Illinois, became aroused in 1873 when they realized that the King mine lacked an escape shaft. A strike broke out immediately. In 1891, the owners of the Bunker Hill mine in the Coeur d'Alene, Idaho, mining district refused to support the union hospital at Wallace. Instead, the management deducted one dollar a month from the pay of each worker and used the money to support a company doctor. When the workers protested against this policy, the company put the question to a referendum vote. But the election was rigged in favor of management. Within a week the miners went out on strike, forcing the company to capitulate. In the aftermath of the famous Cherry, Illinois, mine disaster in 1909, three hundred miners in Spring Valley, Illinois, walked out and refused to return to work until safety conditions were improved. Wildcat action was also threatened at several other mines in the vicinity. Clearly major mine disasters like the Cherry fire intensified the already high safety consciousness of miners and stimulated militant action to secure improvements.[36]

Coal miners have continued the practice of wildcat strikes for safety right down to the present. After a coal refuse dam burst in February, 1972, in Logan, West Virginia the ensuing flood killed 125 people and left four thousand homeless. Four months later three thousand angry miners staged a wildcat strike, demanding back pay for lost work time and improved property and death settlements. And in 1969 threat of wildcat strikes helped compel a reluctant United States President to sign the Coal Mine Health and Safety Act.[37]

IV

Although some students of industrial relations have briefly noted the contribution hazardous working conditions made to the propensity to strike in very dangerous trades,[38] the relationship between occupational safety and labor violence has been ignored by scholars. Research by social psychologists on the character of aggression, along with empirical historical evidence, indicates that the violence of modern technology against the lives and limbs of industrial workers increased their willingness to commit acts of physical aggression generally and made workers more likely to resort to violence during industrial disputes.

Experiments on violence and aggression provide four propositions relevant to this inquiry:

1. Exposure to scenes of assault and battery (aggression) increases the tendency of the witness to resort to aggression against third parties.
2. The tendency to aggression is further enhanced if the witness is shown the pain and physical damage resulting from acts of aggression.
3. If a person is frustrated by the acts of a third party and is then placed in a position to mount aggression against the third party the tendency to aggression is magnified.
4. If a person is exposed to weapons, he or she is more likely to be aggressive towards a third party. This aggressive impulse will be strengthened if the person is told that the weapons placed in view belong to the subject against whom aggression is to be directed.[39]

Industrial workers constantly watched or experienced the assaults made on workers by machines and the natural work environment. They saw the pain and the grotesque physical consequences of accidents. (They also witnessed the psychological trauma and financial adversity experienced by the families and relatives of the injured.) Then they returned to work in the presence of the destructive weaponry of modern technology. Equally important, workers frequently blamed the accidents they observed or suffered themselves on the malice or stupidity of their employers and their job supervisors—men who were their frustrators in matters of safety and in other areas disputed by labor and management.

Workers who witnessed and experienced technological aggression were more likely to be aggressive in all aspects of their lives. They were especially likely to have enhanced aggressive impulses in the aftermath of accidents and in the course of labor disputes resolved by mass action in close proximity to the violent industrial work place. The widespread belief among workers that callous negligence by employers was responsible for large numbers of accidents undoubtedly fueled the anger and frustration of laborers and was translated into violent aggression during labor disputes. Although it is difficult to quantify the effect of industrial accidents on labor violence, this phenomenon was clearly an important source of tension and physical aggression in industrial relations in the United States. In a 1903 interview, John H. Gray, a well-known economist and social reformer, suggested such an analysis of labor violence. Observing that the hazards of industry had workers "fighting for their lives" every day, Gray concluded "I am not in favor of murder, but give us the labor union, with all its murders, its brutality and all its lawlessness rather than a continuation of the evils under which working men of today are compelled to labor."[40]

A Chicago settlement house worker familiar with conditions in the stockyard slaughterhouses also recognized the relation between aggressive behavior and the melieu in which work took place: "One might almost say that the use of violence is the inevitable result of the environment of the worker. Montonously plunging his knife all day long into the throat of the steer, bespattered with blood and inured to the pitiable shrieks of the slaughtered animal . . . the cattle-butcher becomes fierce, brutal."[41]

The frustration-aggression theory just outlined explains the influence of the work environment on individual behaviors and group reactions. In a primitve early American coal mine, two brothers had just finished work for the day. They put their feet into the bucket that was to lift them out of the entry shaft. The engineer operating the steam hoist that lifted the bucket started the machine too quickly, the bucket began to sway dangerously, hit the side of the shaft and toppled over. One brother fell to the bottom of the shaft and was killed. The other brother managed to grab the rope used to lift the bucket. He reached the surface safely. "Crazed with grief, he ran to the engine house to take revenge on the engineer. . . but the engineer realizing what had happened, had fled."[42] Revenge could also be collective. In 1900, in a Biwabic, Minnesota, iron mine, an explosion tore through an underground workroom. Five miners were killed. Blaming their supervisors for the tragedy, the surviving miners saw red. A state mine inspector learned that "the superintendent and shift boss were both in danger of being lynched. . . . The shift boss told me that a number of men laid in wait for him, but being warned in time, he evaded them."[43]

Analysis of the events of the mine disaster in Cherry, Illinois, reveals that employers and public officials through experience had learned to anticipate many of the reactions to "technological aggression" that social science models would predict. About two hundred and seventy men perished in the fire that ignited and quickly swept through the coal mine in Cherry on November 13, 1909. Gross negligence by the managers of the mine and several foremen was responsible for the start of the fire and the high toll of dead and injured miners. Furthermore, many of the men who escaped from the burning mine believed that the hoist men who operated the mine elevators had acted incompetently and negligently after the miners began fleeing from the fire.

The fire began on a Saturday. On Sunday, the Illinois state attorney who had been sent to the scene ordered all the bars in Cherry closed on Monday. He feared violence, especially against the hoist operators, who were placed under guard and escorted out of town. After the initial rescue efforts were abandoned, the mine was sealed. Authorities on the scene wanted to delay reopening the mine and bringing the charred bodies of the dead to the surface because they feared "exciting the people to rash acts." But pressure from the surviving miners—who threatened to open up the mine themselves—forced a quick unsealing. With stories of dynamite plots prominent in the press and with violence expected when the dead were retrieved and could be viewed by relatives and friends, Governor Deneen ordered two companies of the Illinois National Guard to take up positions around the mine before it was reopened. Fortunately, serious violence was averted by the presence of the troops and the fact that twenty-two survivors were found in the mine. However, one miner, apparently crazed with grief, attempted to murder one of the mine foremen.[44]

Here we see that contemporaries sensed that those who viewed technological assault and battery would act aggressively towards the men they perceived as perpetrators and frustrators. The Illinois authorities also understood the aggression would be magnified by exposure to the sufferings of the fire victims.

In a provocative essay on the character of labor violence and labor radicalism in the mining communities of the Rocky Mountains, Melvyn Dubofsky has argued that labor violence was a function of fast econommic growth and was characteristic of the "early stages of industralism." Because Dubofsky's main concern was to explain the radicalism of the miners' unions, he did not systematically develop his ideas on labor violence. He noted the dangerous conditions of the mines only once, in pointing to the role mine hazards played in promoting the group solidarity of the miners who shared a common risk.[45] But Dubofsky's accurate correlation of labor violence with the early stages of the industrial revolution is worth pursuing. One reason for this association was the particular character of work risks in the early stages of industrialization.

During the early industrial revolution, employers were usually ignorant of the economic benefits of accident prevention. They were inclined to blame most accidents on worker carelessness. (Statistics to disprove this assertion were not available.) Safety technology was primitive. Employers had no legal obligation to compensate injured workers. Few workers had unions to fight for safety demands. Consequently employers had less concern for the safety of their workers than they would have in later years. And workers had more anger over industrial accidents and the lack of compensation for their victims. Furthermore, the violent character of Western working-class labor relations should be related to the high risks of the extractive industries in which radical trade unionism flourished. The mining and logging industries in which the Industrial Workers of the World (and their predecessor, the Western Federation of Miners) achieved their greatest successes were, along with railroading, the most hazardous occupations in industrial America. Machine violence against human life and limb made workers in these industries especially willing to resort to violence against the companies they held responsible for their wounds and economic losses.[46]

V

The foregoing analysis indicates that for American industrial workers the new technology of the Industrial Revolution was a mixed blessing. Rising wages, improvements in the quality of consumer goods, and advances in medical care and public health were accompanied by more hazardous working conditions that inflicted economic hardship as well as physical and mental anguish on millions of men and women. Industrial workers reacted to the negative aspects of the new technologies of the Industrial Revolution as individuals and in groups. They sought safer working conditions through unionization and striking. In the aftermath of accidents or in the midst of strikes, industrial workers often responded violently to what they perceived as unnecessary and calculated technological aggression. The fact that workers rarely attempted to destroy the new industrial technologies that assaulted them indicates that workers understood that for the most part, the manner in which technology impacted on producers was a function not of machines but of decisions made by business owners and managers.

Chapter 8

The Labor Boycott and Class Consciousness in Toledo, Ohio

Gregory R. Zieren

I

When the first wave of labor boycotts hit America in the 1880s, the reaction, as gauged from contemporary newspaper accounts, ranged from determined opposition to hysterical denunciation. The Pittsburgh *Commercial Gazette* denounced it as the "despotism of the mob," while a Connecticut editor called it "a scheme of organized revenge." More exotically *The Nation* likened the boycott to "a Malay run amok through an innocent crowd." Many accounts, in fact, stressed its foreign ancestry and branded it as inimical to the spirit of American liberty and America's classless society. The *Brooklyn Eagle*, for instance, detected in the boycott "a smell of Russian prison . . . , a stifling taint of German oppression, a stench of English repression, and a foul odor of Hungarian pauperism"; this foreign pestilence, the boycott, was "a tyranny and a slavery wholly incompatible with the survival of democratic institutions," in words of the *Ohio State Journal*[1].

Yet the imprint of the boycott, "the most dangerous weapon the workingmen ever took into their hands," is scarcely legible in the annals of labor history. The topic of few scholarly articles, the boycott last received book-length attention in 1916. In part the neglect stems from the difficulty of finding sources to document its practice. Quickly shoved into a shadow world of dubious legal standing, the boycott left little record of itself in order to protect its participants against legal attack. Newspapers in general were hostile to the purposes of most boycotts and reported them only to arouse public opinion against them or to record another prosecution. Although statutory proscription failed to stamp out the boycott, the law, which defined the boycott as a conspiracy, clouded its trace for future study.[2]

Two facets of the practice of boycotting make its obscurity especially unfortunate. First, it was a tool which disproportionately aided the organization of the less skilled. Successful boycotts were first imposed to help organize two skilled groups of workers, the printers and the cigar makers. Later, as labor struggles became more numerous and tactically more sophisticated, the boycott won struggles for many other workers. Teamsters, laundry workers, bartenders and waitresses, streetcar men, and hod carriers, who labored without the protection afforded by precious skills, could be organized if their employers were compelled to recognize their unions through coordinated consumer pressure. The determination with which the mainly skilled craft locals of the Toledo Central Labor Union utilized the boycott to promote unionization campaigns of the less-skilled calls into question the traditional picture of the American Federation of Labor as the preserve of a selfish "aristocracy of labor."

The second important facet of the boycott is what it reveals about the behavior of American workers as consumers who obeyed the injunction, "Don't Patronize." Only rarely could a consumer boycott rely exclusively on the buying power of already organized workers. Of necessity boycotters appealed to the broader working class community for support. At this point the study of the boycott goes beyond the focus of traditional labor history on the story of organized workers. All workers were called upon to endorse the wider aims of the labor movement for a decent, humane economic order. The successful boycott, in other words, tapped a vein of discontent with industrial capitalism. As the New York *Commercial Advertiser* observed in 1886, "boycotting can only succeed where a strong public sentiment already exists that only waits for some one to formulate and direct it."[3]

In Toledo the strong public sentiment which sustained the boycott found its strongest expression in the city's working-class neighborhoods and in the retail establishments which served them. The structure of the retail market in nineteenth century cities dispersed and decentralized consumption into hundreds of specialized shops. The purposeful and powerful unity of action that marked the successful boycott made retailers hostage to the demands of their customers. This was especially true of saloons and cigar shops, but greengrocers, laundries, men's furnishing stores, hardware stores, butcher shops, hat shops, shoe stores, and other retail shops could be subjected to the boycott.

The origins of the boycott in Ireland during the agitation of the Irish

National Land League are well known. Irish tenants and shopkeepers simply refused to engage in any social or economic intercourse with certain landlords who had made themselves especially obnoxious to their neighbors. The first of these organized "shunnings" was directed against one Captain Boycott, an agent for an absentee landlord. *The Nation* graphically described the effects of the tactic on its second victim, a landlord on an estate near Cork, a Mr. Bence Jones.

> The process is a very simple one. Under secret orders or warnings, issued, we presume, by the local committee, the obnoxious person is put under a ban. His servants and laborers refuse to work for him; the shopkeepers to sell to him or buy from him; the livery stable keepers to transport him; the blacksmiths to shoe his horses; and he is lucky if his cattle are not driven off his land at night. In order still further to shake his nerves threatening and abusive letters are written to him, and if these fail to produce any effect on him, they are sure to do so on his family.[4]

The most striking point of the account is the totality of the ostracism. To one contemporary only the sentence of excommunication passed by medieval popes conveyed the scope, severity, and effectiveness of the boycott. It evoked images of primordial passions and atavistic practices somehow displaced from the medieval to the modern world. As *The Nation* remarked, the boycott is "a wild and barbarous mode of expressing the reprobation which, in more civilized communities, would find vent in the press and the social influence of a well-to-do industrial middle class."[5] American boycotters, in defense of the practice, claimed it bore an ancient pedigree, with patriotic origins in the eighteenth century when the colonists fought by boycotts against the Stamp Acts and the duties on tea.

Once boycotting became widespread in the 1880s, it was soon identified with attaining specific economic objectives, especially on behalf of the Knights of Labor. Almost immediately boycotting was subject to attacks in the middle-class press, in the legislatures, and in the courts. After 1886, legal definition and proscription outlawed its most extreme manifestations (secondary boycotts and sympathetic strikes) and its most inflammatory usage (against railroads). Twenty cases came before state courts between 1886 and 1888, most of which were decided against the boycotters. In Federal jurisdiction, the first landmark case came in 1893 in a strike and boycott centered around Toledo on the Ann Arbor Railroad, followed by the Pullman boycott in 1894, the Danbury Hatters Case in 1904 and the Buck's Stove and Range

Company boycott in 1907.[6] The weight of legal opinion condemned the boycott as a criminal conspiracy while at the same time defining it precisely for prosecution and narrowing popular usage of the term.

Precise definition of the boycott, paradoxically, obscures both its origin and its true meaning. As it became a weapon in economic warfare, the original sense of the boycott as social ostracism and collective disapproval was lost. Writers in the 1880s used the term boycott to express at least half a dozen related concepts, all suggesting withdrawal of social, economic, or political contact with the offender. The simplest, the primary boycott, entailed an appeal to all parties to cease patronizing a firm because it would not come to satisfactory terms with its employees or with the union representing them. The first important primary boycott, that of the printers against the *New York Tribune* in 1884, resulted from a lost strike; until the mid-1880s the terms strike and boycott were sometimes used interchangeably. A secondary boycott attacks third parties not part of the initial dispute, such as suppliers or wholesale customers of the targeted firm. A hardware dealer who refused to stop selling boycotted stoves, for instance, would find himself the object of a boycott.[7] In a materials boycott, union workmen would refuse to handle nonunion goods. The insistence on a closed shop could be construed as a boycott of union against nonunion workers. Even the "fair list" and "union label" campaigns were boycotts of a sort of firms that did not qualify for the unions' approval.

Legal distinctions, especially those which focused on the boycott as a criminal conspiracy, conveniently ignored one central fact about the successful ones: boycotts relied on the actions of a large number of people. A boycott is a form of mass collective action regardless of the issues involved or the intentions of the parties who called it. Furthermore, boycotting must be considered a rational and purposeful act, the end result of conscious decisions not to consume, work, or fraternize. The targets and the expressed goals of boycotts were usually explicit enough for workers to face clearcut choice of compliance or noncompliance. Well-run boycotts precluded any chance of consumers being ignorant of that choice. Consequently the decision to respect a boycott enables us to infer attitudes towards economic and social concerns of the working class. If the labor boycott is imposed with frequency and effectiveness, we may determine that the community that sustained boycotting demonstrated solidarity with other workers and a willingness to act in pursuit of class goals, that is, class consciousness.

The study of the boycott is ultimately the study of the community that imposed or supported it. One historian has tried recently to establish links between the Irish and American practices of the boycott and suggested that the immigrant community in New York provided the link between Old and New World practices. Studies of Pennsylvania mining communities show that Eastern European immigrants transformed ethnic and community loyalties and norms into powerful sources of group strength when engaged in strikes or boycotts. As Leo Wolman observed in 1916, "where the laboring community is a close-knit, intimate assembly the boycott is waged by collective efforts impelled by a collective consciousness."[8] That description applies to the working-class neighborhoods of Toledo in the 1890s.

II

When Grand Master Machinist James McConnell visited in Toledo in 1897, he complimented the city for its national reputation as "the best organized city in the country." By the late 1890s perhaps a third, certainly one quarter, of the wage earners were organized into craft locals.The leading force in the organizing drive was the Toledo Central Labor Union and its organizing committees. The CLU was established in 1886 when the Knights of Labor were still the leading working-class organization and craft unions existed for only a few of the major trades. Just three crafts—seventy-five to one hundred printers, fifty cigar makers, and two hundred carpenters—made up the CLU at it founding. By 1890, sixteen or seventeen locals with probably fifteen hundred members were represented in the central body, and by the time of McConnell's visit fifty locals with five thousand or so members. For winning new adherents, the boycott, broadly defined, was the CLU's most successful tactical weapon.[9]

The remarkable decade-long organizing campaign exploited opportunities in the late 1880s and 1890s when natural gas discoveries in northwestern Ohio set off an era of rapid economic and population growth. Taking advantage of labor shortages caused by brisk demand for new houses and factories, carpenters and bricklayers worked to organize locals of painters, tinners, plasters, plumbers, stone masons, lathers, and hod carriers between 1886 and 1890. The building trades set up their own central body in 1889 following the success of the CLU's coordinated and centralized operations. Article I of the constitution of the Amalgamated Building Trades Council of Toledo read, "no man can be a true union man who is satisfied to work with a non-union man." Putting this cardinal principle of the boycott into effective practice made the council a model among American building trades councils in the late nineteenth century and added perhaps one thousand workers to the ranks of the organized.[10]

Natural gas also changed the city's industrial landscape and provided a host of new factories for the CLU's organizing committees. The Libbey Glass Company set up its works in Toledo in 1887 and imported a skilled labor force from Boston. As yet barely touched by mechanization, glass workers were artisans with "a long tradition of collective action." Cutters and blowers organized two locals of the American Flint Glass Workers Union and joined the CLU in 1890. Earning more than ministers or college professors, glass workers in Toledo became home owners and respected citizens who were elected to seats on the city council and in the leadership of the CLU.[11]

Bicycle manufacturing, however, was the industry that brought prosperity to the city throughout most of the 1890s and made the largest addition to the ranks of organized workers as well. Metal polishers and machinists, like glassworkers, were drawn from Eastern industrial cities but in insufficient numbers to fill the demand for skilled workers in the new, burgeoning industry. Profiting from labor scarcity, machinists organized their own lodge and the CLU helped the polishers start a local within months of the opening of the first important factory, Lozier and Yost. A CLU-supported strike by metal polishers in 1891 and a national boycott of Lozier and Yost bicycles by the AFL helped consolidate the power of the skilled metal trades workers in Toledo's bicycle factories.[12]

As the city developed into one of the centers of the industry, skilled workers ventured beyond the limits of narrowly circumscribed craft unionism. Machinist and metal polishers helped CLU organizing committees create federal labor unions for lathe operators, grinders and strappers, screw makers, filers, drill press and milling machine hands, drop forgers, and assemblers. These locals formed the Bicycle Trades Council in 1896, patterned after the Toledo Building Trades Council, and founded the International Union of Bicycle Workers which represented them nationally. Union label bicycles were assembled in Toledo in 1897, one of the first machine-tooled mass-consumption items ever to bear the label. The Bicycle Trades Council maintained the closed shop in the major factories and organized perhaps two to three thousand workers.[13]

Boycotting played a more important role than labor scarcity in organizing the city's third growth industry of the 1890s, beer brewing.

Brewery workmen discovered the power of working-class consumers in 1891 while circulating petitions in saloons in support of the demand for recognition and shorter hours; the petition succeeded in swaying the employers after threats of a strike and a CLU offer to mediate had failed. The success of unions in the industry and the "determining consideration" of employers' attitudes toward them depended on "the fact that probably 90% of the product is consumed by working men," according to an estimate by a U.S. Brewers' Association executive. That power was demonstrated locally less than a year after the petition and the implied threat of a boycott had forced recognition. A visiting official of the same association, upon being told of a local boycott on "scab" bread, checked out of his hotel because it served the proscribed item. Following the forward and backward linkages of their industry, brewery workmen used their leverage with consumers to help organize other trades as well. Beer drivers, coopers, firemen, stationary engineers, and bottlers all set up locals behind the protection afforded by the impregnable position of the brewery workmen.[14]

In the course of its organizing campaigns as well as its day-to-day business in the 1890s, few meetings of the CLU passed without a report on the progress of a boycott, the imposition of a new one, or an investigation to determine whether one was warranted. The prominence of the boycott in the local labor movement may stem in part from the role of printers and cigar makers in setting up the CLU. When *Bradstreet's* made the first survey of the boycott in 1885, cigar and newspaper boycotts ranked first and second in frequency. Printers and cigar makers conducted the first boycotts in Toledo in the early 1880s but in the 1890s brewers, barbers, bakers, clerks, flour packers, and a variety of less skilled workers mainly benefitted from the practice.[15] But the boycott's effectiveness always depended on the CLU's influence among working-class consumers.

The Armour boycott of 1897 illustrates the procedural elements of the boycott, the appeal to working-class consumers and the power which accrued to the CLU from its community connections. Before imposing a boycott, usually on request from a local union, the CLU investigated the issue to determine if arbitration or negotiation could resolve the differences. If not, the CLU solicited contributions from the interested locals to pay the cost of the boycott. Thousands of stickers and circulars were printed to inform customers that the Armour Company was unfair to the Machinists and that consumers should buy other brands. The CLU committee then visited retail grocers and butchers to persuade them to stop stocking the product. Of sixty shops visited in the Armour boycott, all but two agreed to comply.[16]

When the CLU determined that Armour was still shipping meat to Toledo, spotters looked for the product at freight depots and followed delivery wagons to their destinations. A second visit to the retailer to confront him with the evidence was often sufficient warning to make him see the error of his ways. If not, his shop and delivery wagons were plastered with boycott stickers and signs that read "Unfair." Local unions, in turn, were charged with reading the names of the offending parties at their own meetings, and the CLU kept a blackboard in its hall with the list of unfair businesses. Some locals established fines against members discovered disobeying the injunction to boycott; repeated offenses brought higher fines. In the case of retail stores, it was common knowledge which neighborhoods contained which factories and crafts, hence which union members were most influential as consumers. In the case of one Mr. MacDonald, who owned a grocery store in the Fifth Ward, he promised, after the second visit, not to handle Armour meats. The committee reported that he "can best be reached through railroad men." A CLU committee contacted the Brotherhood of Railway Trainmen and reported back to the full meeting that the BRT would "do all they could to drive out Armour meats." Grocer W.J. Schultz, whose store served the Nebraska Avenue German community, was one of the two who refused to stop handling Armour meats after repeated visits. Within a month, the boycott committee informed the Central that Schultz was no longer in business.[17]

In the case of the Armour boycott, securing compliance from retailers was a relatively simple matter. Few local merchants wanted to make the troubles of a large corporation—especially a member of the infamous "Meat Trust"—their own. The CLU was capable of making life too bothersome for retailers to consider opposition. As the proprietor of a men's clothing store told the CLU business agent, he "could sell fair goods to everybody but could not do with unfair goods." The manager of the H.M.&R. Shoe Company violated the agreement with the clerks' union and lost the shop card identifying him as a "fair" employer who hired union workers and dealt in union-made goods. He finally had no choice but to give in to the superior power of the CLU and of his working-class customers who boycotted him for his infraction of the rules. After paying ten dollars in costs for the boycott against him, the CLU business agent reported that the manager "received the card and promised not to violate the agreement, remarking that when you wanted to keep a man good you should touch his pocketbook."[18]

Successful boycotts conformed closely to working-class consumption patterns, thus making some merchants more vulnerable to pressure than others. Beer and cheap cigars were the classic items, but stoves, furniture, cheap clothing and shoes, and the services of tailors, barbers, laundries, and certain restaurants were also susceptible because the lion's share of their patronage came from working-class consumers in factory districts. Baker Kugler on Nebraska Avenue was visited about having his wagon repair work done in a union shop and his horseshoeing done in a union livery barn. He told the business agent that "he employed union bakers and most of his bread was sold to union men and he realized that he could not afford to do anything against them." There was even a certain wry humor to the CLU's acknowledged power. The CLU business agent visited a piano dealer who was having his laundry sent to a Chinese shop instead of a union laundry. The man agreed to switch after the business agent commented that the purpose of his visit was "to remind him that Chinamen don't purchase pianos." In 1891, the CLU tried to persuade the Polk Directory Company to switch from a nonunion to a union print shop; when the directory company refused, the CLU instructed its members to give fictitious names to directory solicitors. "Acknowledging that through the antagonism of unionists their efforts were anything but satisfactory in furnishing a reliable directory," the Polk Company signed a five-year contract with a fair firm in 1893.[19]

CLU boycotters were compelled to recognize the limitations of both price and product in their calculations. They quickly gave up on a hatter who sold no product for under five dollars. A master tailor in 1899 told the CLU committee that his workmen were free to join the union but that he would not compel them to. When the committee suggested his business might gain or suffer by his decision, he contradicted them.

> I do not cater to the class of people you represent, most of you have your garments made by cheap tailors or patronize the ready made stores. . . . I get the highest price paid in the city for my work and the question whether I employ union or non-union men never enters the minds of my customers. I have not had a call for the union label since it was introduced eight years ago and do not think my trade is cognizant of its existence.[20]

Merchants catering to the working class trade sang a different tune when CLU committees paid a visit. Saloonkeeper Mickey Shea, after the committee "explain[ed] the condition he was putting himself in," agreed to send back his new National Cash Register, a product the CLU was boycotting, and asked the committee to send the sales representative from a rival firm. The manager of Melvin and Company clothing store told the committee he knew personally of one good customer who stopped patronizing the store when the clerks withdrew their card. Clerks were some of the chief beneficiaries of boycotts, in fact. Their organizing was "no doubt . . . helped by some union men who asked for cards. . . . The same not being shown, they walked out of the store."[21]

Rather than merely threaten, CLU committees sometimes got results by tempting business with the prospects of new customers if they agreed to the demands. Woodworkers were helped in this manner after the breweries signed an agreement to purchase only union-made bar fixtures. Hein Furniture Company then agreed to the union pay scale and union recognition. Brewery workmen, in fact, were masters of the carrot-and-stick approach. When an influx of cheap barrels from a nonunion concern threatened the wage scale of the coopers' union in 1893, the coopers, the brewers' union, and the CLU moved quickly to counter the threat. The coopers visited flour millers in the city and threatened to boycott them if they used the barrels. The brewery workmen informed the boss coopers that the union would not handle cheap, nonunion beer kegs and barrels, and demanded that the breweries purchase only the union-made article. Soon the coopers adopted a stamp so that union-made barrels were recognizable to all.[22]

Retailers recognized that it was good business to stay in the CLU's good graces by sending back orders of boycotted goods and contracting for union-label ones instead. Based on a survey of merchants, one Protestant minister in Toledo called the demand for union-label goods "considerable" and higher than in other cities where similar studies had been done. At CLU meetings, cigar makers and clothing workers harped on the theme of generating greater recognition of and demand for union-label goods. The local survey estimated that union-label goods made up only about ten percent of the demand for some articles, but even ten percent could make or break a store in the competitive retail business. Upon request from the CLU, Milner's Department Store agreed not to stock Rochester-made clothing, boycotted by the United Garment Workers in 1896. Milner's took out a full page advertisement in The *Toledo Blade* announcing their compliance because, the ad confessed, "it was BUSINESS for us to do so. We simply quit buying Rochester clothing because the workingmen of Toledo, who are our friends and whose money we want, requested us to do so." The ad offered to have Milner's compliance tested: "Our books are open. Any committee the CLU cares to appoint can see by them that we have kept the pledge made to the laboring men of this city." Mockett's clothing store, across the street, did not comply with the request and answered Milner's ad the next day. Both ads reflected the bitter competition which prevailed between the two retail stores and even a personal hostility between the owners. Mockett attacked Milner for representing a "foreign" corporation (his first department store was in Kansas City) and pointed out that each of his own expenditures for business improvements "was paid out to Toledo workingmen, not to Kansas City." Somewhat defensively, Mockett claimed to appeal to a different class of customer than that which "judges an article by the price alone. We do not cater to the illiterate Pollock, nor the riffraff and rabble."[23] Mockett's and the carriage trade tailor notwithstanding, many businesses did depend on working-class customers, some of whom called for union label goods, and others who respected the boycott. Determining the mechanics of the boycott were the rational and even cold calculations of the CLU, but the boycott could express class hatreds, resentments and frustrations as well. The more extreme examples of boycotting revealed the extent of working-class grievances against the economic order; these example, in turn, may account for the nearly hysterical accounts in the middle-class press against it and for the legal repression that followed. The boycott, it must be admitted, possessed a cutting edge that was frightening in its effectiveness. More than simply a tool of economic warfare it made people, especially offending workers, outcasts in their own neighborhoods or at work.

The ostracism against scabs hounded them wherever they went. The case of a saloonkeeper who was overly friendly to strikebreakers was reported to the CLU. His indiscretion invited a visit from the business agent and a warning. The CLU attempted to deny strikebreakers all forms of human sustenance in saloons, hotels and restaurants where it had influence, in order to deter manufacturers from importing scabs. A metal polisher once betrayed his union by supplying information to a detective agency. In 1905 he showed up as a pitcher on the Toledo Mud Hens baseball team. The metal polishers insisted he be fired, despite the manager's insistence that the contract had already been signed. Management gave in to the demand, explaining that they could not afford to appear to be "fighting organized labor." The CLU business agent recorded other instances of former union members who had scabbed during a strike being denied its membership, and hence being fired by firms finally coming to terms with the union. Here was a very clear violation of working-class norms. As even Andrew Carnegie noted, several years before the Homestead strike, "There is an unwritten law among the best workmen: 'Thou shall not take thy neighbor's job.' "[24]

In working class neighborhoods where unionism was strong, offenders against the moral code were punished. A plastering contractor in the factory district of Auburndale refused to deal with the plasterers' union in 1900. "As this Mr. Hartman runs a wood and coal yard on Bancroft St., union men should see that Hartman had none of their support," the business agent recommended. When having houses built, union members were expected to have union contractors do the work. When they failed to live up to their obligations, their cases were reported by neighbors to the CLU and to local unions. Union members reported on each other if one was seen patronizing nonunion laundries, buying nonunion cigars or bread, or going to nonunion barber shops. Local unions investigated the charges and sometimes imposed stiff fines on their own members for disobeying their boycotts.[25]

The boycott, like the strike, carried overtones of class warfare in exceptional circumstances. One recurring threat to the social order in major American cities in the late nineteenth and early twentieth centuries was the transit strike and accompanying boycott by working-class passengers. Riots, heavy property losses, injuries, and even death attended streetcar strikes in Detroit (1891), Brooklyn (1895), Milwaukee (1896), Cleveland (1906), Columbus and Philadelphia (1910), and many other cities. As public utilities that amassed revenues larger than those of the cities they served, street railway corporations often stood accused of treating their captive customers with contempt and of corrupting city councils with bribes to obtain favorable franchise terms. Overcapitalization, the abuse of animals on the horsecar network, poor service, excessive fares, and tax evasion were some of the charges leveled against the street railway companies in Toledo.[26]

Public opinion could sometimes shift drastically during the course of streetcar strikes because of the inconvenience to the commuter, business losses to downtown merchants and, most important, the violence that occurred in so many transit struggles. Two points during the course of the strikes held the most potential for violent responses among strikers and sympathizers. The first occasion for violence came with the attempt to run the cars with company officials or loyal workmen. Crowds of strikers and sympathizers typically milled around carbarns to physically prevent any attempt to run the trollies. But where injunctions or action by the police or state militia limited the gatherings, a second and more ominous confrontation could occur. When companies tried to keep the entire system running by recruiting large numbers of strikebreakers, their antagonists declared open season on the cars, which were highly visible targets for attack by stones, bricks, and even gunfire as they passed through working-class neighborhoods. And cars were vulnerable to derailment. After the car left the relatively safe downtown area, patronizing a streetcar during a strike called for foolhardy courage. Strikers and their sympathizers recognized no morally neutral position in the fight against street railway corporations. Every passenger who disobeyed the injunction to boycott the service brought down upon his or her head at least working-class citizens' curses and moral condemnation, if not worse.

Among the best known literary depictions of a streetcar strike is Theodore Dreiser's *Sister Carrie*, an account drawn in part from Dreiser's brief reporting career at The *Blade* during a strike in Toledo in 1894. In his fictional strike, "Cars were assailed, men attacked, police struggled with, tracks torn up, and shots fired, until at last street fights and mob movements became frequent and the city was invested with militia."[27] In fact, the two streetcar strikes in Toledo during the 1890s stopped far short of the violence Dreiser depicts when his character, Hurstwood, goes to work as a scab in the Brooklyn streetcar strike in 1895. Disciplined strikers, cautious corporate officials, vacillating public servants, and the resolute power of workers in Toledo's neighborhoods prevented bloodshed.

The first Toledo strike began on July 15, 1891, on both of the city's systems, the Consolidated and the Toledo Electric, after they had refused wage increases and hours reductions and fired several prominent union members. The union hastily arranged to provide alternative jitney service, but the collection of horse-drawn wagons and carts running once an hour was no substitute for streetcar service. At the same time, the five hundred strikers and hundreds of supporters stationed themselves at the car barns to prevent any movement on the lines. Pickets kept watch around the clock while the streetcar men's union officers and CLU officials made the circuit of the barns, encouraging the men and keeping up morale.[28]

On the second day of the strike, when the Consolidated attempted to run a car, a score of strikers surrounded it, lifted it up a few inches, turned and placed it crosswise on the tracks. But support for the strike among the working class was so strong, one union man declared, that no jury could be found in Toledo to convict the men for violating the Ohio law prohibiting obstruction of the rails. A union painter affirmed, "Until the strikers get their demands not a car will move." He dismissed any effective intervention by the police. "What do the police amount to with the 500 strikers and the 5,000 union labor men who would turn out in a minute to stop the cars of either company." After the CLU endorsed the union, one striker warned, "We do not intend to commit any acts of violence and have not so far; but if they force us to we can call out 5,000 union men within an hour. The Labor unions of this city are right in line with us." Confirming these words, the woodworkers' union resolution promised "the streetcar men our heartiest support, morally, financially, and if need be, physically." With the support of the Central Union and its constituent locals, an officer of the CLU predicted, "There will be bloodshed in this town if those cars are run with non-union help."[29]

Endorsement of the strike by the CLU guaranteed its success or a violent confrontation. A committee of three CLU officials, including two glassworkers and a printer, negotiated with the companies on the fourth and fifth days of the strike and finally won a compromise settlement based on recognition of the union, a twelve-hour day, a ten per cent wage increase, and overtime pay. Once the CLU joined the strikers, The Blade noted, they gained "a reserve force of men ready to call at any time in case of an attempt to take out the cars."[30]

The second strike by streetcar workers, in 1894, was clearly provoked by the management of the smaller of the two lines, the Robison's Toledo Electric. James Robison planned carefully for the confrontation by concluding a contract with the U.S. Post Office to begin handling mail. Consequently, a strike by streetcar workers would disrupt mail service. Robison then fired four prominent leaders of the union for engaging in union business on company time and dismissed the four members of the grievance committee who came to parley the next day. He refused to discuss their reinstatement with the CLU or the international president of the Amalgamated Association of Street Railway Employees, and rejected arbitration of the dispute by the Ohio Board of Arbitration. No doubt he expected a quick victory over the union, which was demoralized and disorganized after accepting a wage cut at the onset of the 1893 depression.[31]

Robison had learned his lessons well from the 1891 strike. When a crowd of strikers and sympathizers gathered in front of the car barn to prevent the first trolley from running, he promptly secured an injunction to keep them off his property and got arrest warrants for four others accused of grounding wires.[32] The movement and size of electric streetcars made them less subject to seizure by crowds, but the expensive equipment was more often the target of sabotage.

Having secured legal help to keep the tracks free of strikers, Robison next faced the crucial test. If passengers would risk riding the cars of the struck line, he could import strikebreakers and defeat the union. But the CLU stepped in to recognize the strike and boycott the line. The effects of the CLU's endorsement, and of public hostility to the company, were swift and unmistakable. A crowd of two thousand gathered on the second day of the strike to watch one of Robison's sons, who attempted to run a car. He collected one fare and then quickly returned to the barn after "a bad smelling egg struck (him) in the face." Every attempt to run a car was met with "hisses, groans and unbecoming epithets. Chunks of mud, small stones and oblong eggs were showered at the copper-colored cars." By the end of the second day the boycott was taking its toll. As the strike's third day began, the local press reported that "the Robison system is thoroughly tied up today. Not a wheel has turned since 9 o'clock last night."[33]

Reporter Dreiser rode the line on the strike's third day but without incident.

> Few persons entered the car or sought to part with a nickel for the sake of such excitement as the thing offered. No violence was attempted by any of the streetcar employees and a large part of the jeering was done by sympathizers of the men.

Motormen from the Consolidated "often slowed and fairly crawled along, making the Robison to travel slow and thus receive the benefit of whatever jeering and hooting might be going on around."[34]

The Consolidated men backed their union colleagues on the Robison line as did the CLU, but it was the streetcar passengers who decided the fate of the strike. The Huron Street line ran north from the downtown area and served the factory district in the First Ward where many glass workers lived. Glass workers were also vocal critics of the company and the service it offered, both on the floor of the CLU and in the crowds that jeered the cars as they passed through working-class neighborhoods. The Robisons were reported as "more afraid of the glass workers than the employees of the line themselves" for fear of what damage they might do. The degree of public support the strike enjoyed equaled that of the strike three years earlier, especially in working-class districts. It guaranteed that the strikers could obey the terms of the Robisons' injunction and still effectively stop service by relying on the boycott of the lines by their supporters.[35]

The 1894 strike ended on the fourth day when the Robisons finally conceded defeat and let a board of arbitration consisting of the CLU president, a company representative, and a public official decide the case. Toledo was fortunate that neither the 1891 nor the 1894 strike escalated to violent confrontations. The success of the union, in both cases, derived largely from the support the strikers enjoyed among the public, especially in the working-class wards. The *Blade* predicted that the company's continued attempts to run the cars in 1894 would bring reactions: "Persistence on their part will be met by firmness on the part of the men." But mob violence did not result because the strikers "had the morals [sic] support of the people of Toledo," who, out of fear or deference to the wishes of the CLU and the streetcar men, boycotted the lines.[36] The toss of a brick or a rotten egg may not have been the worst penalty against those who rode the cars. The power of the boycott in street railway strikes rested ultimately on its directive to workers to help other workers and to shun those who chose the convenience of riding the cars over the assertion of class goals.

III

In the factory, at the building site, and in the neighborhood, the boycott galvanized the collective will of workers to endorse the aims of the labor movement and further the achievement of working-class goals in general. The boycott, by extension, led the CLU into politics when bosses presented themselves for collective judgment at the voting booth. Here was Gompers' simple dictum incarnate of punishing enemies and rewarding friends. In the process of extending the power of consumer persuasion to the political arena, the CLU was drawn by success into a more active role than Gompers would have sanctioned. The boycott taught workers to strike out at miscreants wherever and whenever possible; putting that lesson into practice embroiled the CLU in the fight to elect one of the great Progressive Era mayors, Samuel "Golden Rule" Jones.

The CLU's first political campaign had the essentially negative goal of defeating an open shop printer when he ran for the city council in 1890. A Democrat running in a heavily Democratic ward, he lost nonethless because, as the *Blade* noted, "the labor unionists were out in force and had men working against Batch at every precinct." The CLU took on a more formidable opponent in 1891 when, at the insistence of the cigar makers, a member of a nonunion cigar firm ran for police commissioner on the Republican ticket. It was a banner year for the GOP, which had its entire city ticket elected except for police commissioner. All over the city, the *Blade* reported, "the labor union men cut Nunn at every precinct." Success emboldened the CLU to mark other hostile council candidates for defeat in 1892 and 1894.[37]

After these victories at the polls, the CLU embarked on a quest for political favors, influence, and respectability. When the Board of Education awarded a painting contract to an out-of-town, nonunion firm, the CLU issued a statement pledging itself "to strongly oppose and do its utmost to defeat for office any employer of non-union men." The Board saw the error of its ways and awarded the next contract to a resident union painter; at the same time a printing firm hostile to organized labor lost its contract for city and county printing. In order to help insure that labor's voice was heard, union members, particularly glass workers, printers, and machinists, ran for the city council from working-class wards. By 1896, a former CLU president, a glass worker, was elected president of the Board of Aldermen, a printer became Republican campaign chairman and later city clerk, and several other trade unionists occupied seats on the council.[38] By the late 1890s both political parties were compelled to invite labor representatives to sit on city commissions and boards, court the CLU as one of the most powerful political institutions in the city, and reckon with the power of organized labor in Toledo as a whole.

A powerful political and economic institution, the street railway company, emerged during the decade as the CLU's chief antagonist and villain. The Consolidated thrust the transit issue to the center of Toledo's political stage in 1896 when it bought out its rival, Toledo Electric, and sought a fifty-year franchise for the entire system. Both companies had earned the emnity of the CLU for their hostility to organized labor but Toledo Traction's new franchise terms alienated unorganized workers as well, especially those living in suburban working-class districts, because the proposal abolished the "workingmen's three cent fare." The franchise was stalled all winter in council by members reluctant to face voters over the issue. A CLU officer, meanwhile, warned, "If the council grants a fifty-year franchise to the streetcar company, it will be wiped off the map."[39]

As the political parties approached the mayoral and council elections of 1897, the only issue from labor's point of view was the candidates' stand on the franchise. The CLU worked on behalf of a political unknown, a successful manufacturer with an enlightened record of labor practices, Samuel M. Jones; more important, he pledged to support the three-cent fare and work toward municipal ownership of utilities. Jones won the Republican mayoral nomination and the election with labor's support and the backing of middle-class voters attracted to the idea of a "business administration" of city affairs.[40]

Jones's "business administration" more clearly resembled what the CLU wanted than what the middle class had bargained for. During his first term he campaigned for municipal ownership of the electric light plant, stopped all prosecutions of saloonkeepers and prostitutes, enforced the eight-hour day for city workers, and compelled Toledo Traction to withdraw its franchise proposal. The GOP punished his heterodoxy when party leaders engineered his defeat for renomination by the GOP in 1899. With the official endorsement of the CLU, Jones ran as an independent and won seventy per cent of the vote in a three-way race. Lopsided totals for Jones in immigrant and suburban working-class wards contributed the bulk of his victory margin in 1899 and in subsequent elections in 1901 and 1903.[41]

The boycott in Toledo in the 1890s provided the bridge between political action, as the narrow prosecution of one craft's grievance campaign against an employer, and the broader purpose of politics to promote the interests of workers, organized or not. This movement in the political realm paralleled the function of the boycott in general: it bridged the distance between skilled workers, for whom labor scarcity and organization afforded some measure of defense against the caprice of employers, the uncertainties of the economic system, and the great reserve army of casual and unskilled laborers. The boycott functioned by lining up laboring-class consumers on the side of fellow workers against their employers, sometimes from a distance of hundreds of miles as in the Armour or Rochester Clothing boycotts. Through the mechanism of the boycott, workers asserted control over their economic lives as producers and consumers. The boycott strove for the unity of all workers in the practical quest for higher wages, decent conditions and recognition of the power of class solidarity.

If gauges of working-class solidarity and class consciousness are to be found in American history, they must conform to certain common sense rules of evidence. Such measures should be collective rather than individual, purposeful and persisting rather than episodic, active rather than passsive, and indigenous to American working-class culture; indeed, the labor boycott was one weapon widely admired and copied by European trade unionists during this period.[42] Inferring working-class attitudes toward industrial capitalism from the behavior of boycotters seems risky at best, but concerning the boycott in Toledo in the 1890s, certain conclusions appear to be well grounded. The boycott was an effective tactic for organizing new workers and protecting the status of organized ones because people in sufficient numbers respected its directives. In the hands of the CLU it was a collective and rational activity pursued with clear-cut objectives. Tracing the boycott poses serious problems of evidence, but it seems an especially fitting task to investigate the activities of workers as consumers in this most consumption-oriented of capitalist economies. Conceived by skilled workers, fostered by residents of working-class neighborhoods, and carried out in the interests of wider organization and the pursuit of a more humane economic order, the boycott provides one gauge for worker solidarity and class consciousness.[43]

Reforming Working-Class Play: Workers, Parks, and Playgrounds in an Industrial City, 1870-1920

ROY ROSENZWEIG

"You may take my word for it," landscape architect and horticulturist Andrew Jackson Downing wrote of parks in 1848, "they will be better preachers of temperance than temperance societies, better refiners of national manners than dancing schools and better promoters of general good-feeling than any lectures on the philosophy of happiness." For more than a century social reformers have depicted parks as weapons in the same moral crusade against working-class disorder, degeneracy, and drinking as the temperance movement. "No one who has closely observed the conduct of the people who visit Central Park," boasted Frederick Law Olmsted, the most distinguished and influential landscape architect of the middle and late nineteenth century, "can doubt that it exercises a distinctly harmonizing and refining influence upon the most unfortunate and lawless classes of the city— an influence favorable to courtesy, self-control, and temperance."[1]

The obvious motives of social control and the overt class biases evident in such statements have earned park and playground reformers the disdain of subsequent historians. "Thus it was," charges the author of a recent history of playground reform, "that a movement desiring to release the city's young from the harsher aspects of urban life became one which seemed to prepare them to accept their fate uncomplainingly." Social control was certainly an important and persistent motivation for many reformers, but to focus exclusively on this aspect of the park and playground movement reduces them to rationally calculating social engineers when actually their motivations were much more complex.[2] Early park reformers, for example, were also inspired by naturalistic visions of society, fears about urban disease, and infatuation with European public gardens, as well as by the desire to uplift and quiet the masses.

More important, proponents of the social control paradigm suggest that the object of reform designs—the urban worker—was both inert and totally pliable. By viewing park reform exclusively "from the top down," they ignore the possibility that workers might have taken an active part in conceiving or advocating parks, and assume that workers uncritically accepted the park programs handed down by an omnipotent ruling class. In an effort to explore the ways in which people actively shaped their nonworking lives, this article focuses on the struggles over recreational space and behavior in one industrial city—Worcester, Massachusetts—in the late nineteenth century and the early twentieth.

"Two Distinct and Conflicting Definitions of the Park": The Birth of the Park System

Neither a commercial port nor a company town, Worcester, with a diversified industrial base, a rapid growth rate, and a large immigrant population, was broadly representative of the manufacturing cities where most American workers made their homes at the turn of the century. Worcester's factories turned out a wide range of products, from corsets to carpets, but its most important manufacturing activity was concentrated in the metal industries, a rather heterogeneous category that embraced such products as wire, grinding wheels, lathes, and looms. Along with the capitalization of the city's industries, which multiplied about eight times between 1870 and 1910 (from about eight to sixty-five million dollars), Worcester's population grew rapidly from 41,000 to 146,000. Generally speaking, the owners of the city's factories came from native American, "Yankee" backgrounds, while the workers in those factories were predominantly first- or second-generation immigrants. In 1900, for example, native-stock Americans made up only six percent of the city's manual laborers. Thus, ethnicity and class loyalties, often analytically counterposed by historians, were inextricably intertwined in a city such as Worcester. In the late 1870s and 1880s, most of these immigrants were Irish. Indeed, perhaps half of the city was of Irish heritage in 1880. By 1900, however, substantial numbers of Swedes and French Canadians had entered the city's neighborhoods and factories. And, in the next ten years, Worcester began developing sizeable Jewish, Italian, Polish, and Lithuanian communities.[3]

Despite the numerical predominance of the immigrant working class, the city's Yankee upper class officially controlled Worcester's parks, as they did the factories and most major political offices. In the park system, this elite was represented by Edward Winslow Lincoln, the secretary and chairman of the Parks Commission for most of the late nineteenth century. So complete was his domination of the commission that his death in 1896 necessitated, for the first time, the hiring of a full-time park superintendent. A member of a leading Worcester family, Lincoln spent most of his first forty years seeking a suitable career, first in law and then in journalism. Around 1860, however, he discovered his true vocation in horticulture, and devoted most of his subsequent thirty-six years to the Worcester County Horticultural Society and the city's Parks Commission.[4]

In his elite background, as well as in his career instability and his idiosyncratic personality, Lincoln resembled Frederick Law Olmsted. More important, Lincoln seems also to have shared the conservative social assumptions of Olmsted and other genteel Gilded Age reformers, who insisted on a well-ordered and tranquil society based on hierarchy and professional leadership. Parks, in this view, would, in the same way as tariff or civil service reform, promote social cohesion and order. The quiet contemplation of a park's rural scenery, Olmsted believed, would calm the "rough element of the city" and "divert men from unwholesome, vicious, destructive methods and habits of seeking recreation."[5] But Olmsted's elegant vision of public parks and Lincoln's own less articulated views were not primarily centered on controlling the urban workers. Their main concern was the middle-class urban dweller, whose frayed nerves and exhausted body could be refreshed and renewed by the contemplation of a carefully crafted landscape.

Initially, at least, Lincoln had scant opportunity to implement this Olmstedian vision of the scenic park, for, upon becoming head of the Parks Commission in 1870, he found he had little to rule. Worcester's parkland consisted of an "unsightly" eight-acre Common and a larger twenty-eight-acre tract known as Elm Park, which primarily served as "a handy dumping ground for the Highway Department . . . [and] the casual job-wagon or wheelbarrow."[6] Such inelegant and inadequate public grounds offended Lincoln's horticultural sensibilities; he found them lacking the beauty of the elaborate European public gardens, fountains, and boulevards he admired so much. Their neglect also failed to accord with Olmsted's view of parks as instruments of conservative social reform that might defuse social tensions.

Influenced by these aesthetic and moral visions, Lincoln fought for and won the appropriations needed to begin to shape Elm Park into a fair approximation of the contemplative ideal of Olmsted. Gradually the land was cleared and drained; broad stretches of grass were planted; azaleas, rare trees, and exotic shrubs were artistically arranged; elaborate pools were constructed and arched by intricate wooden bridges.[7]

In pursuit of this ideal, Lincoln sought to banish active uses of Elm Park. Circuses, which had earlier lost their home on the Common, were banned in 1875. Three years later, the soon-to-be familar "keep off the grass" signs were given legal sanction. Baseball playing was left undisturbed, but Lincoln hoped that this "dreary amusement" would soon be removed from his cherished Elm Park to specially designated playfields in "different sections" of the city. Presumably, these fields would be placed closer to the homes of working-class Worcesterites who lived in the southeastern part of the city, not in the more exclusive West Side where Elm Park was located. Lincoln was not necessarily opposed to what Olmsted called the "boisterous fun and rough sports" of the working classes. He simply felt that they did not belong in a scenic park.[8]

This clash between what environmental historian J.B. Jackson calls "two distinct and conflicting definitions of the park"—"the upper-class definition with its emphasis on cultural enlightenment and greater refinement of manners, and a lower-class definition emphasizing fun and games"—continued throughout Lincoln's park regime.[9] His annual Park Reports provide some guarded hints of this class conflict over park usage. In 1876, for example, he petitioned for police patrol of the Common and Elm Park, declaring, "This Commission will exact and enforce that decent behavior from all who frequent the Public Grounds, which is not only seemly in itself but is rightfully expected by the community." Repeated complaints describe correct park behavior as "peaceful," "inoffensive," and "quiet," whereas misbehavior was seen as "rude and boorish" or "disorderly and obscene." The *Worcester Spy* captured Lincoln's notion of proper park usage when it reported approvingly on Elm Park as a "resort for nurses and fond mamas, the former arrayed in the usual white cap and apron, who have brought out the babies for an airing."[10]

This conflict between different styles of parks design and usage climaxed in the 1880s when two contrasting groups asserted new interests. On the one hand, the city's industrialists worked out new, more utilitarian arguments for park development that went beyond the contemplative ideal of Lincoln and the old gentry elite who made up the Parks Commission. They urged additions to the city's parkland to enhance fire protection, health, civic pride, real estate development, paternalism, and social control. On the other hand, a large and rapidly growing immigrant working class raised its own demands for space suited to its more active, play-centered park models. Out of this clash emerged a spatial solution that allowed both groups a measure of autonomy within which to develop their own approaches to park usage and play.

In January 1884, 231 members of Worcester's elite, including several ex-mayors and many leading manufacturers, petitioned the City Council to purchase Newton Hill, a sixty-acre tract adjoining Elm Park. Their motivation, however, was not entirely aesthetic or recreational. They also saw Newton Hill as an ideal spot for a reservoir that would provide fire protection for their fashionable West Side homes.[11] Such political muscle could not be easily resisted. But an unlikely political alliance proved capable of at least temporarily obstructing the Newton Hill acquisition. On the one hand, fiscal conservatives on the Board of Aldermen opposed any new expenditures of public funds. On the other hand, representatives of the so-called lower wards, the immigrant and working-class southeastern section of the city, threatened to block the purchase in retaliation for the earlier defeat of their own efforts to secure public park land for their constituents.

Residents of the East Side confronted the problem of finding play space in a city increasingly crowded by thousands of new immigrants. The expansion of the physical city could not keep pace with such rapid population growth. Before the expansion of streetcar service in the late 1880s and the electrification of the lines beginning in 1891, Worcester workers were sharply limited in their choice of residence. Between 1870 and 1890 the city's population jumped 206 percent, whereas its settled area grew only 29 percent. Consequently, population density increased by more than 50 percent.[12]

The effects of this increasing density were felt most strongly on the working-class East Side. The intensification of land use and the concurrent increases in property values encouraged the development and enclosure of vacant land previously used as play space. In 1882 the city marshal reported that in the absence of "public grounds for children and others for play and amusement, especially in the Southern section of the city . . . boys are driven from streets and fields, and private lands, by officers." Although Worcester's East Side never approached the overcrowding of New York's Lower East Side, in the

1880s play space in that district was clearly losing ground to housing and commercial development. At the same time workers also found themselves barred from slightly more distant play areas that they had traditionally used. "Our suburban retreats," complained a letter writer to the *Worcester Daily Times*, "are dotted all over with notices to 'Keep off under Penalty of Law.'" Noting that only the rich could afford excursions to "seashore and mountain," the letter writer asked: "Where then are the masses of people to seek for rest and recreation, sunshine and the refreshing breezes of summertime?"[13]

Worcesterites of differing social backgrounds were acutely conscious of the class dimensions of these spatial developments. For its part, the city's elite was determined to prevent working-class encroachments into the West Side precincts. When a single family of French Canadians settled on Elm Street in the 1880s, it disturbed "the social serenity of the neighborhood," according to the *Worcester Sunday Telegram*. Soon a "terrible fear" swept "West-side society" in response to a rumor that a "cheap tenement block" filled with "the representatives of all nations" would be erected on the same spot. Only when manufacturer Philip W. Moen purchased the property in 1889 did West Siders heave a sigh of relief. "Elm Street Set in Ecstacy: Philip W. Moen has Removed a Long-Time Nightmare," the *Telegram* headlined its story.[14]

While West Siders sought exclusivity, working-class East Siders complained about unequal treatment. James Mellen, the editor of the *Worcester Daily Times*, repeatedly accused the city government of favoritism and "deference" toward the "well-to-do people" of the West Side, while it ignored the need for providing sewers, streets, and park space in the "workingmen's district." Noting the prevalence of diphtheria among the "cooped up" and "huddled together" East Siders, Mellen demanded municipal action: "We want more outside room, we want every inch of space the city can afford us."[15]

In the context of these class perceptions of spatial inequality, an indigenous movement developed among residents of the Irish working-class East Side (centered in the Fifth Ward) to demand public play space. As early as 1879, letter writers to the *Worcester Evening Star*, then the city's only pro-labor newspaper, complained about the attention lavished on Elm Park—derisively labeled "Lincoln's Patch"—whereas the Common, more accessible to the working class, was neglected. "One who had to stand" maintained that "the people's seats" had been removed from the Common and placed in Elm Park, which he called a "desolate spot where nobody will use them excepting the crows." Another letter writer, similarly perturbed about unequal treatment and impatient with the shaping of Elm Park into a scenic garden, lampooned Lincoln as "the Earle of the frog ponds" and the "grandiloquent Earle of model pools."[16]

By 1882, however, East Siders began to demand not just better care of the Common; they also demanded their *own* park. Irish temperance and civic leader Richard O'Flynn called a meeting "with the thought that interest could be aroused for the establishment of public playgrounds." Around the same time, he gathered the signatures of almost one hundred forty neighbors on a petition asking the City Council to acquire "a few acres of land" for "the less favored children." Desiring recreational space more congenial to active use than that of Elm Park, the petitioners declared, "there is no public ground in that vicinity [the Fifth Ward] where children or young men can resort, either for health or amusement."[17]

The signers of the O'Flynn petition contrasted sharply with the elite Newton Hill petitioners. Their only real social relation to these leading Worcesterites was as employees. Of the ninety-five signers who can now be identified, seventy-five held blue-collar jobs. Even the twenty white-collar signers had little in common with the Newton Hill petitioners: six of them, for example, ran provision or grocery stores, and another three kept saloons.[18] Whereas the West Side industrial elite sought a park reservoir, their East Side Irish employees wanted a play space for themselves and their children.

So strong was the working-class perception of the class basis for Worcester's spatial inequities that their park campaign united sometimes antagonistic segments of the Irish working-class community. Temperance leader O'Flynn led two major petition drives, which netted the signatures not only of local saloonkeepers but also of the Bowler brothers, the city's leading brewers. *Times* editor Mellen, a bitter enemy of O'Flynn's, gave the park drive his enthusiastic support: "A playground for the children is needed, and the work people require an outdoor place of resort, near their homes."[19]

Even more vital backing for the park movement came from the city's two Democratic aldermen, John R. Thayer and Andrew Athy, both of whom at times had been at odds with O'Flynn and Mellen. Indeed, Thayer and Athy were themselves a study in contrasts. Thayer was a wealthy lawyer from old New England stock, an Episcopalian, and a member of the Worcester Fox Club, whereas Athy, a native of Ireland and an ardent Irish nationalist who had joined the abortive Fenian invasion of Canada in 1866, was a former bootmaker who had helped lead the Knights of St. Crispin strike of 1869-70.[20] Despite these differences, both men united in response to pressure from their working-class constituents to hold Newton Hill hostage for the East Side park. When the Board of Aldermen maintained that it lacked the power to purchase East Side parkland and even refused to rent a vacant lot, Athy and Thayer joined with fiscal conservatives on the Board to block the Newton Hill acquisition. "If the city is not willing to provide a breathing spot for women and children who are forced to live in the thickly settled tenement houses, . . . they [the East Siders] shall certainly oppose any addition to the already spacious park areas on the west side where every family has its own door yard and children's playground," reported the *Boston Sunday Herald*.[21]

Thus, the political conflict experienced by the Board of Aldermen reflected the deeper class conflict over the provision, design, and use of public space in Worcester. A letter to the *Worcester Sunday Telegram* contrasted the needs of the city's "wealthy" and its "toilers," and left little doubt about the class basis of the struggle for play space in Ward Five:

> Our wealthy citizens live in elegant homes on all the hills of Worcester, they have unrestricted fresh air and perfect sewage, their streets are well cleared and lighted, the sidewalks are everywhere, and Elm Park, that little dream of beauty, is conveniently near. The toilers live on the lowlands, their houses are close together, the hills restrict the fresh air, huge chimneys pour out volumes of smoke, the marshy places give out offensiveness and poison the air, the canal remains uncovered, the streets are different, the little ones are many. While the families of the rich can go to the mountains or to the sea during the hot months of summer the families of the workers must remain at home.[22]

Despite the weakness of unions and radical parties in Worcester, the struggle over park space fostered at least a neighborhood-based form of class consciousness and class conflict.[23]

The temporary resolution of this conflict was found in a political compromise: the passage of a new Park Act in 1884, which provided funds and authority for acquiring parkland, and two years later the formulation of a comprehensive plan for Worcester parks. The trade-off between East Side and West Side park interests was central to the overwhelming support that Worcesterites gave to the Park Act and the park plan, but other interests—social uplift and control, public health, real estate development, and civic boosterism—also helped infect the city with what one contemporary diagnosed as "Park Fever."[24]

In the summer of 1884 (before the vote on the Park Act), Horace H. Bigelow and Edward L. Davis donated 110 acres to the city to establish a park on the shores of Lake Quinsigamond. There is no specific evidence of the motives of either man, but in a general way such gestures of civic generosity reinforced a paternalist social structure, which gave dominant roles to men like Davis and Bigelow, both of whom were heavily involved in local manufacturing, business, and politics. In addition, some manufacturers and businessmen believed that parks would actually reshape the public behavior of their employees. Hence, Park Commissioner Lincoln, in accepting the gift of Lake Park, noted the Commission's duty "to see that it is made to promote popular enjoyment; to develop a taste for the beauties of nature; and to refine and soften, by cultivating, humanity itself." But such increased refinement might do more than just lessen internal conflict. To many, civic beauty and civic growth were inextricably linked, since a properly arranged city might attract new business. "It will not do," Lincoln wrote, comparing Worcester parks with those in New York and Chicago, "to lag in the rear and fall behind our rivals in the race for supremacy."[25]

For Bigelow, the donation of Lake Park may have gone beyond civic boosterism. As the proprietor of several lakeside amusement enterprises, the operator of the Worcester & Shrewsbury Railroad (the only transportation line to the lake), the owner of extensive lakeside property, and the builder of Lake View cottages, he stood to benefit from growing public use of Lake Quinsigamond.[26] In his Annual Park Reports, Commissioner Lincoln had pointed out that real estate values of land adjoining public parks had skyrocketed in other cities. Indeed, Lincoln, whose family had extensive land holdings in the area around Elm Park, may himself have benefited from the "greening" of the city's parks.[27] Whether or not real estate speculation prompted Bigelow's gift, he seems to have gained financially from his generosity. Between 1870 and 1890 weekend attendance at the lake jumped from one hundred to about twenty thousand per day. In addition, in the two years following his donation, land parcels on the eastern shore of the lake reportedly shot up in value from thirty-five dollars to five hundred dollars per acre.[28]

The public enthusiasm for parks sparked by the gift of Lake Park further ensured the almost unanimous approval—5,094 to 181—of the Park Act in the fall election of 1884. With this mandate and continued prodding from East Siders, the newly established Parks Commission developed a comprehensive park plan, which it unveiled in the fall of 1886. Impressive, in part, because it was one of the first examples of citywide park system planning in the United States, the plan was of even greater local importance because it resolved the class and sectional conflicts over the function and location of Worcester's parks.[29] In effect, if not intent, the Parks Commission opted for a scheme of separate development: The East Side would have its playground; the West Side its scenic parks.

The language of the 1886 park plan reflected the growing commitment of many to the notion of parks as instruments of both social uplift and social control. It argued, for example, that parks might help mold the industrial work force: "Whatever will elevate and refine . . . [the workers'] taste or enlarge their intelligence will increase the excellence of their work." The report also endorsed parks as a setting for "healthful recreation," but it seemed more concerned with social hygiene than with the active fun and games demanded by working-class users. For Lincoln, it was the fear of disease that probably offered the most persuasive reason for the spread of parks to working-class neighborhoods.[30]

The report's conservative social vision notwithstanding, the Parks Commission, in practical and spatial terms, did not impose its view of recreational space on the Worcester working class. Of the six parcels recommended by the report, the two located on the working-class East Side—Crompton Park and East Park—were specifically designated as "playgrounds" rather than as public gardens. In these play areas, workers would have the space to use their leisure time as they pleased. Hence, the enthusiastic working-class support for park reform should not necessarily be seen as an endorsement of the conservative social values of the park reformers. "Even where workingmen made extensive use of the language and concepts of middle-class reformers," labor historian David Montgomery writes in another context, "they infused those concepts with a meaning quite different from what the middle class had in mind."[31] Worcester workers had developed their own distinctive brand of park reform.

In the next few years the park plan was gradually implemented with few modifications and little opposition. And subsequent additions to the city's parklands generally followed the pattern set by the original park plan.[32] Donations provided the city with additional, larger, and more "scenic" parks, whereas play areas for residents of the most densely populated working-class sections of the city came only after petition drives like those that won the original East Side parks. In the late 1890s, residents of the Swedish wireworker community of Quinsigamond Village began campaigning for a park in their vicinity. As with Irish East Siders in the 1880s, the Swedish wireworkers did "not want an elaborate park, simply a playground in the center of the village." When the city finally yielded and created Greenwood Park in 1905, the newspapers proclaimed "This Park for Sport" and noted that "no especial attention will be paid to flowers or shrubbery." As befitted the ethnic character of the neighborhood and the struggle for the park, the July Fourth picnic of the Swedish Methodist Church marked its opening.[33]

Other Worcester ethnic working-class neighborhoods also mounted campaigns for local play space. In 1901, for example, 165 South Worcester residents, more than four-fifths of them blue-collar workers and many of them English carpet weavers employed by the Whittall Carpet Company, petitioned for a playing field on College Hill.[34] Whereas some cultural and recreational issues such as temperance pitted ethnic communities against each other, the parks question tended to focus conflict between workers and elites or between neighborhoods and the city government.

CONFLICTS OVER PARK SPACE AND PARK BEHAVIOR

Although Worcester workers generally won the recreational space they sought in the late nineteenth and early twentieth centuries, struggles continued over issues of park maintenance and behavior. The "separate but equal" parks faced the same problem as did schools founded under that rubric: In a stratified society separate can never be equal. "Most of the park money," charged labor leaders, "has been expended upon parks where the wage workers and their children are least seen, while in East Park, Crompton Park, and the Commons where the most good would be accomplished, the least money is expended and the least improvements made."[35] Even park enthusiasts admitted that Crompton and East parks were "dumps" and one Republican alderman astutely noted that Worcester had created a system of "class parks."[36] But better maintenance alone could not change this basic inequality, since working-class park users also faced overcrowding. "If you want the use of a baseball diamond at Crompton Park, you must sleep on the ground the night before to secure it," one local resident complained in 1904.[37] Such crowding was largely the structural by-product of an industrial city in which large numbers of workers huddled in a small area, and smaller numbers of manufacturers and managers resided in more spacious surroundings. The system of "class parks" meant both autonomy and inequality for Worcester workers.

Moreover, when Worcester workers used parks outside their own neighborhoods, the battle over proper park behavior continued. In the East Side parks, working-class park behavior was usually, but not always, condoned or ignored. But particularly in the parks that drew users from all sections and classes of the city, such as the Common, Lake Park, and Green Hill Park, conflict raged over correct park usage and behavior. Since Worcester's civic and business leaders had sold the public on parks on the grounds that such areas would teach workers "respectable habits" and cultivated manners, they fretted continuously about the obvious persistence of loafing, drinking, and similar habits in these spaces. Parks, they feared, were providing a setting for precisely the sort of behavior they were supposed to inhibit.

As the city's most central and visible park, the Common became the object of repeated middle-class complaints about improper use, particularly by working-class people. Generally, these commentators grumbled about "dirty unkempt people," "bums," and "idlers," who "loiter," "loaf," and even "sleep off drunks." The implication was that these offenders against public decency were habitual drunks or transient hoboes. Although a few probably were homeless drunkards, many seem to have been unemployed workers. During the depression of 1893, for example, one labor sympathizer counted more than four hundred jobless men on the Common on an average afternoon. Indeed, Worcester civic leaders actually confirmed this picture of the Common's patrons when they wanted to stop the building of a new post office on the Common. "This breathing space in the very centre of the city," proclaimed Senator George Frisbe Hoar, Worcester's best-known political leader, "is the comfort and luxury of the very poorest of the people; women who can snatch a few moments from work, . . . men out of work and waiting for work." Perhaps, then, the usual complaints about loafing on the Common reflected middle-class blindness to the large-scale, recurrent joblessness of those years, as well as a broader hostility to any public socializing by the city's workers. Worcester laborers, complained a letter writer to the *Worcester Daily Times*, were insulted with "the epithet of 'loafer' " when using the Commons "for the very purpose . . . for which it was given us." Except when expedient, midafternoon relaxation by workers in the city's most visible park space might be defined as unacceptable park behavior, subject to official repression, including the removal of park benches.[38]

Just as idleness was a common experience for nineteenth-century workers, so was drinking an often indispensable part of their popular culture. Olmsted and other park advocates liked to boast that parks promoted temperance and even put saloons out of business, but drinking actually accompanied workers into the parks. Relatively few users of the Common were drunkards, but more moderate drinking and even covert liquor sales could be readily found in this public space.[39] In addition, reunions and outings at Lake Quinsigamond were usually lubricated by ale and beer—sometimes donated by brewers eager to advertise their products. To reduce drinking at the lake, the Board of Aldermen on several occasions refused to issue liquor licenses to lakeside establishments. But the main impact seems to have been to encourage whiskey drinking, since flasks were more easily transported and concealed than beer kegs.[40]

Naturally, drinking was much more prevalent in the East Side parks, given their proximity to most of the city's saloons. Yet such drinking was less often complained of, in part because middle-class Worcesterites rarely witnessed it. "Crompton Park," noted a newspaper reporter in 1898, "is a place that many people in Worcester have but slight occasion to visit." Consequently, complaints about drinking in East Side parks often emanated from temperance-minded local residents. In 1901, for example, the Reverend James Tuite of St. Anne's Catholic Church urged the Liquor License Commission to restrict the sales of a Shrewsbury Street liquor dealer. Otherwise, he feared, the area would be turned into a "place of orgies . . . on account of the proximity to East Park, which has been and will be made a place, both night and day, by men, women, and boys of carousal, and drunkenness to be avoided by all decent people."[41]

Working-class traditions of collective public leisure, as well as the lack of spacious homes and apartments, pushed working-class drinking into such public places as saloons and parks. Similarly, the lack of privacy in many tenements and three-deckers probably forced some sexual activities into the public parks. In 1879, for example, the *Worcester Evening Star* reported that a twenty-two-year-old Irish immigrant had become pregnant after a "too intimate" acquaintance with a young man in Elm Park. Some years later the *Labor News* guardedly hinted of similar youthful sexual adventures when it reported "young people of both sexes" resented the lighting of North Park.[42]

If parks failed to eradicate patterns of public socializing and drinking, they were even less likely to alter the ethnic basis of working-class social life, despite the Americanization claims of some park promoters. On the contary, Worcester parks probably supported existing ethnically based leisure patterns by providing a convenient location for the outings of ethnic and church organizations. In the early twentieth century, for example, the Chandler Hill and Draper Field sections of East Park seem to have been divided between Swedes and Italians. Chandler Hill, located near the Swedish working-class community of Belmont Hill, was the scene of Swedish temperance rallies. The growing Shrewsbury Street Italian community, on the other hand, dominated the adjoining Draper Field. As recalled by Louis Lomatire, a retired streetcar conductor, it was a "center of activity" for Worcester Italians, with festivals, concerts, fireworks, sledding, skating and swimming.[43] Green Hill Park offered picnic facilities for a wide array of ethnic groups. However, it was not a place for ethnic intermingling: Worcester immigrant picnickers remained segregated into their own fraternal or church organizations. If the parks ever served as a melting pot, it was a rather volatile one. The custodian of the men's bathhouse at the lake warned against overcrowding in the locker rooms: "You take a fellow from French Hill and double him up with a fair haired [Swedish] boy who lives on Belmont Hill, and there will be a fight right away."[44]

The introduction of parks did not "remake" the Worcester working class in the image desired by industrialists and reformers. Neither did it precipitate a new class solidarity or consciousness. While the struggle to win an East Side park had transcended some of the divisions within the Irish working-class community, the actual use of parks revealed continuing antagoisms between ethnic working-class communities. Basically, parks provided a leisure space in which workers expressed and preserved their distinct ethnic cultures. And although these immigrant workers carved out a way of life distinct from that prescribed by the native American middle and upper classes, they rarely mobilized as a class or directly challenged the economic and political dominance of the city's Yankee elite.

THE DISCOVERY OF PLAY

Ironically, at around the same time that Worcester workers were finally winning play space suited to active recreation, the city's middle and upper classes were gradually adopting some of the same preferences for sports and play over repose and contemplation. Although most middle-class people were not sufficiently aware of immigrant, working-class recreation to allow for a process of conscious imitation, occasional exposures could prove revealing. For example, in his memoir of growing up in the native American cultural milieu of the 1890s, literary critic Henry Seidel Canby recalls that the immigrant working people represented the "reality of passion freely expressed which fascinated us." Similarly, in *The Damnation of Theron Ware*, a bestselling novel of the same decade, the book's protagonist, a small-town Methodist minister, is "bored" by his church's annual camp meeting. He drifts over to a nearby Irish-Catholic picnic and witnesses, "in mingled amazement and exhiliration" the "universal merriment" of football, horseshoe tossing, swimming, swinging, dancing, and especially beer drinking. "It is a revelation to me," he tells the Catholic priest with excitement and envy, "to see these thousands of good, decent, ordinary people, just frankly enjoying themselves like human beings. I suppose that in this whole huge crowd there isn't a single person who will mention the subject of his soul to any other person all day long."[45]

Whether it came as a "revelation" or as part of a process of gradual realization, the genteel upper and middle classes were increasingly shedding their old Calvinist suspicion of play—and particularly of active and public recreation. "The immense growth of public sentiment in favor of strictly amateur athletics, as being a healthy occupation for mind and body, is apparent on every hand," observed Worcester's society paper, *Light,* in 1890, "and the chances are that inside of another decade the number of people in the moral and intellectual classes if they may be so styled, who openly favor athletic sport will have doubled." *Light's* comments proved prescient; the 1890s turned out to be the years in which America's middle and upper classes passionately embraced competitive sports and outdoor recreation. But, of course, the change in middle-class and elite attitudes toward leisure was neither begun nor completed in the 1890s. For a sense of the complex and generational process of change, we can turn to Worcester's leading manufacturing family—the Washburns.[46]

In the early nineteenth century Ichabod Washburn established the family fortune in the wire business and led an intensely pious life centered on evangelical Christianity. When his nephew, Charles F. Washburn, settled on the West Side of Worcester, "Ichabod," according to a family memoir, "prayed aloud . . . that Charles . . . not be led out of the Kingdom by his worldly associates in the western part of the town. . . . Even then the spectres of dinner-jackets, the dance and the decolleté stalked before him." Although Charles abandoned Ichabod's religiously proper Union Congregational Church for the socially proper All Saints Episcopal Church, he still strictly observed the sabbath, taught Bible classes, and quietly "spent his leisure hours in the library." The more dramatic change in leisure attitudes and practices came with Charles F. Washburn's son, Robert, who grew up on the West Side in the 1880s and 1890s. Robert joined enthusiastically in the active and secular elite world of the Quinsigamond Boat Club, the Worcester Club (which scandalized some with its allowance of liquor), the Bohemian Club, and the Grafton Country Club.[47]

An even more enthusiastic exponent of these new elite attitudes more approving of sports and active recreation was Robert Washburn's next door neighbor and boyhood friend, Harry Worcester Smith. The scion of an old New England cotton manufacturing family, Smith helped found the Grafton Country Club in 1895 in an effort "to bring within the reach of the West Side, wholesome English out-door life, riding, shooting and hunting." The club's motto, Each to His Pleasure, marked out a "leisure ethic" that contrasted sharply with the Protestant work ethic of the men of Ichabod's generation or even that of his nephew, Charles. Indeed, in occupation, as well, Harry Smith marked out the transition to the new generation and century. Like Ichabod, he was a skilled mechanic, tinkerer, and inventor, but, unlike the deacon, his wealth came not from building up new industrial enterprises but from combining existing ones. He was known nationally as "a 'harmonizer' of industries," a euphemism for his skill at arranging corporate mergers and creating monopolies. Harry Smith also differed from Deacon Washburn in how he chose to spend his money. Rather than financing an evangelical mission, the Mechanics Hall or other Christian charities (as had Washburn), Smith devoted his fortune to his huge country estate, where he was known as "The Master of Lordvale," and to his passion for horses, hounds, and fox hunting.[48]

Smith brought this new upper-class enthusiasm for active sports with him into public life. In 1916 he was appointed to the Worcester Parks Commission, and he almost immediately organized a lavish "Sportsmen Dinner" to honor local track, golf, and tennis stars and to mark a new acceptance of active and competitive sports in the city's parks. Mayor George Wright told the "society" crowd that Worcester's parks were no longer just "sacred spots, places merely to be looked at, they are used. . . [They] are coming more and more to be places of recreation as well as places of rest." To symbolize the new official view, the Parks Commission was reconstituted as the Parks *and Recreation* Commission the following year.[49] In part, this new upper- and middle-class embrace of active recreation reflected a triumph of older working-class leisure attitudes. But important differences remained. The working-class valued active play as part of a process of public socializing, as an end in itself. The middle and upper classes were more concerned with the product, with active play as a means to an end.

This *instrumental* view of play partially emanated from a concern with middle-class behavior. Through more energetic sports and leisure, it was argued, white-collar workers would not only find some release from the tensions and burdens of an urban, industrial society but also learn to cope with, and compete in, the society. Some members of the elite—particularly those like Harry Smith who found their social models among the European aristocracy—probably did not worry as much about the functionality of recreation as did members of the central middle class and their ministers. Still, even among Smith and his circle we can find instrumental notions about play and sport, particularly as embedded in the growing cult of "strenuosity" and competitive sport. It was no coincidence that the man who popularized the notion of "The Strenuous Life"—Theodore Roosevelt—was hosted by Harry Smith in a 1916 visit to Worcester's parks. Men like Smith and Roosevelt believed that athletics would teach young people the ideal of competition and bring America to "true national greatness." Yale students could learn Social Darwinist ideology on the football field under Coach Walter Camp just as they learned it in the classroom from his brother-in-law, Professor William Graham Sumner. "The cult of strenuosity and the recreation movement grew together," historian Daniel Rodgers writes, "minimizing the distinctions between usefulness and sport, toil and recreation, the work ethic and the spirit of play."[50]

Having accepted recreation as a means of self-development and self-control for themselves, the middle and upper classes began— rather more slowly—to perceive its possibilities as a means of social control. Thus, the emerging instrumental view of play also partook of a concern with working-class behavior, a belief that proper play behavior would insure proper behavior in other areas of social life. In the early 1890s Worcester's middle- and upper-class Protestants denounced the efforts of one of their ministers, Frank Vrooman, to provide supervised recreation for the city's workers, but by the early twentieth century a variety of groups had embraced the notion of providing supervised leisure through Boys' Clubs, neighborhood social centers, company-sponsored sports teams, and especially playgrounds.[51] Having finally liberated play from its Puritan cage, middle-class leaders felt it must now be kept on a tight rein, not only for their own class, but especially for the working class.

One of the central figures in creating and publicizing this new instrumental view of play was a prominent Worcester resident—G. Stanley Hall, the president of Clark University and one of the founders of American academic psychology. Hall argued that children's play was essential to normal child development. In his warnings against both the repression and the misdirection of play, Hall revealed the tension between freedom and regimentation common to many play advocates. They sought to eliminate existing constraints on play, but they also sought to impose new constraints of their own devising.[52]

Early psychologists like Hall were not the only writers to urge a more instrumental view of play. Environmentalist social reformers at the turn of the century saw play facilities as part of the social environment that could be reconstructed as a means of reshaping social behavior. They believed that the correct management of the juvenile life cycle and the proper provision of play facilities would socialize children into the roles, behaviors, and values expected of modern urbanites.

PLAYGROUNDS AND SOCIAL REFORM

The conjunction of these new ideas about play and adolescence with growing concern about the urban, immigrant working class made play reform a central project of progresssive reformers. Jane Addams, Jacob Riis, and Lillian Wald, as well as such former students of G. Stanley Hall as Henry Curtis, helped found and staff the Playground Association of America, the leading organization of the play reformers.[53] By concentrating on children and the playground, these reformers believed they could both attack the immediate problem of juvenile delinquency and socialize children into their proper adult roles as workers and citizens. Not only had the studies of Hall and his followers persuaded reformers of the essential role of play in normal child development, but child-centered reform provided a more acceptable outlet for a broader concern with social behavior in general. As Robert Sklar writes in a different context, since reformers "could deal only indirectly or covertly with the issue of class conflict, they made their case on the ground of protecting the young."[54] For many reformers, the entire working class appeared as a group of children whose behavior needed to be reshaped and controlled.

Despite such middle-class goals, in Worcester the first demands for city-sponsored play space came from within the working class. As we have seen, Irish workers in the 1880s sought play areas within the parks system, and such demands escalated around the turn of the century. Growing working-class neighborhoods such as South Worcester, New Worcester, Quinsigamond Village, and Vernon Hill also petitioned the Parks Commission and the City Council for playgrounds. Some of the city's most recent immigrants even began to take matters into their own hands. When Jewish residents of an East Side tenement went on a rent strike, one of their complaints was the lack of play space for children amidst the tenements. Lithuanians considered buying their own enclosed park for the "exclusive use of their people."[55]

Gradually, the Parks Commissioners began to endorse calls for more public play space in the immigrant wards as well as the more affluent areas of the city. The turning point in its acceptance of municipal sponsorship of playgrounds came in 1907. Late that year Parks Commissioner Obadiah Hadwen died, and his death marked the final passing of the old guard of the Worcester Parks Commission. Along with Edward Winslow Lincoln and James Draper, who had died earlier the same year, Hadwen had been a shaping influence on Worcester's Parks Commission for almost forty years. All three men came from elite, landed families and all of them were dedicated horticulturalists with strong ties to groups like the Worcester Horticultural Society, the Grange, and the Massachusetts Fruit Growers' Association. Both Draper and Hadwen made their livings from horticulture.[56] Although they at times supported more active uses of parkland, their deaths in 1907 marked the symbolic close of the era of the contemplative, scenic park.

Manufacturer Peter Baker replaced Draper on the board, and Swedish ticket agent Sven Hanson took Hadwen's seat. In general, the commission remained in the hands of the city's elite families, but the members tended to be manufacturers rather than men whose wealth was in land and whose primary interests were in horticulture.[57] Such men brought with them a more utilitarian view of parks. They would no longer simply serve as "breathing spaces" and natural retreats but also as a structured and controlled environment for play.

Little more than two months after Hadwen's death, James Logan, general manager of the U.S. Envelope Corporation and the newly elected mayor of Worcester, emphasized in his inaugural address "the necessity of playgrounds," and argued that "modern industry and commerce should bear its share of the cost in providing a suitable place, conveniently located near the home of the workman, where, after the day's toil is ended, he can with his wife and children breathe a little of God's pure air." The general population of Worcester seems to have shared Logan's excitement about playgrounds; later in 1908 its voters overwhelmingly (14,570 to 4,849) endorsed the Massachusetts Playground Act, which mandated that cities provide at least one playground for every 20,000 residents.[58]

This growing enthusiasm for play and playgrounds was not confined to the acquisition of new parklands. Beginning around 1905, sections of existing parks were specifically set aside as playgrounds. In conjunction with this development, the Parks Commission began constructing special play facilities for park users, such as baseball fields, tennis courts, wading pools, outdoor gymnasiums, picnic groves, swings, sandboxes, and seesaws. The commission had first installed primitive playground equipment in Crompton Park in 1898; by 1909 it was experimenting with the latest steel gymnastic apparatus.[59]

The provision of playground equipment and play facilities encouraged and fostered play, but it also structured and directed play. In contrast to the original parks, which simply had provided open space, these newer facilities dictated their own use. Carefully graded and laid-out regulation tennis courts could not be easily used for anything but that sport. Nor could children confronted with metal swings and gymnastic apparatus use this equipment or the space on which it stood for much else than its intended purpose. These years also saw the inauguration of an elaborate system of park permits for the use of picnic grounds, ball fields, and tennis courts; the asphalting of parkland; the segregation of play areas by age of users; and the fencing of play spaces. "On the vacant lot we can do as we please," one playground advocate noted disapprovingly, but "when we have a fenced playground it becomes an institution."[60]

The playground promoters' desire to contain and regulate play was usually only implicit in the design and equipping of early twentieth-century playgrounds. It became explicit, however, in the drive to hire playground supervisors. In 1908 the parks commissioners in their annual report had urged "competent supervision" to make play-

grounds "educational centers and not mere resorts." "Mere playgrounds without intelligent and sympathetic supervision of the play
of children will be barren of the best results," they declared. Concerned with similar issues, G. Stanley Hall convened the "Worcester
Conference for Child Welfare" later the following year, and it immediately organized a subcommittee on play and playgrounds. With the
help of the Board of Trade, this committee launched the Worcester
Playground Association in March 1910.[61]

The new Playground Association had the support of a diverse coalition. Wheras the Parks Commission as of 1910 had only included one
non-WASP (a Swede), the directors of the Playground Association
included prominent Worcesterites from Irish, Jewish, and French-
Canadian, as well as Swedish backgrounds. The rising ethnic middle
class, based in the second generation of immigrants, joined the native
middle class in its enthusiasm for play reform. The "new" professional middle class—particularly schoolteachers and school principals—
also played a leading role in the playground movement. Of course,
many of the members of the "new" middle class had roots in the old
elite as well as in the emerging group of ethnic entrepreneurs. Lizette
Draper, the principal of Bloomingdale School and the daughter of
former Parks Commissioner James Draper, was a Playground Association director, as was Ellen Murphy, a local schoolteacher and the
daughter of the city's first Irish alderman. While some children of the
elite joined the Playground Association out of their professional commitment to teaching through play, others apparently signed on because of their enthusiasm for active sports. For example, Samuel E.
Winslow, the son of the skate manufacturer and former mayor, was an
early leader of Harry Smith's Grafton Country Club as well as a star of
the Harvard baseball team.[62]

Although the Playground Association managed to attract ethnics,
women, teachers, manufacturers, lawyers, businessmen, sportsmen,
priests, and ministers, it was not composed of a cross section of the
city. No blue-collar workers, trade unionists, or representatives of the
city's recent Italian, Polish, and Lithuanian immigrants were among
the approximately thirty directors of the association. Worcester's
working class had joined actively in movements for public play space,
but it took no part in the movement to supervise and control play.

To build broader public support and to raise money for a summer
program of supervised playgrounds, the association hired playground activist Henry S. Curtis to spend five weeks in Worcester.
With the assistance of the movement's leading local boosters, like the

Worcester Gazette editor, George F. Booth, and the St. Anne's Church pastor, John J. McCoy, Curtis generated substantial support and enthusiasm for the playground idea among local businessmen and clergy, and helped raise more than ten thousand dollars.[63]

The success of Curtis's playground crusade enabled the Playground Association to undertake an ambitious program of supervised play in the Summer of 1910 at twenty different locations around the city—half of them school yards and the rest parts of existing city parks and playgrounds. A paid staff of fifty and eight volunteers oversaw a diverse play program, which included organized athletics, ring and singing games, gardens, cane seating, basketry, raffia, sewing, drama, folk dancing, and storytelling. More then sixty-five hundred children daily joined in these activities during the two-month playground season.[64]

For all the fanfare, the Playground Association added little additional play space to the existing Worcester park system. The essential new ingredient was *supervision*. "The playground is something more than a mere means of pleasant diversion," explained George Booth in a *Worcester Gazette* editorial. "It is, in fact, a school, where instruction of no less value than that of the school proper is given." And there was little that these play schools would fail to teach: Loyalty, courtesy, justice, helpfulness, friendship, courage, sympathy, morality, cleanliness, citizenship, seriousness, patience, honesty, mutual understanding, and higher ideals were among the virtues promised Worcester playground graduates.[65] Such catalogues of proper conduct and high moral standards tended to be rather vague, and playground advocates thus claimed three more specific benefits of their work: a decrease in juvenile delinquency, an improvement in work habits, and the rapid assimilation of immigrants.

The specter of juvenile crime was a staple of the playground movement from its inception. Movement leaflets luridly asked: "Shall We Provide a Playground? Or Enlarge the Jail?" Such arguments found a ready echo in Worcester. "Experience has shown," proclaimed Mayor James Logan, "that when city children are playing in the places prepared for them, under proper supervision, they are not on the back alleys learning to become criminals."[66]

In addition to becoming law-abiding citizens, playground users would become compliant workers. "In our playground we did not forget to teach children to work as well as to play," Father McCoy reported at the end of the first Worcester playground season. In part, play leaders sought to teach specific job-related skills. The aim of the playground sewing course, according to its instructor, was "to teach the girls high standards, habits of accuracy and thrift so much needed when the girl enters the business life or becomes a homemaker." But playground advocates also believed that playing itself would make better workers. "As a child plays," noted Booth, "so will he later work."[67] "The boy without a playground is the father to the man without a job" became a leading slogan of the playground movement.

In these objectives, playground reformers revealed their preoccupation with working-class conduct. Juvenile delinquency in Worcester was almost entirely concentrated in the poor, working-class district known as the Island. Proper assembly line demeanor hardly needed to be taught to middle-class children headed for business or the professions. But it was the playground movement's obsession with Americanization that most suggested its interest in reforming and controlling the working class, since in Worcester immigrants were the predominant constituents of that class. Thus, the effort to Americanize immigrants was a frontal assault on the dominant characteristic of their defensive culture: the separateness and impermeability of the ethnic worlds within which they lived. "We have got to make Americans of these children," insisted Booth. Although other twentieth-century Americanizers saw the schools or evening citizenship classes as the shortest route to assimilation, in Booth's assessment only the playground would "bring pure gold out of the melting pot." Even Irish pastor McCoy assented: The public school (a hostile environment for many Catholics) was not always a successful Americanizer, "but he who says that the *playground* is the 'melting pot' will tell the absolute truth."[68]

PLAYGROUNDS AND WORKING-CLASS BEHAVIOR

There is little doubt then that Worcester playground advocates promised to reshape not just children's play in general, not just working-class play but working-class life in general. Their success in achieving these goals is more questionable. The limited available evidence suggests that instead of being reshaped by playgrounds, workers and their children actually reshaped the playgrounds (as they had the parks) according to their own needs and values.

Despite the many proclamations to the contrary, the Worcester playground system, at least initially, did not serve as a "great melting pot." Quite the opposite, it seems to have offered play space for the preexisting, separate, ethnic communities to affirm their own identities. On August 26, 1910, the Playground Association took a census of that day's playground users. The census showed that the playgrounds were quite effective in reaching their intended immigrant constituency. Fully 85 percent of that day's thirty-four hundred playground users were of foreign background , although only 71 percent of the total city population was of foreign stock in 1910.[69] Immigrant children came to play at Worcester playgrounds, but not with the children of other immigrant categories . Of the twenty playgrounds in operation in 1910, fifteen were dominated by a single immigrant group. In some cases other immigrant groups were all but excluded. For example, Greenwood Park was 86 percent Swedish, Institute Park, 79 percent Irish, and the Ledge Street School Yard, 75 percent Jewish. In part, these figures reflected Worcester's ethnic neighborhood structure: Greenwood Park was located in heavily Swedish Quinsigamond Village, the Ledge Street School Yard in the midst of the Providence Street Jewish ghetto. Since 82 percent of the children who attended a particular playground lived within a quarter mile, Worcester playgrounds necessarily mirrored their surrounding communities. Regardless of the cause, the effect was still the same: Worcester playgrounds, although intended to break down ethnic exclusivity, actually reinforced the existing pattern of immigrant enclaves.

A further analysis of the 1910 Playground Census suggests that this ethnic exclusivity may have been a matter of choice as well as a product of social geography. Comparing playground attendance by nationality with the overall 1910 population census figures suggests that some ethnic groups were overrepresented on the city's playgrounds, while others were underrepresented. Significantly, it was the city's largest ethnic groups (Irish, French Canadians, Swedes, and Jews) that were overrepresented and its smaller ethnic groups (Italians, Germans, Finns, English Canadians, and Scots) that were underrepresented. What this pattern may indicate is that those ethnic groups that had sufficient numbers in a particular locality to dominate a playground adopted it as a local institution, whereas smaller ethnic groups, fearful of being outnumbered on the playground, tended to stay away.[70] The city's largest immigrant group, the Irish, was also the group that most heavily patronized the playgrounds.

Although the playgrounds did not promote ethnic intermingling, they may have had a more subtle and more limited Americanizing and assimilating impact. It is possible that the patriotic songs, American games, and Anglo-American folk dances taught at the playgrounds helped to bring immigrant working-class children closer to the American mainstream, or at least made them more aware of its existence. It is intriguing to note the important role played by second- and third-generation immigrant young people—particularly Irish Americans—as playground supervisors and teachers. These college students and recent college graduates may have served as intermediaries in the long-term process of partially integrating immigrants and their children into the dominant American culture.[71]

Although the impact of the playgrounds on Americanization remains unclear, it is evident that Worcester playgrounds never diminished juvenile crime. Since arrestable offenses were socially determined and might include loitering on the streets, playgrounds could immediately lower the arrest rate simply by shifting the location of juvenile activity. But Worcester playgrounds failed to produce even a lower arrest rate. In 1933 sociologist Paul Shankweiler, a professor at Clark University, concluded that "in Worcester supervised summer play activities have little or no bearing on the incidence of juvenile delinquency."[72]

The persistence of ethnic segregation and juvenile delinquency points to the rather unsurprising conclusions that manipulating or controlling play would not alter working-class behavior, and that neither children's play in general nor working-class children's play in particular was as easily reshaped as playground reformers had anticipated. As one recent student of the history of play has pointed out, "There is evidence that children are not easily influenced and select elements from the adult culture to fit their particular needs and values."[73] In Worcester, at least, this subversion of the intentions of play reformers appears to have been the general rule.

In 1912 the *Worcester Telegram* ran a series of articles critical of the Worcester playgrounds as a needless extravagance aimed at taking the fun out of play. The *Telegram* articles included what purported to be twenty interviews with children who had used the city's playgrounds. In all cases, the children expressed disdain for the adult efforts to teach them how to play, and many said that they either no longer paid any attention to play leaders or had stopped attending the playgrounds altogether. "I can't go to the playgrounds now," complained one eleven-year-old living near Crompton Park. "They get on me nerves with so many men and women around telling you what to do." "I can't see any fun playing as school ma'ams say we must play," explained a fourteen-year-old boy. One group of boys asserted their independence by organizing their own baseball team outside the playground league and proclaimed that their team could "defeat the playground baseball team with its paid umpires and balls furnished by the city." Often the children's disdain for the playground coexisted with an outward compliance with external forms. Some children found the playground storytelling inane, but still applauded the stories since they were told they must. Others told of being drafted into the annual playground festival because of a shortage of performers. Even some behavior that playground advocates promised to eliminate seems to have flourished on its grounds. A fifteen-year-old resident of the Island neighborhood reported that he had never seen an ambulance at Crompton Park until the playground began. "They say they don't let the kids fight," he grumbled. But "I know [a] . . . kid that got swiped over the bean with a beer bottle some of the bums had left from the night before."[74]

As with the parks, the efforts of social reformers to uplift, refine, and control the working class through the provision of supervised playgrounds did not significantly diminish the autonomy Worcester workers exercised over their leisure time and space. Indeed, in both cases, Worcester workers were able to turn reform efforts to their own advantage. Parks provided them with free space within which to pursue their active conception of leisure activity. Within that unstructured context, workers were able to affirm their ethnic cultures and their alternative values. Even the tighter supervision and reform designs of the playground advocates were often ignored or subverted by Worcester workers and their children. Working-class recreational space and recreational behavior thus remained largely under working-class control.

Given the nature of economic relationships and power in Worcester society, however, this working-class recreational autonomy existed only within limited boundaries and under substantial constraints. East Side Parks, for example, never received the appropriations and the care lavished on their West Side equivalents; hence, working-class park space in Worcester was often poorly maintained and heavily overcrowded. In addition, although the various attempts to mold working-class recreational behavior were never fully successful, some of these efforts, such as the removal of park benches from the Commons, the banning of liquor sales at the lake, the establishment of a permit system for baseball and picnics, and the structuring of play space through the provision of steel apparatus and the asphalting of grounds, did have an impact on working-class life. Workers could, for example, smuggle liquor to the lake but that was neither as simple nor as pleasant as purchasing it there.

The most fundamental constraint on working-class recreation, however, was work itself. In 1890 the *Worcester Evening Gazette* described in detail how Worcester workers played freely in Institute Park during lunchtime:

> Before the 12:05 whistle blows, the crowd begins to arrive from Washburn and Moen's, the envelope shops, electric light station, and many other establishments north of Lincoln Square. After eating, a good romp is indulged in by the girls, running and racing about, with now and then a scream of laughter when some mishap, a fall perhaps, occurs to one of their numbers. Some of them wander about in pairs or groups, exchanging girlish confidences, or indulging in good-natured banter with their masculine shop-mates. Occasionally a boat is secured by some gallant youth, who rows a load of laughing maidens about the pond, the envied of their less fortunate friends.
>
> The younger men try a game of base ball or a little general sport, jumping, running, etc., while their elders sit about in the more shaded spots, smoking their pipes. But when the whistles blow previous to 1 o'clock there is a general stampede to the shops and in a few minutes all of those remaining can be counted on one's fingers.[75]

No matter how much autonomy Worcester workers achieved in their leisure space and time, they still had to confront the factory whistle. Its sound returned them to a sphere of life in which power and control resided outside their class.

CHAPTER 10

Dance Madness: New York City Dance Halls and Working-Class Sexuality, 1900-1920

KATHY PEISS

In the early twentieth century, dancing was a popular form of recreation for New York City's working-class youth. Observers estimated that thousands of men and women flocked to the dance halls each week. Greater New York recorded over five hundred public dance halls in 1914; more than one hundred dancing academies provided instruction to an estimated one hundred thousand pupils each year. In the words of one observer of working-class life, "the town [was] dance mad."[1] These dance halls catered to a particular subculture of young men and women whose leisure time was oriented around commercial amusements, rather than forms of recreation based on immigrant traditions, familial celebrations, and community networks. These amusements offered their young patrons the opportunity to participate in the forms of "modern" social life newly available in the metropolis. An essential component of this new life style involved distinctive patterns of sexual behavior. Analysis of dancing styles, patrons' behavior, and the cultural trappings of the halls provides insight into the sexual norms and social relations of some working-class youth.[2]

Dance madness thrived in the backrooms of dingy saloons, in large neighborhood halls, and in the brightly lit pavilions of popular amusement resorts. The character of dances varied widely, from immigrant weddings and fests attended by young and old, to masquerade balls in which prostitutes and underworld figures mingled with the working-class crowds. The most common form of dance in the late nineteenth century, however, was the "racket" or "affair." Usually held in a rented hall or neighborhood saloon, affairs were sponsored by fraternal lodges, mutual aid societies, political clubs, and other voluntary organizations. Offered on an annual or occasional basis, these balls raised money for charitable purposes or mutual aid, while providing a large festive social gathering for members. Attendance was regulated by invitation, and whole families would customarily attend. Integrated into the texture of the working class and ethnic community, rackets involved a measure of neighborhood and familial control; as one investigator reported, "greater respectability is maintained, because there is a close acquaintance among those who attend."[3]

In the 1890s, dances run by social or "pleasure" clubs emerged alongside the traditional racket. Sporting such fanciful names as "The Fly-by-Nights," "The East Side Crashers," and "The Lady Millionaires," pleasure clubs rented halls and organized dances strictly for fun and personal profit. Such associations marked a new development in the organization of working-class leisure time. The youth-oriented social clubs separated leisure activity from the provision of social services and discouraged family participation. Dances sponsored by social clubs involved extensive advertising, the indiscriminate sale of tickets, and large crowds of dancers, and, unlike the lodge dance, were not as concerned with controlling patrons' activities and protecting young women.[4]

The growth of the club and lodge entertainment contributed to the expansion of dance halls in the city. Saloon owners converted adjacent back rooms or the second stories of tenements into dance halls, hired cheap bands, and rented the space to organizations at nominal fees. While the club's profits derived from the sale of tickets, the hall owner's came from the sale of alcohol to thirsty dancers. This source of profits is clearly reflected in the typical dance program, which allowed brief dance periods, often as short as three or four minutes, interspersed with lengthy intermissions for rest and refreshment at the bar.[5]

In the early 1900s, the popularity of dancing encouraged entrepreneurs to build halls specifically for dancing and to operate without the sponsorship of a social club or organization. Such halls were open nightly to anyone paying the price of admission. Dancing academies sprang up throughout the city, alternating instruction nights with public dance evenings. In 1911, the first large-scale dance palace, the Grand Central Palace, was built near Grand Central Station in midtown Manhattan. Five other palaces, ranging in capacity from 500 to

3000 patrons, were erected in the next ten years, primarily along Broadway, the leading amusement zone in the city.[6]

This expanding network of commercial dance halls and amusement resorts catered specifically to a subculture of working class youth. One survey indicated that single young men favored dance halls over saloons and poolhalls. Similarly, unmarried women filled the halls, but as one settlement worker wrote, "when marriage comes, regular attendance upon balls ceases." While girls who were strictly guarded by parents went to an occasional wedding or racket with their families or approved escorts, other young women regularly attended public dances and club parties at least once a week. Women with a passion for the dance were highly visible to observers of urban life. Hutchins Hapgood, a journalist who wrote extensively about working-class life, described a group of East Side shop girls who "dance every night, and are so confirmed in it that they are technically known as 'spielers.' "[7]

In her memoir, Dorothy Richardson described with astonishment her sister factory workers who took their dancing costumes and shoes to work, partied through the night, then returned to the shop the next morning:

> A girl was already bending over her paste-pot, and the revelers of the "Ladies' Moonlight Pleasure Club" came straggling in by twos and threes. Some of the weary dancers had dropped to sleep, still wearing their ball-gowns and slippers and bangles and picture-hats. . . . Others were busy doffing Cinderella garments, which rites were performed with astounding frankness in the open spaces of the big loft.[8]

Who were these working-class dance hall habitués? No ethnic enclave seems to have had a monopoly on dance halls. Russian and Polish Jews delighted in balls, and the Lower East Side was riddled with dance houses and dancing academies; a 1901 survey counted one dance hall for every two and a half blocks. Other neighborhood surveys found that dancing was a highly popular amusement whether the locale was an upper East Side block of Jews and Italians, or a West Side tenement district inhabited by American, German, and Irish working people.[9] Much recent scholarship demonstrates the strength of cultural traditions in affecting women's behavior, and we would anticipate that those immigrant parents who usually supervised closely the social lives of their daughters, e.g., the Italians, forbade their attendance at dance halls. At the same time, ethnicity did not *determine* participation, since dance hall observers mention the presence of Italian women at some balls.[10]

While ethnic traditions must have played a significant role in the propensity of women to visit dance halls, the conditions of urban existence dictated the place of dancing in young women's and men's lives. The popularity of the halls was closely tied to the changing nature of courtship and leisure in the city. Single people "adrift" in the city depended on new urban institutions to feed, house, and entertain them; dance halls provided a convenient means of meeting the other sex. The density of the metropolis made the business of amusement profitable. Overcrowded tenements, tiny rooms in lodging houses, and disapproving landladies helped to push recreation and courtship into the streets and amusement resorts.[11] Some second generation women also turned to commercial amusements in opposition to old-world customs, and the attractions of an "Americanized" life style could easily become a sphere of controversy within the family. Negotiating with parents over spending money or free time, some wage-earning daughters might demand more independence in the realm of "personal life" while still upholding the centrality of the family economy. Within some families, observed reformer Lillian Betts, "tacitly it is agreed that [in return] for the complete control of wages the wage-earner shall be given freedom. The young wage-earner goes and comes, often without control or attempt to control on the part of the parent."[12] An example of the potential conflict within some working-class families is suggested by the case of Louisa, a young girl with a taste for fine clothing and fancy dancing who used her salary to gain leverage within the family: "The costume in which she steps out so triumphantly has cost many bitter moments at home. She has gotten it by force, with the threat of throwing up her job."[13]

The dance halls that lured these young men and women embodied a culture in which the promiscuous intermingling of strangers, free sexual expression, and close physical contact defined "appropriate" behavior. At one Turnverein ball, for example, a vice investigator described the scene of respectable working-class men and women in the hall's barroom:

> I saw one of the women smoking cigarettes, most of the younger couples were hugging and kissing, there was a general mingling of men and women at the different tables, almost every one seemed to know one another and spoke to each other across the room, also saw both men and women leave their tables and join couples at different tables, they were all singing

and carrying on, they kept running around the room and acted like a mob of lunatics let lo[o]se.[14]

In another dance hall, the investigator asserted that the easy familiarity of asking strange women to dance or drink did not represent vice or prostitution, and that "this changing of tables was not a case of open soliciting but just a general mixing." He noted with some frustration, "I was here about 45 minutes and tried hard to make some of the women but there was nothing doing." At another dance run under the auspices of the National Brotherhood of Bookbinders, such "unruly" and familiar behavior as kissing, singing, and shouting across the room was common.[15]

The ambience of the dance halls permitted easy sexual expression. Advertising for dances, for example, was accomplished by the social club or hall distributing "throwaways" or "pluggers," which were small cards printed with the time and location of the dance along with snatches of popular songs, pictures, and verses. In the words of one offended middle-class reformer, the printed lyrics and scenes "all appeal to the sex interest, some being so suggestive that they are absolutely indecent." Yet these "suggestive" advertisements were carefully preserved and valued as mementoes of the dance by its young patrons.[16]

The openness in sexual expression is best indicated by an analysis of the dominant working-class dancing styles. While waltzes and two-steps were common around 1900, the most popular dance style in the more unrestrained commercial halls was known as "pivoting" or "spieling." In this dance, the couple, grasping each other tightly, would twist and spin in small circles on the dance floor. One observer at a Coney Island dance house described two stereotypical "pivoters":

> Julia stands erect, with her body as rigid as a poker and with her left arm straight out from her shoulder like an upraised pump-handle. Barney slouches up to her, and bends his back so that he can put his chin on one of Julia's shoulders and she can do the same by him. Then, instead of dancing with a free, lissome, graceful, gliding step, they pivot or spin, around and around with the smallest circles that can be drawn around them.[17]

Pivoting, a loose parody of the fast waltz, was in intention diametrically opposed to the waltz. While in nineteenth century high society the waltz was initially scandalous because it brought men and women into closer contact than in earlier dances, the dance room itself countered that closeness with injunctions toward stiff control and agile skill. The speed of the waltz demanded self-control and training to achieve the proper form. The spieling dance, in parodying this form, was performed not with self-control, but as a dance out of control, its centrifugal tendencies unchecked by proper dance training or internalized restraint. The wild spinning of spieling couples promoted a charged atmosphere of physical excitement, often accompanied by shouts and singing. Of all the so-called "vulgar" dances, noted one observer, the spiel was especially popular. Supposedly, spieling "particularly cause[d] sexual excitement" through "the easy familiarity in the dance practiced by nearly all the men in the way they handle the girls."[18]

The sexual emphasis in working-class dance was even more pronounced in a genre of dance known as "tough dancing," which became popular after 1900. Tough dancing had its origins in the houses of prostitution on San Francisco's Barbary Coast, and gradually spread, in the form of the slow rag, the turkey trot, and the bunny hug, to the "low resorts" and dance halls of major metropolitan areas. Ultimately, these dances were transformed (and tamed) in the 1910s, into the mainstay of the middle-class dance craze, the one-step. In the commercial halls, though, unrestrained versions of the grizzly bear, Charlie Chaplin wiggle, and "shaking the shimmy" were joyously danced to the popular ragtime tunes of the day.[19]

Tough dances differed significantly from other round dances like the waltz or polka, in which partners were also in close contact. Simple to learn and appropriate for a small crowded dance floor, they were performed either in a stationary or walking position. The movements ranged from a slow shimmy, or shaking of the shoulders and hips, to boisterous animal imitations, and they permitted endless variations. Most important, however, was their suggestion of sexual contact. As one dance investigator noted, "what partcularly distinguishes this dance is the motion of the pelvic portions of the body, bearing in mind its origin [i.e., in houses of prostitution]."[20] What troubled such reformers was that the dance, whether wild or tame, became an overt symbol of sexual activity that the dancers, operating outside the usual conventions of dance, were free to control:

> Once learned, the participants can, at will, instantly decrease or increase the obscenity of the movements, lowering the hands from shoulders to the hips and dancing closer and closer until the bodies touch.[21]

In celebrating animality, sexuality, and raucous fun, tough dances came under severe criticism from numerous representatives of middle class morality, including moral and civic leaders, reformers, journalists, and dancing masters. These middle-class men and women voiced a fear that such dancing promoted sexual promiscuity, irresponsible freedom, and social disorder. These concerns mirrored the broader middle-class effort of the Progressive Era to control and regulate the behavior of working-class people in both their work and leisure time.

While the new dances were performed by the avant-garde of the wealthy and middle classes, they remained highly controversial until dancers like Irene and Vernon Castle tamed them and made them respectable for the dominant culture. The dancing mania which swept the middle class in the 1910s points to a new—but still restrained and controlled—level of sensuality and expressiveness within middle-class culture.[22] Popularizers of the new one-step or Castle Walk maintained that it should bear "no relation or resemblance to the once popular Turkey Trot, Bunny Hug, or Grizzly Bear." They asserted that the sexual potential of the dance must be deemphasized, insisting that "our new dances do not require 'hugging' and crossed arms to make them enjoyable." In conclusion, admonished the dancing masters, "do not rag these dances."[23] Although such prescriptions should not be equated with behavior, the middle-class line seems to have been drawn between the sexually explicit tough dancing and other, less overtly suggestive forms of close dancing. This distinction may be seen in a description of a businessman and his expensive date at a high-society cabaret: "They dance, the girl with her arms around the fellow's neck—the way many society girls do it now a days. It is not exactly tough but it brings the cou[pl]e rather close together."[24]

Control over dance styles was only one aspect of the larger problem of controlling relations between men and women at dance houses. Halls differed in the kinds of behavior their managers would tolerate or risk. Despite legal threats and vice reformers' infiltration, the commercial halls favored by working-class youth erected few barriers to spontaneous behavior. At one wild New Year's Eve dance, for example, "the manager was on the floor all the time but did not interfere or prevent [the dancers] from doing what ever they pleased." In the dark corners of the halls and in the balconies, women often sat on men's laps, smoking, hugging, kissing, and caressing.[25]

The problem of control was heightened by the fact that working-class youth usually did not attend dances as heterosexual couples. Rather, young men and women arrived at the halls alone or with members of their own sex, expecting to "couple off" during the dance. One particular ritual known as "breaking women" reflected this process. As the music commenced, women danced with each other; then, as one observer described it, "The boys step out, two at a time, separate the girls and dance off in couples." No introductions were required, and the etiquette of the hall demanded that a woman remain with her partner at least until the dance had ended. Some East Side dance houses even employed men called "spielers" to dance with and entertain unattached women. Waiters also played powerful roles in matching up and introducing young men and women, though they were not always successful as informal regulators of sexual morality. As one waiter ruefully observed, "The way women dress today they all look like prostitutes and the waiter can some times get in bad by going over and trying to put someone next to them, they may be respectable women and would jump on the waiter."[26]

Unlike the working-class dance hall, the popular middle-class resorts, cabarets, and cafes tended to limit promiscuous contact and sexuality by imposing regulations on their clientele. Cabarets often banned the attendance of unescorted men and women, discouraged the intermingling of strangers, and outlawed suggestive dancing. The proprietors of one high-class cafe, the Parisien, would not "allow men from different tables to take women for a dance and won't allow anyone to change tables." Moreover, the placement of tables and the stage in such resorts created a structure that limited contacts between unacquainted men and women.[27]

This structuring of leisure affirmed the participation of mixed-sex couples, rather than single individuals or large groups, in middle-class urban night life. The "couple" provided a way to control the heterosocial relations of women and men, as well as regulate the potentially promiscuous sexuality implied by the new dances. This institutionalization of the couple was *not* a crucial aspect of the commercial hall, by contrast. Indeed, when a working-class man or woman found a "steady," their attendance at the dance hall tended to drop off.[28]

Within the hall's unstructured world of close female-male interactions, popularity became a hotly pursued goal for women. Besides dancing ability, dress and accessories played a large role in achieving this end. While Chicago women were said to place powder puffs in their stocking tops to be drawn out ostentatiously in the hope of attracting male attention, it is doubtful that New York women were bested in flamboyance. The cultural style of the dance hall habitués demanded that they deck themselves in the flossy finery available in the Grand Street shops. As one observer noted rather critically, "gilt rings, bracelets and bangles, frizzes, bangs and cheap trimmings of every order, swallow up her earnings."[29]

Popularity also depended on the willingness to drink. In many dance halls, men ostracized women who refused to drink. Since profits were pegged to the sale of liquor, economic considerations militated against such behavior: in some halls, the management requested an abstaining woman to leave, while in others, prizes were awarded to the woman with the most drinks to her credit. Moreover, positive inducements, in the form of ingenious cocktails and expensive mixtures, rather than five-cent beer, helped to make drinking in dance halls an acceptable female activity. The connection between popularity and drinking in the company of male friends put such pressure on women that, between dances, "girls not being entertained at the tables rush over to the dressing-rooms to avoid being seen on the floor."[30]

Dance hall habitués measured popularity in terms of "treating," a customary practice in which men paid for women's drinks and refreshments, admission fees, and other incidentals. While women might pay their own dance hall's entrance fee or carfare to an amusement resort, they could rely on men's treats to see them through the evening's entertainment. Such treats were highly prized; as one observer remarked, the announcement to one's friends that "he treated" was "the acme of achievement in retailing experiences with the other sex."[31]

This enthusiasm for treating made a cultural virtue out of women's economic exploitation. Sexual segmentation of the labor market, the concentration of women in semiskilled, seasonal employment, and the demands of the family economy structured women's wage-earning so that few could afford the price of commercial amusements. In 1910, few women earned a living wage, which was then nine to ten dollars a week. Self-supporting women living in the furnished-room districts of the city consumed their meagre earnings in lodging, board, and dress, and had little cash left over for recreation. The vast majority of working women, who lived at home, usually turned over their pay envelopes to their parents. Daughters typically received twenty-five to fifty cents as spending money each week. While they often increased that amount by skipping lunch or walking to work to save carfare, these sums were barely enough to pay for entertainment. Treating thus allowed women to participate in a social life oriented around commercial amusements.[32]

Treating was not a one-way proposition, however. Financially unable to reciprocate in kind, women offered sexual favors—ranging from flirtatious companionship to sexual intercourse—in exchange for men's treats. Engaging in treating ultimately involved women's negotiating between their desire for social participation and their adherence to cultural standards that discouraged premarital sexual intimacy. One investigator, commenting on women's dependency on men in their leisure time, aptly observed that "those who are unattractive, and those who have puritanic notions, fare but ill in the matter of enjoyments. On the other hand, those who do become popular have to compromise with the best conventional usage."[33]

The nature and extent of the social and sexual relations surrounding treating are difficult to establish. Middle-class categories of "respectability" and "promiscuity" do not adequately describe the apparent flexibility and ambiguity of working-class sexual norms, norms that were complicated further by ethnic and generational differences. While some communities stigmatized women who attended "dubious resorts" or bore illegitimate children, attitudes toward premarital sexual relations were less harsh among many young working-class women. As one explained, "a girl can have many friends, but when she gets a 'steady,' there's only one way to have him and to keep him; [and] I mean to keep him long."[34]

Many working-class women probably received conflicting messages in their work, family life, and social activities about the virtues of virginity. Despite parental and religious instructions, the systems of sexual control faced antagonistic forces. Crowded tenement homes caused women to pursue social life in the "promiscuous" space of the streets. Women's work in factories and stores often entailed forms of school harassment that encouraged and coerced women to exchange sexual favors for economic gain. Further, women's work culture in many jobs involved elaborate discussions of dates and sexual exploits, stories which would speed the long working day.[35]

Within the dance halls there existed a subculture of working women who bought into the system of treating and sexual exchange, by trading sexual favors of varying degrees for gifts, treats, and a good time. These women were known in underworld slang as "charity girls." Unlike prostitutes, the charity girls did not accept money in their sexual encounters with men. As a vice investigator reported after a visit to a dance hall, "Some of the women . . . are out for the coin, but there is a lot that come in here that are charity."[36] A waiter at "La Kuenstler Klause," a restaurant with music and dancing, remarked that "girls could be gotten here, but they don't go with men for money, only for [a] good time." Vice investigator Kahan described the women at this resort in some detail: "Most of the girls are working girls, not prostitutes, they smoke cigarettes, drink liquers and dance dis[orderly] dances, stay out late and stay with any man, that pick them up first." At another bar, an investigator named Odgen met two women who "are both supposed to be working girls but go out for a good time and go the limit." These women had clearly accepted the full implications of the system of treating and the prevailing cultural style of the dance halls.[37]

While this evidence points to the presence of charity girls, it tells us little about their numbers, social backgrounds, working lives, or relationship to family and community. The investigators' reports indicate that charity girls were generally young, some not over 16, and they often lived with their families. For example, one man in a dance house remarked that "he sometimes takes them to the hotels, but sometimes the girls won't go to [a] hotel to stay for the night, they are afraid of their mothers, so he gets away with it in the hallway."[38] The vice reformers estimated that charity girls comprised as many as half of the dancers at the halls and resorts they investigated. Significantly, these studies were done in the larger halls oriented to a metropolitan clientele. We do not know whether charity girls could be found in the smaller neighborhood halls and social centers, and therefore cannot be sure of the degree to which this behavior was acceptable for young people within the working-class communities. However, in the anonymous space of the large commercial hall, this subculture was a viable option for some working women in New York.[39]

Beyond the charity girls, many more women must have been conscious of the need to negotiate the sexual encounters inherent in treating, if they wished to participate in commercial amusements. This awareness is apparent in a dialogue between the hat girl at Semprini's dance hall and a vice investigator. Answering his propsal for a date, she "said she'd be glad to go out with me but told me there was nothing doing [i.e., sexually]. Said she didn't like to see a man spend money on her and then get disappointed." Reflecting the complexity of sexual norms, she then remarked of the charity girls, "these women get her sick, she can't see why a woman should lay down for a man the first time they take her out. She said it wouldn't be so bad if they went out with the men 3 or 4 times and then went to bed with them but not the first time."[40]

An indication of women's efforts to control the terms of the "sexual exchange" lies in the phenomenon of the female friendship. According to one social worker, these were structured relationships with specific obligations and rituals. A young woman usually had a "lady friend" who supplied companionship at the dance halls and generally enhanced social occasions. Lady friends performed a more important function, however, by providing mutual protection during the process of "coupling off" at dances and amusement resorts. The presence of the lady friend helped to deflect unwanted sexual attentions, as one investigator discovered at a racket of the Driver's Sick and Benevolent Fund: "I tried to get next to some of the women but couldn't, they travel in pairs and its hard for one man to pick any of them up."[41] Moreover, the lady friend symbolized respectability at a point in women's lives when contact with men was potentially at its most promiscuous, as women were meeting prospective "steadies" and husbands. The single woman alone might be taken for a prostitute; hunting in pairs, however, permitted the maintenance of respectability *and* the aggressive pursuit of pleasure.

The working women described here adopted flexible sexual norms that kept them outside of the realm of prostitution while at the same time permitting greater sexual freedom and expressiveness. As historian Judith Walkowitz has recently observed, such women constituted a vanguard for whom sexual activity symbolized a new level of personal autonomy.[42] However briefly, some working-class women in their adolescent years rejected traditional gender roles and rebelliously challenged familial control.

The historical evidence available does not indicate how young women thought about this process. But it is clear that the dance hall phenomenon contributed to the breakdown of Victorian gender relations and blurred the sharp definition of sexual spheres. Through their provocative behavior and sexual style, dance hall women helped to define the emergent "manners and morals" of the 1910s and 1920s. Dance halls were among many new cultural institutions in the city that reinforced the sexual freedom of young women and provided space for an alternative life style that stressed more individual control over heterosexual relations. In their efforts to gain a new audience, apostles of mass leisure incorporated the sexuality expressed by this vanguard of working women, tamed it and made it palatable for a broad middle and working-class audience. Not only dance halls, but movies and amusement parks reveal this process of cultural transmission involving in part the transformation of working-class social and sexual forms.[43] The new sexual expression, through commercial leisure and mass consumption, had by the twenties spread throughout American society—as the social phenomena of flappers, adolescent dating, and the controversy over petting indicate. At the same time, the process of cultural change did not homogenize sexual norms and behavior. For example, popular romance magazines such as *True Story* appealed primarily to working-class, not middle-class, women.[44] And sociological studies of working class families from 1950 to 1975 suggest that the ideology of romantic companionship, which controlled and delineated contact between middle-class women and men after the breakdown of Victorian gender spheres, may not have been internalized by working class people until the 1960s and 1970s.[45] Once they were married, the working women who unconsciously helped initiate the greater sexual freedom of the new morality may not have experienced the kind of heterosexual romance and companionship they had enjoyed as single adults.

Chapter 11

Women Workers, Work Culture, and Collective Action in the American Cigar Industry, 1900-1919

BY PATRICIA COOPER

"What manufacturers require," noted a 1902 issue of *Tobacco Leaf*, a cigar industry trade journal, is "female labor—cheap hire, which responds so favorably to the cost of production in modern competition."[1] Women had been employed in large numbers in the cigar industry beginning in the 1870s, but it was not until the first two decades of the twentieth century that women came to outnumber men in the craft of making cigars. In 1900, women were about thirty-three to thirty-six percent of the industry's workers. In 1920, they accounted for about fifty-eight percent.[2] The proportion of women workers increased as newly emerging large firms, employing as many as a thousand or more cigar makers, universally adopted the practice of dividing up the labor process and hiring women exclusively. These firms sought to neutralize the Cigar Makers' International Union of American (CMIU), a male craft union affiliated with the American Federation of Labor (AFL), and acquire a cheap, pliant, controllable labor force. Increasingly, however, manufacturers found their own policies inadequate and unsatisfactory. Women's shopfloor work culture—the system of ideas, values and practices in the work place through which the workers adjust, mediate, and resist the limits and pressures of their wage work—frequently operated against manufacturers' own interests.[3] Ultimately, only changes in the work process and the labor force itself could sufficiently meet employers' goals.

This work culture, which proved so troublesome, differed considerably from that of the male unionists. Both men and women were working for wages and had interests unlike and opposed to their employers, yet women were also living their lives within the framework of institutional male dominance. In the work place, women were devalued, paid less money, and often treated as children. At home women attended to household responsibilities men did not have and held a lower status than male kinsmen. For women cigar makers, this system of male dominance defined their place as workers in the industry and complicated their relations with male workers and thus the possibility for unified protection of their class interests. Yet women's work culture actively resisted employers' policies and imposed its own cultural system, which included the possibility of collective action. This essay examines manufacturers' design of the work process, and the nature of women's work culture within this structure.[4]

Before the Civil War, the American cigar industry had been miniscule, but during the Gilded Age, the cigar became the country's favorite tobacco product, and cigar production increased dramatically. Domestic manufacturers produced nearly five billion cigars a year and employed approximately eighty thousand cigar makers at the turn of the century. The factory system had become firmly established in the late nineteenth century, but even in 1900 the industry remained highly decentralized and competitive. Thousands of one-man shops operated alongside a growing number of larger factories, a few employing hundreds. Signs of concentration were appearing, however. Between 1896 and 1904, the number of factories decreased for the first time— from 30,000 to 25,700—while production doubled. Still, the industry seemed fairly resistant to the forces creating monopolies in other industries. Between 1901 and 1904, James B. Duke's American Tobacco Company (ATC) tried to take over cigar making as it had the rest of the tobacco industry, but ATC's subsidiary, the American Cigar Company, never accounted for more than sixteen percent of U.S. production.[5]

Duke believed, and government studies confirmed, that the high degree of decentralization and diversity in the industry reflected the nature of the production process—work was still performed largely by hand. Large firms had identifiable, but not substantial, advantages over smaller firms. In 1901 Duke organized the American Machine and Foundry Company (AMF, today known for selling bowling equipment) with the express mission of developing cigar machinery. Yet none of his engineers could come up with a way of duplicating mechanically the intricate motions and steps needed to produce a cigar fine enough to shake consumers' resolute prejudice in favor of handmade goods. Still, the American Cigar Company took its place alongside several other larger companies beginning to hold an important place in the industry. By 1912, the ten largest firms, less than one percent of the total, accounted for twenty-three percent of U.S. cigar production.[6]

Labor in the industry fell into three broad categories corresponding to the type of cigar manufactured and the scale and method of production. Although there were scores of exceptions, women tended to work in the larger factories, under a division of labor known as the team system, which at times utilized the elementary machinery then available. Most women made cigars using domestically grown tobaccos (with some imported leaf), which retailed for five cents or less. Cigars selling for ten cents or more were sometimes made by women, but more often by male craftsmen, members of the CMIU, without machinery or any division of labor, using a finer grade of imported and locally grown tobaccos. Founded in 1864, the CMIU had established itself as a considerable force within the industry by the 1890s. Its members accounted for roughly thirty to forty percent of the country's cigar makers between 1900 and 1919. The premier cigars made in the U.S. were the Clear Havanas—handrolled by Cuban, Spanish, and Italian workers (primarily men, but including some women) using tobaccos grown in Cuba. The center of the U.S. Clear Havana industry, which rivaled even Havana, was located in Tampa, Florida.[7]

Manufacturers' work and labor policies defined the structure of the work process and the context of social relations on the shop floor. Cigar manufacturers who hired women did so consciously in order to lower costs, to avoid the influence of the CMIU, and to reduce the possibility of strikes and confrontations. Women were "cheaper" and "more easily controlled." The manufacturers hired young, single immigrant women for the most part—many cigar makers began working as girls aged twelve to fifteen. A majority of women cigar makers could be found in the largest cities of the East and Midwest, especially the "cigar belt" which ran from New York City down through New Jersey, then through Philadelphia, ending about one hundred miles west of the city. York County, Pennsylvania (and to an extent, Lancaster County) was a special case. Here, every town and hamlet in the county made cigars, and people still stemmed tobacco and rolled cigars in their homes. The area was isolated and much more rural than most other centers of cigar manufacture, but in 1920, twenty percent of U.S. cigar production came from York County, Pennsylvania. Illinois, Indiana, Michigan, and Ohio also served as areas of women's employment. In each region or city, the ethnic composition of the labor force might be different—Italian and Hungarian women in New

Jersey, Jewish and several Eastern European nationalities in Philadelphia, Bohemian and Jewish women in New York, Polish and Slovak women in Detroit, Pennsylvania Dutch in York County. Nationally, a majority of women cigar makers were foreign-born or the children of foreign-born, but in 1910, less the one percent were Black.[8]

To assist in holding down wages, which ranged from five to twelve dollars a week,[9] cigar manufacturers frequently located factories in areas where they would be least likely to encounter competition from higher-paying industries and where pools of female labor might be available, a policy of "taking the factory to the workers." Detroit, Michigan, for example, had a fairly small cigar industry employing primarily men before 1900, but after the turn of the century many larger factories began moving into the Polish neighborhoods, whose male residents worked in the city's heavy industry, and provided employment for thousands of women. Once the idea caught on, the Detroit cigar industry mushroomed as scores of new factories moved near the labor supply.[10]

Certainly not all manufacturers could follow this localizing pattern and avoid competition for labor; large factories operated in the midst of New York City, Philadelphia, and Chicago. However, many such firms maintained branch factories in smaller, less urban areas. For example, the Philadelphia-based companies of Otto Eisenlohr, Bayuk, United Cigar Manufacturers, and Bobrow Brothers had several branch factories elsewhere in the state, particularly in York and Lancaster counties, or nearby in New Jersey and Ohio. The Deisel-Wemmer Company of Lima, Ohio, began branching out in 1907, and had fifteen factories within a fifty-mile radius of Lima by 1912. John Swisher and Company followed a similar pattern in eastern Ohio. The branch factory system permitted manufacturers to find cheaper labor, and it helped minimize disruption caused by strikes. If operations were halted in one factory, production could shift to another.[11]

Although the process of cigar making was still largely unmechanized by the beginning of the twentieth century, several elementary machines, primarily for five cent cigars, did lower costs of production. The division of labor itself, without any special tools or machines, cut expenses, because it took less skill to perform only part of the work and less time to train someone to do it. The team system divided the work process in half, into "bunching"—making the initial bunch of tobacco formed from long pieces of filler tobaccos encased inside a coarse binder leaf—and "rolling"—applying a thin elastic wrapper leaf to the outside of the cigar. Most frequently the team system incorporated use of a wooden shaping block, called a mold, which held about twenty cigars and pressed the bunches into the desired shape before rolling. Bunching machines were simply metal frames with a sheet of canvas attached, operated by hand. Gradually, several of the largest firms, particularly the American Cigar Company, began using power-operated suction tables which simplified the process of cutting the wrapper leaf to shape. Together these machines did not appreciably augment output or efficiency; rather, they provided "the opportunity of employing girls at low wages."[12]

A few of the largest manufacturers such as the American Cigar Company and various Detroit companies, adopted elements of what might be termed "modern" managerial practices. That is, to reduce employee turnover and keep workers away from unions, several firms adopted employee welfare programs. These included providing pianos for noontime entertainment, cafeterias, and showers for employees. Many companies did little more than hold dances or annual picnics, but a few went so far as to set up benefit associations and profit-sharing plans.[13]

Such welfare benefits were not widely offered in the industry, however, and most companies relied more on the stick than the carrot. Disciplinary penalties ranged from fines to dismissal. The American Cigar Company tended to have the most refined managerial structure and the most rigid regulations regarding work. Unlike much of the rest of the industry, several of its plants monitored hours and breaks, and a few even prohibited women from talking to each other while working. More common was the practice of fining employees and deducting money from their pay. Many companies did not pay learners at all until they had completed several months of training, so that the companies could gain some return on their investment. Dismissal served as manufacturers' ultimate method of discipline, especially in cases where employees attempted to organize a union.[14]

Factory buildings usually rose no more than three or four stories high and housed all of the operations in cigar making from the initial tobacco preparation and stemming to packing and shipping. In most cases work areas were less than pleasant environments. Investigations in many cities found them universally dusty, poorly ventilated, and crowded. Toilets were often uncared for, and cafeterias and first aid rooms (where they existed) were not always clean and sanitary. Factories where welfare benefits were emphasized doubtless improved on these conditions, but most factories did not have such amenities. In summer a cigar factory could be unbearably hot. The odor of tobacco was strong, and many who could not ignore it and overcome their nausea had to quit. The work itself was dirty and the tobacco smell lingered inside clothing long after the workday had ended. Anna Bartasius, a Lithuanian cigar maker in Philadelphia, took the streetcar home each day and never doubted that fellow riders easily guessed where she worked.[15]

The area for cigar making itself might take up an entire floor of a large factory. Since cigar makers needed light, factories were usually built with tall windows on all four sides. Cigar makers sat at benches, which were wooden tables with raised edges on three sides. The back of the bench rose higher than the two sides and formed a shelf, just at eye level, for the seated cigar maker. A canvas sack for catching tobacco scraps and cuttings was usually tacked to the open side of the bench. The benches were attached back to back in long rows, so that a cigar maker sat with people on either side and across from her. These rows extended across the floor, broken by one or two aisles.[16]

Under the team system, two "rollers" sat on either side of a "buncher." The buncher took the long, dry filler leaves and broke them off to the proper size and thickness, cupping them in her left hand and arranging them with her right. "You have to feel in your hand," one cigar maker explained. Each cigar had to be the exactly the same shape, size and weight as the next one. Cigar makers saw the work as skilled: "You had to know just what you were doing." Once the buncher shaped the bunch, she usually placed it in a wooden shaping mold, locked the top on and put it, along with several other molds, into a press. She kept ahead of the rollers who removed the bunches from the molds after ten to twenty minutes. Using special tobacco, the roller cut the delicate wrapper leaf to the exact shape needed, judging how much leaf to use and how to cut around a tear or hole. She began at the lighting end and rolled the bunch up inside the wrapper leaf, spiraling it around the filler. If she were working at a suction table, she had fewer decisions to make, but still had to position the leaf carefully so as to bypass imperfections. At the end of the wrapper, she cut a sort of flag from a bit of the tobacco, which wound around the head end of the cigar and sealed with a special glue, creating a completely rounded, smooth surface. She placed the finished cigar in the "bundler," a wire rack on the shelf in front of her.[17]

Management's requirement of careful use of tobacco weighed in each cigar maker's mind as she rolled or bunched cigars. In the stock room, one or two employees dispensed stock and punched cigar makers' cards according to the number of preweighed packages of filler, binder, and wrapper leaves each worker received. Factories set rigid schedules as to the number of cigars they expected from a specific amount of tobacco. "They just made their mind up that we had to make 100 cigars out of the pack that they gave you," noted Detroit cigar maker Helen Pikowska. At her factory, women who failed to meet the quotas were fined and lost anywhere from twenty-five cents to three dollars from their weekly pay envelopes. Other factories did not fine cigar makers for these offenses, but all paid careful attention to the matter and warned those who used tobacco inefficiently. As Anna Bartasius explained about her work in Philadelphia, "They give hell to you: . . . Do better." A cigar maker might not like this treatment, but feelings "don't matter. . . . You want to work, you have to take it." When the tobacco stock was poor, as it often was for cheaper cigars, the problems of working quickly and using as little tobacco as possible were intensified.[18]

Cigar making was almost universally piece work—wages were based on the number of cigars made. The pressure to make more money could "make a nevous wreck out of you," noted a cigar maker in Evansville, Indiana, who worked at the H. Fendrich Company.[19] In Detroit in 1908, women could make as much as ten dollars a week, but only if they worked steadily. There and elsewhere, the pressure to take more pay home meant that many women ate their lunches at their benches, rather than in the cafeteria or a nearby restaurant. For example, Frances Salantak of Detroit took "no lunch hour." Manufacturers did not require this work pace, but their low piece rates encouraged it.[20] Wages were calculated from the total production of the team and then split proportionally between bunchers and rollers. If a buncher came in late, her two rollers had no work unless they could fill in for someone else. Thus the team system encouraged women to report for work punctually. It could also be a source of conflict and division among women. Foremen assigned team members, and if a buncher or roller could not keep up, the other members of the team suffered.

In most factories, the foreman who inspected the work could remove as many cigars as he wished from the bundler as seconds, and cigar makers lost all payment for them, although the seconds could be sold anyway, albeit at a lower price. Thus speed did not ensure top earnings. In order to earn enough under the piece rate system, women had to work both carefully and quickly. Even then, they had no guarantee that the foreman might not simply remove a few cigars anyway without justificiation.[21]

In some ways, manufacturers could feel satisfied with the results of hiring women and structuring work in this way. Women cigar makers rarely joined the CMIU, and if they did, they seldom remained in it for long. Nor did they form alternative organizations of comparable strength.[22] The CMIU, composed of male craft unionists, remained ambivalent at best and often openly hostile to the organization of women. Institutionalized male dominance reinforced manufacturers' class-based power by keeping women out of unions.[23].

Even in 1915, when the CMIU actively tried to organize women because of increasing competition and the men's own deteriorating position, women cigar makers found the union essentially unappealing. They were hardly encouraged by the men's lack of enthusiasm. Male attitudes fluctuated between chivalry and condescension—women were thought of as either helpless victims or prostitutes.[24] Union traditions and customs had little relationship to women's own experience of work. Most important, the CMIU reflected a very specific work culture—a patriarchal craft culture. This made it nearly impossible for women to feel integrated into the life of a male-dominated union local, or, if the women formed their own local, into the CMIU as a whole.[25]

It is useful to compare the relative sources and privileges of male unionists and nonunion women within the industry during these years. Belonging to the union meant a financial cushion of benefits and strike payments. These, along with other union traditions, reinforced a sense of collective strength. Newcomers were initiated into the CMIU with stories of past struggles and a group history. Male unionists shared a tradition of geographic mobility which not only put them in contact with each other and militated against isolation, but fostered a sense of belonging to a larger group. Cigar makers' "tramping" also gave them a better understanding of the structure and operation of the industry as a whole. Women had none of these supports and thus had more obstacles to viewing themselves collectively. They were also more isolated than male unionists. Too, while "manhood" offered legitimacy for men's challenging managerial authority, the cultural constrictions of "womanhood" did not customarily permit such a claim, and indeed, often contradicted it.[26]

Despite these factors, manufacturers' policies regarding women did not, in the long run, prove satisfactory. Women's work culture emphasized their own interests in the work place, and the limits of factory discipline provided opportunities for women to modify or even resist the exploitation they encountered. Much of women's work culture remains invisible in the documents of the cigar industry; but interviews with women cigar makers in Detroit, Philadelphia, York County, and Lima, Ohio, along with industry trade journals and state investigations, reveal its outlines.

Piece work, as we have seen, clearly operated as a form of exploitation, but piece work also had its advantages for women. Workers did not always place maximum earnings as a first priority, and piece rates allowed them a degree of control and flexibility. A study of women cigar makers in Philadelphia in 1917 found that "it is the habit of women workers to come late in the mornings, to take extra time at the lunch period, and at times to leave early in the afternoons." Since few factories kept any records of employees' hours, federal efforts to collect wage and hour data in the cigar industry were continuously thwarted by workers' frequent coming and going. Using their freedom, women could interrupt monotonous work schedules to make time for other activities. Or they could simply assert their claim on their own time. Philadelphia manufacturers in 1900 complained when hundreds of women stayed home during the intense heat wave that summer. If July 4th fell on a Wednesday, manufacturers might have only half their work force during the entire week. In York County, Pennsylvania, cigar makers frequently abandoned work on spring and summer afternoons in order to attend baseball games. Their outside interests made it "difficult to keep them at work, no matter how pressing the demands of cigar orders might be," noted one observer of the trade in Binghamton, New York. In Detroit, women refused to work during the Polish holidays, and the factories were "all compelled to shut down."[27]

Piece work also served as a strategy for combining work and home roles. Mothers could stay home with sick children, or single daughters could help out with household tasks. Women could also quit their jobs and return a few months later in most factories, and manufacturers were always glad to rehire someone who was already trained. Piece work was coercive, but women used it in important ways to serve their own interests. While it could work at cross-purposes with manufacturers' needs, it also satisfied and reinforced the needs of the patriarchal family by freeing women's time in the household.

The team system, as we have seen, could promote conflict within teams and divide workers from each other, but it contained elements that could at times act as a resource for women. Since the team was paid according to its entire production and since the work process itself required coordination and cooperation within the team, the organization of work could act to emphasize the importance of the group rather than the individual. As a team worker, a woman could understand the concerns of the woman next to her. She worked not only for herself, but for her coworkers as well. To gain control over time, women cooperated and negotiated their schedules with each other. Often a buncher might come in a little early to have some work ready when rollers arrived. They in turn stayed a little later to finish up the last few bunches. If anyone wanted to leave ahead of schedule, "You'd talk it over with your girls and you'd go home." A buncher who anticipated being late the following morning might stay on and make several extra bunches for her coworkers to start on in the morning. "It was the partnership or nothing," explained Rose Purzon in Detroit. If a buncher ran short of tobacco, the rollers got more for her. As one buncher recalled, when she had bunched enough, she "helped the girls rolling the cigars." Many women prided themselves on learning the other operation in addition to their own. Thus the team system had a contradictory impact. It could divide workers and extract the maximum amount of work for the lowest wage, but it could also build solidarity and a sense of interdependence.[28]

Because of turnover and absenteeism, however, the composition of teams did not usually remain the same for long periods, although there were cases where women "worked for quite a few years together." In Hanover, a small city in York County, Pennsylvania, Pauline McKenney worked with two sisters for several years. In Detroit, two women who worked well together might apply for jobs together. Turnover provided the opportunity to meet new people and widen the circle of acquaintances.[29]

The team system and seating arrangements helped to facilitate warm social ties among cigar makers. "We were all talkers," noted Natalie Nietupski. "Some of the girls would sing," recalled Editha Mattingly of Hanover. Anna Bartasius recalled that many of the women in Philadelphia factories where she worked engaged in conversation, although she did not because it slowed her down and she made more mistakes. Instead, she only worked and then would "run home" to begin preparing dinner for her family. Jokes and pranks could also relieve boredom. In McSherrystown every year at Halloween, some of the cigar makers at one factory stole the outhouse. Friendships formed and were reinforced by the spirit of mutual help which the teams fostered. Rose Purzon of Detroit explained that "you were always in a bunch. It was like a family. Not only that you knew them, but your family knew them too." Close ties developed at work were often reinforced by ethnic or neighborhood communities outside the factory, as in Detroit, where women might share a walk home and a visit to the corner store or gather again at the church or at Dom Polski, the Polish Ladies Hall. In the small towns of York County, Pennsylvania, women shared skating parties, picnics, or local sports events. In factories where all the workers were women and all managers were men, the gender division could simply reinforce male dominance and female deference, yet the same division could also cement a kind of gender solidarity.[30]

Throughout the working day, cigar makers adjusted the ideal model of the work process to better accommodate their own needs. There were shortcuts in the work that added to speed, but they had to be concealed from the foreman. A cigar maker, for example, might quickly lick the flag at the head of the cigar instead of reaching for the paste cup. Biting off the ends of the tobacco instead of taking time to use the knife shaved off several seconds as well. Since most factories carefully monitored the use of wrapper leaf, cigar makers developed ways to reach acceptable averages of cigars made from the tobacco allotted. Lucille Schmidt in Lima, Ohio, recalled that "you really got the dickens" for not making a high enough average. While some workers found it easy to do, Schmidt had more trouble. Workers with extra tobacco quietly shared with her and others like her. Neva Fake in Windsor, Pennsylvania, recalled that those who were "close" wrapper cutters used to give wrappers to those who were not, but unfortunately for her "the ones that I sat aside of were as bad as I was." Too, women might also regulate the average informally among themselves. Pearl Hume in Lima noted that shopmates called down a woman who consistently had a higher average than everyone else. "She made it harder for everybody. . . . A lot of them was really mean to her." Hume herself aimed for an average in the middle, "not too low or too high."[31]

Male cigar makers, particularly unionists and Tampa workers, insisted upon the observance of an old custom in the cigar factories. Each day, each cigar maker was allowed three free cigars, called smokers. Manufacturers employing women liked to boast that they had no "free-smoker nuisance," but women saw the matter differently. In Detroit, women removed cigars each day for their boyfriends and husbands, carefully concealing the cigars so "no one could see it." Such pilfering undoubtedly took place elsewhere. One woman in New York City was caught trying to leave work with 250 cigars concealed in her bloomers.[32]

Other aspects of women's work culture exploited weak points in the labor system which women could use to augment their control. Labor shortages and job turnover predictably worked to their advantage. Manufacturers in some areas raised wages to attract enough workers. Anna Bartasius noted that in Phildelphia, where there were so many factories, one could always get a job, if not in one factory, then in another. In Detroit, women "just quit in one place and they went to the other place." Rose Purzon explained that "if anything got too bad in one place, you know, like the tobacco wouldn't be just right or something—they tried to save money on that—you tell them to go to hell and go someplace else. . . . They were always desperate for help." A 1919 survey of New Orleans manufacturers suggested that only 36 percent of women who quit did so for "personal" reasons. The responses of women employees questioned, however, revealed that 64 percent of those who had quit had cited working conditions. Sometimes several factors combined to augment women's power. In 1910, a strike in Tampa, Florida, caused orders in Detroit to reach record highs. An industry spokesman, using imagery which degraded women, complained that "all the available girls were employed and they are as independent as a hog on ice, refusing to work if they don't feel like it because they know they can get as good a job at a moment's notice at another factory."[33]

Despite manufacturers' goals and rules governing the work process, and the pressure on women for accommodation and "consent,"[34] women's work culture expressed a concern with controlling work and included the possibility of collective action. Accurate, comprehensive data on women's strike activity in the cigar industry between 1900 and 1919 is not available, but references to these confrontations surface in the union journals, industry publications, and state reports on labor. Annual reports of the New Jersey Bureau of Statistics of Labor, for example, chronicled major labor disputes in the state between 1900 and 1917. Women cigar makers, according to these reports, struck 24 times during this period, and the frequency increased markedly after 1914, reflecting national strike trends. Of the twenty four, seven were at least partially successful. In most cases, the strikes lasted only a few days, although two continued for two months. Fifteen involved wage increase demands; two resulted from threats of a wage cut; three related to reinstatement of a foreman; and two others stemmed from the discharge of fellow employees. The rest had to do with fines, hours, work rules and poor tobacco stock. These reasons were similar to those reported in the trade press between 1900 and 1919—strikes against a change in method of work, for increased wages, against "tyranny of their foreman," or to retain a foreman who was liked.[35]

Poor tobacco stock frequently precipitated strikes. Women working at the Eisenlohr factory in Lancaster County, Pennsylvania, in 1906, for example, began talking at lunch one day in March at a restaurant near the factory. A few drafted a notice on a piece of brown paper: "Notice: Cigarmakers, are we going to continue working these small wrappers? Do you know the result? Nervous and physical wreck is the result. Are we going to continue, cigarmakers? Let us all say no. Therefore at 3 o'clock let us all go to the stock counter and demand more wrappers. Remember the time." The note circulated in the shop after lunch and at the appointed hour all but three went to the counter with the demand, the CMIU reported. The superintendent promised to take the matter up with management, but the company soon announced that the branch factory would close.[36]

Ethnic division sometimes caused conflict among women workers and prevented solidarity during strikes. In at least two strikes in New Jersey where women of different ethnic backgrounds worked together in the same factories, strike activity broke down along ethnic lines. In both cases, the strikers were Hungarians, while Polish, Italian, and some "American" women did not join. However, several nationalities participated in the Newark strike of 1916, including "Jewish, Polish, and Italian" workers. In a 1908 strike in Newark, a state report commented on women's mutual aid. "An interesting circumstance in connection with this strike is that practically all the women and girls employed in other manufactures of cigars in and about the city of Newark have contributed regularly every week a certain percentage of their earnings to assist the strikers."[37]

Resistance sometimes involved physical force and sabotage. During the New York City strike of 1900, women left water faucets running overnight before they walked out of one factory. Strikers in Kingston, New York, in 1903, angered by the company's refusal to pay their back wages once they had struck, broke into the factory, and attacked fifty workers who had remained at work. Police were unable to clear the building for several hours. Strikers argued that they had a right to occupy the building until the company paid the back wages owed to them. Many of the incidents involved strikers' attacking scabs or anyone who broke the solidarity of the strike. During a 1907 strike involving women at the Rosenthal Brothers factory in New York City, several women strikers arrested for attacking those who had continued to work and for violating an injunction against picketing. In a 1909 strike in New Brunswick, New Jersey, women strikers threw rocks at women who crossed the picket line. In the 1915 South River, New Jersey walkout, strikers appeared at the factory the day after the strike began and began as if they were ready to return to work. Once inside, they made a "furious" attack on those women who had continued to work. Police arrived and took half an hour to clear the building .[38]

Between 1916 and 1922, the incomplete record suggests that women participated in a greater number of strikes than ever before. A startling strike of seven thousand women in Detroit during the summer of 1916 inaugurated this phase. Because Detroit had been featured as a showcase for the entire industry and had been without labor strife, the strike caused a shock wave through the entire industry. Unlike other large manufacturers, Detroit companies had not followed the branch factory system, but the strike confirmed the need for such factories and illustrated the folly of keeping "all their eggs in one basket," according to *Tobacco Leaf*. By early 1917, most Detroit cigar manufacturers of any size had a string of auxiliary factories in Pennsylvania and Ohio.[39]

The Detroit strike had only been the opening salvo, however. During the years from 1917 through 1919, three-quarters of the industry's workers went out on strike—joining the 4 million other U.S. workers who had walked off their jobs in 1919 alone. Despite problems, the movement represented the best effort yet at cooperation between male and female cigar workers; much of the activity took place outside formal union structures. The branch factory system was rendered ineffective, since the strike spread from branch to branch and the strikers were successful in shutting down most production in the largest firms in the industry during the late spring and early summer of 1919. The country's manufacturers were thoroughly shaken by this massive strike wave—not only because of its size and its demonstration that women could strike in great numbers, but also because it raised the spectre of class-wide organization.[40]

Industry trade journals decried the "dictatorial attitude" of strikers and searched for a solution to the difficulties rocking the industry. There were hints of change to come. One editorial recounted the strikes during 1917 and 1918, and noted that "rarely do we hear of labor trouble in the cigarette business. . . . Eventually machinery will solve the cigar-making problem just as it solved the cigarette making problem."[41] The strike movement subsided during the late summer as the wartime labor shortages disappeared and economic conditions changed. Furthermore, in August, the American Machine and Foundry Company succeeded in its twenty-year quest for an automatic cigar-making machine. The new device helped to break one strike and demoralize others. By early 1920, the labor movement had been completely defeated.[42] A few more strikes took place, the last in February, 1922, when two thousand women in Lima, Ohio, walked out of the Deisel-Wemmer factories to protest a change in the organization of work. They lost the strike and manufacturers soon installed machinery and closed the many branch factories in nearby towns.[43]

Women's work culture and their participation in collective action called into question the manufacturers' assumptions and policies— women had struck as much or more than men, and strikes spread throughout the branch factories. In the 1920s, manufacturers adopted new methods to achieve their goals. They consolidated their hold on the industry, closed branches, and concentrated operations in large, mechanized factories under one roof. Many also began consciously drawing on a new pool of women workers, those with no previous ties to the industry. Women's work culture had reflected the labor process and the nature of the cigar industry during the early twentieth century. It had been shaped by women's experience both as workers and as women. As the nature of these factors shifted after 1919, so too did the form and content of women's work culture.

CHAPTER 12

Not So "Turbulent Years": A New Look at the 1930s

MELVYN DUBOFSKY

Our conventional view of the 1930s was aptly caught in the title of Irving Bernstein's history of American labor during that decade, *Turbulent Years*, a title that the author borrowed from Myron Taylor's annual report to the Board of Directors of the United States Steel Corporation in 1938. That liberal historians and corporate executives perceive the 1930s as a "turbulent" decade should today occasion no surprise. For the American business elite especially, their social, economic, and political world had turned upside down during the Great Depression and New Deal. After nearly a full decade of corporate hegemony, class collaboration, and trade union retreat, the United States during the 1930s seemed chronically beset with class conflict, violence, and ubiquitous labor radicalism. In the words of one of the decade's radicals, Len DeCaux, a "new consciousness" awakened workers from lethargy. "There was light after the darkness in the youth of the movement," exulted DeCaux. "Youth that was direct and bold in action, not sluggish and sly from long compromise with the old and the rotten. There was light in the hopeful future seen by the red and the rebellious, now playing their full part in what they held to be a great working-class advance against the capitalist class. There was light, and a heady, happy feeling in the solidarity of common struggle in a splendid common cause."[1]

The picture one has of the 1930s, then, whether painted by a liberal scholar such as Bernstein, an activist like DeCaux, or a tycoon like Taylor, is of conflict and struggle. The foreground is filled with militant and radical workers, the masses in motion, a rank and file vigorously, sometimes violently, reaching out to grasp control over its own labor and existence.

Given the conventional portrait of the American 1930s, conventional questions arise, the most obvious of which are the following: (1)
Why did labor militancy decline? (2) Why did militant, radical rank-
and-file struggles produce old-fashioned, autocratically controlled
trade unions in many cases? (3) Why did the turbulence create no
lasting, mass radical political movement?

Before seeking to answer such questions, even assuming they are
the best ones to ask about the thirties, I am reminded of a lesson
contained in an American cartoon strip. A caveman reporter informs
his stone-age editor that he has both good news and bad news. "Let's
have the bad news first," says the editor. "There's only good news,"
responds the reporter. Need I add that American journalists had a
field day during the 1930s and that their editors rejoiced in an abun-
dance of "bad news;" frontpage headlines shrieked class war and wire
photos depicted strikers in armed conflict with police and troops.

But were class war and violent pitched battles the reality of the
1930s? And, if they were, how do we explain the absence of a mass
radical political movement?

Frankly, all of us realize how difficult it is to create or grasp historical reality. As historians, we work with the available evidence, always,
to be sure, seeking to discover more about the past, but always aware
that the *total* record of what happened is beyond our recall or recreation. Ultimately, then, just as man through his thoughts and actions
makes history, historians, in the process of research and writing,
create their own history.

In examining the 1930s, how should we go about creating the history of that era? Two convenient models are at hand. In one we can seek
lessons for the present in an instrumental view of the past. That
approach suggests the might-have-beens of history. If only Communists had behaved differently; if nonsectarian radicals had pursued
the proper policies; if the militant rank and file had been aware of its
true interests (as distinguished from the false consciousness inculcat-
ed by trade-union bureaucrats and New Deal Democrats); then the
history of the 1930s would have been different and *better.*[2] The second
approach to our turbulent decade has been suggested by David Brody.
"The interesting questions," writes Brody, "are not in the realm of
what might have been, but in a closer examination of what did happen."[3] Brody's approach, I believe, promises greater rewards for
scholars and may even be more useful for those who desire to use the
past to improve the present and shape the future. As Karl Marx noted
in *The Eighteenth Brumaire*, man indeed makes his own history, but

only "under circumstances directly encountered, given and transmitted from the past. The tradition of all the dead generations weighs like a nightmare on the brain of the living."[4]

One more preliminary observation must be made about recreating the past in general and the American 1930s in particular. We must be zealously on guard against falling victim to what Edward Thompson has characterized as the "Pilgrim's Progress" orthodoxy, an approach that, in his words, "reads history in the light of subsequent preoccupations, and not in fact as it occurred. Only the successful . . . are remembered. The blind alleys, the lost causes, and the losers themselves are forgotten."[5] In light of what I intend to say below and also what such theorists of "corporate liberalism" as Ronald Radosh and James Weinstein have written about the history of the American labor movement, it is well to bear in mind Thompson's comment that history written as the record of victors and survivors is not necessarily synonomous with the past as experienced by all of those who lived it and created it.[6]

I

Let us now see if we can uncover or glimpse the reality of the American 1930s. Certainly, the turbulence, militancy, and radicalism of the decade existed. From 1929 through 1939, the American economic and social system remained in crisis. Despite two substantial recoveries from the depths of depression, unemployment during the decade never fell below 14 percent of the civilian labor force or 21 percent of the nonagricultural work force.[7] Those workers who once believed in the American myth of success, who dreamed of inching up the occupational ladder, acquiring property of their own, and watching their children do even better occupationally and materially, had their hopes blasted by the Great Depression. As Stephan Thernstrom's research shows for Boston, the Great Depression thwarted occupational and material advancement for an entire generation of workers.[8] And what was true in Boston most likely prevailed elsewhere in the nation. If, in the past, American workers had experienced marginal upward social and economic mobility, during the 1930s they could expect to fall rather more often than to climb.

The thwarted aspirations of millions of workers combined with persistent mass unemployment produced a decade of social unrest that encompassed every form of collective and individual action from mass marches to food looting. One historian has pointed out that between February 1930 and July 1932, at least seventeen separate incidents of violent protest occurred. In Chicago in 1931, after three persons were killed during an anti-eviction struggle, sixty thousand citizens marched on City Hall to protest police brutality. Indeed in nearly every city in which the unemployed organized and protested, violent confrontations with the police erupted.[9]

More important and more threatening to the established order than protests by the unemployed and hungry, which punctuated the early depression years, were the more conventional forms of class struggle which erupted with greater incidence after the election of Franklin Roosevelt and the coming of the New Deal. In 1934, after twelve years of relative quiet on the labor front, industrial conflict broke out with a militancy and violence not seen since 1919. In Toledo, Ohio, National Guardsmen tear-gassed and drove from the city's streets Auto-Lite Company strikers who had the support not only of the radical A.J. Muste's American Workers party and Unemployed League, but also of the citywide central labor council, an AFL affiliate. And the following month, July 1934, witnessed still more violent struggles. A strike by maritime workers in the San Francisco Bay area brought battles between police and longshoremen, several dead strikers, and the dispatch of state troops. In protest, the San Francisco central labor council declared a citywide general strike for July 16. Here, too, a labor radical, Harry Bridges, an Australian immigrant and a Marxist, led a strike unsanctioned by the AFL. Only a day after the San Francisco general strike ended, Americans read in their newspapers of July 21 that on the previous day in Minneapolis, Minnesota, fifty men had been shot in the back as police fired on strikers. Within a week of the bloody July 20 battle between police and teamsters in the city's main square, Minnesota Governor Floyd Olson placed the Twin Cities under martial law. Once again, in Minneapolis, as earlier in Toledo and San Francisco, left-wing radicals led the strike, in this instance the Trotskyists, Farrell Dobbs and the brothers Vincent, Miles, Grant, and Ray Dunne. And only a week after the shootings in Minneapolis, on July 28, 1934, deputy sheriffs in the company town of Kohler, Wisconsin, killed one person and injured twenty in what the New York *Times* characterized as a "strike riot."[10]

Few areas of the nation seemed untouched by labor militancy in 1934. In the spring a national textile strike called by the United Textile Workers of America brought out 350,000 workers from Maine to Alabama, and violent repression of the strikers proved the rule in the South's Piedmont mill towns. Throughout the spring auto and steel workers flocked into trade unions, like coal miners the previous year, seeming almost to organize themselves. And when auto manufacturers and steel barons refused to bargain with labor, national strikes threatened both industries. Only direct presidential intervention and the equivocal actions of AFL leaders averted walkouts in autos and steel.[11]

If 1934, in Irving Bernstein's chapter title, amounted to an "Eruption," 1937 experienced an epidemic of strikes. The year began with the famous Flint sit-down strike in which the United Auto Workers conquered General Motors; saw United States Steel surrender to the Steel Workers Organizing Committee (SWOC)-CIO without a struggle less than three weeks after the General Motors strike ended; and culminated in the late spring with perhaps the most violent and bloodiest national strike of the decade: the Little Steel conflict that led to the Memorial Day "massacre" outside Republic Steel's South Chicago plant. In between Flint and Little Steel, more than four hundred thousand workers participated in 477 sit-down strikes. Twenty-five sit-downs erupted in January 1937, forty-seven in February, and 170 in March. "Sitting down has replaced baseball as a national pastime," quipped *Time* Magazine.[12]

The labor militancy and strikes of 1934 and 1937 created a solidarity that hitherto eluded American workers. During the 1930s, it seemed, the United States had developed a true proletariat, more united by its similarities than divided by its differences. Mass immigration had ended in 1921, and hence the last immigrant generation had had more than a decade to integrate itself into the social system and for its children to have been "Americanized" by the public schools and other intermediate social agencies. Male-female role conflicts appeared notable by their absence, and strikers' wives provided their husbands with substantial assistance as members of women's auxiliaries. "I found a common understanding and unselfishness I'd never known in my life," wrote the wife of one Flint sit-downer. "I'm living for the first time with a definite goal. . . . Just being a woman isn't enough any more. I want to be a human being with the right to think for myself."[13] "A new type of woman was born in the strike," noted an observer of the struggle in Flint. "Women who only yesterday were horrified at unionism, who felt inferior to the task of speaking, leading, have, as if overnight, become the spearhead in the battle for unionism."[14]

Even racial tensions among workers seemed to diminish during the 1930s, especially after the emergence of the CIO whose "new union-

ists" often crusaded for civil rights as vigorously as for trade unionism. The changes wrought by CIO led two students of black labor to
conclude in 1939 "that it is easier to incorporate Negroes into a new
movement . . . than to find a secure place in an older one." Surveying
the impact of depression, New Deal, and CIO on black workers,
Horace Cayton and George S. Mitchell suggested that

> in the readjustment of social patterns and ideologies, we find
> reflected a profound transition in Negro life as well as in the
> economic outlook of American workers generally. What has
> been for generations a racial stratification in occupations is, un-
> der present-day conditions, in process of transformation. Class
> tensions and class solidarity have measurably relaxed racial ten-
> sions and, by so doing, have mitigated the divisive effects of ra-
> cial antagonism.[15]

One must not, however, romanticize working-class solidarity and
thus lose sight of the tensions that continued to pit American workers
during the 1930s against each other rather than a common enemy. In
New Haven, Connecticut, American-born workers still denigrated
Italians as "wops," and "it's dog eat dog all right," retorted an Italian-
American machinist "but it's also Mick feeds Mick!"[16] A Hollywood
film of the late 1930s, *Black Legion*, starring Humphrey Bogart as a
frustrated white American-born Protestant machinist, captured the
still lingering resentment harbored by the American-born against the
foreign-born (and even their children), and depicted the sort of worker more likely to listen to Father Coughlin than to John L. Lewis,
Franklin D. Roosevelt, or perhaps William Z. Foster. Or, listen to an
official of an AFL union with jurisdiction in an industry that employed many Afro-Americans. "I consider the Negroes poor union
men. You know as well as I do that they are shiftless, easily intimidated and generally of poor caliber. . . . What should have happened is
what is being done in Calhoun County, Illinois, where Negroes are
not allowed to stay overnight. As a result there are no Negroes there
and no Negro problem."[17]

But it was the CIO, not the AFL, that symbolized the labor upheaval
of the 1930s. And in 1937 when CIO-organized autos, steel, rubber,
and other former bastions of the open shop, between three and a half
and four million workers joined the labor movement, a larger number
than the entire AFL claimed as of January 1, 1937. Now, for the first
time in its history, organized labor in America wielded power in the
strategic core of mass-production industry, and it did so under the

aegis of a labor federation (CIO) whose leaders consciously repudiated the AFL tradition of class accommodation and collaboration. The CIO during the late 1930s exemplified solidarity rather than exclusiveness, political action in place of nonpartisanship, biracialism and bisexualism instead of racial and sexual chauvinism, and militancy rather than opportunism. "CIO started as a new kind of labor movement," recalled Len DeCaux in his autobiography. "A challenge to the old AFL and the status quo it complacently guarded. It was new in its youth and fervor, new in the broad sector of the working class it brought into action, new in the way it accepted and integrated its radicals, new in its relative independence of corporate and government control, new in its many social and political attitudes."[18]

DeCaux was not alone among radicals in looking to CIO as the instrument through which to build a new America. Powers Hapgood, the Harvard-educated son of a wealthy Midwestern family, who worked as a coal miner in order to share the worker's plight, felt compelled in 1935 to seek an accommodation with his ancient enemy John L. Lewis, who was then organizing the CIO. "It's surprising how many radicals think I ought to see Lewis," Hapgood informed his wife, "saying it's much less of a compromise to make peace with him and stay in the labor movement than it is to get a government job and cease to be active in the class struggle." To reject a reconciliation with Lewis in 1935, concluded Hapgood, would let the left wing down.[19] After the CIO's first national conference in Atlantic City in October 1937, Adolph Germer, a former ally of Hapgood and then a Social Democrat evolving into a New Deal Democrat, wrote to an ex-associate in the Socialist Party of America: "I attended the Atlantic City conference and I assure you it was an educational treat. There was as much difference between that meeting and the A. F. of L. conventions I have attended as there is between night and day."[20] And Lee Pressman and Gardner Jackson, the former an ex-Communist and the latter a left-wing, socialist-inclined reformer, both of whom worked closely with Lewis from 1936 through 1940, observed that Lewis seemed a changed man in 1937, that the CIO experience had transformed him from "a labor boss of the most conventional kind, and a discredited one at that" into an eager, dedicated leader of a movement encompassing blue- and white-collar workers, farmers, small professionals, and all sorts of "little people." Lewis, Pressman and Jackson believed in 1937, might well lead an independent populist or farmer-labor political movement in the event Roosevelt and the Democrats failed to implement full-employment policies and a welfare state.[21]

Had Lewis decided to lead such an independent political movement, the time never seemed riper. The Great Depression and the New Deal had wrought a veritable political revolution among American workers. Masses of hitherto politically apathetic workers, especially among first-generation immigrants and their spouses, went to the polls in greater numbers. And Roosevelt broke the last links that bound millions of workers across the industrial heartland from Pittsburgh to Chicago to the Republican party.[22] Lewis exulted at the results of the 1936 election in which for the first time since the depression of the 1890s, Democrats swept into power in the steel and coal towns of Pennsylvania and Ohio, winning office on tickets financed by CIO money and headed by CIO members. A new consciousness appeared to be stirring among the nation's industrial workers. A social scientist sampling attitudes and beliefs among Akron rubber workers at the end of the 1930s discovered that the vast majority of CIO members valued human rights above property rights and showed little respect or deference for the prerogatives and privileges of corporate property. Akron's workers, and also many residents characterized as middle class, apparently distinguished between purely personal use-property and property as capital, which afforded its possessors power over the lives and labor of the propertyless.[24] Such an altered consciousness fed the dreams of Popular Fronters and third-party activists.

All this ferment, militancy, radicalism, violence, and perhaps even an altered working-class consciousness were part of American reality during the 1930s. Yet, as we know, American socialism expired during the depression decade, communism advanced only marginally, Roosevelt seduced the farmer-laborites and populists, the CIO came to resemble the AFL, and John L. Lewis once again reverted to behaving like a "labor boss of the most conventional kind." Why? To answer that question we have to examine other aspects of social, economic, and political reality during the 1930s.

II

Just as one can claim that the 1930s represented a crisis for American capitalism that expressed itself most overtly in the eagerness and militancy with which workers challenged their corporate masters, one might just as easily assert that for most Americans, workers included, events during the decade reinforced their faith in the "justness" of the American system and the prospects for improvement without fundamental restructuring. For many workers capitalism never collapsed; indeed, for those employed steadily, always a substantial proportion of the work force, real wages actually rose as prices fell. For other workers, the tentative economic recovery of 1933-34 and the more substantial growth of 1937 rekindled faith in the American system. The two great strike waves of the decade, 1934 and 1937, erupted not in moments of crisis, but when hope, profits, employment, and wages all revived. Crisis, in other words, induced apathy or lethargy; economic recovery, a sign that the system worked, stimulated action. And when the recovery of 1936-37 was followed by the "Roosevelt depression," a more rapid and deeper decline than the Great Crash of 1929-33, the number of strikes diminished markedly and the more militant CIO affiliates concentrated in the mass-production industries suffered severe membership and financial losses.[25] Perhaps this final crisis of the depression decade left unresolved might have snapped whatever bonds still tied workers to the American system. That, however, remains a problematic historical might-have-been, as the coming of World War II resolved the contradictions in American capitalism and substituted patriotic unity for class conflict.

An analysis of the statistics of working-class militancy during the 1930s—the incidence of strikes, the number of workers affected, the man-days lost—also leads to divergent interpretations. One can stress the high level of strike activity, the fact that only 840 strikes were recorded in 1932 but 1,700 erupted in 1933, 1,856 in 1934, 2,200 in 1936, and in the peak strike year, 1937, 4,740.[26] One can argue that no area of the nation and, more importantly, no major industry escaped industrial conflict. For the first time in United States history, strikes affected every major mass-production industry and paralyzed the towering heights of the economy: steel, auto, rubber, coal, electrical goods; the list goes on and on. For the nation and its workers, the 1930s were indeed "turbulent years."

But the statistics of industrial conflict reveal another story, an equally interesting one. When the 1934 strike wave erupted, President Roosevelt sought to understand its origins and implications. He asked the Commissioner of Labor Statistics, Isidore Lubin, to analyze and interpret the 1934 outbreak. Lubin prepared a report that he transmitted to the President in late August 1934. Seeking to place the 1934 strikes in historical perspective, Lubin acted logically. He compared what had happened in the first half of 1934 to the last previous year in which the United States had experienced such massive labor militancy, 1919. And he concluded that the 1934 strike wave could not match 1919 in intensity, duration, or number of workers involved. More than twice as many strikes began each month in the first half of 1919, reported Lubin, than in the same period in 1934; moreover, more than two and a half times as many workers were involved in the 1919 strikes. He then proceeded to assure the President that July 1934, the month of the San Francisco and Minneapolis general strikes, witnessed no mass working-class upheaval. Only seven-tenths of one percent, or seven out of every thousand wage earners, participated in strikes. Only four-tenths of one percent of man-days of employment were lost as a result of strikes. "In other words," Lubin reassured the President, "for every thousand man-days worked four were lost because of strikes." Selecting ten major industries for analysis, Lubin observed that only one-half of one percent of the total number employed struck in July 1934. "Comparing the number employed with the number actually involved in strikes, one reaches the conclusion that for every thousand workers employed in those industries only five were affected by strikes. In terms of the number of man-days lost . . . it is estimated that for every thousand man-days worked . . . seven days of employment were lost because of strikes." And, in a final note of reassurance for the President, Lubin observed that the "recent strikes have been relatively short lived," less than half as long as the average duration during 1927 (24 compared to 51 days), a time of labor peace.[27]

But what of 1937, the decade's premier strike year, when more than twice as many workers struck as in 1934? Well, according to official statistics, only 7.2 percent of employed workers were involved in walkouts (practically the same percentage as in 1934) and their absence from work represented only 0.043 percent of all time worked.[28]

Questions immediately arise from a reading of such strike statistics. What was the other 93 percent of the labor force doing during the great strike waves of 1934 and 1937? More important, how were they affected by the upsurge of industrial conflicts which did not involve or affect them directly?

Such questions are especially important when one bears in mind the continental size of the United States. Geography could, and did, easily dilute the impact of industrial conflict nationally. The United States lacked a London, Paris, Berlin, or Rome, where massive, militant strikes affected the national state directly as well as private employers. Few of the major strikes of the 1930s occurred even in state capitals, most of which were isolated from industrial strife. When teamsters tied up Minneapolis and longshoremen closed down San

Francisco in July 1934, truckers continued to deliver goods in Chicago and Los Angeles, and waterfront workers remained on the job in New York, Baltimore, and San Pedro. For trade unionists and radicals it was exceedingly difficult, as Roy Rosenzweig has shown for A.J. Muste's Unemployed League, to transform well-structured local and regional organizations into equally effective national bodies.[29] Just as the millions of unemployed during the 1930s did not experience the shock of joblessness simultaneously, so, too, different workers experienced industrial conflict at different times and in different places. As we will see below, what workers most often experienced in common—participation in the American political system—was precisely what most effectively diluted militancy and radicalism.

Despite the continental size and diversity of the American nation, it is possible to glimpse aspects of working-class reality in local settings that disclose uniformities in belief and behavior which do much to explain the dearth of durable radicalism in the United States. We are fortunate that two truly excellent, perceptive sociological field studies were completed during the 1930s that dissect the social structure and culture of two characteristic smaller American industrial cities. We are even more fortunate that the two cities investigated—Muncie, Indiana, and New Haven, Connecticut—proved so unlike in their economic structures, population mixes, and regional and cultural milieus. Muncie was dominated by two industries—Ball Glass and General Motors—characterized by an almost totally Americanborn, white Protestant population, and situated in the heartland of American agriculture, individualism, and evangelical Protestantism. New Haven, by contrast, claimed no dominant employers, encompassed a population differentiated by nationality, race, and religion as well as class, and was set in a region traditionally urban (also urbane) and non-evangelical in culture. Yet after one finishes reading Robert and Helen Lynd on Muncie and E. Wight Bakke on New Haven, one is more impressed by the similarities rather than the differences in working-class attitudes and behavior.[30]

Let us examine Muncie first. The Lynds had initially gone to Muncie in the mid-1920s in order to discover how urbanization and industrialization had affected American culture, how the city and the factory had altered beliefs and behavioral patterns developed in the country and on the farm.[31] They returned a decade later in order to see what impact, if any, the "Great Depression" had had on local culture and behavior. Surprisingly, for them at least, they found labor organization weaker in 1935 than it had been in 1925, yet the Muncie business class seemed more united and more determined than ever to keep its city open shop (nonunion). The Lynds discovered objectively greater class stratification in 1935 than in 1925 and even less prospect for the individual worker to climb up the ladder of success (see Thernstrom on Boston's depression generation workers for similar findings), yet they characterized Muncie's workers as being influenced by "drives . . . largely those of the business class: both are caught up in the tradition of a rising standard of living and lured by the enticements of salesmanship." As one Middletown woman informed the sociologists: "Most of the families that I know are after the same things today that they were after before the depression, and they'll get them the same way—on credit."[32]

Union officials told the Lynds a similar tale of woe. Union members preferred buying gas for their cars to paying dues, and going for a drive to attending a union meeting. Local workers were willing to beg, borrow, or steal to maintain possession of their cars and keep them running. Despite seven years of depression, Muncie's workers, according to the Lynds, still worshipped the automobile as the symbol of the American dream, and, as long as they owned one, considered themselves content.[33]

"Fear, resentment, insecurity and disillusionment has been to Middletown's workers largely an *individual* experience for each worker," concluded the Lynds,

> and not a thing generalized by him into a "class" experience.
> . . . Such militancy as it generates tends to be sporadic, personal, and flaccid; an expression primarily of personal resentment rather than an act of self-identification with the continuities of a movement or of a rebellion against an economic status regarded as permanently fixed. The militancy of Middletown labor tends, therefore, to be easily manipulated, and to be diverted into all manner of incidental issues.[34]

So much for Muncie—what of New Haven with its more heterogeneous and less culturally individualistic working class that, in some cases, the investigator could interview and probe after the CIO upheaval of 1936-37? Again we see in Bakke's two published examinations of the unemployed worker in New Haven an absence of mass organization, collective militancy, or radicalism, despite an apparent hardening of class lines. New Haven's workers, unlike Muncie's, apparently did not share the drives of the business class and they did in fact develop a collective sense of class. "Hell, brother," a machinist told Bakke, "you don't have to look to know there's a workin' class. We may not say so—But look at what we do. Work. Look at where we live. Nothing there but workers. Look at how we get along. Just like every other damned worker. Hell's bells, of course, there's a workin' class, and it's gettin' more so every day."[35] Yet New Haven, like Muncie, lacked a militant and radical working class. Why?

Bakke tried to provide answers. He cited the usual barriers to collective action and working-class radicalism: ethnic heterogeneity; fear of the alien; fear of repression; and capitalist hegemony that was cultural as well as economic and political.[36] Yet he also discovered that answers to the absence of militancy and radicalism lay embedded deep within the culture of New Haven's workers. In most cases, their lives had disproved the American dream; rather than experiencing steady upward mobility and constantly rising material standards of living, Bakke's interviewees had lived lives of insecurity and poverty. They regularly had had to adjust their goals to actual possibilities, which almost always fell far below their aspirations. As one worker after another informed Bakke, life involved putting up with it, grinning and bearing it, and using common sense to survive. Explaining how the unemployed managed in a period of general economic crisis, a brass worker noted in a matter of fact fashion, "The poor are used to being poor."[37]

As Eugene Genovese has remarked in a different context, an attempt to explain the relative absence of slave rebellions in North America,

> Only those who romanticize—and therefore do not respect—the laboring classes would fail to understand their deep commitment to "law and order." Life is difficult enough without added uncertainty and "confusion." Even an oppressive and unjust system is better than none. People with such rich experience as that of the meanest slaves quickly learn to distrust Utopian nostrums. As Machiavelli so brilliantly revealed, most people refuse to believe in anything they have not experienced. Such negativity must be understood as a challenge to demonstrate that a better, firmer, more just social order can replace the one to be torn down.[38]

Just so with New Haven's workers. For the majority of them, alternatives to the existing system seemed most notable for their absence. The only alternatives the city's workers cited, German Nazism, Italian Fascism, and Soviet Communism, none of which to be sure they had experienced, held no allurement, promised them "no better, more just social order." Workers repeatedly referred to Soviet Russia to explain both Socialism's and Communism's lack of appeal.[39]

Lacking an alternative to the existing system, New Haven workers grabbed what few joys they could in an otherwise perilous existence. One worker explained his own resistance to Socialism in the following manner. He had fought enough losing battles in his life. But he knew one place where he could celebrate as a winner. As a Democrat or a Republican, at least once in a while he could get drunk on election night and act the part of a winner. But Socialists, he sneered, "when do you think they're goin' to have a chance to get drunk?"[40]

Ah, one might say, Muncie and New Haven were atypical and their working class more so.

Look at Flint and Youngstown, Akron and Gary, Minneapolis and San Francisco. In those cities workers acted collectively and militantly. But a closer look at even such *foci* of labor struggle reveals a much more complex reality than suggested by conventional romanticizations of working-class solidarity and rank-and-file militancy.

Without militants, to be sure, there would have been no Flint sit-down strike, no San Francisco general strike, no walkout by Akron's rubber workers. Without rank-and-file participation, that is, collective struggle, there would have been no union victories. Yet, in reality, solidarity rarely produced collective action; rather, more often than not, action by militant minorities (what some scholars have character-ized as "sparkplug Unionism"[41]) precipitated a subsequent collective response. And rank and filers frequently resisted the radicalism of the militant cadres who sparked industrial confrontations. In Flint, as Sidney Fine has shown, only a small minority of the local workers belonged to the UAW and paid dues on the eve of the strike, and the sit-down technique was chosen consciously to compensate for the union's lack of a mass membership base.[42] The story was the same in Akron. When that city's rubber workers gained CIO's first major victory in March 1936 after a strike against the Goodyear Tire and Rubber Company, Powers Hapgood disclosed the following to John L. Lewis: "Confidentially, I can tell you that it was a minority strike, starting with only a hand full of members and gradually building a membership in that Local Union to a little over 5000 out of 14,000 workers."[43] Lee Pressman, general counsel to the Steel Workers Orga-nizing Committee, recalls that as late as the spring of 1937, after the UAW's success at Flint and United States Steel's surrender to SWOC, labor organizers had still failed to enrol in SWOC more than a sub-stantial minority of the steelworkers employed by firms other than

United States Steel.[44] For most rank and filers, then, militancy consisted of refusing to cross a picket line, no more. As one observer noted of the Flint sit-downers, a group more militant than the majority of auto workers, "Those strikers have no more idea of 'revolution' than pussy cats."[45]

Even the most strike-torn cities and regions had a significantly internally differentiated working class. At the top were the local cadres, the sparkplug unionists, the men and women fully conscious of their roles in a marketplace society that extolled individualism and rewarded collective strength. These individuals, ranging the political spectrum from Social Democrats to Communists, provided the leadership, militancy, and ideology that fostered industrial conflict and the emergence of mass-production unionism. Beneath them lay a substantial proportion of workers who could be transformed, by example, into militant strikers and unionists, and, in turn, themselves act as militant minorities. Below them were many first- and second-generation immigrant workers, as well as recent migrants from the American countryside, who remained embedded in a culture defined by traditional ties to family, kinship, church, and neighborhood club or tavern. Accustomed to following the rituals of the past, heeding the advice of community leaders, and slow to act, such men and women rarely joined unions prior to a successful strike, once moved to act behaved with singular solidarity, yet rarely served as union or political activists and radicals. And below this mass were the teenage workers caught halfway between liberation from their parental families and formation of their own new households, more attracted to the life and rituals of street gangs and candy-store cronies than to the customs and culture of persistent trade unionists and political activists.[46]

A word must now be added concerning those scholars who have argued that during the 1930s a spontaneously militant and increasingly radical rank and file was either handcuffed or betrayed by bureaucratic and autocratic labor leaders. For those who accept the Leninist thesis that trade unions are, by definition, economist and hence nonrevolutionary, there is no problem in comprehending the behavior of American trade unions and their members during the 1930s. But for those who seek to understand why the militant beginnings of the CIO terminated in an ideological and institutional deadend, why, in Brody's words, "the character of American trade unionism . . . made it an exploiter of radicalism rather than vice versa"—questions remain.[47] And it may seem easiest to answer, as Art Preis, Ronald

Radosh, James Weinstein, and Staughton Lynd have done, that the blame for the failure of radicalism rests with such labor leaders as John L. Lewis and Sidney Hillman who sold out to the New Deal, collaborated with employers, and restrained rank-and-file militancy through the instrument of the nonstrike union contract. That hypothesis, commonly subsumed under the rubric "corporate liberalism," contains a grain of truth.[48] But the small truth tends to obscure a greater reality. As J.B.S. Hardman observed a half century ago, labor leaders are primarily accumulators of power; and, need it be said, no man was more eager to accumulate power than John L. Lewis.[49] A businessman's power flowed from his control of capital; a politician's from influence over voters and possession of the instruments of government; and a labor leader's power derived from his union membership, the more massive and militant the rank and file, the more influential the labor leader. Bereft of a mass membership or saddled with a lethargic rank and file, the labor leader lost influence, and power. All labor leaders, then, necessarily played a devious and sometimes duplicitous game. Sometimes they rushed in to lead a rebellious rank and file; other times, they agitated the rank and file into action; whether they seized leadership of a movement already in motion or themselves breathed life into the rank and file, labor leaders obtained whatever power they exercised with employers and public officials as a consequence of their followers' behavior. Yet, while they encouraged militancy, labor leaders also restrained their troops, in John L. Lewis's phrase, "put a lid on the strikers." They did so for several reasons. First, not all rank-and-file upheavals promised success; and nothing destroyed a trade union as quickly or diluted a labor leader's power as thoroughly as a lost strike. Second, leaders had to judge at what point rank-and-file militancy would produce government repression, an ever-present reality even in Franklin D. Roosevelt's America. Third, and more selfishly, rank-and-file upheavals could careen out of control and threaten a labor leader's tenure in office as well as strengthen his external power. Throughout the 1930s such labor leaders as John L. Lewis alternatively encouraged the release of working-class rebelliousness and "put the lid back on." The labor leader was truly the man in the middle, his influence rendered simultaneously greater and also more perilous as a result of working-class militancy.[50]

A final word must also be said about the union contract, the instrument that allegedly bound workers to their employers by denying them the right to strike. With historical hindsight, such seems to be the end result of the union-management contract under which the union promises to discipline its members on behalf of management. But one must remember that during the 1930s ordinary workers, the romanticized rank and file, risked their jobs, their bodies, and their lives to win the contract. And when they won it, as in Flint in February, 1937, a sit-down striker rejoiced that it "was the most wonderful thing that we could think that could possibly happen to people."[51]

IV

Paradoxically, the one experience during the 1930s that united workers across ethnic, racial, and organizational lines—New Deal politics—served to vitiate radicalism. By the end of the 1930s, Roosevelt's Democratic party had become, in effect, the political expression of America's working class. Old-line Socialists, farmer-labor party types, and even Communists enlisted in a Roosevelt-led "Popular Front." Blacks and whites, Irish and Italian Catholics, Slavic- and Jewish-Americans, uprooted rural Protestants and stable skilled workers joined the Democratic coalition, solidifying the working-class vote as never before in American history. Roosevelt encouraged workers to identify themselves as a common class politically as well as economically. As with David Lloyd George in Britain's pre-World War I Edwardian crisis, Franklin D. Roosevelt in the American crisis of the 1930s found revolutionary class rhetoric indispensable. It panicked the powerful into concessions and attracted working-class voters to the Democratic party. Just as Lloyd George intensified the earlier British crisis in order to ease its solution, Roosevelt acted similarly in New Deal America. By frightening the ruling class into conceding reforms and appealing to workers to vote as a solid block, Roosevelt simultaneously intensified class consciousness and stripped it of its radical potential.[52]

The dilemma of John L. Lewis showed just how well Roosevelt succeeded in his strategy. During the 1930s, no matter how much Lewis preferred to think of himself as an executive rather than a labor leader, however little he associated personally with the working class, he functioned as the leader of a militant working-class movement. Whereas Roosevelt sought to contain working-class militancy through reforms, militant workers pressured Lewis to demand more than the President would or could deliver. The more evident became the New Deal's economic failures, the more heatedly labor militants demanded a fundamental reordering of the economy and society,

demands that Lewis, as leader of CIO, came to express more forceful-
ly than any other trade unionist. "No matter how much Roosevelt did
for the workers," recalls DeCaux, "Lewis demanded more. He
showed no gratitude, nor did he bid his followers be grateful—just
put the squeeze on all the harder."[53] But Lewis, unlike the British
labor leaders of Lloyd George's generation who found in the Labour
Party an alternative to the Prime Minister's "New Liberalism," had no
substitute for Roosevelt's New Deal. In the United States, the President easily mastered the labor leader.

Lewis's lack of a political alternative to the New Deal flowed from
two sources. First was the refusal of most American leftists to countenance a third-party challenge to the Democrats and the intense
loyalty most workers felt to Roosevelt. Between the winter of 1937-38
and the summer of 1940, however much Lewis threatened to lead a
new third party, his public speeches and private maneuvers failed to
create among workers a third-party constituency. It was Lewis's radical speeches that made his eventual endorsement in 1940 of Wendell
Willkie so shocking to many of the labor leader's admirers. Had those
Lewis sycophants known that in June 1940, the CIO president plotted
to win the Republican nomination for Herbert Hoover, they might
have been even more startled.[54] And it was his support first of Hoover
and then of Willkie that exposed the second source for Lewis's lack of
a radical alternative to the New Deal. That was the extent to which
Lewis, other labor leaders, and perhaps most workers had assimilated
the values of a business civilization. This union, Lewis told members
of the United Mine Workers at their 1938 convention, "stands for the
proposition that the heads of families shall have a sufficient income to
educate . . . these sons and daughters of our people, and they go
forth when given that opportunity. . . . They become scientists, great
clergymen . . . great lawyers, great statesmen. . . . Many of our former members are successful in great business enterprises." And two
years later in 1940, he told the same audience: "You know, after all
there are two great material tasks in life that affect the individual and
affect great bodies of men. The first is to achieve or acquire something
of value or something that is desirable, and then the second is to
prevent some scoundrel from taking it away from you".[55] Notice the
substance of Lewis's remarks to a trade-union crowd, the combination of urging the children of the working class to rise above it, not
with it, and the materialistic stress on possessive individualism. Lewis, the most militant and prominent of the depression decade's labor
leaders, remained too much the opportunist, too much the personifi-

cation of vulgar pragmatism and business values to lead a third-party political crusade.

What, then, follows logically from the above description of the 1930s and the implied line of analysis? First, and perhaps obviously, however turbulent were the American 1930s, the depression decade never produced a revolutionary situation. Second, one observes the essential inertia of the working-class masses. Once in motion, the mass of workers can move with great acceleration and enormous militancy—but such movement remains hard to get started. Such social inertia combined with the inability of most workers and their leaders to conceive of an alternative to the values of marketplace capitalism, that is to create a working-class culture autonomous from that of the ruling class, was more important than trade-union opportunism, corporate cooptation, or New Deal liberalism (though the last factor was clearly the most potent) in thwarting the emergence of durable working-class radicalism. Third, and finally, it suggests that a distinction must be drawn between class struggle as a historical reality and workers as a class fully aware of their role, power, and ability to replace the existing system with "a better, firmer, more just social order [than] the one to be torn down."

CHAPTER 13

Fighting on the Domestic Front: Black Steelworkers During World War II

DENNIS C. DICKERSON

Although expanded employment opportunities emerged for Black workers in the steel industry of western Pennsylvania during World War II, pervasive racism tended to retard their occupational advancement. The involvement of the federal government and growing militancy among Black laborers, however, increased the hiring and promotion of Negro workmen in the Pittsburgh area. Employers and union representatives, despite their public declarations against discriminatory treatment, at times colluded to deny Black steelworkers better jobs and working conditions. Only the intervention of the federal Fair Employment Practices Committee (FEPC) and strikes by Black laborers restricted the influence of company and union officials unsympathetic to Black aspirations.

World War I, which reduced European immigration to the United States and generated increased defense production, stimulated a massive Black migration from the agricultural South to northern mills and factories. Although Blacks had labored in Pittsburgh area steel plants since 1875, their numbers had reached only 789 in the Smoky City in 1910, when they comprised a miniscule 3 percent of the industry work force.[1] The wartime migration boosted the number of Black steelworkers in the region to over seven thousand by 1916 and to over fourteen thousand in 1919. In 1923, 16,900 Black mill laborers constituted 21 percent of all steelworkers in western Pennsylvania.[2]

Despite the broad availability of employment in the steel industry in the 1910s and 1920s, Black employees usually worked on jobs shunned by most whites. Hard, dirty, and dangerous labor at open hearth furnaces, in labor gangs, and in coke-making facilities awaited the majority of prospective Black workers. Promotions were rare, and opportunities to transfer to other departments where pay was higher and working conditions more favorable eluded most Black steel employees. Nonetheless, even the relatively lower wages they received in segregated mill departments exceeded their earnings in the South, and this factor fostered the Black migration to western Pennsylvania into the 1920s.

The Great Depression of the 1930s devastated Black communities throughout the Pittsburgh area. Disproportionate percentages of Blacks populated relief rolls and the ranks of the unemployed. In Pittsburgh, for example, in October, 1933 Blacks comprised 8 percent of the population, but 43.4 percent were on relief. In Allegheny County in February 1934, Blacks constituted 40 percent of the unemployed, while foreign-born and white workers were respectively 28 percent and 32 percent unemployed.[3]

Encouragement of independent union activity by the federal government and such AFL dissidents as John L. Lewis of the United Mineworkers produced the Congress of Industrial Organizations (CIO), which organized workers in the mass-production industries in 1936 and 1937. A few years earlier Blacks had joined the revived Amalgamated Association of Iron and Steel Workers, a group which by then had eschewed its anti-Black behavior in the 1918 steel strike. Amalgamated leaders recognized the importance of interracial solidarity and gladly sought support from Black leaders, especially the clergy, as the principal spokesmen for Black steelworkers in 1934. When the CIO's Steelworkers Organizing Committee (SWOC) absorbed the Amalgamated Association, Blacks continued to play an important role, especially as organizers. After U.S. Steel, Jones & Laughlin, Crucible, and other steel firms recognized the union, Black members won election to various offices in SWOC (later United Steelworkers of America) locals. Black union leaders replaced company-employed Black welfare officers and other timid Black steelworkers.[4] Their experience in union affairs and awareness of federal support in developing the CIO prepared Black working-class activists to fight against employment discrimination during the Second World War.

The revival of employment opportunity in the steel industry during World War II eased Black unemployment in western Pennsylvania and stimulated another Black migration from the agrarian South to the Pittsburgh steel district. Migrants flocked into racially segregated residential areas, overcrowding already limited and substandard housing facilities and expanding the ranks of unskilled and semis-killed Black laborers in the mills. Despite the greater availability of jobs in the steel industry after a decade of depression, discrimination in hiring, promotion, and work assignments persisted. However, the urgency of securing the cooperation of Black workers during the war made the federal government through its FEPC particularly respon-sive to their complaints about discrimination, especially when the United Steelworkers of America apparently defaulted in adjudicating such disputes. Moreover, increasing racial militancy, which generally characterized Afro-Americans during World War II, prompted Black steelworkers to stage "wildcat" strikes and work stoppages, and to protest to the FEPC about racial discrimination in the steel mills of western Pennsylvania.[5]

As in World War I, manpower deficiencies during the Second World War required steel managers to search beyond their immediate envi-rons for additional mill employees to assist them in meeting expand-ed production demands. Local mill officials followed previous prac-tices and sent recruiters to the South to attract Black workers to the Pittsburgh steel district. The Homestead steel works, for example, rehired Grover Nelson, a former welfare official, to bring in Black Southerners to work in its mills.[6] Blacks were recruited throughout the South, particularly from Tennessee, Alabama, Georgia, and Tex-as.[7] Most were like Calvin Ingram, whose disenchantment with farm labor caused him to leave Camden, South Carolina, in 1943. He and other Black Southerners flocked into Washington, D.C., where war-time government jobs were especially plentiful. Ingram secured a job building and maintaining army camps in and around the District of Columbia. However, he and Henry Truesdale, after three months in the capital area, were recruited into the western Pennsylvania mills by a hometown acquaintance, Johnnie Johnson. All three became steel-workers at the Carnegie-Illinois facilities in Duquesne.[8] Bartow Tip-per, a veteran employee at Jones & Laughlin in Aliquippa, told his cousins in Pelham, Americus, and La Grange, Georgia, about new employment opportunities in western Pennsylvania.[9] They, like other Black migrants, were lured to the Pittsburgh vicinity because of the "higher wage scales" in local mills and foundries.[10]

Several government agencies, including the United States Employ-ment Service, the War Manpower Commission, and the War Produc-tion Board, assisted local managers in securing Black workers for the Pittsburgh steel district. During the war, two open hearth furnaces at the Farrell Works of Carnegie-Illinois Steel were reopened for production. Plant officials quickly notified the War Manpower Commission of their need for ninety-five men to refurbish these dormant facilities, and for another 141 laborers to fill other unskilled positions. The inadequate supply of local laborers in Farrell made the search for "in migrants" to work in the mills an absolute necessity.[11] The Wyckoff Drawn Steel Company in Abridge, which reported a "bottleneck" in its shipping department in 1943, asked the War Production Board whether "any available negro laborers . . . could be hired . . . to alleviate the manpower shortages."[12] Labor deficiencies at the Carnegie-Illinois facility in Clairton also proved an impediment to steel production. A local mill official wrote the War Manpower Commission, urgently requesting Black workers from "inter-regional recruitment . . . in Southern States." He noted that such efforts "brought good results in [the] past."[13]

Consequently, Black Southerners by the "hundreds" began migrating to western Pennsylvania.[14] During the war, approximately 10,595 Black newcomers settled in Pittsburgh and the surrounding mill towns.[15] By 1944, the rehiring of furloughed Black employees, together with these newly arrived Black laborers, brought the number of Black steelworkers to at least 11,500 workmen, and they comprised 14 percent of the total work force. At most area mills, the percentage of Blacks usually exceeded 10 percent. In some cases, they made up more than 25 percent of all plant employees.

Housing was already inadequate for Blacks at the beginning of World War II. Wartime plant expansion aggravated this problem further. In many mill communities, the construction of additional steel-making facilities required the complete demolition of entire Black neighborhoods. In Homestead, where tank and naval armor were produced, most Blacks lived "below the tracks" in an area directly adjacent to the local steel works.[16] Shortly after the war began, leveling of these residential areas commenced. Several open hearth furnaces, a forge and machine shop, a plate mill, and other facilities were to occupy these now-vacant spaces.[17] By late January, 1942 over 60 percent of these twelve hundred homes had been destroyed, and only one thousand of the ten thousand inhabitants still remained. Indeed, the "population was thinning rapidly," and by early February, "the wrecking of lower Homestead approached its final stages."[18] Similarly, in Duquesne, plans had been made to build three electric furnaces, a conditioning plant, and a heat-treating facility.[19] As in Homestead, this meant that more than twenty-five hundred people living in Castle

Garden, an area bordering the Duquesne steel works, had to vacate their homes to make way for these new facilities.[20]

Housing shortages from mill expansion and renewed Black migration to western Pennsylvania were partially allayed by building government-sponsored housing. However, at no time during the war were housing accommodations sufficient for Blacks in the Pittsburgh area. Only one housing project, Steel City Terrace, was built in the Farrell-Sharon vicinity. Blacks occupied 50, or 33 percent, of the 150 units.[21] However, even these were not adequate. Local residents filled them so quickly that none were "available for in-migrants." Instead, Farrell's Black newcomers had to reside in buildings that had been converted into living quarters, but these were also in short supply. Although "40 trailers" were likewise made available to "in-migrants and their families," none without spouses or children were "permitted to rent" these dwellings.[22] The Cochrandale project in Duquesne included 83 units, and the Blair Heights development in Clairton had 148 units, all of which were occupied by Black tenants.[23] Yet housing for Blacks in both towns remained limited, and in many cases overcrowded. Consequently, Blacks imported by Carnegie-Illinois Steel to its Clairton works were provided with rooms in Pittsburgh, over twenty miles from where they worked. Other Blacks working at the Clairton coke facility lived at the Quonset Barracks in Duquesne, seven miles away. Black migrants in Duquesne had similar difficulties in arranging for lodging. In addition to the vacancies at the local mill dormitory, officials at the Duquesne steelworks found "35 rooms in 'nice homes' for Black newcomers." However, an investigation by the Urban League of Pittsburgh revealed "that after a period of a month or two, the men who had been placed in rooms by the plant were expected to have found other accommodations and were forced to move for more incoming men."[24] Housing shortages existed also in Pittsburgh. Shortly after the war, the Pittsburgh Housing Association reported that Blacks needed over nine thousand additional dwelling units "to meet their present deficiencies."[25] Throughout western Pennsylvania, in spite of governmental efforts, housing remained sharply limited for Blacks.

Racial discrimination also persisted in the steel industry itself. At the end of World War II, forty percent of all industrial firms in Allegheny County still denied any employment to Blacks.[26] In 1942, the Urban League of Pittsburgh hired Jesse Hawkins, a young Black, to apply at several mills in the Carnegie and East Pittsburgh area for a job as a common laborer. Officials at Superior Steel and Columbia

Steel rebuffed him by simply saying, "We're not hiring." Bethlehem Steel and American Steel Band both emphatically stated that "no colored labor" was used in their mills. Shortly thereafter, a local League official concluded in a letter to Robert C. Weaver of the Fair Employment Practices Committee "that there are still plants in this area which refuse to hire Negroes even as common labor."[27]

Discrimination kept Blacks who did find work in Allegheny County primarily in the ranks of the unskilled. Although the proportion of Blacks in semiskilled positions began to equal that of whites, at 41.4 to 46.5 percent respectively, whites continued to outstrip Blacks in the skilled categories. Approximately 41.9 percent of all employed whites worked as skilled laborers, while 16.7 percent of all employed Blacks held such positions. On the other hand, 42 percent of all Blacks worked in unskilled positions, compared to only 11.6 percent of all whites.[28] The experiences of Percy Foster and Theodore Spencer, who both sought skilled positions in local steel firms, was common for most Blacks. Foster tried to get hired as a chipper at the Blaw Know Steel Company in Pittsburgh. Despite his four years of experience in that trade, he was offered a laborer's job "on the grounds that [the] company did not hire Negroes as chippers." Spencer had extensive training as a machinist. After suffering an injury while on active duty in the Marines, he spent an eight-month convalescence in a hospital. Soon thereafter, the United States Employment Service referred him for a job at the Mackintosh & Hemphill Company in Midland. A telephone interview with a company official revealed that Spencer qualified for a vacant position consistent with his skills. However, when he appeared at the plant, his race was evident and he was informed that the job had just been taken. Nonetheless, a position "sweeping" was immediately offered to the young Black veteran.[29]

Blacks already employed in area steel facilities frequently encountered discriminatory practices from both plant officials and white fellow workmen. J. Burrell Reid, a migrant from Virginia, had become a chauffeur to an official of the Jones & Laughlin Steel Company in 1927. When his employer died in 1936, Reid secured a job as a janitor in the all-white metallurgy department at Jones & Laughlin's South Side plant in Pittsburgh. Later, the wartime draft led to a high turnover of young men in the department, and consequently a friendly mill official persuaded Reid, now in his forties, to inquire about one of the vacant positions. To Reid's great dismay, the foreman in that department flatly refused to consider him for such an advancement.[30] Howard Lee, another Black employee at the South Side mills, tried to get a better job, either as a "rigger, sheeter, strip mill worker, or pipefitter helper," but he met with no success. Lee, a former employee at the Pittsburgh Coal Company mine in Library, stated that:

> white men who formerly worked with him and with the same experience were transferred to these jobs while he was told by his foremen [that] there was no point in referring Negroes to those departments as they would not be acceptable because of race.[31]

Louis Causby, a Black steelworker at Jones & Laughlin's Aliquippa Works, had the same trouble securing a promotion. He had ten years of experience as a straightener's helper in the 14-inch mill. In 1943 Causby tried to become a straightener himself, but opposition from the foremen blocked this attempt. Soon thereafter, two whites, who both lacked Causby's experience, were hired as straighteners.[32]

When Black women became steelworkers in western Pennsylvania, they too encountered the same discrimination which had checked the progress of their sons, husbands, and fathers. Unlike white women, female Blacks had initial difficulties just in getting hired. In 1943, nineteen-year-old Frances Stanton needed to support herself and her infant daughter while her husband served in the armed forces. However, she complained that the Clairton steel works was hiring white women "everyday in the week," while totally ignoring her employment inquiry.[38] Another Black woman, Mrs. William Scott, who had a son "booked for the Navy," expressed her dismay about job discrimination in a letter to President Franklin D. Roosevelt:

> They don't seem to be hiring colored women in Washington County at all. There are two plants close by, one in Washington, that is Jessop Steel, and the one in Bridgeville, but they will hire the white girls but when the colored girls go there they always refuse them.[34]

Several women applied for jobs at the Homestead steel works and a few other defense plants in the Pittsburgh area, and found that white women received preference in hiring. One of these Black women, Ruth Boyd, believed it was ridiculous to get relief "when there is so much defense work in demand." She wondered "how is it I cannot have a chance to work . . . [?]"[36]

Like Black men, female Blacks, if they did secure jobs in the mills, frequently encountered unfair treatment, particularly in their job assignments. At Jones & Laughlin in Aliquippa, Black women received strenuous assignments pushing wheelbarrows full of bricks for the blast furnaces, while white women received lighter assignments.[37] Ethel Cotton worked as a grinder at the Crucible steel plant in Midland. This physically exacting position had "no regulated rest periods," and eventually caused her to injure her wrist. When she saw that white women were being assigned to "lighter work" as paint girls, she too requested a transfer to that department. However, her superior bluntly told her to accept either "grinding" or no job at all![38] Bessie Simmons had a similar position in the ordnance department at the Carnegie-Illinois steel facility in Farrell. She also wanted to leave her job as a grinder in the burr gang. When she asked Sam Ruieko, her foreman, "if colored girls could get better jobs," he told her that they were simply not "wanted" in other departments.[39] In 1943, the Carnegie-Illinois plant in Clairton hired Bessie Martin, Florence Carr, and Lucretia Hamlin as jamb cutters in the mill batteries. Their boss promised them that they would perform these duties for only four of the eight hours on their shift. They would spend the remaining time "on less arduous toil away from the batteries." After working there for six days, their boss approached them again to inquire whether they would work the full eight hours as jamb cutters. When they replied negatively, he fired them. Likewise, when they asked for transfers, he told them, "unless you cut jambs, there is no other place here for you." Although plant officials customarily transferred white women to other departments after three days in this section of the mill, they refused to inaugurate the same practice for Black women.[40]

Discriminatory treatment in the mills stimulated an unprecedented militancy among Black steelworkers. Their protest to employers was part of a general mood of defiance which characterized Black behavior during World War II. In 1933, Blacks had completely staffed the coke division of the Carnegie-Illinois by-products plant in Clairton. But at that time, company officials had begun to require Black veterans to teach newer white workers how the coke division operated. When this task had been accomplished, whites replaced their Black instructors, who were "transferred to other departments and jobs of a lower classification." These and other similar experiences continued into the war period and eventually prompted a series of work stoppages among Black Clairton steelworkers between December 1943 and February 1944. These lasted from one to four hours. Finally, on February 25, at midnight, over 600 Black workmen "claiming that they were being denied promotions and actually being passed over by white men with far less seniority," went on a much longer strike. Since the coke and gas made at the Clairton by-products plant were piped to

several Carnegie-Illinois mills which lined the banks of the Mononga-
hela River, this walkout threatened to idle close to thirty thousand
steel employees. Consequently, the swift return of these striking
Black workers to the coke and gas-making operations became a matter
of crucial importance. At the instigation of the Fair Employment Practices Committee, the local steelworkers' union formulated a compromise that allocated 20 "top machine jobs" equally between Black ad
white steelworkers. The acceptance of this formula allowed Carnegie-
Illinois Steel to resume normal production in all of its nearby mill
facilities.[41] Promises from representatives of the Office of Price Administration to investigate high rents and an assurance from Carnegie-Illinois Steel that it would construct another housing project
brought Black strikers back to work.[42]

Similar kinds of racial unrest also appeared among Black Jones &
Laughlin employees in western Pennsylvania. In 1943, 450 Blacks in
the 14-inch bar mill at the Aliquippa plant went on strike, protesting
the company's refusal to promote two Blacks to the positions of inspector and straightener.[43] In 1944, thirty Black clearners "shut down
operations in the Rod and Wire Mill," idling 2,800 workers. Dissatisfaction with their wages and working conditions caused these Aliquippa Blacks to walk off their jobs.[44] As elsewhere, Black steelworkers at Jones & Laughlin's Pittsburgh plants relied on strikes whenever
they encountered discrimination. In 1943, Black boiler firemen at the
South Side Works discovered that their white counterparts at the
Eliza plant received 93 cents per hour in wages, while they earned
only 82 cents per hour. Finally in 1945, after repeated failures by the
union and the FEPC to eliminate this differential in negotiation with
company officials, twenty-eight Black firemen walked off their jobs.
As a result, the entire power plant at the South Side Works shut down
and eleven thousand workmen were idled. [45] The grant of a 5-cent
increase in wages finally ended the strike.

The presence of Black unionists in western Pennsylvania and a well-
articulated national policy against racial discrimination prompted local unions to pay special attention to the condition of Black steelworkers. At the Duquesne steel works, Thomas McIver, Edward Campbell,
John Campbell, Carl Dickerson, Roger Payne, Jim Grinage, and other
Black unionists were conspicuous in their support of Local 1256 in its
many disputes with plant officials. Similarly, "Bus" Taylor played an
active role in union affairs at the Carnegie-Illinois plant in Homestead.[46] In recognition of Black participation in the Clairton steel
union, Local 1557 began contributing to the local NAACP.[47] At Jones

& Laughlin's Aliquippa Works, the president of Local 1211 gave vigorous support to eight Black laborers denied promotions in the plant's 14-inch mill. Moreover, he vehemently denounced the firm to the War Manpower Commission when it refused to employ 150 Black female applicants "except as dishwashers in the [plant] restaurant."[48] Midland workers, both Black and white, supported a Black steelworker in his conflict with Mackintosh-Hemphill because they believed he had suffered discrimination "because of his union activities."[49] James McCoy, a Black employee at the Continental Roll and Steel Foundry in Coraopolis, served in several union offices before becoming president of his steelworkers' local. Consequently, when Black employers met "with subtle and flagrant forms of segregation," white unionists threatened to walk off their jobs to protest company discrimination.[50] United Steelworkers President Philip Murray also made an important gesture to Blacks when in 1942 he appointed Boyd L. Wilson as his special assistant for Negro affairs. Murray, who also headed the CIO, appointed Wilson to the federation's Committee for the Elimination of Racial Discrimination.[51]

Yet, in spite of these gestures, Blacks could not totally rely on the United Steel Workers of America to lift the yoke of discrimination from them. In some cases, local unions were ineffective in presenting Black grievances to employees. In other instances, the local union leaders and the rank-and-file workers held the same racial prejudices as the managers of the steel companies. William Fountain, a Black employee at Crucible Steel in Midland, became especially frustrated with the United Steel Workers of America. In 1942, he attended the organization's convention in Cleveland, and came away impressed with its outspoken stand "against Hitlerism, both at home and abroad."[52] However, his optimism changed once he returned to Midland. Plant officials at Crucible Steel hired Blacks almost exclusively in the coke works and in labor gangs. They did not allow Blacks to enter any skilled occupations or to work in the shell factory, except when extra men were needed "to get out production." Fountain complained that "repeated requests to . . . union officials . . . to look into upgrading for Negro workers have been ignored." He accused Edward Melvin, the president of Local 1212, and Bert Hough, the United Steelworkers district director for the Beaver Valley, of having a "do-nothing attitude" which was causing a "growing resentment" among Black laborers toward the United Steelworkers.[53]

At the Clairton steel plant, Blacks in the coke works had gone on strike because management had completely replaced Black machine operators with whites. In December 1943, the local union concluded an agreement with Carnegie-Illinois Steel which established a line of promotion "from laborer straight . . . to the top machine job." Blacks felt that this new contract provided displaced Black machine operators with no opportunity to regain their jobs, and represented the union's tacit approval of the company's recent discriminatory practices. Although the matter was finally adjudicated to the satisfaction of all parties, Local 1557 had clearly failed to conduct an "educational program" about the new agreement which was sensitive to the concerns of its Black members.[54] Local 1049 at the American Steel Band Company in Pittsburgh raised no protest when a Black applied for a position in the production department and was told by the personnel officer that "Negroes . . . were used solely as janitors and window washers." The acting district director, John F. Murray, responded by saying that the issue of whether to hire Blacks was "a matter for the Company to decide." William Evans, the president of the local union, dismissed the episode by declaring that "we have never had any negroes in our plant and when that negro came for a job we didn't have any kind of opening for him or anyone else." He went on to indicate that his local would take a stand on Black employment at American Steel Band when "our union is confronted with such a situation."[55]

Without the United Steelworkers of America as a reliable advocate, Black laborers in western Pennsylvania frequently looked to the Fair Employment Practices Committee to solve the problem of discrimination. Responsibility for receiving complaints and settling disputes rested with the agency's Division of Field Operation. The agency had twelve regional offices located in key cities throughout the nation. Pittsburgh and its environs were included in Region III, and Black steelworkers in the area made their charges of discrimination to the Region III Philadelphia office. In each case, a field investigator went to the plant in question, and tried to secure voluntary compliance from all parties on an agreed-on settlement.[56] In November, 1944 Roger Williams, a Black employee at the Jones & Laughlin Works in Pittsburgh, was placed in charge of a small group of track laborers. He received no raise in pay for performing this extra duty. However, the white man who succeeded him did get a pay bonus for doing the same job as Williams. The FEPC intervened after receiving a complaint from this aggrieved Black steelworker. After conferring with plant officials, the field investigator announced that Williams would be restored to his job as gang leader and receive a retroactive increase in pay.[57] John Anderson, a Black soldier, was released from duty along with four whites to work at the Union Steel Castings Company in Pittsburgh. Eventually each of the four whites was given a chance to do skilled work, while Anderson remained a molder's helper earning 78 cents per hour. The FEPC, along with an army ordnance official, stepped in and secured a better job for Anderson, making cores at $1.19 per hour.[58]

FEPC investigators arranged conferences and made inquiries about the employment policies of mills and foundries in western Pennsylvania holding defense contracts. When the C.G. Hussey Steel Company allegedly discriminated against Black women, two field operators went to Pittsburgh to inquire about the charge. After talking with plant officials and to union representatives, the FEPC learned that both had become advocates of "hiring Negro women."[59] Black steelworkers at Local 1592 in Pittsburgh told the FEPC that they were "paid less than white workers." Consequently, a field examiner came "to discuss the future plans of the union in regard to seniority rights and pay rates" of these Black workmen.[60] A FEPC representative also traveled to Sharon to confer with a United Citizens Committee about "the employment problems of the Negroes in [that] community." During his stay in the area, the examiner visited the Carnegie-Illinois Steel plant in nearby Farrell, which had been charged with discrimination against Black women. Since "Negro girls" had been recently assigned to the disputed department, the FEPC official declared it "a correction of [the] original complaint" and closed the case.[61]

The FEPC clearly helped to stem the tide of racial discrimination in area mills and foundries. With this in mind, the "colored citizens" of Blairsville wrote the agency in 1945, inviting its cooperation in seeing that "negro men and women be hired at a local defense plant." After asking FEPC officials to "make adequate means in helping us," they received a rather dismal reply. Since the status of the FEPC was uncertain in Congress, all "regional and subregional offices [are compelled] to curtail their field trips."[62] However, agency officials made plans to open a subregional office in Pittsburgh.[63] In 1946, despite protests by Black leaders, Congressional appropriations for FEPC expired. Although the agency had existed only briefly, it had tried to reverse the pattern of discrimination which kept Blacks in lower-echelon jobs and denied them pay equal to most whites. Although it met with remarkable success in performing these tasks, the FEPC did not survive long enough to complete its work.[64]

Postwar cutbacks generally spared long-time Black steelworkers in the Pittsburgh steel district. But the problem of racial discrimination persisted after 1945. An Allegheny County race relations survey in

1946 revealed that the majority of Black workers remained disproportionately concentrated within unskilled and semiskilled occupations.
Over half of all firms in the county continued to segregate Blacks into
special job categories that usually paid less than assignments given to
whites.[65] John Hughey, who in 1947 began to work at the Carrie
Furnaces in Rankin, witnessed a more subtle form of racial discrimination. In 1947, Black steelworkers predominated in the sintering
plant, the blast furnaces, and the open-hearth department. Between
1947 and 1950, Carnegie-Illinois Steel updated its equipment and
machinery. Although these technological advances eased the work of
most plant employees, they required a reduction in the number of
Carrie furnaces from six to four. Few men were displaced, but new
jobs became scarce. When senior employees in these "solid Black"
departments began dying and retiring, they were almost always replaced by whites.[66]

Although racial discrimination was not new to the steel industry,
the refusal of Blacks to endure it without organized protest meant that
times had changed. The World War II period gave Black steelworkers
a legacy of activism that manifested itself in the postwar period in
continued work stoppages to protest unfair employment practices. In
1946 and 1947, Blacks at the Jones & Laughlin mills in Pittsburgh
staged wildcat strikes to protest company discrimination. One Black
striker remarked:

> The men knew that they were risking their jobs in this walkout
> . . . but they had got worked up to the point where this didn't
> seem so important . . . They were tired of never getting pro-
> moted, and they were tired of being treated like dogs by . . .
> white foremen. . . .[67]

During the 1950s, Blacks at the Clairton steel plant went on strike
because a Black with sufficient seniority failed to become a skilled
pusher. With backing from Local 1557, the strike won a promotion for
the aggrieved Black employee.[68] Despite the absence of a federal FEPC
and only the occasional support of the United Steelworkers of America, Black steelworkers remained militant. They fought discrimination
by staging wildcat strikes, by informational picketing, and by signing
protest petitions that were presented to company and union officials.
In western Pennsylvania Black steelworkers continued to use collective action to advance their interests, even if they had to challenge the
trade unions that did not always represent all the men and women
who were members of the steel industry's labor force.

CHAPTER 14

Life at the Rouge: A Cycle of Workers' Control

NELSON LICHTENSTEIN

To attempt a historical account of working-class militancy in an era of widespread trade union retreat may seem an exercise in presumption or nostalgia. Yet even as the employers' offensive and the concession bargaining of the 1980s have brought an end to one era of union history, so have these hard times simultaneously raised one of the central issues of all social history: who controls the work place? As the American economy undergoes a massive economic and technological transformation, the distribution of power and authority in office and factory has again become an issue of serious political and ideological debate. How far does management's writ extend, and upon what resources can the working class call to advance its own frontier of control? Since these issues are hardly new, there may yet be some profit in taking a closer look at the cycle of shop-floor conflict that once engulfed what was the world's premier manufacturing facility in the middle third of the 20th century.

Built and expanded in the two decades after 1917, the Ford Motor Company's giant River Rouge complex at Dearborn represented perhaps the most advanced example of the early twentieth century revolution in industrial technology and work reorganization. Characterized by the massive use of electrically-driven machine tools and the most elaborate deployment of assembly-line production methods, the Rouge, wrote historian Allen Nevins, "brilliantly realized Ford's dream of continuous, integrated manufacture." Coal and iron ore were unloaded on the docks, and thirty-three hours later they had been transformed into a Ford automobile that scooted off the assembly line under its own power.[1]

The Rouge plant was undoubtedly the largest concentration of machinery and labor anywhere in the world. By 1940 there were nineteen separate units at the Rouge, many of which could have stood alone as very large factories or mills in their own right. The most important facilities at the Rouge were the power plant, a fully integrated steel mill, a glass production facility, a foundry, a stamping plant, the motor building, the assembly plant, and a large tool and die room. A giant fifteen-thousand-worker Pratt and Whitney Aircraft Building was constructed just before the war. Almost eighty thousand production workers labored at "the Rouge," in a huge complex that sprawled for more than two square miles on the south side of the Rouge River. Set apart from the rest of the Detroit metropolitan area by a series of highways, canals, and railroad tracks, the Rouge stood as a mighty industrial city that seemingly dwarfed the thousands of workers who streamed in and out of its gates each day. As early as 1932 the great Mexican artist, Diego Rivera, captured some of the imaginative power, the physical complexity, and the sheer brutality of this enterprise in his famous series of murals painted on the walls of the Detroit Art Institute.[2]

Control of materials and men was central to the Ford managerial vision, but the highly integrated character of the production process at the Rouge did not mean that Ford managers had achieved that "technical control" of the work force which Richard Edwards and other sociologists have recently described as a primary characteristic of semiskilled production work in the first half of the twentieth century.[3] Although Henry Ford and his brilliant production chief, Charles E. Sorenson, spurned incentive pay schemes as unnecessary in a thoroughly mechanized production process, the overwhelming majority of Ford Motor Company workers did not labor under the coercive work regime of the moving assembly line itself. Probably eighty percent of Rouge employees worked in an environment which was functionally, but not physically, linked to other elements of the production process. For example, in the motor building several hundred individual operations were necessary to machine an engine block and then assemble it. Although completed in sequence, no mechanized conveyor moved the block past each worker as was the case with the assembly of the car chassis and body. In motor assembly each worker determined, within limits, the pace at which his operation would be completed and the block manhandled on to the next work station. Photographs of this production process in the 1930s show a densely packed row of workers on both sides of the engine line.[4]

Since the technical process of production was incapable of maintaining labor discipline and productivity, this burden fell upon the foremen and building superintendents within the various units at the Rouge. Although Ford had stood at the forefront of "progressive" personnel administration in their period of the First World War, the Ford management style had become increasingly authoritarian and parochial in the 1920s and 1930s. The famous five-dollar day, which Ford had so dramatically inaugurated in 1914 as a means of reducing labor turnover and accommodating workers to an intensified work regime, had long ago been eroded by the inflationary surge of the First World War and then the wage reductions of the Depression. Ford paternalism had declined as well. When Ford's early efforts to reshape immigrant workers to an "American standard" collapsed, the corporation turned to more directly coercive methods to create a disciplined work force. Tight supervision and draconian work rules—no talking or sitting down, little personal relief time—were standard in the plant.[5] At the same time little uniformity existed in the way building superintendents handled labor in their various departments. Religious and ethnic favoritism was rife in hiring, promoting, and firing workers. The Masons were a particularly strong force within the supervisory ranks. Many Protestant workmen joined the order in hopes of advancing their career or at least protecting their job during the next layoff. Foremen, selected for their mechanical aptitude as well as their ability to "handle" the men, were instructed to get out production at the very lowest cost. Under pressure from their own superiors, they in turn used a series of intermediaries—straw bosses, leading men, and pushers—to force the pace of production in their departments.[6]

Simultaneously, the Ford Service Department operated as a parallel source of authority. Employing over two thousand individuals, the Service Department recruited many of its key personnel from outside the usual sources of factory manpower: the white-collar unemployed, small entrepreneurs gone bankrupt, the Detroit underworld, and parolees from the prison population. Run by Ford confidant Harry Bennett, the Service Department functioned as part spy organization, part old-fashioned patronage machine. Over the years the Department became increasingly integrated into the hierarchy of production itself. Ordinary workers were recruited into its ranks to serve as spies and goons even while they performed their daily tasks. And among the individuals who beat up auto union officers Richard Frankensteen and Walter Reuther at the well-photographed "Battle of the Overpass" in 1937 were Sam Taylor and Wilfred Comment, Ford foremen later promoted to building superintendents.[7] C.L.R. James once remarked that the internal work order at the Rouge came to resemble in America the closest equivalent to the labor discipline imposed by Stalinist or fascist regimes abroad. Many workers concurred in this assessment. Their popular name for Service Department personnel was the "Gestapo."[8]

The ethnic composition of the vast Ford work force provides a key to understanding the initial unionization process at the Rouge. In 1940 a least half of Ford workers were either black or first- and second-generation immigrants. Concentrated in the foundry and in unskilled maintenance occupations, about 12 percent of the Ford work force were black. Five percent were born in the British Isles and an equal proportion in Italy, 4 percent in Poland, 2 percent in Germany and in Austria, and those from Hungary, Romania, Russia, Yugoslavia, Lithuania, Malta, Syria, and Turkey each provided one percent or slightly less of the work force. Of the nearly fifty-two thousand (62%) which a 1940 Ford census of the Rouge listed as American-born, a sizable but unknown proportion were certainly second-generation immigrants who still identified strongly with their ethnic community.[9]

The ethnic and occupational divisions in the Ford work force provide a rough guide to the hetrogeneous level of union consciousness that existed at the Rouge in the late Depression years. British and German immigrants, many with Socialist or union backgrounds in their native labor movements, were concentrated in the seven-thousand-man tool and die unit at the Rouge. With their plant-wide mobility and articulate intelligence, these skilled workers naturally took on leadership roles in the union-organizing drive and in the new Ford local. In the 1930s and 1940s, craft pride often merged with and reinforced a sense of class consciousness. Three of the first six presidents of the local were skilled workers; a total of four were from Britain or Scotland.[10]

Estimates of the number of Poles at the Rouge run as high as ten thousand of the first and second generation, and Italians probably accounted for about the same number. Semiskilled workers from these nationality groups dominated two of the larger units at the Rouge, the nine-thousand-man motor building and the eight thousand employees in the pressed-steel unit. Along with other Southern and Eastern European Catholics, these two ethnic groups provided much of the social terrain upon which the battle for the organization of the Rouge would take place. Most of the nine thousand blacks at the Rouge labored in either the foundry or in unskilled maintenance jobs spread throughout the plant. During the UAW's initial organizing effort, they remained remarkably loyal to the company. Ford was the major employer of black labor in Detroit; compared to other available work, employment at the Rouge was highly desirable in the black community. Moreover, Ford maintained a close relationship with the black churches and with such community groups as the Urban League and the NAACP, both of which remained decidedly anti-union until the early 1940s.[11]

When it finally took place, the union breakthrough at the Rouge came with a rush. In 1937 the UAW had probably organized about twenty thousand Ford workers, but this initial campaign had been smashed by wholesale firings, Service Department intimidation, and internal union factionalism. In November 1940 the UAW and the CIO reopened the Ford organizing drive with a well-coordinated, well-financed campaign administered directly by the national CIO itself. The organizing drive was notable for the sensitivity with which it targeted Ford's ethnic workers. Meetings were frequently held in the churches and fraternal halls of the Polish, Ukranian, Finnish, and Italian communities. The CIO established separate committees to target workers in the Italian and black communities, where union sentiment seemed weak. The International Workers Order, a Communist-oriented fraternal organization, played a particularly active role, laying the foundations for the considerable following the Party would command at the Rouge a few years later.[12]

Until February 1941 this organizing effort was modestly successful, with recruitment taking place on a one-to-one basis, usually at off-plant locations. ("I got my Ford Worker" buttons were distributed throughout UAW ranks.) In December 1940, the union secured repeal of a restrictive Dearborn handbill ordinance; then in February the U.S. Supreme Court upheld a National Labor Relations Board decision that forced the company to rehire several unionists who had been fired in the years since 1937. Returning to the motor building with union buttons prominently displayed, these UAW cadre made a powerful impression throughout the Rouge. A steward system sprang up in virtually every department, and the Ford membership drive, which had been recruiting about one thousand a month since November, now exploded, with more than twenty thousand signing up in February and March 1941. During these two months, managerial and Service Department authority was repeatedly challenged, with sitdown strikes taking place in the rolling mill, the motor building, and the B

building (automobile assembly). When the company fired key unionists in late March, almost the entire plant shut down on April 1 in the
great walkout that finally forced Ford to bargain with the UAW.[13]

The Ford-UAW contract signed in June 1941 proved virtually
unique in heavy industry. It covered workers not only at the Rouge,
but at all Ford factories, even in far-flung assembly plants with little
union presence in 1941. Moreover, the contract mandated a full union
shop and dues checkoff, which the rest of the auto industry did not
concede until the 1950s. The new contract sharply reduced the power
of the Service Department by including all nonmanagement plant
protection men in the union and providing that they must wear uniforms at all times. Finally, and perhaps most significantly, the Ford
agreement provided for a system of full-time union committeemen, at
a ratio of one for every 550 employees. This full recognition of a
powerful shop representation system differed markedly from the situation at both General Motors and Chrysler, where management
strongly resisted and only grudgingly conceded the growth of such
"released-time union representation."[14] This unique committeemen
system had many ramifications at the Rouge: in the early years it
seemed to legitimize and advance the direct exercise of union power
on the shop floor itself. Moreover, the existence of a corps of more
than one hundred fifty full-time union activists in a single plant provided the social and institutional basis for the continuously high level
of political factionalism that characterized Local 600 during the next
several years.

The UAW would certainly have settled for less, so why did Ford
agree to this extraordinary contract? We can certainly discount the
widely reported but highly debatable personal influence of Edsel and
Clara Ford, son and wife of the company founder, who are thought to
have taken a more liberal view of industrial-relations problems. Undoubtedly of more significance was the inability of Ford managers like
Harry Bennett to conceive of any system of authority in the plant
which was not of a unitary character. In other words, if building
superintendents did not control the work force, then this responsibility must be handed over to someone else. In fact, there is some
evidence that the strong measures the UAW International took in
suppressing the "wildcat" North American Aviation defense strike in
early June 1941 may have prompted Ford negotiators to expect a
similar union disciplinary effort at the Rouge. At the same time, and
in a somewhat contradictory vein, Ford strategists thought union
strength was fragile and transitory. Bennett certainly hoped that if all

Ford workers were automatically enrolled in the union, those loyal to the old regime would gradually increase their influence in the new locals, possibly transforming some of them into pliant company unions.[15]

If this was management's expectation, it proved a fantasy. Ford's recognition of Local 600 touched off a virtual revolution on the shop floor, which generated a condition that can only be described as one of industrial "dual power." Production standards were everywhere cut back, petty shop rules that regulated smoking, loafing, eating, and talking were suspended and unpopular foremen were often physically forced out of their departments. Ford loyalists who ran for union posts were overwhelmingly defeated. Although the contract mandated a four-step grievance procedure, UAW committeemen functioned less as grievance processors and more as roving troubleshooters. In the motor building, where supervision has always been particularly tight, Local 600 education director Frank Marquart reported that workers chose as their representative a man who had done an outstanding job as a picket captain during the strike.

> When he was elected committeeman, he walked over to the foreman, pointed to his shiny committeeman's button, and exclaimed: "Do you see this?" The foreman replied, "Ah yes, you are the new committeeman, congratulations." The Committeeman snapped, "Congratulations hell, I'm running this department now—you scram the hell out of here."[16]

Although strike statistics are not always an accurate guide to worker consciousness, they are the most readily available quantative measure of shop-floor conflict with management. During the course of World War II, when neither the UAW nor the Ford local formally authorized any stoppages, there were some 773 strikes of all kinds at the Rouge. In the 22 months following June 1942, 303 such wildcats took place, costing 932,000 hours of work. About 70 percent were protests over discipline, supervision, and working conditions, issues intimately associated with the structure of authority in the plant. Although these stoppages decreased after the war, the level of wildcat or unauthorized strikes remained about six times higher at Ford than at industry leader General Motors. Between 1950 and 1955, an era not notable for union militancy, some 185 unauthorized strikes took place at the Rouge, involving 635,000 lost hours of work. Most of these strikes were so-called "quickie" stoppages involving anywhere from half a dozen to a few hundred employees who halted work for a shift or less in duration. They typically began when management retimed an operation or changed a job assignment, then insisted that the employees meet the new standard or duty. If they refused or proved sluggish, foremen took disciplinary action against those who failed to meet the new level of work intensity. At this point the issue in the strike became less the original grievance than the discipline itself, and committeemen might "adopt" such a protest, leading an entire department out in defense of those penalized. During these brief strikes a good deal of physical conflict often took place, involving strikers, foremen, and plant protection men. Unit-wide stoppages took place throughout the 1940s and early 1950s, especially in the foundry, open hearth, aircraft, motor, and B buildings.[17]

Job actions of this sort were not counterposed to the union infrastructure, nor were they simply due to the wave of industrially-undisciplined workers who surged into wartime factories. Rather, they represented an extracontractual dimension of union influence and power. In Local 600's early years, most of the serious wildcat strikes were either led or condoned by union committeemen or veteran union activists.[18] Thus in March 1944, after a particularly disruptive "riot" staged by Aircraft Unit workers in the building personnel office, Ford discharged twenty leading participants, including eleven committeemen whom management considered most responsible for the maintenance of order among their fellow workers. "Who are these [fired] members?" asked *Ford Facts*, the organ of Local 600: "Militant union leaders, district and building committeemen, the backbone of the UAW-CIO."[19]

Despite their opposition to wartime strikes, the Communists were among the chief beneficiaries of the union breakthrough at the Rouge. Because of the Party's size and ethnic composition, a steady trickle of Ford workers had joined the Party since the early 1920s when communists first distributed clandestine shop newspapers. In 1932 the CP had been the chief organizer of the "Ford Hunger March" during which four participants had been killed by Service Department and police bullets. In the late Depression years there were about thirty-five to fifty Communists active at the Rouge, of whom the most important was Bill McKie, a Scottish skilled worker who did much to build the "underground" UAW there. Communists gained additional credibility in the organizing drive of 1940 and 1941 when perhaps a quarter of the paid staffers were Party members or closely associated with its politics. The union breakthrough made it possible for the

Communists to function as a more or less legitimate part of the union scene, especially during World War II when they enthusiastically endorsed the CIO's brand of patriotic productionism. The Party's numerical strength grew rapidly after 1941 and by the end of the war probably numbered close to four hundred fifty throughout the entire Rouge. Many more workers looked to the Communists for political leadership on a wide range of trade union issues.[20]

The Party maintained fractions or clubs in most of the major buildings at the Rouge, frequently taking top leadership posts in the motor, plastics, pressed steel, tool and die, axle, and foundry units. McKie, one of the few white Communists to openly assert his political affiliation, was repeatedly elected a local trustee, while John Gallo, a Communist who was also the former Golden Gloves champion of Michigan, used his many connections in the Italian community to help him win plant-wide elections throughout the 1940s and early 1950s. Led by the enormously talented Paul Boatin, the Motor Building became known as one of the most highly politicized and militant units at the Rouge, but the single most important center of Party strength was among the black workers in the foundry. Although many blacks had actually served as strikebreakers during the April 1941 walkout, the process of unionization worked an enormous transformation in the consciousness of these first-generation industrial workers. For the next decade at least, the Rouge foundry was the center of civil rights militancy in the Detroit area and a training ground for a generation of black leaders. The communist Party, whose advocacy of black rights figured so prominently in this era, was an integral part of this social transformation. The two most open communists in the Ford plant were black foundrymen Nelson Davis and Joe Bullips, while Shelton Tappes, a "fellow traveler" from the foundry, was regularly elected Local 600 Secretary-Treasurer during World War II. As late as 1948 Davis could sell several hundred subscriptions to the *Daily Worker* in the Rouge foundry each year, while another black Communist, Art McPhaul, boasted that about half the members of this department in Pressed Steel read the Communist paper regularly.[21]

Although other UAW locals were sometimes led outright by Communist or fellow-traveling unionists, it was only at the Rouge that the Party achieved something close to a mass base among rank and file unionists. The Party was able to do this less by virtue of any particular "Party line" it propagated at the Rouge, than by the skillful fashion with which it merged its organizational identity with that of the union and the social aspirations of the Rouge work force. Until the late 1940s, the Party did not "colonize" the Rouge: Party members there were organically rooted in the ethnic and working-class structures of the plant and surrounding community. At the Rouge the Party seems to have tempered, in practice if not in rhetoric, its World-War-II defense of the CIO no-strike pledge. This deviation from official policy accommodated the militant attitude of the Ford work force. As elsewhere, the Party sought to maintain a "center-left" alliance with the top leadership, and for more than a decade it succeeded, playing an influential role in Local 600's political and organizational affairs. But the Party's importance lay not so much in the specific offices or posts its members held. Rather, more crucial was the degree to which the Party's presence helped sustain an ideological and activist political environment, thereby encouraging a level of debate and rank-and-file mobilization rarely matched in other UAW locals. It was in partial tribute to this influence that, when Harry Bennett appointed Ford's first officer in charge of overall industrial relations, he chose John Bugas, an FBI man familiar with labor radicalism.[22]

Another important index of the new relationship of forces at the Rouge came with the dramatic decline in prestige and power of the four thousand foremen who worked there. In prewar years Ford foreman had been noted for their often brutal and capricious exercise of power, and as long as they got production out, they retained virtually unchallenged authority in their respective departments. Preunion foremen often took enormous pride in their mastery of the technology of production, but they also inhabited a world of insecurity and fear. No grievance procedure, seniority system, or standard pay and promotion scale existed. Administrative lines of authority were indistinct and overlapping, employment records often went unrecorded, and a Masonic "job trust" controlled many managerial posts.

The unionization of the Rouge struck this massive but archaic supervisory structure like a whirlwind. "We noticed a very definite change in attitude of the working man," recalled one supervisor. "They got very independent. It was terrible for a while . . . the bosses were just people to look down on after the union came in."[23] Some foremen were physically forced out of their departments, but all foremen felt their power ebb as the UAW developed a set of uniform regulations to govern shop-floor working conditions. Seniority rules, job bidding, and grievance procedures gave workers an elementary sense of job security because these contractual devices sharply limited the foreman's ability to either reward or punish his subordinates. Meanwhile, UAW committeemen often short-circuited the foremen's power, taking grievances directly to the various building superintendents where the real power lay. Ford executives initially cooperated with this process, either because they doubted the loyalty of their foremen or because they considered union problems far too important to be left to these lowly management representative. The union finally effectively stripped line foremen of the various helpers, assistants, and straw bosses who had provided them with the human tools they had relied upon to enforce discipline and production standards. The UAW insisted that any individual who worked on production had to be a union member, so these intermediate categories were either upgraded to full foreman status or redefined as utility or relief workers.[24]

These dramatic changes sparked an enormously successful unionization effort among Ford foremen themselves. Organization began in August 1941 in the new Pratt and Whitney Aircraft Building. In this massive but still incomplete facility, the technical landscape seemed as chaotic as the shop-floor social relations were explosive. To staff the new facility, Ford managers had recruited fifty of their most proficient foremen from the rest of the Rouge, but when they arrived at the still-incomplete Aircraft Building they found machine tools scattered everywhere, an inexperienced but militantly led work force, and a set of blueprints that required clever shop-floor modification before actual production of the complicated, precision-tooled Pratt and Whitney engines could begin. With all the headaches associated with setting up a new operation under wartime conditions, many foremen were working seven days a week, ten hours a day, but their pay, they soon found, varied not according to their new work assignment but remained linked to their prewar job assignment.

All this offended their sense of order, efficiency and justice. Led by 28-year-old Robert Keys, a few aircraft unit foremen met as a social club in late summer, but by early fall they had begun holding larger Rouge-wide meetings. A November assembly of twelve hundred foremen formally established the Foreman's Association of America, which quickly won even more substantial support from supervisors throughout the Rouge, other Ford plants, and then much of the Detroit-area auto industry. Four thousand were enrolled at the end of 1941, nine thousand by the end of the next year. The FAA "comes as close to being a spontaneous development as anything that requires organization can be," admitted *Business Week* in 1942. By the time it reached its peak at the end of the war, the FAA had enrolled more than thirty-three thousand and extended throughout much of union-organized heavy industry.[25]

The FAA sought many of the same things as the UAW: seniority rights, a grievance procedure, a rational wage structure, but also the reorganization of the production hierarchy on a basis that would give foremen the authority and recognition they felt they deserved. FAA leaders were universally contemptuous of Ford's strife-ridden top management and they retained an almost Veblenesque sense of their centrality in the production process. "We are trying to establish a program in the plants where we work that the employers themselves have failed to establish," Keys told a House Committee in 1943, "a program of harmony, cooperation and efficiency."[26] Although individual foremen might feel hostile to the newly empowered rank and file, they now found distasteful the disciplinary tasks top management assigned them. In fact, the actual process of building a union drove the FAA into an increasingly intimate collaboration with the UAW as an institution and with rank-and-file workers as individuals. The Association conducted several departmental strikes at the Rouge to protest disciplinary action against its members, and in June 1943 disrupted production in a Rouge-wide stoppage by pulling most supervisors off the job. This led to negotiations with Ford management and a signed collective bargaining agreement in May 1944. The UAW welcomed formation of the FAA, and although rank-and-file union members crossed FAA lines during the war, they refused to take over foremen's supervisory tasks once inside the factory.[27] Of course, this informal UAW-FAA alliance represented a practical recognition that the new trade unions were the only force powerful enough to enable the Association to survive in their struggle with Ford and other major corporations. But on the wider arena of class politics, the foremen's turn to the working class proved a profound tribute to the ability of an aggressive union movement to sweep into its orbit whole social strata that in more socially quiescent periods might have stood against it.

If the foremen's abdication of management status symbolized something of a revolution in shop-floor social relations at the Rouge, then the counterrevolution was not long in coming. Beginning in late 1943, Ford managers began a decade-long effort to rewin control of the shop-floor work environment. By this time war production had actually passed its peak at the Rouge, and managers could afford to "take a strike" if their disciplinary efforts were resisted. More important, the old autocratic, short-sighted supervisors of the Harry Bennett stripe were being replaced by the new management team Henry Ford II had begun to assemble. Determined to emulate General Motors' corporate strategy and its "firm but fair" labor policy, the younger Ford and his new managers adopted a long-range program designed to bureaucratize industrial relations and reestablish labor discipline. In 1944 John Bugas took labor relations out of the hands of individual building superintendents and transferred them to a centralized personnel office. "Clearly defined policies were set out," reported labor relations lawyer Malcolm Denise, "particularly with reference to meeting out of disciplinary action and enforcement of production and other similar items. . . . It was established as an inflexible rule that no member of supervision would be removed as a consequence of union pressure, nor could any grievance requesting such actions be entertained."[28]

This policy was strongly endorsed by the new UAW-Ford umpire, Harry Shulman, who sought to establish a uniform system of shop-floor industrial jurisprudence. Shulman, a Yale Law School professor and former mediator in the heavily unionized clothing industry, had been installed as impartial grievance umpire by the National War Labor Board, which hoped that such third-party arbitration might improve Ford's wartime strike record. During the twelve influential years he served as umpire under the Ford contract, Shulman "tutored" both labor and management in what he considered responsible industrial relations. He insisted that Ford management rationalize its often chaotic system of shop discipline and respect the union's interest in determining job assignments and wage standards.[29] But Shulman also maintained that a mature relationship between management and workers could only succeed if the union helped suppress the tradition of shop-floor activism that had so rapidly become part of the industrial scene at the Rouge and other Ford plants. Local 600 committeemen who led or condoned wildcat strikes manifested "a romantic expression of a perverse and debasing view of the committeeman's obligations," argued Shulman.[30] Management's right to organize production and take the initiative in the maintenance of shop discipline stood at the core of Shulman's conception of industrial democracy. In a widely-read 1944 umpire opinion, this liberal jurist framed the issue in almost metahistorical terms:

> In any industrial plant, whatever may be the form of the political or economic organization in which it exists, problems are bound to arise. . . . These are not incidents peculiar to private

enterprise. They are incidents of human organization in any form of society. . . . But an industrial plant is not a debating society. Its object is production. When a controversy arises, production cannot wait for exhaustion of the grievance procedure; . . . production must go on. And someone must have the authority to direct the manner in which it is to go on until the controversy is settled. That authority is vested in Supervision. It must be vested there because the responsibility for production is also vested there; and responsibility must be accompanied by authority.[31]

This policy looked forward to postwar union-management cooperation, and in his famous "Human Engineering" speech of January 1946, Henry Ford II outlined a "progressive" labor policy in keeping with Shulman's perspective. "We do not want to destroy the union," he asserted, nor were any harsh legislative restrictions on the unions contemplated by the Ford Motor Company. Rather, Ford sought to help trade union leaders "assume the responsibilities they must assume if the public interest is to be served. It is clear, then, that we must look to an improved and increasingly responsible union leadership for help in solving the human equation in mass production. . . ."[32] Thus, in the crucial 1946 contract negotiations Ford readily agreed to renew the union shop and match the best contract the UAW could secure from strike-bound GM, but the corporation insisted upon a "company security" clause codifying management perogatives in elaborate detail. Bargaining for the UAW, Ford Director Richard Leonard demanded that the company have the contractual right to discipline those it considered guilty of unauthorized work stoppages. Keenly sensitive to the charge of irresponsibility, the UAW agreed to deny wildcat strikers use of the grievance machinery unless the entire local undertook a special investigation of the work-stoppage incident.

On the issue of production standards, the company also won stronger language. The original 1941 Ford-UAW agreement had ignored the issue, thus allowing committeemen and cohesive work groups considerable latitude when they actually bargained over the pace of work. The 1942 contract merely set forth the principle of a "fair days' work for a fair day's pay," but the 1946 contract contained the first specific clause giving management the right to determine, maintain, and enforce work standards. The Ford Motor Company could now fire any employee who refused to meet established standards or who engaged in any attempt "to participate in any plan to control or limit the amount or speed of production." Local 600, like other UAW locals, had the right to strike over production standards once they had exhausted the grievance procedure and won International Executive Board authorization, but shop-floor slowdowns, protests, and wildcat stoppages were now rigidly proscribed under the terms of both the new contract and the numerous grievance arbitration decisions Shulman offered in the 1940s.[33]

The next year Ford further increased its ability to enforce a greater level of work discipline when it broke the Foremen's Association at the Rouge. Even before passage of the Taft-Hartley Act, which excluded foremen unions from NLRB protection, Ford management had reached the conclusion that any foremen's organization that functioned along union lines could not be tolerated.[34] In May 1947, therefore, Ford withdrew its recognition of the FAA and sustained a 47-day strike to smash the fledgling organization. Fearful that the FAA and the UAW would soon merge, Ford defended its intransigent policy in terms of the need to enforce a tighter postwar work order on its production work force. "We must rely upon the foremen to try and keep down those emotional surges of the men in the plants and urge them to rely on the grievance procedure," argued one Ford spokesman. "If we do not have the foremen to do that, who is going to do it?"[35] In the next few years management increased the loyalty of the several thousand foremen at the Rouge through a program that tried to draw a sharp line between their status and that of the men they supervised. Foremen were put on salary, given promotion opportunities, told to wear ties and white shirts, provided desks and special parking privileges, and indoctrinated in management-oriented "human relations."[36]

During the first postwar decade Ford also reduced the effective economic leverage of Rouge workers by undertaking a multibillion dollar program of expansion and modernization. In 1946, company engineers considered the Rouge, then employing more than 60 percent of the total Ford work force, as choked by obsolescent equipment and overcrowded activity. Although the company operated more than a score of assembly and parts plants throughout the country, almost all manufacturing facilities for gears, motors, axles, and camshafts were located at Dearborn, mostly in the Rouge complex. Moreover, Ford's new managers estimated that as a result of union-era erosion of production standards, unit productivity at the Rouge had declined some 25 percent. Wages were also about 5 percent higher than in outlying plants.[37]

The Ford expansion program ended the Rouge "bottleneck." Ford's postwar automobile production nearly doubled in the first ten postwar years, but while its work force grew to almost two hundred thousand, the company built its new production capacity to duplicate and then supplant the Rouge output. As a consequence, Rouge employment fell from about sixty-five thousand in the first postwar years to something under thirty thousand in the 1960s. In building their new facilities in Cleveland, Buffalo, Canton, and Cincinnati, Ford made no effort to escape the union or to pay other than standard wages. Nor did they find the work force at these new plants particularly docile. Nevertheless Ford Local 600 accurately called the decentralization program "Operation Runaway"; indeed, the new facilities decimated the work force in two of the largest and most militant buildings at the Rouge. In the early 1950s, the Motor Building, which had employed upwards of nine thousand workers, was reduced to only four thousand, first by removal of much production to the new facilities in Cleveland, later by the automation of motor block production. At the foundry the same process took place. A facility which had employed more than eight thousand workers was first reduced in size and later eliminated entirely. Both of these buildings had been strongholds of militant, often Communist-led unionism: their virtual elimination in the 1950s gave Ford the vital "breathing room" the corporation needed to dilute and push back union power at Dearborn.[38]

Ford's use of "automated" machinery in some of its postwar facilities also helped to intensify the pace of work and put unionists on the defensive. At the time, the new automation techniques were heralded as a spectacular innovation, but in essence, the new technology was merely an extension of assembly line principles to link several transfer-type machines together with automatic materials-handling devices. Extensively deployed in the company's new or remodelled foundry, stamping, and engaging manufacturing operation, the automation of the 1940s and 1950s represented the simple coordination of machining and materials-handling operations into large and rigid processes employing a much smaller work force than had hitherto been required. First installed at Cleveland and then at the motor building of the Rouge, a linked series of boring machines and transfer devices cut engine-block labor time by about 90 percent. But the chief saving Ford engineers sought to gain from the new technology was not through direct reduction of labor. Instead, as the *American Machinist* put it, the corporation sought "to operate its equipment at maximum rate in order to achieve planned production goals."[39] To help achieve this end Ford reorganized and greatly expanded its production engineering department, which then inaugurated a massive program to do time studies of virtually every job at the Rouge. From the worker's point of view this postwar surge of corporate Taylorism amounted to a chronic sense of speed-up as work standards were enforced and machine-paced production became ever more widespread.[40]

Meanwhile, these were the years in which the Reuther leadership of the UAW consolidated its control of the union, reached a working accommodation with the major auto corporations, and established a system of pattern bargaining that would determine the character of union-management relations in the industry for the next quarter century. National leaders of the UAW increasingly focused their attention on those elements of the bargaining which could be most easily quantified and monetized—generally wage and fringe benefit improvements in the national contract. Those chronic, daily conflicts involving speed-up, management prerogatives, work assignments, and the like were not ignored, but from the leadership perspective they took a necessarily subordinate place in the bargaining agenda with Ford and other large corporations. In this context the shop-floor traditions maintained by maverick and highly politicized locals like 600 would prove a threat to the UAW's larger bargaining strategy.[41]

The union's fight for pensions at Ford provides a good example of how the UAW's quest for broad contractual innovations could subvert the shop-floor struggle itself. Although such fringe-benefit bargaining in the late 1940s was hailed by most observers as yet another index of union power, the process by which such welfare benefits were secured had important costs on the shop floor. The course of events surrounding Local 600's famous "speed-up strike" of May 1949 provides a spectacular example of the very real conflict that could develop between a local's determination to resist management's shop-floor offensive and the larger bargaining strategy of the national union to which it belonged.

In late 1948 the Ford Motor Company finally swung into mass production of its first complete postwar model. Since a car-starved public eagerly snapped up anything on four wheels, the company wanted to expedite production. In the B Building (automobile assembly), Labor Relations director John Bugas authorized foremen to increase the line speed above the daily standard to make up for those minutes when routine breakdowns had halted the conveyor. Committeemen denounced this policy and opened a fruitless series of negotiations to modify it. In January the company disciplined twelve men for failure to meet production standards, and in March the union chairman of the B Building, then in the midst of a hard re-election campaign, instigated a brief work stoppage on the paint line by telling some workers not to follow company rules. In April the Building voted to strike over the production standards dispute. Although the dispute had begun in a building dominated by Reuther partisans, the Communists and other anti-Reuther elements in the Rouge championed the speed-up dispute as a platform upon which to mobilize the work force.[42]

This conflict put Walter Reuther in serious difficulty. The lynchpin of Reuther's 1949 national bargaining strategy was the pension program he hoped to win from Ford. This would bring the UAW abreast of other major unions like the United Mine Workers and the United Steelworkers of America, who had recently won company-funded pensions, set the pattern for the rest of the automobile industry, and also aid Reuther in finally building a real base of support at the Rouge, the most important remaining bastion of opposition to his uncontested leadership of the UAW. But Reuther found the prospects of a Rouge-wide shutdown over the shop-floor distribution of power subversive of his larger bargaining agenda. Reuther therefore sent a fact-finding delegation to the B Building in early May to resolve the dispute. But instead of settling the issue, the presence of top UAW officers touched off a wildcat strike. When Ford then fired some fourteen committeemen whom they held responsible for the walkout, the dispute escalated into a Rouge-wide confrontation. Following an impressive strike vote, the UAW International authorized a work stoppage, and in the first complete shutdown since 1941, some sixty-two thousand workers struck the Rouge for twenty-four days in May.[43]

"When the Strike appeared inevitable Reuther was right out in front leading the parade," observed the *Detroit Free Press*. "In fact, he gave the appearance of a man running hard to keep ahead of the mob."[44] But because of his reluctance to make the stoppage a full-scale showdown with Ford, Reuther was relieved when Ford executives agreed that the issue go before a special arbitration panel chaired by Harry Shulman. This postponed the issue for several weeks, took both Reuther and local union officers off the hook, and allowed the UAW to get on with what its president certainly considered the central task: renegotiation and improvement of the national agreement. When more than a month later the Shulman panel promulgated a decision, the award proved anticlimactic, and, from the ordinary worker's view-point, largely ineffective. In an extraordinarily complex decision, the panel ruled that Ford had no right to run its lines faster than 100 percent of "standard" at any given time; but the decision did nothing to resolve the long-range problem because the production standard issue had always been one involving not only line speed but also work assignments, manning schedules, production mix, and the evaluation of new technology. These remained largely the prerogative of man-agement. The annual model change and the daily variation in auto body mix and options on the moving assembly line kept the fight against speed-up one of Sisyphean struggle. No arbitrator's formula alone could insure a humane work environment.[45]

The 1949 speed-up strike proved a turning point in the history of Local 600. Ford managers complained bitterly to the national officers of the UAW that the level of wildcat strike activity at the Rouge threatened to undermine good-faith bargaining at the highest levels. In turn, Reuther told Ford executives: "Have you ever thought that to get control the leadership must fight to get the machinery necessary for control?"[46] And for the next few years the UAW International would fight desperately to capture the political control of Local 600. A direct assault on the maverick local proved a failure in the early 1950s, but the UAW national leadership won a more subtle long-range victo-ry as the very structures of the postwar industrial relations system in the auto industry brought the practice of trade unionism at the Rouge more closely in line with Reuther-era unionism in the rest of the industry.

When Carl Stellato won the Local 600 presidency on a militant anti-Communist platform in 1950, Reuther must have thought he had finally begun to bring the Rouge into the Administration camp. Since 1944, Stellato had been an International Representative, and he cam-paigned for office in Local 600 with backing from the Reuther camp. But Stellato and Reuther soon found that even at the height of the Cold War, anti-Communism alone proved insufficient to mobilize a solid constituency. In July 1950, Stellato pushed resolutions through the Local's General Council backing the Korean War and condemning the Soviet Union and its satellites. All elected and appointed officers of the Local, including shop committeemen, were called upon to sign non-Communist loyalty pledges. In August, five prominent local offi-cials associated with the Party were charged with being subservient to the policies and programs of the Soviet Union and its Communist Party and thus subject to removal from office under a nine-year-old

UAW constitutional provision. Among the five were Paul Boatin, the motor building president, who was perhaps the local's foremost opponent of the Ford decentralization program, and Nelson Davis, charismatic vice president of the Production Foundry and the leader of the important group of black Communists at the Rouge.[47]

However, the lengthy trial of these five proved that the Rouge Communists could not be isolated and destroyed, as they were in so many other unions at the height of the Cold War. With the anti-Communist trial as the central issue, General Council elections in the fall of 1950 turned into a referendum that substantially weakened the Reuther-Stellato forces in the local. The Stellato group now broke with the UAW International and formed an informal alliance with what remained of the Communist grouping at the Rouge. Attacking current UAW policy, Stellato agitated against the Ford decentralization program, renewed the attack on the company speedup, rejected the UAW call for a general dues increase, and began a campaign for a 30-hour-week at 40 hours' pay. He also invited John L. Lewis, not Reuther, to keynote Local 600's 10th anniversary celebration in June 1951. Although Communists played a relatively subordinate role in all this, the top UAW leadership used the Local's failure to convict the five accused Party members as an excuse to impose an Administratorship in March 1952. This was a major blunder. Stellateo and his slate were swept back into power at the next general election. For much of the next decade Local 600 continued as a center of opposition to the UAW International.[48]

Underlying much of Reuther's failure at the Rouge were two characteristics of the politically conscious Rouge work force that made it unique among the UAW locals of the early 1950s. First, Reuther never succeeded in building a corps of loyal "Reutherites" at the Rouge. By the 1950s, when Reuther dominated the UAW International, he found the ordinary bureaucratic powers of his office insufficient to create his own machine in Local 600. The Rouge was so big and so well staffed that local presidents like Carl Stellato could easily maintain a political apparatus independent of International patronage. Moreover, since being a Reutherite at the Rouge did not insure one's election to local office, many of the UAW Administration's most talented supporters found their way onto the International staff, thus removing them from direct participation in the Local's political affairs. Second, anti-Communism never took hold at the Rouge to the extent it did in other UAW locals. With extensive and overlapping ties in Detroit's ethnic and black communities, the Communist Party maintained something of a mass base at the Rouge all through the early 1950s, and this provided the basis for the maintenance of a "center-left" alliance with Stellato and other opportunist politicians. The Party therefore was partially insulated from the winds of the Cold War. When the House Committee on Un-American activities conducted a series of highly publicized hearings in Detroit in March 1952, radicals, both Communist and non-Communist, were often assaulted and pushed out of their plants. But such persecution was notably absent at the Rouge, despite the Committee's focus on Communist activities there.[49]

However, the political independence enjoyed by the local was insufficient to stem the larger tide in postwar industrial relations. The union-wide influence of the local declined in the 1950s, first because of the Ford Motor Company's decentralization program, and second because Local 600 remained generally isolated within the UAW. Despite the fact that it contained 40 percent of the vote in UAW Region 1A, Carl Stellato was unsuccessful in winning a place on the International Executive Board.[50] The UAW Ford Department, firmly controlled by the International, became the focus of contract negotiations with the Ford Motor Company while the rank and file and the Local's leadership were increasingly left in the passive role of approving or disapproving contracts presented to them as a complete package. Thus by 1955 Ford labor relations officer John DeMotte could offer a revealing assessment of the new bargaining process. During that year's negotiations, Ford faced a committee composed of both local union leaders and UAW international officers accompanied by their research staff aides. The latter handled the major economic issues and captured the newspaper headlines, but the former, with little previous experience in national bargaining, concentrated their effort upon changes in the local working agreement.

> Their solution to most of the things they are unhappy about in the shop is the simple one of eliminating by contract most of management's rights to exercise its discretion or to take unilateral action. They would substitute for these management rights, either rigid rules or a requirement of union consent. They are at a loss to understand how their predecessors could have been cajoled out of providing this obvious remedy in past negotiations. And they are determined not to be similarly hoodwinked. But, in a very real sense, it is necessary in each set of our contract negotiations to argue out all over again the vital necessity for

preserving those areas of management flexibility and discretion which are basic to the effective and efficient conduct of our business. . . .[51]

Political infighting remained intense at the Rouge, but it was divorced from an immediate shop-floor context. Committeeman John Sarri noticed the gradual demobilization of rank-and-file workers, especially after the UAW signed its famous five-year contract with Ford in the summer of 1950. Ford committeemen gradually played a less aggressive role vis-à-vis lower levels of management. Subject to the harsh penalties decreed under the "company security" clause of the Ford contract and partially insulated from shop floor pressures by their status as full-time grievance handlers, many committeemen came to see their work as little more than that of contract administration. Although in the early 1940s the system of full-time committeemen had been a symbol of the local's shop-floor strength, by the mid 1950s it became a sign of union bureaucratization. Many committeemen served as numbers runners: in the early 1950s the yearly take at the Rouge was estimated at about $7 million.[52]

Of course industrial conflict still took place at the Rouge, but in the 1950s it was increasingly confined to routine and narrow channels, essentially defensive in nature. For example, among the most bitterly contested issues at the Rouge was the insistence by the skilled trades workers there that lines of craft demarcation be rigidly enforced, even when technological change blurred work categories. The rearguard battle they waged over this issue slowed the company's efforts to dilute their skills, but it also provided at least part of the basis for the growing craft consciousness of the skilled trades at the Rouge; a sentiment which would erupt in a right wing revolt against UAW-style industrial unionism in the late 1950s.[53] Production workers had no craft skills to protect, but they too sought precise job definitions as a protective shield against management power. By the early 1950s Ford had increased the foreman-worker ratio by about 50 percent, so first line supervisors who took an occasional hand at production labor were strongly resented, both for the work they stole and for the more intimate managerial control of production it facilitated. Thus grievances against "foreman working" soared in the 1950s, to become the second most important category by the end of the decade.[54]

Along with other UAW locals the Rouge still had the right to negotiate and strike over unresolved grievances and local working conditions, but after 1949 these issues were clearly subordinated to the

UAW's larger collective-bargaining agenda. The union adopted an informal policy authorizing stoppages on such issues only after the negotiation of a national contract had been completed, thereby severely limiting the effective power of local officials. In 1955, and again in 1961, 1964, and 1967, many Ford locals, including 600, conducted strikes on local issues after Reuther and Bugas had initialed the national accord. From the International's perspective these strikes were politically useful, for they gave the rank and file a chance to blow off steam, and they enabled local officers to horsetrade difficult grievances that might otherwise fester during the remainder of the contract. But the strikes did not seriously threaten the larger pattern of managerial control. In the boom years of the 1960s and early 1970s the International pressured the few recalcitrant locals to return to work after they had held up company-side production for about a month.[55]

Shop floor militancy that unfolded at the Rouge had almost completed its cycle by the early 1960s. The general bureaucratization of collective bargaining at both the shop floor and national levels had broken the power of the lower-level union cadre and restored many of the prerogatives management had enjoyed in the pre-union era. Meanwhile, the erosion of the work force at the Rouge and the massive layoffs of the 1958-1961 recession scattered the generation of auto workers who had built a tradition of workers' power in the 1940s. The ethnically-based Communist grouping in the Rouge gradually dissolved, while such prominent opposition leaders as Carl Stellato and Paul Boatin eventually made their peace with the Reuther leadership of the UAW.[56] When a new cycle of militancy began in the mid-1960s it would have as its base a working class with a very different social composition, and it would encounter problems and possibilities of a new order.

CHAPTER 15

Office Workers and Machines: Oral Histories of Rhode Island Working Women

VALERIE QUINNEY

How do people who actually use office machines feel about them? How does new office technology affect health, personal relationships at work, work satisfaction, and home life at the end of the day? A group of women who were members of Rhode Island Working Women (an affiliate of the national Nine to Five movement) decided during the summer of 1981 to carry out oral history interviews with office workers in their small state. They wanted answers to these and other questions strictly from the workers' point of view and in the workers' own words. They were seeking, not short answers to questions on a survey questionnaire, but interviews in which the individual could elaborate on her work experience and give her reflections on it. The purpose of the project was formally stated: "to record the history of working women, especially office workers, in Rhode Island; to gather information in order to understand their own past; to give them the opportunity to tell their stories and review their life's experiences; and to record working women's unique experiences for their families, their friends, their co-workers, and society."

The thirty office workers who came forth to tell their stories represented a sprinkling of ethnic groups: seven of them came from Swedish, Italian, French-Canadian, Greek, or French families, but the majority were white, native-born of native-born parents. These proportions are consistent with statistics on the clerical work force in Rhode Island.[1] And the census data since 1890 reveal that nationwide 90 percent of female office workers have been native-born women.[2] Only one male office worker recorded his story, and only one black woman. While black women are a small percentage of all office workers, and men are only 20 percent, still this sample is not representative of these categories of workers. A range in age was deliberately sought: the oldest workers entered the work force before World War I and the youngest entered the work force in the 1970s. They came from different situations: they worked in small offices, insurance companies, banks, corporations, small businesses such as local trucking companies and oil distributors, state offices, and educational institutions. Although social class is hard to ascertain in a few cases, class origin seems to be approximately 50 percent working class and 50 percent lower middle class.[3]

These thirty life histories comprise a rich source of information for many aspects of office work. In this paper I will concentrate on the answers given to questions about office work and technology. The topic has several ramifications that will be explored here: (1) the historical relationship of new office machinery to the increase of women in the clerical work force, (2) the ways that socialization for office work in business schools and high school commercial courses stressed adaptation of worker to machine, (3) ways that principles of scientific management determined the use of new machines, (4) the social situation in the office that affected feelings about office work and the machines that were a part of it, and (5) current health problems caused by new office technology.

First of all, office work for the last one hundred years has been characterized by changes in technology. From the fourteenth to the nineteenth century, skills necessary for office work consisted of an ability to copy in a legible hand and to understand double-entry bookkeeping. Offices were small: they usually consisted of owner, bookkeeper, copyist, and office boy—all male. In the mid-nineteenth century clerical workers were a negligible proportion of the total work force. Then Frederick Remington invented the typewriter and started manufacturing them in 1863. Writing machines had been around, but his was the first viable machine. By the 1890s the typewriter was widely used, and other machines were being introduced. The dictaphone was developed to complement the typewriter and was in use as early as the 1880s and was steadily improved. Carbon paper was in use in the 1870s. Offices started using mimeographing machines in 1890, the Burrough's adding machine in 1892. And the tabulator was invented to count the 1890 census.[4]

The typewriter made the copyist obsolete. Adding machines, calculators, and tabulators made the bookkeepers a diminishing proportion of the clerical work force. Machine operators were a growing proportion, and women became the machine operators.

It was the typewriter which first came to be used in offices mainly by women. Why did women quickly become the majority of typists in the clerical work force? Assumptions have been made that women could operate sewing machines and play the piano and that therefore they were naturally fitted for the typewriter: they had manual dexterity and could sit still for a long time. Judith Smith has shown that this rationalization became current *after* women became a majority of typists within the clerical labor force.[5] A small number of women were already being employed as copyists in offices about the time of the Civil War. In fact, the United States Government employed women during the Civil War and paid them one-half to two-thirds what it had paid men. After the war, businesses expanded: they needed a quick way to write out their more voluminous records and correspondence. The typewriter became a necessity in the office in the last decades of the century. Elyce Rotella argues that when an office manager added a typist to the office, it was cheaper to hire a woman.[6] On the supply side of the argument, women were entering the urban labor force in increasing numbers in the last decades of the nineteenth century. Public high school and commercial schools were offering office training to both men and women, but men more often took courses leading them to management. Compared to the other kinds of jobs available to men, stenographer/typist/clerk jobs were not so lucrative, so men trained for higher-paid jobs. The supply of men available for clerical work diminished.

For women, office work paid well compared to other work that they could get. In Rhode Island in 1889, a saleswoman made $6.36 a week; a tailoress made $7.87; a woolen mill worker, $5.38; but a stenographer made $11.12.[7] In 1939, women office workers made about the same as nurses, between $19 and $24 a week.[8] Mill workers were making $11 to $15 a week, and saleswomen were making about $15. By 1950 the median income for office workers was $36.36 a week; nurses made $39 a week; textile mill workers, $32; saleswomen, $25.[9] Other nationwide research shows consistent decline in the relative salary advantage that clerical workers once had. By the 1970s the average male or female office worker made less than the average male or female blue-collar worker.[10] According to a special report of the United States Department of Labor in January 1981, 1 in 7 women office workers who headed households in 1980 had incomes below the official poverty level of $8,450 for a family of 4.[11] A single parent who recorded her life history said:

I was 25 and they were 3 and 5 when I got my divorce. When I came back here in 1968, I got a job at a corporation where, by the time I brought my paycheck home, paid my babysitter, I had $45 a week to live on. With that I had to pay food, rent, clothing, everything. It was a tough time. I was getting $150 a month child support. That meant the difference between eating and not eating. I was still dependent on my husband. (Mrs. P.G.)[12]

Yet in spite of the fact that office workers' salaries did not maintain their advantages relative to other alternatives for women, the myth remained that office work offered good pay.

Women continued to enter this occupation. These workers' testimony reveals the reasons why many young women become office workers. Four of the thirty people interviewed said they grew up wanting to be office workers, that they were interested in the work itself. Mrs. E.B., who started working before World War I, said that since childhood she had wanted to work with figures and be a businesswoman. Mrs. Y.M., who grew up in the 1940s, said, "I had an idea about management: I didn't have an idea about what I wanted to manage, but I had the idea that I wanted to direct." She is now an office manager.

Most people who graduated from high school in the 1930s and 1940s gave an account similar to this one, by Mrs. V.G., of the influence of expectations for women:

I was always encouraged to take a commercial course in high school. I did not balk at it; I just went ahead and did it because that was the way it was. Everybody thought that boys should be more educated than girls and this was accepted by me.

Mrs. E.P., who worked in offices all her life, said,

Their mode of thinking at that time was that the girls would go as far as high school and get married and have children. The boy was the one that should go to college and have the career. But it didn't work out that way for me.

Another woman summed up the expectations for women:

I grew up in the fifties: You get out of high school, get married and have babies. That's what I did, just the way you were supposed to do it. (Mrs. P.G.)

Unbiased, competent vocational guidance was often lacking in high school. Young women did not know about alternatives. In many cases this accounts for their choice of office work:

> I just graduated from Hope High School and didn't want to go on to school. I was an honor student, but something in me just had to go out and go to work and be independent. In those days—when I graduated from high school, it was 1949—all I heard was nurse, secretary. They didn't really talk about speech therapist. (Mrs. M.R.)

Parents often pressured their daughters to become clerical workers. A woman who first worked for the telephone company and then went into office work observed sadly:

> I had wanted to be a nurse, but my father was, as I said, really old-fashioned, and he didn't believe in women working nights and Sundays and holidays, so I went to work for the telephone company and I worked nights and Sundays and holidays. Even to this day, I wish I'd been a nurse. (Mrs. M.W.)

Mrs. R.D., who was an office worker for many years, told this story:

> At Aldrich High School they had a course called JBT, which was Junior Business Training, and I guess they taught them a lot about how to conduct yourself in an office and things of that sort as well as the bookkeeping and other skills that you would need. I told my mother I hated typing and I never wanted to study typing, but she really was insistent upon it and said that I really should at least do that. It was an elective and I did so poorly in it that—I remember the teacher's name was Miss Pearson—she made me promise that if she would pass me in the course, I would never go into business. (Laughs) I was more interested in reading and literature and things of that sort than I was in doing anything as dull as office work.

She added, "I did hope that I would be able to go to college, but they didn't have all of the financial aid type things in those days."

Often lack of confidence and a poor self-concept made professions requiring college training seem too formidable. Some women just said, like Mrs. J.E., "I didn't feel that I was really college material." Mrs. L.P. said, "Hardly anybody in my class was going to college; well, maybe some of the boys went." She added, "I guess my family thought maybe I wasn't that much of a student, and perhaps a business course was good for me."

Summing up, few clerical workers talked about interest in the actual work itself, yet women flocked to it. Parents saw advantages for their daughters in entering an occupation that seemed to offer good pay. Office work was regarded as clean, safe, and respectable. And a commercial course in the last couple of years in high school or nine months' education in a business school was sufficient training.

The tuition for courses in commercial or business schools was relatively inexpensive. Mrs. E.B.'s parents paid $10 a month in 1908 when they sent her to Rhode Island Commercial School. She made that much per week when she got her first job in 1909. Shorthand, typing, filing, Business English, arithmetic, and Business Law were the essential courses. Gregg had introduced his shorthand method into the United States in the 1890s. The ten-finger touch system of typing had become current in 1888. So young people needed these skills and were willing to pay business schools for the learning opportunity and for assistance in getting them jobs.

Running a business school was lucrative. The first business school in Providence was started in 1846—Scholfield's. Then in 1863 two midwesterners, Henry Bryant and Henry Stratton, founded a business school in Providence with the idea of attracting Civil War veterans with their mustering-out pay.[13] They had a chain of such schools in the Midwest. Soon after the Civil War, business schools all over the country started recruiting women students. The 1877 circular for Bryant and Stratton's school in Providence listed forth-eight "lady students" along with its 403 "gentleman students."[14] The proportion of women steadily increased from then on. By 1914, women were 57 percent of all students enrolled in clerical work courses across the nation.[15]

Women started their own schools. Katharine Gibbs found herself a widow with two small sons to bring up. She took some courses at Simmons College and told friends she meant to earn her living doing office work. They said she would not make much money doing that. They advised her to start a school to teach other women how to take shorthand and type. In 1911, she sold her jewelry and rented a room in an elegant building in downtown Providence. She made so much money in Providence in two years that she founded schools in Boston and New York.[16] In 1914, Gertrude Johnson and Mary Wales also started a school in Providence devoted to business education for women.

In that year there were five commercial schools located in downtown Providence in the heart of the business district. All of them acted as employment agencies as well as educational institutions. Public schools in the Providence-Pawtucket area had started offering commercial courses in 1906,[17] and they, too, tried to get their students part-time work while they were in school so they would have prospects for full-time jobs when they graduated. Contacts with businesses were assiduously cultivated. Especially the private commercial schools' reputations depended on their demonstrating their efficacy in getting their graduates jobs. To do this, they had to supply workers skilled in operating the machines that businesses adopted. An advertisement for Bryant and Stratton in the *Providence Board of Trade Journal* in 1908 is typical of commercial school advertising: "Commercial education means more than a superficial knowledge of business forms; it requires a thorough training in Actual Business Practice and a familiarity with every mechanical labor-saving device used in the modern office."[18]

The business school student learned to operate office machines, but was not encouraged to question the way that new machines were used or to think in terms of their effect on the quality of the work experience. Rather, the schools taught women that respect for authority, promptness, dependability, and loyalty were the characteristics that would enable them to keep their jobs. Mrs. K.A. described the attitudes she imbibed:

> I remember so well the teacher telling us at Hill College: "Remember the businessman does not want to pay you *anything* because you're not *producing* anything. But he can't run his business without office help. So, therefore, you have to make yourself invaluable." And you did it by being on time, doing your work well, and therefore you would be sure to have a job.

All of the secretarial programs featured personal improvement courses, sometimes called professional development. For example, the *1947-53 Bulletin* for Bryant College described a course in Personal Improvement offered by specialists from the John Roberts Powers Organization of New York. There were lectures on the right way to walk, speak, dress, and wear makeup and one on "orientation," which was explained as "adjustment of the individual to surrounding society and circumstances."[19]

Business schools and high schools thus supplied businesses with trained office workers, and the demand remained high as businessmen tried to keep up with the volume of paper work their growing companies generated. The clerical work force grew spectacularly. In 1870, clerical workers were only six-tenths of one percent of the total work force; they were 18 percent of the work force in 1970. Within this growing occupation, the proportion of women steadily increased. Women were half of all clerical workers by 1920; in 1979 they made up

79 percent of clerical workers.[20] The United States Census lists three major clerical suboccupations: (1) bookkeepers, cashiers, and accountants, (2) clerks, and (3) copyists (in early censuses), stenographers, and typists.[21] At first women were a majority of the clerks, stenographers, and typists, and men were the bookkeepers, cashiers, and accountants. But women became a majority even in these latter suboccupations as office machinery was introduced and the level of skill and pay were lowered. Today one out of every three working women is an office worker.

At the beginning of the century, office situations varied. There were many offices where one woman operated all the machines and did all the manual and brain work. Mrs. E.B. worked in a one-woman office from 1909 to 1915; her company was the Auto Car Company. She described the work:

> I did a variety of things—I answered the telephone, kept the books, kept records, filed, took dictations, typed. I enjoyed it.

There were also offices with a clerical work force of ten or more people where each one performed special tasks. And in large companies, especially banks and insurance companies, the office work force was organized in departments where workers might do the same thing all day. Mrs. M.C. worked for Rhode Island Hospital Trust Bank in the early 1920s. The office staff numbered 238.[22] She was in the filing department and she liked the work. She said she pulled the files, typed entries, and refiled. When pressed to say what she liked about the work, she said she liked the people she worked with.

In the mid-1920s, however, division of labor, specialization of tasks, and control of workers became much more extensive. It was in this context that new office technology was introduced. For the human beings who worked with the machines, the assumptions of "scientific management" made all the difference.

Margery Davies, in her recent book *A Woman's Place Is at the Typewriter,* surmised that the growth in the amount of office work as companies expanded left office managers frantically searching for ways to get it done.[23] They needed some way to organize workers so that they could keep up with the increased work load. They also thought that work would be done more efficiently if they had control over each worker. "Scientific" principles of management such as Frederick Taylor had developed for metal fabrication were applied to office work in 1918 in texts such as *Office Management: Its Principles and Practice.*[24] First, the work was divided into distinct operations. Then each operation was scrutinized to find out how it could be done with the least expense of effort and time. Finally, the person with the least skill needed was assigned to each operation. Routines were set and rigidly adhered to so that as soon as one operation was finished, the piece of work was handed to the next person, and so on. In theory each task was performed at the lowest level of skill necessary and for the lowest possible rate of pay; in practice, workers brought more skills than the job description stipulated but the pay scale was based on the job description, that is, on the least skill.

These ideas are still the bases for office management. What are their effects on the office worker? Harry Braverman has pointed out that office work was becoming proletarianized, that is, the mental tasks were being separated from manual tasks, with only a few at the top of the hierarchy really understanding what the work was all about.[25] The office workers in this study had a lot to say about that. One woman described the bank she works in: "Behind the scenes, it's a glorified factory." (Mrs. B.W.) A woman who was a typist in a typing pool in an insurance company described her work:

> I hated it because I sat there and had to type up forms and I didn't know what I was doing. I had to type in a foreign language and I had no training in that language. . . . I was told, "Just put this block in this block." (Mrs. P.G.)

A woman who is office manager in an insurance company admitted:

> I am obliged . . . to hire people who are not too demanding, who can do the work without caring to do more. There are some women who are like that, satisfied to do the routine situation every day. They do not require too much, just to be employed. The type of work my employees do, they can do it without comprehending. (Mrs. Y.M.)

Constant supervision is required to produce a document quickly so as to keep the flow of work moving to the next level. This results in a lack of autonomy, responsibility, and even freedom of movement. Contact between workers is prohibited. Mrs. M.C., who filed all day, liked the job because she enjoyed the interaction with the other women. Scientific management dictates decreased interaction. Still, workers try to circumvent the rules. Mrs. G.M. gave an example:

> As you came in the door, there was the first row of desks. The supervisor sat in the center. And then there were three rows all the way down—just the whole length of the office. It was very systematic. But yet, I liked it. I liked the girls. [They said] you

mustn't talk to the girl next to you. (Laughs) Of course, there's always a way. Sometimes I'd bring candy or something. They'd put it in the waste paper basket and it would go all through the line.

The way one woman in a small office used a time-motion study to her advantage is interesting. She gave an unusual twist to Taylorism:

My actual job description, when I sat down and wrote it out, took six pages, and I also did a study of how much time I spend on each of these tasks so I know exactly what my job consists of. . . . So what my supervisors did, is that they took my job description as I wrote it and my time study and went to personnel and said, "Look, this woman is working hard, do something." They studied it and turned it inside out and analyzed it and came up with a job title for me called "Staff Assistant." And as Staff Assistant, it was a considerable raise and promotion. (Mrs. P.G.)

Some of the women in this study worked in small offices, had some autonomy, had contact with people, and understood the goals of the company and how their work fit in. They expressed satisfaction with their work. Mrs. K.A. was an administrative secretary in a career development center. She worked closely with the director and with people coming in for training programs. She said,

We weren't just selling widgets. We were dealing with people, offering training to people. You'd see them come in; then in a few months you'd see them change, they'd have an ability they didn't have when they started.

She added that she loved the job.

Another woman said,

I have no complaint about my working situation. I have a very free and easy day. I do my work; no one tells me what to do first. It is definitely my choice, how I want to do my work. (Mrs. V.G.)

She is an administrative secretary, a category at the top of the clerical hierarchy. Like others at the top, she has variety in tasks, person-to-person contacts, responsibility, decision-making power and personal autonomy. Administrative secretaries often expressed satisfaction in their work, unless the relationship with their boss was stressful. But there were many more women in routinized, repetitive jobs who lacked decision-making power, autonomy, and personal contact and felt little work satisfaction.

Principles of scientific management have influenced office managers in their planning for new office technology. Now in large offices no alternatives are visible. But it was not inevitable that each new machine introduced into the office would result in greater specialization of personnel and more monotonous work. In small offices one person might use several machines in the course of a day's work. In such a situation, the machine was often seen as a godsend. One women, a harassed secretary in the main office of an engineering firm, explained:

> I was the secretary to five men—the president, vice-president, secretary-treasurer, office manager, and draftsman. I did all the work except the bookkeeping. . . . I was there six months, and I took a day off because I was tired, there was just too much work. He told me, "Young lady, when you come in, we're going to have a talk. . . ."

> So, when I came in he wanted my notice because he said I was a one-girl office and I had to be there all the time. I told him that "you dictate and I do all the work, and there is so much work to it that I just can't keep up." I told him, "Why don't you get a dictaphone?" He accepted my resignation. I worked my two weeks' notice.

> In two weeks he came back and said, "I was talking to my wife, and would you consider staying? We will get a dictaphone." So they did.

Comptometers were not easy to learn to operate: sometimes all ten fingers had to be pressing down on the machine. Mrs. G.M. said that when her office got a comptometer just before World War I, it was a help:

> Now, if you wanted to multiply $1.25—1-2-5—by 12, you'd press it twice, move over, press it once, and your total sat down at the bottom. We seldom used 9 or an 8, we'd just press 4 twice. And that kept both hands down on the lower part of the machine. Of course, you could divide and subtract and everything on those things.

> I got used to using it. I was adapted to it, you know. I didn't have to be shown it. It didn't seem any puzzle to me. I used it from then on.

Many people praised the invention of the Xerox photocopier, especially women who had had to work with carbons to get multiple copies. Mrs. M.C., who worked in a bank in th early 1920s, said,

You had to type everything with carbons. Oh yes, everything was triple, and it was quadruple if you wrote a policy covering a dwelling that had a mortgage on it. You had to make the original for the mortgagee; a copy went to the customer. And then we had a copy and the company had a copy. You'd have to be careful of your typing. No mistakes. Yes, it all had to be lined up, dear. Everything.

The situation was even worse if the typist worked for the government or the armed forces:

The Navy would bid on certain items they would want to buy from suppliers, so this was what we would be typing mostly. Bids with a lot of figures on them, that's what we did and many, many copies of them. That was a big problem when I first started. I knew how to type and all that—but to line up seven or eight carbons—and there were lines on the paper and they could slip after you got them in the typewriter. (Mrs. R.D.)

The alternative was to use the duplicating machine:

I don't know what they call it. I think it was a duplicating machine. But it was the dirtiest thing. And it had a special kind of ink in it. If you got that on your clothes, well that was the end of them. You never got it out. It was purple; and it was filthy— and I hated that. Thank God somebody invented Xerox. (Mrs. J.E.)

Office workers became even lyrical in their descriptions of the electric typewriter and especially the built-in eraser:

I first ran into electric typewriters when I was working at the Shipyard and my boss brought one in. He wanted me to get something out in a hurry. For a change, he was working. And I don't know if you know anything about electric typewriters, but you just breathe on it. With a manual you have to hit hard. (Mrs. J.E.)

Another woman exclaimed:

I have a beautiful Selectric now. That's another thing, your eraser tape comes in the machine now. That was the greatest invention! (Laughs) Ah! (Mrs. E.J.)

A secretary described the difference a machine made (she had been working on an old typewriter):

I explained to him [the office manager] that the typewriter was a part-time typewriter and I did a full-time job on it and that I

thought it had gone the mileage. Two weeks later I had a brand
new typewriter. It's a beautiful typewriter; it has some automatic gauges. I notice now I don't leave my desk half as much as I
did. It's taken about fifty percent of my frustration away from
me, and it's very comfortable. (Mrs. L.M.)

In describing a job she had in the late 1940s, one woman explained
why she thought a word processor could be a liberating instrument in
the office:

It cuts out so much of the drudgery. And it *was* drudgery. . . .
The boss sent the same letter to all his customers. He dictated it
to me once and that was the end of my shorthand duties for
that one because I typed the same letter, letter after letter, after
letter, getting addresses off the 3-by-5 cards and typing a different address for each one. Not only that, but each letter ended,
"Thanking you for your future valued favors, I remain, Yours
Truly."[26]

She wishes she had had a word processor then: she could have put
the letter on the machine and pulled off as many originals as she
needed. She said that she would have used the time saved to help her
boss organize conferences. Executive secretaries liked the word processors in their offices, and they especially praised the computers for
the convenience of easy, quick retrieval of information.

To be sure, there was some fear of machines. One woman described
the way she felt about computers coming into the office:

Everything is computerized and if I don't learn it soon, I'm going to feel way behind. I'm in awe of them! And I'm sure there's
so much more of that going on, and technology—frankly it
scares people who have never worked with that. You feel like
you're being replaced by automation. And I think [technology]
will be a little scary to conquer. (Mrs. M.R.)

Introduction of computers meant for one woman learning a new
skill, and that brought her a lot of satisfaction—but no increase in
salary:

I was hired under the title of service secretary but the actual
work I did was that of dispatcher. At that time I was given very
extensive training and I became knowledgeable within the field
itself. We moved from the small East Providence office to a larger building that incorporated not only the commercial division
but also the computer division. By the time I left, there were 14
servicemen that I was dispatching, which is quite a crew.

I was promoted to Dispatcher, which is what I was doing all along anyway, and they developed an entirely new system, a computer-generated service program. It was an entirely new system; I had to learn my job from scratch. Everything was computerized. I learned it so well that I trained people from the Providence office and Boston. Unfortunately, I never got re-warded for it; I never got recognized for it; I never got a promo-tion out of it. I didn't get days off; I didn't get anything. What I did get was the respect of my peers and my own self-satisfac-tion that I did this and did it well. (Mrs. P.G.)

If new technology is not in itself hateful, if machines are even thought of as helpful, why isn't mechanization of office work a good thing? In 1961 a researcher on the effects of office automation, Ida Hoos, observed: "It must be noted that the very purpose of mechani-zation is to break down systems into such repetitive fragments that the machines can perform them with a minimum of human participa-tion."[27] In large offices introduction of machinery always meant the further division of labor, specialization of tasks, and routinization of the work. These workers in their oral histories described a process whereby workers used fewer and fewer skills and were finally phased out. The dictaphone was used very early to facilitate division of labor; its use made the typing pool in large companies a standard feature.[28] With this machine, the stenographer became unnecessary. But the typist who used a dictaphone did need to know how to type, how to punctuate, paragraph, and spell. Now the word processor eliminates the need for spelling, punctuating, and paragraphing. The boss can select standard parts of his business letters from all the possible for-mats. Quantities of these canned paragraphs are run off. Sometimes the machine even supplies the addresses. It's a purely mechanical job. In this situation, many typists who would have typed each letter can be replaced by a person needing less skill.[29]

In the past, people who were key-punchers or who operated tabula-tors and collators were necessary even though the machines did a lot of the work; mental and manual processes were necessary to prepare the information, collect it, and process it. When computers were introduced, these processes became obsolete, along with the people who did them. This meant that workers who used these machines were either retrained or fired. Mrs. K.A. said that the boss just in-formed her that he was going to send the stuff out to be put on computer, and that was the end of her job.

The easy retrieval of information that executive secretaries praised is made possible by the work of data-entry clerks who sit at the computer all day, typing information. One narrator recounted a conversation she had with the head of the office where data was put on computer:

> The computer required more work because you had to learn a whole new method of putting that information into the machine. There were a lot of mix-ups; trucks would appear several times a week at the same house to deliver oil. The people who programmed didn't know anything about the oil business. It was a leased thing—we sent the information out. I complained to the boss about the computer, about the girls who put the information in, the data-entry clerks. I said, "They're not even thinking." He said, "I don't pay them to think." (Mrs. K.A.)

Data entry is not just monotonous; it's a dead-end job. There is no upward mobility. Typing meaningless numbers from a Fortran card doesn't increase one's understanding so that one can rise in the business to become a computer programmer or an analyst.[30] As Mrs. B.W. remarked, "If you sit there for twenty years, you'll be doing the same thing." Sometimes women just quit and go somewhere else. They do the same thing at the new job, but they can relieve their boredom temporarily by changing environments. However, some are reluctant to quit the company because they lose all their accumulated benefits. They are stuck. Mrs. M.R. expressed the feeling very poignantly:

> I was very brave when I was younger—always felt there was tomorrow. I would just pick up and go. If something bothered me—I was very smart when I was younger—I'd leave. As you get older, you get more cautious. You need more security. You're afraid to try new things. So I lost that boldness and that courage, and I'm afraid sometimes I put up with things that I didn't like that weren't good for me.

Workers talked about their need for personal freedom and the way a computer deprives them of a sense of freedom. Work pacing forces the operator to keep up with the machine: She has a limited time to complete a project. The computer records the time a worker takes to complete a project. If she turns off the machine to go to the bathroom, it records the times the machine was turned off and turned on again. No human supervisor could be so stringent and unrelenting.[31]

Being unable to make decisions about one's work and being under constant supervision results in a high level of stress. A survey of video-data-terminal operators conducted by the National Institute of

Occupational Safety and Health revealed that office workers have "higher levels of job stress than have ever been observed on assembly lines."[32]

Attitudes about machines can only be understood if one understands that machines are used according to the dictates of scientific management. But the social environment may be just as important in influencing attitudes about machines. Office workers are at the bottom of the hierarchy, and they feel it. Mrs. E.J. said, "Many of the secretaries or clerical workers feel that they're kind of low-echelon." Mrs. L.M. described the situation this way: "They would ask you very impossible things and you were always supposed to say, 'Yes,' you were never to backtalk." She recalled one conversation in her office:

> There was too much work and everybody on the phone used to holler, and I asked the purchasing agent one day, "Why is everybody hollering? My God, I can't stand this, everybody hollers, hollers, hollers."
>
> He said, "Because that's management, from management they holler all the way down."
>
> I said, "When they get to me, I don't holler back, but it upsets me."

Often the subservient position is enforced in a subtle way:

> I was called by my first name, and yet I called the male supervisors by "Mr.", whereas, in the department where I work now, in academia, I call the professors by their first name.
>
> It gets to the point where you are calling a 25-year-old man "Mr." and he is calling you your nickname even though you are older. I just hadn't thought about it. As I became more aware of it, I began to realize that it emphasized my being in a subservient position. In the position that I am in now, I am not made to feel like such a servant. (Mrs. V.G.)

Often in the offices these workers described, the supervisors were men, the office workers were women. Mrs. J.E. said, "I wouldn't say there was any discrimination because the men all had the top jobs and the girls were just secretaries or typists or file clerks." In situations where the supervisor is male and the office workers are all women, subservience makes the woman worker vulnerable to both open and subtle sexual harassment. Sometimes it is not blatant, but vaguely troubling:

But who do you tell about these things? What do you do about these things? I was asked to do personal favors, and then the boss would come over to me while typing and put his arm around me and ask, "Oh, would you please do this for me?" and pinch your cheek. It wasn't anything blatant. It was subtle, but it was there. I saw a picture one time describing sexual harassment, and the boss had his arm around his secretary as she was sitting at the typing desk and I thought, "Oh, my God, that was me!" (Mrs. P.G.)

Sometimes the harassment is blatant indeed, as Mrs. Y.M. described:

They felt that they could do almost anything because I was the only woman there. Yes, they could dominate, they could make remarks about almost anything. They could pinch your arm, they felt very free to act. Whatever they felt like saying at the time was fine. Sometimes it was totally out of place and un-called for.

Because I was the female, they felt they could allow them-selves. Sometimes I would go to the manager who was a man also and I would tell him I did not need this sort of thing, that I did not have to take it. He would say, "Oh, you are right; you do not have to take that." But at the same time he did nothing about it.

The annoyance of it was wearing. Mrs. L.M. recounted the daily routine in her office:

Every day he would ask me, "Did you get laid last night?' Every morning I could be sure that with my coffee I got *that* because he knew I was a single woman.

Some women referred to situations where they did the work and the male bosses got the credit. Mrs. J.E. said,

I got a job as secretary to the Purchasing Agent. And that was a racket. He was the head Purchasing Agent and he had all these underlings—all men, of course. Women weren't allowed to have a job as Assistant Purchasing Agent. Every Assistant Pur-chasing Agent—he must have had a couple of dozen of them—had a secretary to do the work. My boss spent all his time out at the Narragansett Race Track.

Subservience and stress experienced on the job have an effect on the worker that continues when she goes home at the end of the day. Mrs. Y.M. described her interaction with her children:

> Well, number one, I have been very tired. I do not have patience. If you have something to tell me, it has to be very important for me to listen. I don't have the patience nor do I have the time nor do I have the interest. A lot of pressure is put upon me and sometimes I really do not want to hear, especially if it is not important. I have not done badly so far, but it has been very hard.

This situation—stress, subservience, lack of recognition—was often but not always the one these workers experienced. In some offices where the interpersonal relationships were not based on dominance/subservience but rather on mutual help and appreciation, workers described very different feelings. This statement was typical of workers who liked their jobs:

> It's a good feeling to know that you are accepted and that your work is liked and admired. I mean, whenever there're bonuses, they've included me, even though I'm a part-time worker. Because it's appreciation that I like. The fact that they can see that you're conscientious. Even if it's just a word or a kind card or a note—it's appreciation that means so much to me as a person. (Mrs. M.R.)

In offices where managers realize that support of fellow-workers is essential to a sense of well-being and positive feelings about the job, they allow some social interaction. The importance of this was raised again and again. Mrs. M.R. expressed feelings typical of those described by nearly everyone:

> That's what's important to me. In my life, the best reward I've ever had from jobs is the friends I've made from it, really.

Organization of work and social environment creates a context in which workers view machines. However, beyond these, there are real health hazards to consider from machines. Office technology has been potentially harmful since the introduction of duplicating machines and type-cleaning fluids. Both create exposures to chemicals that are irritants, that cause burning of eyes and membranes, headaches and dizziness. There is triolene in type-cleaning fluids; trichloroethane in duplicating fluid, plus ammonia, ethanol, and methanol. Some of the paper used in copiers contains or is coated with harmful substances; the fluids in the copiers contain chemicals which can cause sickness if they escape—trinitrofluorenone in some IBM copier printing drums, and nitropyrenes in Xerox photocopiers.[33] A harmful chemical, ozone, is produced when oxygen molecules come into contact with the high voltage elements used in photocopiers.

With video data terminals, the problem, in addition to stress, is that the operator has to constantly refocus her eyes because the letters are small and the image flickers. These machines are moved into existing office environments where no changes have been made to make it easier to work with them. The same overhead fluorescent lights are used and the walls remain bright; this situation produces glare on the screen. A worker talked about the results of her environment:

> I learned in two months how to computer-input. . . . But there were fluorescent lights there and also the lights from the computers, and my eyes started to go. I made a doctor's appointment and I told him I was working on computers. He said, "Is that the green screen?"
>
> I said, "Yes."
>
> He said, "Are there fluorescent lights there?"
>
> "Sure," I said, "there are fluorescent lights all over the ceiling." I had to get very strong glasses. (Miss. J.G.)

The operator tries to sit and hold her head in such a way as to reduce glare. This results in back pain and shoulder strain. In 1979 the National Institute for Occupational Safety and Health surveyed workers in offices that were computerized: their subjects were 250 video-data-terminal operators and 150 control subjects in four large offices. They found that terminal operators had a considerably higher proportion of complaints of eye strain, burning eyes, blurred vision, painful or stiff neck and shoulder, and back pain.[34] When Rhode Island Working Women conducted a survey of its members who worked steadily at computers or word processors, a large majority reported eye pain (83%), neck pain (77%), and back and shoulder pain (60%).[35] These findings are similar to those of research findings in such European countries as Sweden.[36]

Office work has been considered safe in the past and is still considered safe by many people. Informational interviews with educators in four colleges and business schools in Rhode Island indicate that only one was aware of the health hazards in office work.[37] There were no sections in the curricula devoted to informing the student of the health hazards in the occupation for which she was training.

Clerical workers took it for granted that there would be eye strain.

As one woman remarked, "That just goes along with the job." (Mrs. K.A.) Another said,

> I wouldn't have considered eye strain a thing to worry about. I never got hurt at work. If I had fallen down the stairs or something like that, I would have complained.

The effects of health hazards are slow in showing up: they are not immediate and directly attributable to the work as are accidents in a mine or on a construction job. Therefore, it may sometimes be difficult even for the office workers themselves to identify the causes of those effects.

Businesses which bring new technology into their offices have a history of viewing machines as efficient and as cheap because they save human labor costs. They have not concerned themselves with other aspects of machine use. When the Rhode Island Department of Health and Safety wrote letters to sixteen companies in the state asking if they had a health policy governing the use of video-data terminals, not one replied. A follow-up telephone call resulted in many noncommittal answers. Only a small percentage of companies in the state had formulated a policy.[38] However, in Norway and Sweden there are laws prohibiting workers from using video terminals more than two hours at a time and more than four hours a day.[39] The Harvard Medical School Health Letter in April 1983 reviewed research in this country on the video data terminal (VDT) and made this statement in summary:

> The VDT is not just another piece of office equipment; it changes the nature of the work people do. Most potential health problems caused by VDTs can probably be averted by planning that takes account of the operators' needs.[40]

Workers expressed apprehension about job loss due to computerization of their offices. Research in Sweden reported at a recent conference on Office Work and New Technology indicated that in companies where computerization had occurred, the clerical work force had been reduced.[41] Others argue that availability of information creates a need for more information and that such information will be more widely distributed within a company. Just as the typewriter and carbon paper made it possible to put copies of a document into the hands of several people and the Xerox machine made it possible to give hundreds access to copies of the document, computers will make it so easy to retrieve information that everybody on the system will get used to working with complete, up-to-date information. Information will be sent electronically to specified destinations over telephone lines. People will define this as a need. Office managers will buy more computers and hire more coders and data-entry clerks. But even if the need for data-entry clerks is maintained, the boring job of typing in meaningless information and of being monitored by a machine will remain.

There are alternatives to scientific management in organizing work and using machines. Some unionized European workers recently demanded and received the power to discuss their employers' adoption of computers and word processors, to base their choice on health and safety considerations, and to participate in decisions on the use of the machines.[42] They have devised a workday which limits the time any worker has to spend at video terminals, and they have structured a variety of tasks and periods of relief into the eight hours. Instead of wholesale firing of workers when the new technology has made their jobs obsolete, they have insisted on natural attrition as workers retire or find jobs elsewhere and on the retraining of workers so they can remain with the company if they choose. A concern for the dignity, well-being, and security of the individual has guided their decisions, which they make jointly with company executives. In Rhode Island, only a minority of office workers belong to unions. The subservient, vulnerable position of many office workers makes it difficult for them to demand decision-making power over the introduction of new technology in their offices.

Office workers who had variety in their work and some degree of autonomy and responsibility liked their jobs and felt good about the new technology they were learning to use. They were particularly positive in their attitudes about machines when there was a supportive work group and when they were treated with respect and their good work was acknowledged. Women who worked in offices where their work was routine, repetitive, and boring, and where they were watched, denied freedom of movement, forbidden communication with other workers, and forced to work at an imposed pace, hated their jobs. They hated the machines which provided all-day monotony and which forced them to keep up a strenuous, nonvarying pace.

In the socialization process for office work and in the actual work situation, the adjustment of the worker to the office environment has most often been emphasized by educators and psychologists. We have not developed a critical view of technology based on the opposite assumption, that the work environment should be adjusted to the human being. The testimony of Rhode Island's clerical workers points to the need for such a humanistic approach in office management. Office workers do not hate new machine technologies *per se*, but they often complain that the way work technologies are used exploits workers physically and mentally.

Notes

CHAPTER ONE: NOTES

Note: Quotations in the Introduction which are not cited are from the essays in this volume.

1. Charles Tilly, "The Old New Social History and the New Old Social History," *Review* 7 (Winter 1984), 363–406.

2. See, for example, E.J. Hobsbawm, *Labouring Men* (London, 1957); E.P. Thompson, *The Making of the English Working Class* (London, 1963).

3. Ira Katznelson, *City Trenches: Urban Politics and the Patterning of Class in the United States* (New York, 1981), p. 16.

4. Bruce Laurie and Mark Schmitz, "Manufacture and Productivity: the Making of an Industrial Base, Philadelphia, 1850–1880," in Theodore Hershberg, ed., *Philadelphia: Work, Space, Family and Group Experience in the Nineteenth Century—Essays Toward an Interdisciplinary History of the City* (New York, 1981).

5. Alan Dawley, *Class and Community: The Industrial Revolution in Lynn* (Cambridge, Mass., 1976).

6. Massachusetts Bureau of Labor Statistics, *Annual Report, 1870* (Boston, 1971).

7. C.R. Dobson, *Masters and Journeymen: a Pre-History of Industrial Relations, 1717–1800* (London, 1980); John Rule, *The Experience of Labour in Eighteen-Century English Industry* (New York, 1981).

8. U.S. Congress. 1885. Senate. Committee on Education and Labor, *Report upon the Relations Between Labor and Capital, and Testimony Taken by the Committee.* (Washington, 1887).

9. For a thorough discussion of issues related to workers' control see David Montgomery, *Workers' Control in America; Studies in the history of work, technology, and labor struggles* (New York, 1980).

CHAPTER TWO: NOTES

1. Alan Dawley, *Class and Community: The Industrial Revolution in Lynn* (Cambridge, Mass.: Harvard University Press, 1976), Paul G. Faler, *Mechanics and Manufacturers in the Early Industrial Revolution: Lynn, Massachusetts, 1780–1860* (Albany: State University of New York Press, 1981), Howard B. Rock, *Artisans of the New Republic: The Tradesmen of*

New York City during the Age of Jefferson (New York: New York University Press, 1979) are three such works. The most far-reaching analysis of artisan rituals has been done by Sean Wilentz; see his "Artisan Republican Festivals and the Rise of Class Conflict in New York City, 1788–1837," in Michael H. Frisch and Daniel J. Walkowitz, eds., *Working-Class America: Essays on Labor, Community, and American Society* (Urbana: University of Illinois Press, 1983), and his book, *Chants Democratic: New York City and the Rise of the American Working Class, 1789–1850* (New York: Oxford University Press, 1984).

2. See William H. Mulligan, Jr., "The Family and Technological Change: The Shoemakers of Lynn, Massachusetts, during the Transition from Hand to Machine Production, 1850–1880" (Ph.D. dissertation, Clark University, 1982), esp. ch. 2.

3. Henry F. Tapley, "An Old New England Town as Seen by Joseph Lye, Cordwainer," *Register of the Lynn Historical Society,* 19 (1915), p. 42.

4. *Vital Records of Lynn, Massachusetts, to the End of the Year 1849,* 2 vols. (Salem, Mass.: Essex Institute, 1905), 1, p. 249; 2, p. 530; and Tapley, passim.

5. These obituary accounts are in the *Register of the Lynn Historical Society,* 1 (1897) –22 (1918–1921), passim.

6. Ibid. 8 (1903) p. 49.

7. Ibid. 10 (1905), p. 56. Lewis was born in Lynn in 1823 and died there in 1905.

8. Ibid. (Luther Johnson), 18 (1914), p. 43; Johnson was born at Nahant in 1841 and died in Lynn in 1914; ibid. (George Albert Breed), 21 (1917), p. 17; Breed was born in Lynn in 1841 and died there in 1917.

9. William Stone, "Lynn and Its Old Time Shoemakers' Shops," ibid., 15 (1911), p. 84.

10. This close relationship between the occupation of the head of the household and other employed males extended to boarders as well. When the occupation of male boarders is compared to that of the head of the households in the 1850 census sample, a strong relationship, i.e., well over 80 percent, is found.

11. Formula from John F. Rees, *The Art and Mystery of a Cordwainer; or an Essay on the Principles and Practice of Boot and Shoe Making* (London, 1813). I am grateful to Kenneth Carpenter of the Harvard University Libraries for calling this item to my attention.

12. *The Awl,* July 17, 1848, p. 2.

13. *Register,* 7 (1902), p. 31.

14. Ibid., 18 (1914), p. 48.

15. Johnson, *Register of the Lynn Historical Society,* 18 (1914), p. 336-38.

16. Mary H. Blewett, "'I am Doom to Disappointment, . . .': The Diaries of a Beverly, Massachusetts, Shoebinder, Sarah E. Trask, 1849–1851," *Essex Institute Historical Collections,* 117 (1981), pp. 192–212. See also her, "Shared But Different: The Experience of Women in the Nineteenth-Century Workforce of the New England Shoe Industry," in *Essays From the Lowell Conference on Industrial History 1980 and 1981* (Lowell, Mass.: 1981), pp. 77–85.

17. Ibid., p. 200.

18. Massachusetts Bureau of Labor Statistics, *Second Annual Report* (Boston 1871), 93–98; *Fourth Annual Report* (Boston, 1873), 304–6. For a fuller discussion of mechanization see Mulligan, "Family and Technological Change," ch. 4 and "Mechanizing the Gentle Craft: The Introduction of Machinery into the Lynn, Massachusetts Shoe Industry, 1852–1883," in *Essays from the Lowell Conference on Industrial History 1980 and 1981* (Lowell, Mass.: 1981), pp. 33–45.

19. Lynn *Reporter,* reprinted in *Scientific American,* July 4, 1863, p. 4.

20. W.H. Richardson, comp. and ed., *The Boot and Shoe Manufacturers Assistant and Guide . . .* (Boston, 1858), p. 11. Emphasis in original.

21. *Annual Report of the Massachusetts Bureau of Labor Statistics for the Year 1875* (Boston, 1876), p. 249.

22. Fred A. Gannon, *A Short History of American Shoemaking* (Salem, Mass.: Newcomb & Gauss, 1912), p. 34.

23. "One of the Mrs. _____ Victims," *Superintendent and Foreman*, Oct. 27, 1896, p. 5.

24. Ibid.

25. "Learn It in the Factory," *Superintendent and Foreman*, Nov. 10, 1896, p. 7.

26. See Edith Abbott, *Women in Industry* (New York: Appleton, 1913); J.B. Andrews and W.D.P. Bliss, *History of Women in Trade Unions* (Washington, D.C.: U.S. Government Printing Office, 1913); Annie Marion MacLean, *Wage-Earning Women* (New York: Macmillan, 1910); and Helen L. Sumner, *History of Women in Industry in the United States* (Washington, D.C.: U.S. Government Printing Office, 1910).

27. Neil J. Smelser, *Social Change in the Industrial Revolution* (Chicago: University of Chicago Press, 1957) and "Sociological History: The Industrial Revolution and the British Working Class Family," *Journal of Social History,* 1 (1967). For a critique of Smelser and his model, see M.M. Edwards and R.L. Jones, "N.J. Smelser and the Cotton Factory Family: A Reassessment," in *Textile History and Economic History,* ed. by N.B. Harte and K.G. Ponting (Manchester: Manchester University Press, 1973).

CHAPTER THREE: NOTES

An earlier version of this essay was written with the aid of a grant from the Merrimack Valley Textile Museum, North Andover, Mass. I would like to express my gratitude to the Museum and its director, Thomas W. Leavitt, for supporting my research, and to the staff of the MVTM, particularly Helena Wright, for their invaluable help. I would also like to thank Robert Asher and Matthew Roth for their comments on a previous draft. Elizabeth C. Sholes contributed substantially to the form and content of the analysis presented here, and her constant support was crucial.

1. Much of the recent discussion of these issues has been informed by a revitalized Marxian analysis. See Harry Braverman, *Labor and Monopoly Capital* (New York: Monthly Review Press, 1974); David Gartman, "Marx and the Labor Process: An Interpretation," *The Insurgent Sociologist,* 8, nos. 2 and 3 (Fall 1978), pp. 97–108; Dan Clawson, *Bureaucracy and the Labor Process* (New York: Monthly Review Press, 1980), particularly ch. 1; Stephen A. Marglin, "What Do Bosses Do? The Origins and Functions of Hierarchy in Capitalist Production," in Anthony Giddens and David Held, eds., *Classes, Power, and Conflict* (Berkeley and Los Angeles: University of California Press, 1982), pp. 285–98; David Stark, "Class Struggle and the Transformation of the Labor Process: A Relational Approach," in Giddens and Held, pp. 310–29.

2. Raphael Samuel, "The Workshop of the World: Steam Power and Hand Technology in Mid-Victorian Britain," *History Workshop,* 3 (Spring 1977), pp. 6–72, is a spellbinding account of this process which has greatly influenced my own interpretation.

3. David Montgomery, "Workers' Control of Machine Production in the Nineteenth Century," *Labor History,* 17, no. 4 (Fall 1976), pp. 485–509.

4. David J. Jeremy, *Transatlantic Industrial Revolution: The Diffusion of Textile Technologies between Britain and America, 1790–1830* (Cambridge, Mass.: MIT press, 1981), 12-13, pp. 84–86.

5. On artisan production in a different metropolitan setting, see the occasionally conflicting interpretations of Howard B. Rock, *Artisans of the New Republic* (New York: New York University Press, 1979), ch. 6, 9, and 10, and Sean Wilentz, "Artisan Republican Festivals and the Rise of Class Conflict in New York City, 1788–1837," in Michael H. Frisch and Daniel J. Walkowitz, eds., *Working-Class America* (Urbana: University of Illinois Press, 1983), esp. pp. 39–43.

6. Gary B. Kulik, "The Beginnings of the Industrial Revolution in America: Pawtuck-

et, Rhode Island, 1672–1829" (unpub. Ph.d. dissertation, Brown University, 1980) gives an excellent and conceptually sophisticated analysis of this point in the community where the textile and textile machinery industries got their start.

7. William R. Bagnall, "Sketches of Manufacturing Establishments in New York City, and of Textile Establishments in the Eastern States," typescript, Victor S. Clark, ed., 4 vols. (1908), 3, pp. 2342–43, Baker Library, Harvard University (hereafter, BL).

8. David Wilkinson, "Reminiscences," *Transactions of the Rhode Island Society for the Encouragement of Domestic Industry in the Year 1861* (Providence, 1862), pp. 100–18; Jonathan Thayer Lincoln, "The Beginnings of the Machine Age in New England: David Wilkinson of Pawtucket," *New England Quarterly,* 6 (1933), pp. 716–32; John P. Johnson, "David Wilkinson" (unpub. M.A. thesis, Bridgewater State College, Mass., 1978); BL, Nathan Sweetland & Company, Ledger (1811–1816).

9. For a summary of the industry's development, see John W. Lozier, "Taunton and Mason: Cotton Machinery and Locomotive Manufacture in Taunton, Massachusetts, 1811–1861" (unpub. Ph.D. dissertation, Ohio State University, 1978), pp. 25–38. Older accounts are available in Victor S. Clark, *History of Manufactures in the United States,* 3 vols. (New York: Peter Smith, 1949), 1, pp. 434–35, 518–21, and in Jonathan Thayer Lincoln, "The Cotton Textile Machine Industry," *Harvard Business Review,* 11 (1932), pp. 88–96. On the early woolen machinery shops of Worcester, see also [Louis McLane,] *Report of the Secretary of the Treasury, 1832, Documents Relative to the Manufactures of the United States,* 2 vols., Doc. 308 22nd Cong., 1st Sess., (Washington, D.C.: Duff Green, 1833); Arthur H. Cole, *The American Wool Manufacture,* 2 vols. (Cambridge, Mass.: Harvard University Press, 1926), 1, pp. 99 n1, 124; Barnes Riznik, "New England Machine-Building Shops for Manufacture of Wool Carding, Picking, Napping, and Shearing Machines, 1800–1840" (Old Sturbridge Village, Mass.: Research Report, 1965).

10. T.E. Leary, "Industrial Archaeology and Industrial Ecology," *Radical History Review,* 21 (1979), pp. 171–82.

11. Rhode Island Historical Society Library, Providence, R.I. (hereafter, RIHS), Zachariah Allen Manuscripts: Miscellaneous Papers, List of Cotton Mills in Rhode Island in 1811 (copy at Slater Mill Historic Site, Pawtucket, R.I. [hereafter, SMHS]); Johnson, "Wilkinson," p. 35.

12. Frederick M. Peck and Henry H. Earl, *Fall River and its Industries* (New York: Atlantic Publishing and Engraving, 1877), p. 14.

13. Thomas Mann, "A Plat of the Blackstone River and Sargent's Trench . . . 13 June 1823." Original document filed in connection with the Sargent's Trench case (Tyler et al. versus Wilkinson et al., 24 Fed. Case 472, 474 [no. 14, p. 312]), Federal Records Center, Waltham, Mass. Copy in files of SMHS and reprinted in *The Flyer* [publication of SMHS], 9, no. 5 and 6 [Sept.–Dec., 1979]); Massena Goodrich, *Historical Sketch of the Town of Pawtucket* (Pawtucket, R.I.: Nickerson, Sibley, 1876), p. 64; Robert Grieve and John Fernald, *The Cotton Centennial, 1790–1890* (Providence: J.A. & R.A. Reid, 1891), p. 51.

14. Bagnall, "Sketches," pp. 2154, 2158, 2354; George S. Gibb, *The Saco–Lowell Shops* (Cambridge, Mass.: Harvard University Press, 1950), pp. 69–70.

15. Gibb, *Saco–Lowell Shops,* p. 82. A sketch of the Lowell shop's foundry in the mid-1840s may be found in Merrimack Valley Textile Museum, North Andover, Mass. (hereafter, MVTM), Essex Company Manuscripts: MS 306, Memoranda Made during a Tour of Inspection among Various Machine Shops . . . March 16–22 (1846). (My thanks to Duncan Hay and Helena Wright for this reference.) On foundry construction by other New England textile machinery companies during the 1830s and 1840s, see Lozier, "Taunton and Mason," pp. 144–45. On the comparative militance of foundry workers and machine operators in certain late 19th century industries, see Daniel Nelson, "The American System and the American Worker," in Otto Mayr and Robert C.

Post, eds., *Yankee Enterprise* (Washington, D.C.: Smithsonian Institution Press, 1981), pp. 174–76.

16. Sequence of construction taken from BL, Lowell Machine Shop Manuscripts: TC–1, List of Tools (1883).

17. On the decline of the locomotive manufacture at Lowell, see Gibb, *Saco–Lowell Shops*, 195; Lozier, "Taunton and Mason," pp. 493 n 40, 501.

18. *The New England Textile Mill Survey: Selections from the Historic American Buildings Survey*, No. Eleven (Washington, D.C.: Historic American Buildings Survey, U.S. Department of the Interior, 1971), pp. 57–64; Peter M. Molloy, *The Lower Merrimack River Valley: An Inventory of Historic Engineering and Industrial Sites* (Washington, D.C.: Historic American Engineering Record, U.S. Department of the Interior, 1976), pp. 33–34.

19. Lozier, "Taunton and Mason," p. 346.

20. Thomas R. Navin, *The Whitin Machine Works since 1831* (Cambridge, Mass.: Harvard University Press, 1950), pp. 36–37.

21. MVTM, Barlow's Insurance Survey no. 4063 (1876); Gary B. Kulik and Julia C. Bonham, *Rhode Island: An Inventory of Historic Engineering and Industrial Sites* (Washington, D.C.: Historic American Engineering Record, U.S. Department of the Interior, 1978), p. 150; Stephen J. Roper, *Pawtucket, Rhode Island: Historical Preservation Report P-PA-1* (Providence, R.I.: Rhode Island Historical Preservation Commission, October 1978), p. 53.

22. Charles G. Washburn, *Industrial Worcester* (Worcester, Mass.: Davis, 1917), p. 87.

23. MVTM, Davis & Furber: MS 67.47, Letter Book (1833–1841). Description of Property at Auction, June 14, 1841; S.F. Rockwell materials on Davis & Furber Company history: MS 231.1, p. 128A; Barlow's Insurance Survey no. 3436 (1874). See also Molloy, *Lower Merrimack*, pp. 92–93.

24. For a brief overview, see Daniel Nelson, *Managers and Workers* (Madison: University of Wisconsin Press, 1975), pp. 13–14, 17–18.

25. Matthew Roth, *Connecticut: An Inventory of Historic Engineering and Industrial Sites* (Washington, D.C.: Society for Industrial Archeology, 1981), pp. xxiii–xxiv.

26. See James B. Jefferys, *The Story of the Engineers* (1945; reprint New York: Johnson Reprint, 1970), pp. 12–15 for an analysis of the situation in Britain.

27. Eugene S. Ferguson, ed., *Early Engineering Reminiscences [1815–1840] of George Escol Sellers* (Washington, D.C.: Smithsonian Institution Press, 1965), p. 34.

28. Samuel Smiles, ed., *James Nasmyth, Engineer: An Autobiography* (New York: Harper, 1883), pp. 201–2.

29. Ibid., p. 311.

30. See Monte A. Calvert, *The Mechanical Engineer in America, 1830–1910* (Baltimore: Johns Hopkins University Press, 1967), and David F. Noble, *America by Design* (Oxford: Oxford University Press, 1977), particularly ch. 1–3.

31. James Nasmyth, "Remarks on the Introduction of the Slide Principle in Tools and Machines Employed in the Production of Machinery," Appendix B of Robertson Buchanan, *Practical Essays on Mill Work and Other Machinery*, 3rd ed. (London: John Weale, 1841), p. 401.

32. See Robert S. Woodbury, *Studies in the History of Machine Tools* (Cambridge, Mass.: MIT Press, 1972); L.T.C. Rolt, *A Short History of Machine Tools* (Cambridge, Mass.: MIT Press, 1965); W. Steeds, *A History of Machine Tools* (Oxford: Clarendon Press, 1969); Ian Bradley, *A History of Machine Tools* (Hemel Hempstead, Hertfordshire: Model and Allied Publications, 1972).

33. On Maudslay's work, see Woodbury, "History of the Lathe to 1850" in Woodbury, *Studies in the History of Machine Tools*, pp. 96–108; Rolt, *Short History of Machine Tools*, pp. 83–91; Steeds, *History of Machine Tools*, pp. 14–15, 22–23, 28–30; Bradley, *History of Machine Tools*, pp. 11, 19. For an analysis of the limitations of Maudslay's early designs

based on artifacts in the Science Museum, London, see K.R. Gilbert, *The Machine Tool Collection: Catalogue of Exhibits with Historical Introduction* (London: H.M. Stationery Office, 1966), pp. 37–39.

34. My thanks to Matt Roth for clarifying this point. Also see Samuel Smiles, *Industrial Biography: Iron-Workers and Tool-Makers* (Boston: Ticknor & Fields, 1863), pp. 261–62.

35. Wilkinson, "Reminiscences," pp. 102–3.

36. Ibid., pp. 106–9; Woodbury, "History of The Lathe," pp. 89–93; Rolt, *Short History of Machine Tools*, pp. 162–63; Steeds, *History of Machine Tools*, 22. Compare with Merritt Roe Smith, *Harpers Ferry Armory and the New Technology* (Ithaca, N.Y.: Cornell University Press, 1977), pp. 122–23.

37. See the following lathes in the collections of SMHS: Accession numbers 70.094, 70.169, 71.007, 73.003, 73.030.

38. RIHS, Henry B. Dexter Manuscripts: George Clark Diary, Apr. 4, 1852, (reprinted in *The Flyer*, [SMHS], 4, no. 1, [Jan. 1973]) pp. 10–11.

39. On the early planer (c. 1836) at the Gay & Silver shop, see "Observations in an Old Shop," *Machinery*, 2, no. 6 (Feb. 1896), pp. 167–68. Compare with Lozier, "Taunton and Mason," pp. 145–46.

40. For example, see MVTM, Essex Company Manuscripts: MS 306, Box 3, List of Tools in Amoskeag Company Shop, Feb. 7, 1846, and Mr. Marvel's Estimate of Tools for Machine Shop, Oct. 7, 1846; Davis & Furber Manuscripts: MS 67.20, Purchase Ledger: Tool Account (1860–1864); Gibb, *Saco–Lowell Shops*, pp. 636–37.

41. Wilkinson, "Reminiscences," pp. 107–8; Goodrich, *Historical Sketch*, p. 48; James L. Conrad, Jr., "The Evolution of Industrial Capitalism in Rhode Island, 1790–1830: Almy, the Browns, and the Slaters" (unpub. Ph.D. dissertation, University of Connecticut, 1973), pp. 176–77; Gary Kulik, Roger Parks, and Theodore Z. Penn, *The New England Mill Village, 1790–1860* (Cambridge, Mass.: MIT Press, 1982), p. 92 n8.

42. Gibb, *Saco–Lowell Shops*, pp. 25, 49.

43. MVTM, Trade Catalogues: "Machinery and Machinists' Tools Manufactured by the Lawrence Machine Shop" (Lynn, Mass.: Reporter Office, 1855).

44. Ibid., "Machinery and Machinists' Tools . . ."

45. Nasmyth, "Remarks," p. 410.

46. MVTM, John Rogers Letters (originals at New-York Historical Society): MS 223, Rogers to his father, Nov. 9, 1850.

47. Gibb, *Saco–Lowell Shops*, p. 81.

48. On measurement in the Lowell Machine Shop, see Paul Uselding, "Measuring Techniques and Manufacturing Practice," in Mayr and Post, *Yankee Enterprise*, pp. 114–15.

49. Gibb, *Saco–Lowell Shops*, pp. 89, 145–47, 217, 296, 359, 646–47; Navin, *Whitin*, pp. 139–49; Nelson, *Managers and Workers*, pp. 36–38; Clawson, *Bureaucracy and the Labor Process*, pp. 71–125.

50. E.J. Hobsbawm, "The Labour Aristocracy in Nineteenth-Century Britain," in *Labouring Men* (Garden City, N.Y.: Doubleday, 1967), pp. 351–54. For an analysis of the work force in the Oldham textile machinery industry which also relies on the concepts of the labor aristocracy and coexploitation, see John Foster, *Class Struggle and the Industrial Revolution* (New York: St. Martin's Press, 1974), pp. 224–29.

51. For example, Gay, Silver & Company in North Chelmsford was a quintessential jobbing shop in the 1830s, making textile machinery, millwork, woodworking machinery, machine tools, and agricultural machinery to order. They even undertook to hang a stove door for the local Baptist Society. See Gay, Silver & Company, Day Book (1836–1842) in the private collection of Warren G. Ogden, North Andover, Mass. I am most grateful to Mr. Ogden for allowing me to examine this source and for giving me on numerous occasions the benefit of his expertise in the field of machine tools and their history.

52. On contracting in the federal armories, Smith, *Harpers Ferry Armory*, pp. 64, 134–36, 239–40.

53. George Clark Diary, Feb. 6, 1853, reprinted in *The Flyer*, 4, no. 5 (May 1973), p. 11. Clark was employed at the Farrel Foundry in Ansonia, Connecticut, whose product line consisted of heavy machinery and millwork. On the Farrel works, see Roth, *Connecticut*, p. 165.

54. George Clark Diary, Mar. 10, 1853, reprinted in *The Flyer*, 4, no. 6 (June 1973), p. 11.

55. Ibid., Aug. 6, 1852, reprinted in *The Flyer*, 4, no. 3 (Mar. 1973), p. 10. Upon receiving his raise to $2.00 per day (from $1.80) he had remarked, "My wages are now more than I ever expected to receive as a journeyman mechanic, and I feel every way satisfied with my pay."

56. One can begin to understand the contributions of the military in stifling democracy in the modern American work place by consulting Merritt Roe Smith, "Military Entrepreneurship," in Mayr and Post, *Yankee Enterprise*, pp. 63–102, and Alfred D. Chandler, "The American System and Modern Management," in Mayr and Post, pp. 153–70.

57. A convenient introduction to this topic is Jonathan Thayer Lincoln, "Origin of Piece Work Revealed in Early Loom Building," *Textile World*, 81, no. 3 (Jan. 16, 1932), pp. 20–21.

58. Bagnall, "Sketches," 2351; BL, Proprietors of Locks & Canals Manuscripts: Case S-1, Orders to Job Hands by George Brownell (1826–1828).

59. Navin, *Whitin*, p. 146.

60. Clawson, *Bureaucracy and the Labor Process*, pp. 79–81, 114.

61. Jefferys, *Story of the Engineers*, pp. 23, 35, 63–64, 100; James B. Jefferys, "The Wages, Hours, and Trade Customs of the Skilled Engineer in 1861," *Economic History Review*, 17, nos. 1 and 2 (1947), pp. 40–49; Montgomery, "Workers' Control," pp. 492, 494.

62. George S. White, *Memoir of Samuel Slater* (Philadelphia: no publisher, 1836), p. 254. On the wages of English and American machinists during this period, see White, p. 340 and Nathan Rosenberg, "Anglo-American Wage Differences in the 1820s," *Journal of Economic History*, 27 (1967), pp. 221–29.

63. Nathaniel W. Everett, Personal Account Book: Work Account (1831–1872). In possession of Judith Malone, Newton Upper Falls, copy at SMHS. (My thanks to Patrick Malone for calling this valuable source to my attention.)

64. Davis & Furber Manuscripts: MS 67.40, Cost of Labour Book (1860–1861).

65. Gibb, *Saco–Lowell Shops*, p. 89.

66. Navin, *Whitin*, p. 65.

67. For the early experiences of George Richardson at the Lowell shop, see Gibb, *Saco–Lowell Shops*, pp. 644–46.

68. Bagnall, "Sketches," p. 2405.

69. Ibid., p. 2406.

70. MVTM, MS 86.2: Indenture of John McGarrigle (Oct. 1, 1855). For Slater's indenture, see White, *Memoir*, facing p. 33.

71. MVTM, MS 7: William Burke to Dr. O. Dean, Manchester, N.H., July 16, 1844. Burke did note that apprenticeship policies in the foundry differed from those common among machinists.

72. Gibb, *Saco–Lowell Shops*, p. 147.

73. George Clark Diary, Nov. 19, 1851, reprinted in *The Flyer*, 3, no. 10 (Oct. 1972), p. 11.

74. John Rogers Letters, Rogers to his father, July 19, 1850.

75. Rogers to his sister Laura, Sept. 22, 1850, and to his father, Nov. 9, 1850.

76. Rogers to his sister Ellen, Mar. 23, 1851.

77. Rogers to his sister Ellen, Oct. 2, 1853.

78. Rogers to his mother, Nov. 17, 1850, and to his father, Jan. 4, 1851.

79. Rogers to his mother, July 28, 1850.

80. Rogers to his father, July 22, and Sept. 1, 1850. Compare this opinion with the earlier account of O.H. Moulton.

81. Rogers to his mother, July 28, 1850, and to his father Sept. 1, 1850.

82. Rogers to his father, July 22, 1850.

83. Eliza A. Chase, "Being Somebody," *Andover Advertiser,* Sept. 10, 1853.

84. MVTM, Samuel F. Rockwell collection on Davis & Furber Company history: MS 231.1, 47.

CHAPTER FOUR: NOTES

I wish to express my appreciation for support from the Robert Starobin Memorial Fellowship. I am also grateful to Harold Wechsler, Charles Stephenson, Bob Asher, and Susan Greenberg for their valuable criticism.

1. Stephan Thernstrom, "Urbanization, Migration, and Social Mobility in Late Nineteenth-Century America," in Barton Bernstein, ed., *Towards a New Past: Dissenting Essays in American History* (New York: Vintage Books, 1969), and Stephan Thernstrom and Peter Knights, "Men in Motion: Some Data and Speculations about Urban Population Mobility in Nineteenth-Century America," *Journal of Interdisciplinary History* (Autumn 1970).

2. Eric L. McKitrick and Stanley Elkins, "Institutions in Motion," *American Quarterly* (Summer 1960), and Rowland Berthoff, "The American Social Order: A Conservative Hypothesis," *American Historical Review* (Apr. 1960).

3. Alexis de Tocqueville, *Democracy in America,* 2 vols. (1835; reprint New York: Vintage Books, 1945), 2, p. 114.

4. See Herbert G. Gutman, "Work, Culture, and Society in Industrializing America, 1815–1919," *American Historical Review* (June 1973), p. 567; Alan Dawley and Paul Faler, "Working-Class Culture and Politics in the Industrial Revolution: Sources of Loyalism and Rebellion," *Journal of Social History* (June 1976); David Montgomery, "The Shuttle and the Cross: Weavers and Artisans in the Kensington Riots of 1844," *Journal of Social History* (Summer 1972); and Stanley Aronowitz, *False Promises: The Shaping of American Working-Class Consciousness* (New York: McGraw-Hill, 1973).

5. "Worldly asceticism" is Max Weber's term, presented in the *Protestant Ethic and the Spirit of Capitalism* and discussed by Eric Foner in *Free Soil, Free Labor, Free Men: The Ideology of the Republican Party before the Civil War* (New York: Oxford University Press, 1970), pp. 12–13.

6. In *Free Soil,* Foner discussed the importance of free labor ideas in the formation of the Republican Party. Also see David Montgomery, *Beyond Equality: Labor and the Radical Republicans, 1862–1872* (New York: Knopf, 1967), pp. 30–31. This article is part of my study, *Worker and Community: The Social Structure of a Nineteenth-Century American City, Albany, New York, 1850–1884* (Albany: State University of New York Press, 1985) in which I deal with the impact of free labor ideas on the full range of workers' political, social, and economic activities within the political, ethnic, religious, and institutional structures of the community. Thus, the free labor ideas presented here are not unique to fraternal societies but reflect basic social values.

7. Noel P. Gist, "Secret Societies: A Cultural Study of Fraternalism in the United States," *University of Missouri Studies* (Oct. 1, 1940). Gist calls the IOOF and the Masons models, in terms of how they functioned, for other fraternal societies that developed in the United States. Although industry, particularly small manufacturing, was important

in Albany, the city was primarily a commercial, not an industrial, one. For example, its wealthiest and most influential citizen during these years, Erastus Corning, was president of the Albany City Bank, the Albany Mutual Insurance Company, and the New York Central Railroad. He also developed a large hardware business in Albany and set up the New York Central Railroad shops in West Albany. But he built the Albany Nail Factory and the Rensselaer Iron Works in Troy, New York, not Albany. See Irene D. Neu, *Erastus Corning: Merchant and Financier, 1794–1872* (Ithaca, N.Y.: Cornell University Press, 1960).

8. Gist, "Secret Societies," pp. 31–32; Fergus MacDonald, *The Catholic Church and Secret Societies in the United States* (New York: Catholic Historical Society, 1946), p. 100. Of the six million names, many were probably duplicates. An individual could join more than one fraternity, and there is evidence that this was done by members of the Albany fraternities.

9. Theodore A. Ross, *Odd-Fellowship: Its History and Manual* (New York: M.W. Hazen, 1888), pp. 9–10; MacDonald, *Catholic Church and Secret Societies*, p. 6; Henry Stillson, ed., *The Official History and Literature of Odd Fellowship, The Three-Link Fraternity* (Boston: Fraternity Publishing, 1897), p. 754.

10. Ross, *Odd-Fellowship*, pp. 12–27, 32–37.

11. Reverend A.B. Grosh, *The Odd-Fellow's Improved Manual: Containing the History, Defence, Principles and Government of the Order. . .* (New York: Clark and Maynard, 1873), p. 72. The national body was originally called the Supreme Grand Lodge.

12. The "unwritten" work refers to the rituals and ceremonies that were secret, whereas the "written" work includes much of the actual functioning of the order, such as the names and lessons of the degrees, the benefits, and the regalia, which could be found in the histories and manuals of Odd-Fellowship.

13. Ross, *Odd-Fellowship*, pp. 573, 251. In my discussion of the symbols and rituals of the order, it can be assumed that the practices in Albany were those described in the manuals.

14. The order provided financial assistance to the families of deceased Odd Fellows, including aid for the education of orphans, and relief for a brother in distress because of sickness or unemployment.

15. Once he had been a member for at least four weeks, an Odd Fellow could apply for a higher degree, pay the fees, and go through the appropriate ritual testing his knowledge of the lessons of that degree. In addition to the five degrees in the subordinate lodge, Odd Fellowship had a Patriarchical Degree, begun in 1829. Membership in this degree was open to Scarlet Degree Odd Fellows. The Patriarchs met outside the lodge in Encampments. In 1851 the Rebekah Degree was established for women, and in the 1880s a military degree, the Patriarchs Militant, was introduced.

16. James L. Ridgely, *History of American Odd Fellowship: The First Decade* (Baltimore: By the author, 1878), p. 492. The Masons had similar restrictions but also barred eunuchs from membership.

17. Ross, *Odd-Fellowship*, p. 538.

18. Stillson, *Official History*, pp. 234, 257; Ross, *Odd-Fellowship*, p. 2.

19. In 1911 the Albany Odd Fellows' temple burned, and most of the records were destroyed. The lists I used are available in the New York State Library. The disparity between the 1845 list and the later scattered records prevents meaningful comparison, and therefore I have avoided the use of statistical evidence. Nevertheless, I have checked the names on the available records and on the lists constructed from the records of the State Grand Lodge against the appropriate Albany city directories for the occupational status of these men. The point I want to make in this article—that members of all of Albany's social classes participated in Odd Fellowship—is supported by the evidence as it stands.

It is perhaps worthwhile to note one final methodological problem. In the 1845

Albany city directories many Odd Fellows either are not listed, are not given an occupational reference, or have a common name, meaning that more than one occupational reference is possible. For example, of the seventy-eight names of members of Hope Lodge No. 8 in 1845, thirty-three (42%) fit into one of these categories, and similar gaps in information exist for all of Albany's Odd Fellow lodges. This situation undermines any meaningful statistical description of the social composition of Odd Fellowship in Albany.

20. Using the specific occupations listed in the city directories, I assumed that a carpenter or molder was a skilled worker and that unskilled laborers were listed separately. For a discussion of the problem of occupational classification, see Clyde Griffen, "Occupational Mobility in Nineteenth Century America: Problems and Possibilities," *Journal of Social History* (Spring 1972), pp. 310–30. Former chief officers of the subordinate lodges, or Noble Grands, were referred to as Past Grands.

21. The membership of Hope Lodge No. 3 included Robert Pruyn, Cornelius Ten-Broeck, Abraham Van Vechtan, and other noted Albany attorneys; C.W. Bender, the city chamberlain; Joel Munsell, a book and job printer and local archivist and antiquarian; and Rufus King, assistant editor of the *Albany Evening Journal*, the city's leading Republican newspaper.

22. William E. Rowley, "Albany: A Tale of Two Cities, 1820–1880" (Ph.D. dissertation, Harvard University, 1967), pp. 168–75, Appendix (Tables 1–5).

23. I used membership lists from Mountaineer Lodge No. 321 for 1872 and American Lodge No. 32 for 1882 to examine the socioeconomic structure of Albany's Odd Fellows after 1845. There is also a list of members for American Lodge No. 32 in 1850, but I found this was similar to the 1845 list.

24. It is interesting that a large number of foremen were Odd Fellows, particularly at a time when control over labor was largely informal and left to the foremen—but this evidence is only suggestive as it is limited to American Lodge No. 32.

25. Irish Catholics may not have joined the Odd Fellows in great numbers because they had their own distinct ethnic, social, and benevolent organizations like the Hibernian Provident Society. See Rowley, "The Irish Aristocracy of Albany, 1798–1878," *New York History* (July 1971), pp. 275–304.

26. Gist, "Secret Societies," p. 70.

27. Ridgely, *History of American-Odd Fellowship*, pp. 2, 10; Ross, *Odd-Fellowship*, p. 600. Emphasis in original.

28. Ross, *Odd-Fellowship*, p. 44. In a paper presented in a workshop at the American Historical Association Convention in December 1976, I endeavored to show how the activities and philosophy of fraternal societies—the provision of traveling cards and practical benefits, the universality of their symbolic "secret work," the emphasis on brotherhood, and their perception of themselves as a family—illustrate the portability of nineteenth-century American voluntary institutions. Odd Fellowship is one example of an institutional network that developed to give a volatile people a sense of community. See also Don H. Doyle, "The Social Functions of Voluntary Associations in a Nineteenth-Century American Town," *Social Science History* (Spring 1977), pp. 333–55.

29. Stillson, *Official History*, p. 101.

30. Ridgely, *History of American Odd-Fellowship*, p. 319. MacDonald (*Catholic Church and Secret Societies*) claimed that the break with the Manchester Unity resulted from the English chartering of a Negro Odd Fellow Lodge in the United States. The literature of American Odd-Fellowship, however, does not mention this; moreover, the literature accounts for the break as reform. Ridgely, as grand secretary for over thirty years, was the leader of this reform movement.

31. Ridgely, *History of American Odd-Fellowship*, pp. 264, 320. Although this reform was spoken of in terms of its moral influence, Odd Fellows seemed unaware of its significance for their social position. Also see Stillson, *Official History*, p. 103.

32. *Journal of Proceedings of the Right Worthy Grand Lodge of the Independent Order of Odd Fellows of Northern New York State for 1858, held in the City of Syracuse* (Syracuse: Curtiss and White, 1858), p. 36.

33. Stillson, *Official History,* p. 817.

34. James L. Ridgely and Paschal Donaldson, *The Odd Fellows' Pocket Companion: A Correct Guide in All Matters Relating to Odd-Fellowship* (Cincinnati: W. Carroll, 1867), p. 321.

35. Grosh, *The Odd-Fellow's Improved Manual,* p. 34.

36. *Constitution and By-Laws of Union Lodge No. 8 of the Independent Order of Odd Fellows* (Albany, 1845), p. 4; *Constitution, By-Laws and Rules of Order of American Lodge No. 32, of the Independent Order of Odd Fellows of the City of Albany* (Albany: Joel Munsell, 1850), p. 16.

37. The "lessons" of the emblems appear throughout Odd Fellow literature. For example, see Stillson, *Official History,* pp. 874–77; Ross, *Odd-Fellowship,* pp. 574–78; and Grosh, *The Odd-Fellow's Improved Manual,* pp. 86–172.

38. Grosh, *The Odd-Fellow's Improved Manual,* p. 109.

39. Ezra Cook, *Five Standard Rituals: Odd-Fellowship Illustrated, Knights of Pythias Illustrated, Good Templars Illustrated, Exposition of the Grange, Ritual of the Grand Army of the Republic and the Machinists' and Blacksmiths' Union* (Chicago: Ezra Cook, 1880), p. 29. Cook opposed secret societies, and in this collection of five pamphlets he published their "secret" rituals. Gist claimed that Cook's information was substantially correct. On the expulsion or suspension of members for drunkenness, see, for example, the *Constitution of . . . American Lodge No. 32,* p. 37. Other causes for suspension and expulsion included neglect of family, abuse of benevolence, gambling, and conduct unbecoming an Odd Fellow. See *Journal of Proceedings of the Annual Communication of the Right Worthy Grand Lodge of Northern New York, held at the City of Auburn, August 1852* (Utica: Curtiss and White, 1852), pp. 193–95.

40. Grosh, *The Odd-Fellow's Improved Manual,* p. 52.

41. *Constitution . . . of American Lodge No. 32,* pp. 10–11.

42. *Constitution . . . of Union Lodge No. 8,* p. 26; *Mountaineer Lodge No. 321,* p. 27.

43. *Constitution . . . of Union Lodge No. 8,* p. 3.

44. Grosh, *Odd-Fellow's Improved Manual,* pp. 88–89.

45. Gist, "Secret Societies," p. 66.

46. Ridgely, *History of American Odd-Fellowship,* p. 495.

47. Stillson, *Official History,* pp. 874–77; Ross, *Odd-Fellowship,* pp. 574–78; Grosh, *Odd-Fellow's Improved Manual,* pp. 86–172.

48. *Constitution . . . of Union Lodge No. 8,* p. 3.

49. Gist, "Secret Societies," p. 142.

50. In *Worker and Community* I argue that free labor values formed the basis of the "community consciousness." Reflecting their belief in a mutuality of interests, adherents of the free labor ideology sought to foster loyalty to the community rather than to class among employers as well as workers. Free labor values were thus the core of a communally acceptable norm for all groups. The question of modification of employer behavior through participation in community associations like the Odd Fellows is a critical one and merits its own study.

51. *Argus,* Apr. 15, 1867.

52. *Albany Evening Journal,* May 3, 1867.

53. See *Mountaineer Lodge No. 321,* pp. 5, 7; *Constitution . . . of American Lodge No. 32,* p. 13.

54. Ross, *Odd-Fellowship,* p. 569.

55. *Mountaineer Lodge No. 321,* p. 20.

56. Gist, "Secret Societies," p. 120.

57. Dawley and Faler, "Working-Class Culture," p. 2.

58. See Irwin Yellowitz, *The Position of the Worker in American Society, 1865–1896* (Englewood Cliffs, N.J.: Prentice-Hall, 1969), p. 1; and Douglas T. Miller, *Jacksonian Aristocracy: Class and Democracy in New York, 1830–1860* (New York: Oxford University Press, 1967), p. 23. It should be noted that I am merely presenting here the tenets of the success ethic and not making any claims for high vertical mobility in American society in these years. Moreover, as Albany workers' efforts in behalf of producers' cooperatives and the eight-hour day demonstrate, workers could in fact think of equality as a leveling process.

59. *The Covenant,* 4 (May 1845), pp. 227–28.

60. Ridgely, *History of American Odd-Fellowship,* pp. 492–93.

61. Ibid., p. 497.

62. Stillson, *Official History,* p. 545.

63. Gist, "Secret Societies," p. 67.

64. Ross, *Odd-Fellowship,* p. 207.

65. Ridgely and Donaldson, *Pocket Companion,* p. 304. Emphasis in original.

66. Stillson, *Official History,* pp. 874–77; Ross, *Odd-Fellowship,* pp. 574–78; Grosh, *Odd-Fellow's Improved Manual,* pp. 86–172.

67. Grosh, *Odd-Fellow's Improved Manual,* p. 108.

68. Ridgely and Donaldson, *Pocket Companion,* p. 13. Emphasis in original.

69. The Order spent over $50,000 on relief in New York State in 1870, and in 1875 almost $150,000. For Albany alone over $1,600 was spent in 1870 and in 1875 almost $7,000. The figures for Albany represent relief to members only, not including aid to widows for funerals or for support of the education of orphans. The figures for New York State represent the total amount spent on relief. See Ross, *Odd-Fellowship,* pp. 614–15; George R. Howell and Jonathan Tenney, *Bi-Centennial History of Albany: History of the County of Albany, New York, from 1609 to 1886* (New York: W.W. Munsell, 1886), p. 720.

70. Ross, *Odd-Fellowship,* p. 135.

71. Ridgely, *History of American Odd-Fellowship,* p. 495. Emphasis in original.

72. Quoted in Ross, *Odd-Fellowship,* pp. 257–57.

Chapter Five: Notes

The quote in the title is from Gertrude Barnum, "The Story of a Fall River Mill Girl," *The Independent* (February 2, 1905). The epigraph is from Elyakum Zunser, "For Whom is the Gold County?", in Abraham J. Karp, *Golden Door to America* (New York, 1976), p. 122. I would like to thank Suzanne Schnittman for research assistance on this essay.

1. Ptirim Sorokin, *Social Mobility* (New York, 1927).

2. Stephan Thernstrom, *Poverty and Progress: Social Mobility in a Nineteenth Century City* (Cambridge, Mass., 1964), p. 238.

3. See especially Thernstrom, "Urbanization, Migration, and Social Mobility in Late Nineteenth-Century America," in Barton J. Bernstein, ed., *Towards a New Past: Dissenting Essays in American History* (New York, 1968), and "Working Class Social Mobility in Industrial America," in Melvin Richter, ed., *Essays in Theory and History: An Approach to the Social Sciences* (Cambridge, Mass., 1970). See especially his discussion of "Men on the Move," pp. 85–90 in *Poverty and Progress.*

4. See especially Chapter Four, "Property, Savings,and Status," pp. 115–137.

5. Ibid., pp. 223–224.

6. Ibid., pp. 31–32.

7. Thernstrom, "Urbanization, Migration," pp. 169, 173.

8. Stephan Thernstrom, *The Other Bostonians: Poverty and Progress in the American Metropolis, 1880–1970* (Cambridge, Mass., 1973).

9. Michael J. Katz, *The People of Hamilton, Canada West: Family and Class in a Mid-*

Nineteenth-Century City (Cambridge, Mass., 1975); Katz, Michael J. Doucet, and Mark J. Stern, "Migration and the Social Order in Erie County, New York: 1855," *Journal of Interdisciplinary History* 9 (1978), 669–701, and *The Social Organization of Early Industrial Capitalism* (Cambridge, Mass., 1982); much of their article is drawn from Chapter Three of the book.

10. Katz, *People of Hamilton*, pp. 24–42.

11. Katz, "People of a Canadian City: 1851–2," *Canadian Historical Review* 17 (1972), pp. 402–426, and *People of Hamilton*, pp. 302–426.

12. David Gagan, "Geographical and Occupational Mobility in a Nineteenth Century City" (Paper presented to the Great Lakes Regional History Conference, 1975), p. 14; "Geographical and Social Mobility in Nineteenth Century Ontario: A Micro Study," *Canadian Review of Sociology and Anthropology* 13 (May 1976), 152–164.

13. Katz, *People of Hamilton*, p. 44; emphasis added.

14. Robert Wiebe, *The Search for Order* (New York, 1971), p. xiii.

15. Vance Packard, *A Nation of Strangers* (New York, 1972), p. 1 and front page [unnumbered].

16. Howard I. Kushner, "Immigrant Suicide in the United States: Toward a Psycho-Social History," *Journal of Social History* 18 (1984), 6, 18, 19. More recently Kushner has hypothesized that diet also might be involved: "[t]he carbohydrates in potatoes and pasta may be keeping untold numbers of Irish and Italians from killing themselves," he says! *Hartford Courant*, September 27, 1985, C5.

17. Samuel Hays, Review of Thernstrom's *The Other Bostonians, Journal of Social History* 10 (1976), 413.

18. See, for example, my "A Gathering of Strangers? Mobility, Social Structure, and Political Participation in the Formation of Nineteenth Century American Working Class Culture," in Milton Cantor, ed., *American Workingclass Culture: Explorations in American Labor and Social History* (Westport, Conn., 1979).

19. See Stephenson, "Migration and Mobility in Late Nineteenth- and Early Twenti-eth-Century America," Ph.D. dissertation, University of Wisconsin, Madison, 1980.

20. Thernstrom, *Poverty and Progress*, p. 31.

21. Howard M. Gitelman, *Workingmen of Waltham: Mobility in American Urban Industrial Development, 1885–1890* (Baltimore, 1974), p. 181.

22. James A. Henretta, "The Study of Social Mobility: Ideological Assumptions and Conceptual Bias," *Labor History* (1977), p. 174 n20.

23. Katz, *People of Hamilton*, p. 49.

24. Hays, "Review," p. 410.

25. David Montgomery, "The New Urban History," a review of Alan F. Davis and Mark H. Haller, *The Peoples of Philadelphia: A History of Ethnic Groups and Lower-Class Life* (Philadelphia, 1973), in *Reviews in American History* 2 (1974), 502.

26. Margo Anderson Conk, "Occupational Classification in the United States Census, 1870–1940," *Journal of Interdisciplinary History* 9 (1978), 128, 129 and "Social Mobility in Historical Perspective," *Marxist Perspectives* 3 (1978), 53, 55.

27. Henretta, "Social Mobility," 165, 173, 174, 176 n4, 167. See Montgomery, "New Urban History," and William H. Sewell, Jr., "Social Mobility in a Nineteenth Century European City: Some Findings and Implications," *Journal of Interdisciplinary History* 8 (1976), 217–233.

28. John Bodnar, *Workers' World: Kinship, Community, and Protest in an Industrial Society, 1900–1940* (Baltimore, 1982), 166, 177, 185, 166.

29. See, for example, David Montgomery, "Strikes in Nineteenth-Century America," *Social Science History* 4 (1980), 81–104.

30. Montgomery, "New Urban History," 502.

31. See the discussion of the free labor ideology in Brian Greenberg, *Worker and Community: Response to Industrialization in a Nineteenth-Century American City, Albany,*

New York 1850–1884 (Albany, 1985), Chapter One and thereafter; and Eric Foner, *Free Soil, Free Labor, Free Men: the Ideology of the Republican Party Before the Civil War* (New York, 1970), especially the introduction and Chapter One.

32. Greenberg, *Worker and Community,* pp. 2–4.

33. Quoted in Richard Hofstadter, *The American Political Tradition and the Men Who Made It* (New York, 1948), p. 105.

34. Quoted in David Montgomery, *Beyond Equality: Labor and the Radical Republicans 1862–1872* (New York, 1967), p. 31, from Lincoln, *Works,* III, 479.

35. Quoted in Foner, *Free Soil,* p. 16; pp. 17, 15.

36. The phrase is from Montgomery, *Beyond Equality,* p. 447.

37. Greenberg, *Worker and Community,* Introduction.

38. See, for example, the work of Herbert Gutman, particularly his discussion in "Work, Culture, and Society in Industrializing America," in *Work, Culture, and Society in Industrializing America: Essays in Working-Class and Social History* (New York, 1976).

39. Herbert G. Gutman, "The Reality of the Rags-to-Riches 'Myth': the Case of the Paterson, New Jersey, Locomotive, Iron, and Machinery Manufacturers, 1830–1880," in Stephan Thernstrom and Richard Sennett, eds., *Nineteenth-Century Cities: Essays in the New Urban History* (New Haven, 1969), pp. 121–122.

40. Bruce Laurie, "'Nothing on Compulsion': Life Styles of Philadelphia Artisans, 1820–1850," *Labor History* (1974), p. 26; E.P. Thompson, *The Making of the English Working Class* (New York, 1965), p. 249; Irwin Yellowitz, *Industrialization and the American Labor Movement, 1850–1900* (Port Washington, N.Y., 1977), p. 26.

41. Laurie, "Life Styles," p. 341; Thernstrom, *Poverty and Progress,* p. 20; Virginia Yans-McLaughlin, "A Flexible Tradition: South Italian Immigrants Confront a New Work Experience," *Journal of Social History* 9 (1975), 458; see also her *Family and Community: Italian Immigrants in Buffalo, 1880–1930* (Ithaca, N.Y., 1977), p. 433; B.B. Adams, Jr., "The Every-day Life of a Railroad Man," *Scribner's* (November 1888), p. 556; Leon Stein, *Out of the Sweatshop* (New York, 1977), pp. 161–163; Abell quoted in Stephen Meyer III, *The Five Dollar Day: Labor Management and Social Control in the Ford Motor Company, 1908–1921* (Albany, 1981), p. 80.

42. R.M. MacIver, *Labor in the Changing World* New York, 1919), p. 84; Karp, *Golden Door,* p. 258; Jacob Riis, *How the Other Half Lives* (New York, 1890), pp. 58, 59; Medinkoff quoted in Karp, *Golden Door,* p. 143; Daniel T. Rodgers, "Tradition, Modernity, and the American Industrial Worker: Reflections and Critique," *Journal of Interdisciplinary History* 8 (1977), 669 (emphasis in the original)—see also his *The Work Ethic in Industrial America* (Chicago, 1978); John T. Cumbler, *Working-Class Community in Industrial America* (Westport, Conn., 1979), p. 52; W.M. Leiserson, "The Problem of Unemployment Today," *Political Science Quarterly* (1916), p. 15.

43. Quotation in Rexford B. Hersey, *Workers' Emotions in Shop and Home* (Philadelphia, 1932), p.178.

44. See especially Yans-McLaughlin, "Flexible Tradition" and *Family and Community,* and Cumbler, *Working Class.*

45. Cumbler, *Working Class,* p. 53.

46. Patricia Cooper, "Traveling Cigarmakers: the Journey of Discovery," *Journal of Social History* (1983).

47. Karl Marx, *Capital* 1 (New York: 1977 reprint), 785–786, 789.

48. Leiserson, "Unemployment," p. 12.

49. Whiting Williams, *What's on the Workers' Mind* (New York, 1920), pp. 39, 8–9, 53.

50. Ibid., pp. 5–6.

51. David Brody, *Steelworkers in America: the Nonunion Era* (Cambridge, Mass., 1960; reprint, New York, 1969),p. 105, 106; Samuel Gompers, *American Federationist* (March 1913), pp. 8–9.

52. Rodgers, "Tradition, Modernity," p. 663.

53. Meyer, *Five Dollar Day*, pp. 84–85.

54. See especially the discussion in Stephenson, "Migration and Mobility"; quotations in Meyer, *Five Dollar Day*, p. 81. "Stealing a trade" describes the practice of some workers trying to develop a skill 'on the job' by taking a job requiring that skill rather than spending the requisite time in training.

55. Quoted in Benita P. Eisle, ed., *The Lowell Offering* (Philadelphia, 1977), pp. 73, 160.

56. Mary P. Antin, *At School in the Promised Land* (Boston, 1928), pp. 93, 101.

57. Riis, *The Other Half*, pp. 24, 126.

58. Mother Jones recounted the experience of coal workers: "Men who joined the union were blacklisted . . . their families thrown out on the highways. Men were shot. They were beaten. . . ." (Mary P. Antin., ed., *Autobiography of Mother Jones* [Chicago, 1925]). In *The Steel Workers* (New York, 1910; reprinted New York, 1969), John A. Fitch reported: "married men cannot jeopardize the interests of their families by leaving the known for the unknown . . . married men dare not quit, and so do not make trouble"; and August Sopies said of Philadelphia that "there the workmen are . . . in slavery. . . and they are afraid to belong to a labor organization, as they might be discharged, and put on the so-called black list . . . [their] ambition [is] to have their own home. . . ." (Philip S. Foner, ed., *Haymarket Martyrs* (New York, 1969), p. 164.

59. Rogers, "Tradition, Modernity," p. 663; emphasis added.

60. John W. Briggs, *An Italian Passage: Immigrants to Three American Cities, 1890–1930* (New Haven, 1977). See Katz, Chapter Four, "The Entrepreneurial Class," in *People of Hamilton*, and his article on the same topic in the *Journal of Social History* (1975), 1–29; Stephenson, "Migration and Mobility." Quotation in Hersey, *Workers' Emotions*, p. 179.

61. Cumbler, however, characterizes much of this property mobility as encouraged primarily by the middle class who "pushed it as a panacea for the working class." *Working-Class Community*, p. 61.

62. Louis Adamic, *Laughing in the Jungle: An Autobiography of an Immigrant in America* (New York, 1910; reprint, New York, 1969), pp. 17, 20, 99, 240.

63. John T. Cumbler, "Immigration, Ethnicity, and the American Working-Class Community," in Robert Asher and Charles Stephenson, eds., *Ethnicity and the American Worker* (Forthcoming); John Benson, *The Penny Capitalists. A Study of Nineteenth-Century Working-Class Entrepreneurs* (New Brunswick, N.J., 1983); Clyde and Sally Griffen, "Small Business and Occupational Mobility in Mid-Nineteenth-Century Poughkeepsie," in Stuart W. Bruchey, *Small Business in American Life* (New York, 1980), p. 128; see Gutman's discussion in "Class, Status, and Community Power in Nineteenth-Century American Industrial Cities: Paterson, New Jersey: A Case Study," in *Work, Culture, and Society*.

64. See John Bucowczyk, "The Transformation of Working-Class Ethnicity: Corporate Control, Americanization, and the Polish Immigrant Middle Class in Bayonne, New Jersey, 1919–1925," *Labor History* (1985).

65. See Henretta's discussion in "Social Mobility."

CHAPTER SIX: NOTES

1. David Lightner, "Labor on the Illinois Central Railroad, 1852–1900" (Ph.D. dissertation, Cornell University, 1969), pp. 163–64.

2. Thomas C. Cochran, *Railroad Leaders, 1845–1890: The Business Mind in Action* (Cambridge, Mass., 1953); Alfred D. Chandler, Jr., "The Railroads: Pioneers in Modern Corporate Management," *Business History Review*, 34 (Spring 1965), pp. 16–40.

3. This paper will deal only with operating railroad workers. Construction laborers,

especially in the first decades of rail transport development, were usually hired, managed, and paid by local, small-scale construction entrepreneurs, who contracted with
the companies to build portions of the line. They will be excluded from this study of
pioneer workers in bureaucracy, as will Pullman porters.

This paper will pursue a different kind of approach to the study of labor history. The
primary focus will not be on strikes and trade unionism—matters of concern to traditional labor historians; nor on working-class consciousness, community, and culture—
the grist of so-called "new" labor historians. Rather, this will be an investigation into
changes in the nature and organization of work. I have written about the contribution
of new labor historians and the potential and meaning of labor- or work-process studies
in "Labor Economics and the Labor Historian," *International Labor and Working Class
History,* 2 (Spring 1982), pp. 52–62, and "Divisions of Labor History," *Reviews in American History,* 12 (June 1984), pp. 278–85.

4. Jonathan Knight and Benjamin Latrobe, *Report upon the Locomotive Engines and the
Police and Management of Several of the Principal Railroads in the Northern and Middle States*
(Baltimore, 1838), p. 3.

5. Report on the Running of the Road, June 12, 1838, Western Railroad Papers, Case
1, Baker Library, Harvard University.

6. Stephen Salsbury, *The State, The Investor and the Railroad: The Boston and Albany,
1825–1867* (Cambridge, Mass. 1967), pp. 185–86.

7. *Regulations for the Transportation Department of the Western Rail Road* (Springfield,
Mass., 1842).

8. Hank Bowman, *Pioneer Railroads* (New York, 1954), p. 66; Chandler, "The Railroads," p. 23.

9. *Organization of the Service of the Baltimore & Ohio Railroad under the Proposed New
System of Management* (Baltimore, 1847), p. 20.

10. The two standard histories of the Erie Railroad are Edward Mott, *Between the
Ocean and the Lakes: The Story of the Erie* (New York, 1899), and Edward Hungerford, *Men
of the Erie: A Story of Human Effort* (New York, 1946).

11. New York and Erie Railroad Company, *Organization and General Regulations for
Working and Conducting the Business of the Railroad and Its Branches* (New York, 1852).

12. Chandler, "The Railroads," pp. 28–33.

13. Ibid., p. 33.

14. Ibid., p. 35.

15. Chandler, "The Railroads," p. 36; Lightner, "Labor on the Illinois Central Railroad," pp. 67–69; Paul Black, "The Development of Management Personnel Policies on
the Burlington Railroad, 1868–1900" (Ph.D. dissertation, University of Wisconsin,
1972), pp. 60–64. The New York Central Railroad represents a major exception: The road
was run in an ad hoc fashion with a general superintendent directly overseeing all
operations. Chandler, "The Railroads," p. 39.

16. The bureaucratic principles and structures introduced by American railroad companies did not materialize spontaneously or full blown, nor were they the work of some
invisible hand. The installation of bureaucratic administrative procedures on the railroads progressed in stages and involved a good deal of trial, error, and variation. In fact,
at the same time that one group of executives were developing bureaucratic methods,
another smaller group of railway managers were deliberately looking for nonbureaucratic solutions. The most widely discussed and important alternative considered was
the contract system, in which operations were parceled out to independent providers of
services (locomotive engineers on several railroads actually ran trains under contracts).
Where implemented, this system did not survive the Civil War; independent contractors could not cope with severe wartime inflation. For more on this interesting experi-
ment with nonbureaucratic solutions, a chapter usually bypassed by students of American business history, see Walter Licht, "Nineteenth-Century American Railwaymen: A

Study in the Nature and Organization of Work" (Ph.D. dissertation, Princeton University, 1977), pp. 16–25.

17. As Thomas Cochran has written, early railroad executives for the most part viewed their respective companies as "financial entit[ies] belonging to the stockholders, rather than as . . . service structure[s] composed of . . . employees." Cochran, *Railroad Leaders*, p. 92. Most studies indicate that on nineteenth-century American railroads, employees' wages amounted to about 60% of operating costs and 40% of revenues. See Marshall Kirkman, *Railway Expenditures*, 1 (Chicago, 1880), p. 97; Black, "The Development of Management Personnel Policies," pp. 12, 549. On differences of opinion about labor-related matters, see Cochran, *Railroad Leaders*, pp. 33, 52–53, 174–77, 427–30, 449–50; Licht, "Nineteenth-Century American Railwaymen," pp. 25–35.

18. Francis Bradlee, *The Eastern Railroad* (Salem, Mass., 1922), p. 18; petition to the directors of the Atlantic & St. Lawrence Railroad, March 6, 1848, Atlantic & St. Lawrence Railroad Papers, Correspondence, 1845–1848, Bowdoin College Library; Henry Carter, L.M. Goodwin, John Down, and George Emery to the President of the Atlantic & St. Lawrence Railroad Company, July 10, 1849, ibid., Correspondence, 1849–1855.

19. *Rock Island Magazine*, 17 (Oct. 1922), p. 12.

20. The following correspondence in the archives of the Atlantic & St. Lawrence Railroad in the Bowdoin College Library provided evidence about the recruitment of white-collar workers: Samuel McCobb and C. Barnes to the directors of the Atlantic & St. Lawrence Railroad, Dec. 6, 1848; S.J. Corser to same, Apr. 3, 1848; John M. Adams to same, Aug. 9, 1849; H.G. Hitchcock to same, Dec. 25, 1838. Similar letters of application can be found in the Baltimore & Ohio Railroad Papers in the Maryland Historical Society, the Nashua & Lowell Railroad and Boston & Lowell Railroad Papers in Baker Library, (hereafter, BL), and the Illinois Central Railroad and Chicago, Burlington & Quincy Railroad Papers in the Newberry Library (hereafter, NL).

21. *Railroad Record*, Dec. 23, 1869, p. 450.

22. For recruitment of early engine drivers, see Alvin Harlow, *The Road of the Century: The Story of the New York Central* (New York, 1947), p. 12; Stephen Holbrook, *The Story of American Railroads* (New York, 1947), p. 22; Licht, "Nineteenth-Century American Railwaymen," pp. 47–51.

23. Lightner, "Labor on the Illinois Central Railroad," pp. 50, 77; Account for service, 1843, Western Railroad Papers, Case 4, BL; Howard Dozier, *A History of the Atlantic Coast Line Railroad* (Boston, 1920), p. 90.

24. J.C. Davis to J.W. Garrett, July 17, 1865, Baltimore & Ohio Railroad Papers, File 6837, Maryland Historical Society; Andrew Anderson to James Hamilton, Feb. 22, 1866, Baltimore & Ohio Railroad Letterbooks, Maryland Historical Society; Taylor Hampton, *The Nickel Plate Road: The History of a Great Railroad* (Cleveland, 1947), p. 138. While literary and statistical evidence points to a general pattern of labor adequacy and even a labor surplus for the railroads, there were two exceptions: Southern railroads throughout the early years of rail transport development faced severe problems in meeting their needs for skilled and unskilled manpower, and during the Civil War, railroads both in the Confederacy and the Union were hard pressed on account of the drafting of railway workers. See Samuel Derrick, *Centennial History of the South Carolina Railroad* (Columbia, S.C., 1930), p. 124; John Stover, *The Railroads of the South, 1865–1900: A Study in Finance and Control* (Chapel Hill, N.C., 1955), p. 18; Robert C. Black III, *The Railroads of the Confederacy* (Chapel Hill, N.C., 1952), pp. 29–30, 128–30; Thomas Weber, *The Northern Railroads in the Civil War* (New York, 1952), pp. 18, 63, 130–33; Lightner, "Labor on the Illinois Central Railroad," pp. 93–99.

25. Turnover figures for the Hartford & New Haven Railroad, 1845–1847, 1851–1853, 1868–1870, Cleveland & Toledo Railroad, 1864–1866, Western Railroad, 1842, Eastern Railroad, 1836–1847, Boston & Maine Railroad, 1849–1868 and the Chicago, Burlington & Quincy Railroad, 1861–1862, and 1877 can be found in Licht, "Nineteenth-Century

American Railwaymen," pp. 95–107. Identical figures on turnover also have been calculated recently for the Atchinson, Topeka & Santa Fe Railroad in the late nineteenth century. See James Ducker, "Men of the Steel Rail: Workers on the Atchinson, Topeka & Santa Fe" (Ph.D. dissertation, University of Illinois at Champaign-Urbana, 1980), pp. 132–42. While on an average, 50 percent of the employees traced remained with their firms for a maximum of six months, turnover varied by job grade. Workers in high-level positions stayed longer than lower-grade employees.

26. Minutes of directors' meetings, pp. 215–16, 2, p. 20, 3, pp. 45–46, Boston & Worcester Rail Road Papers, BL; see also B.A. Botkin and Alvin Harlow, eds., *A Treasury of Railroad Folklore* (New York, 1953), p. 158.

27. Chandler, "The Railroads," p. 29; Black, "Development of Management," p. 191.

28. Chauncey del French, *Railroadman* (New York, 1938), p. 32.

29. Charles George, *Forty Years on the Rail: Reminiscences of a Veteran Conductor* (Chicago, 1887); Harvey Reed, *Forty Years a Locomotive Engineer* (Prescott, Wash., 1915); Gilbert Lathrop, *Little Engines and Big Men* (Caldwell, Id., 1954); Otis Kirkpatrick, *Working on the Railroad* (Philadelphia, 1949).

30. K.I. Kimpton to George Stark, Jan. 1, 1858, Nashua and Lowell Railroad Papers, 203, BL; *Report of the Board of Managers to the Stockholders of the Mine Hill and Schuylkill Haven Railway Company, 1864* (Philadelphia, 1864), p. 7; John Kendall, "The Connecticut and Passumpsic Rivers R.R.," *The Railway and Locomotive Historical Society Bulletin*, no. 49 (May 1939), p. 31.

31. Illinois Central Railroad, *History of the Illinois Central Railroad and Representative Employees* (Chicago, 1900).

32. Ducker, "Men of the Steel Rail," p. 52.

33. Historians of the family have emphasized the important role played by kin in job procurement. See Michael Anderson, *Family Structure in Nineteenth-Century Lancashire* (Cambridge, 1971) and Tamara Hareven, *Family Time & Industrial Time: The Relationship between the Family and Work in a New England Industrial Community* (New York, 1982). A recent analysis of survey research conducted in Philadelphia during the 1930s indicates that upwards of a quarter of the work force relied on family members to secure initial employment, but that relatives played a diminishing role in later efforts at obtaining work. See Walter Licht and David Hogan, "Getting Work in Philadelphia: An Historical Perspective" (paper at the convention of the Organization of American Historians, April 1982).

34. George Emery to the President and Directors of the Atlantic & St. Lawrence Railroad, Aug. 9, 1849, Atlantic & St. Lawrence Railroad Papers, Correspondence, 1849–1855, Bowdoin College Library.

35. Quoted in Richard Reinhardt, ed., *Workin' on the Railroad: Reminiscences from the Age of Steam* (Palo Alto, Calif., 1970), p. 129.

36. Dan Mater, "The Development and Operation of the Railroad Seniority System," *Journal of Business of the University of Chicago*, 13 (Oct. 1940), p. 400; George, *Forty Years on the Rail*, pp. 60, 75; U.S. Eight-Hour Commission, *Report* (Washington, D.C., 1918), p. 307.

37. James Sullivan to J.W. Garrett, May 2, 1868, Baltimore & Ohio Railroad Papers, File 3089, Maryland Historical Society.

38. Robert Harris to H. Hitchcock, May 6, 1868, and July 24, 1871, Chicago, Burlington & Quincy Railroad Papers, 3H4.1, NL; C.E. Perkins' Memorandum of July 10, 1878, Chicago, Burlington & Quincy Railroad Papers, 3P4.92, NL.

39. Mater, "Development and Operation," pp. 400–401.

40. Warren Jacobs, "Early Rules and the Standard Code," *Railway and Locomotive Historical Society Bulletin* no. 50 (Oct. 1939), pp. 29–55. A large collection of early railroad rule books can be found in Baker Library. For a lengthy discussion of employee regula-

tions on the railroads, see Licht, "Nineteenth-Century American Railwaymen," pp. 109–25.

41. Reed Richardson, *The Locomotive Engineer: 1863–1963, A Century of Railway Labor Relations and Work Rules* (Ann Arbor, Mich., 1963), pp. 94–95, 225; Salsbury, *The State*, p. 116; Hank Bowman, *Pioneer Railroads*, pp. 70, 95.

42. Cited in Charles Clark, "The Railroad Safety Movement in the United States: Origins and Development, 1869–1893" (Ph.D. dissertation, University of Illinois at Urbana, 1966), p. 17.

43. Allen Pinkerton, *Tests on Passenger Conductors Made by the National Detective Agency* (Chicago, 1870), p. 4; for a lengthy discussion of labor discipline problems on American railroads before 1880, see Licht, "Nineteenth-Century American Railwaymen," pp. 130–55.

44. For commentary on the unsystematic nature of disciplinary procedures, see C.E. Perkins to Robert Harris, Dec. 15, 1877, Chicago, Burlington & Quincy Railroad Papers, Papers Concerning Employees, 1877–1898, CBQ–33 1870 3.6, NL. Information on reasons for discharge are contained in Circular Notice, Mar. 31, 1873, Erie Railway Company Papers, Letter Book of Incoming Correspondence and Miscellaneous, Syracuse University Library, and "Record of Discharged Employees from the Service of the C.B. & Q. and Leased Lines, February 1877–June 1892," Chicago, Burlington & Quincy Railroad Papers, CBQ – 33 1870 3.4, NL.

45. Master of Machinery to J.W. Garrett, June 26, 1867, Baltimore & Ohio Railroad Papers, File 1573, Maryland Historical Society.

46. Cited in Reinhardt, *Workin' on the Railroad*, pp. 122–26.

47. On the personalities of early railroad foremen, see Richardson, *The Locomotive Engineer*, pp. 246–47; George, *Forty Years on the Rail*, p. 167.

48. For a comprehensive analysis of railwaymen's wages before 1880, see Licht, "Nineteenth-Century American Railwaymen," pp. 176–94, 417–18.

49. *Fifth Annual Report of the Commissioner of Labor, 1889. Railroad Labor* (Washington, D.C., 1890), p. 21; Lightner, "Labor on the Illinois Central Railroad," p. 125; Black, "Development of Management," pp. 285, 335, 343–44; Holbrook, *The Story of American Railroads*, pp. 116, 269, 340; Bowman, *Pioneer Railroads*, p. 99. Fringe benefits and means of supplementary income are discussed in depth in Licht, "Nineteenth-Century American Railwaymen," pp. 194–209.

50. *Holley's Railroad Advocate*, May 2, 1857, p. 4.

51. Reed, *Forty Years a Locomotive Engineer*, pp. 33–34.

52. Bowman, *Pioneer Railroads*, p. 121.

53. Richardson, *The Locomotive Engineer*, pp. 45, 112–18, 144, 155–56, 196, 208–9.

54. W.P. Smith to C.W. Perviel, Jan. 17, 1859, Baltimore & Ohio Railroad Papers, File 1461, Maryland Historical Society.

55. G.B. McClellan to L.H. Clarke, Nov. 18, 1858, Illinois Central Railroad Papers, McClellan Out-Letters, IC-IM2.1, NL.

56. *Fifth Annual Report of the Commissioner of Labor, 1889. Railroad Labor*, p. 82. Hours of work also varied dramatically for pioneer railroad workers, especially trainmen. For details see Licht, "Nineteenth-Century American Railwaymen," pp. 257–65.

57. Memorandum of C.E. Perkins, Jan. 30, 1886, Chicago, Burlington, & Quincy Railroad Papers, President's Memoranda, 1878–1900, CBQ-3P4.92, NL.

58. A detailed study of promotions and career ladders can be found in Licht, "Nineteenth-Century American Railwaymen," pp. 209–238.

59. U.S. Eight-Hour Commission, *Report*, p. 307.

60. Cochran, *Railroad Leaders*, p. 307.

61. Quoted in James Stevenson, "The Brotherhood of Locomotive Engineers and its Leaders, 1863–1920" (unpub. Ph.D. dissertation, Vanderbilt University, 1954), p. 7.

62. Quoted in Clive Stott, "Robert Harris and the Strike of 1877" (unpub. M.A. thesis, University of Western Ontario, 1967), p. 185.

63. *Second Annual Report on the Statistics of Railways in the United States to the Interstate Commerce Commission for the Year Ending June 30,1889* (Washington, D.C., 1890), pp. 36–38.

64. Licht, "Nineteenth-Century American Railwaymen," pp. 280–82.

65. *Second Annual Report to the ICC*, pp. 279–80.

66. Stover, *American Railroads*, pp. 151–52.

67. Quoted in Robert Bruce, *1877: Year of Violence* (New York, 1959), p. 45.

68. Clark, "The Railroad Safety Movement," pp. 219–33; Robert Asher, "Workmen's Compensation in the United States, 1880–1935," (Ph.D. dissertation, University of Minnesota, 1971), pp. 32–47.

69. Mott, *Between the Ocean and the Lakes*, p. 401; Lightner, "Labor on the Illinois Central Railroad," pp. 125–26; Black, "Development of Management," pp. 379–80.

70. Paul Black, "Robert Harris and the Problem of Railway Labor Management" (unpublished paper in this author's possession), p. 27.

71. H. Evans to James Howison, Jan. 14, 1863, Baltimore & Ohio Letterbooks, Maryland Historical Society.

72. Minutes of directors' meetings, 3, pp. 217–218, Boston & Worcester Railroad Corporation Papers, BL.

73. *First Annual Report of the Baltimore and Ohio Employees Relief Association* (Baltimore, 1881), pp. 3, 10, 14–15, 77; Emory Johnson "Railway Departments for the Relief and Insurance of Employees," *Annals of the American Academy of Political and Social Science*, 6 (Nov. 1895), 64–108; a comprehensive survey of early efforts to establish insurance programs can be found in Licht, "Nineteenth-Century American Railwaymen," pp. 300–6.

74. French, *Railroad*, p. 195. For efforts of pioneer railwaymen to secure private insurance and their reliance on brotherhood programs, see Richardson, *The Locomotive Engineer*, pp. 132, 146; Stevenson, "The Brotherhood of Locomotive Engineers," p. 91; Hamblen, *The General Manager's Story*, pp. 220–21; Lightner, "Labor on the Illinois Central," p. 128.

75. Standard accounts of the railroad strikes mentioned can be found in the following sources. For the railroad strikes of 1877: Bruce, *1877: Year of Violence* and Philip Foner, *The Great Labor Uprising of 1877* (New York, 1977). For the Gould strikes of 1885–1886: Henry Pelling, *American Labor* (Chicago, 1960), pp. 70–72, and Philip Foner, *History of the Labor Movement in the United States, 2: From the Founding of the American Federation of Labor to the Emergence of American Liberalism* (New York, 1955), pp. 50–53. For the Burlington strike of 1888: Donald McMurray, *The Great Burlington Strike of 1888: A Case History in Labor Relations* (Cambridge, Mass., 1956). For the Pullman strike and boycott of 1894: Almont Lindsey, *The Pullman Strike* (Chicago, 1942). For the Harriman strike of 1911–1914: James Green, *The World of the Worker: Labor in Twentieth-Century America* (New York, 1979), p. 107; David Montgomery, *Workers' Control in America* (New York, 1979), pp. 107–108; and Carl Graves, "Scientific Management and the Santa Fe Railway Shopmen of Topeka, Kansas, 1900–1925" (unpub. Ph.D. dissertation, Harvard University, 1980), pp. 310–11. For the threatened strike of trainmen in 1916 and the passage of the Adamson Act: Arthur S. Link, *Woodrow Wilson and the Progressive Era, 1910–1917* (New York, 1954), pp. 235–39. For the railway shopmen's strike of 1922: Green, *The World of the Worker*, pp. 120–21; Graves, "Scientific Management," pp. 263–90.

76. The dramatic strikes of the post-1877 era should not obscure the reality of relations between railway workers and managers in the early years. In addition to the daily individual confrontations which occurred between railwaymen and their supervisors over such matters as recruitment practices, training, discipline, compensation, work loads, promotions, and accidental injury and death benefit awards, the pre-1877 period

was also marked by organized group conflict. Strikes occurred almost yearly. For a catalogue of early organized job actions, see Licht, "Nineteenth-Century American Railwaymen," pp. 360–66.

77. Herbert G. Gutman, "Trouble on the Railroads in 1873–1874: Prelude to the 1877 Crisis?", *Labor History,* 2 (Spring 1961) pp. 215–35; and "Workers' Search for Power: Labor in the Gilded Age," in H. Wayne Morgan, ed., *The Gilded Age: A Reappraisal* (Syracuse, 1963) pp. 36–68; Shelton Stromquist, "Community Structure and Industrial Conflict in Nineteenth-Century Railroad Towns" (unpublished paper read at the convention of the Organization of American Historians, 1978, New York, in possession of author).

78. *Locomotive Engineers' Journal,* Dec. 1875, p. 640.

79. Quoted in Richardson, *The Locomotive Engineer,* p. 165.

80. Quoted in Richard Edwards, *Contested Terrain: The Transformation of the Workplace in the Twentieth Century* (New York, 1979), p. 60.

81. Ibid., pp. 58–61.

82. Ibid., p. 61.

83. Ibid.

84. Information on union formation, the number of workers enrolled, and contracts signed can be found in Mater, "Railroad Seniority System," p. 395; Clark, "Railroad Safety Movement," pp. 188–89.

85. C.E. Perkins to J. Forbes, Aug. 2, 1877, Chicago, Burlington & Quincy Railroad Papers, Perkins Letterbook, NL.

86. For a discussion of railroad executives' reactions to the labor unrest of the late nineteenth and early twentieth centuries, see Licht, "Nineteenth Century American Railwaymen," pp. 381–90.

87. Robert Harris to J.N. Griswold, Aug. 2, 1877, Chicago, Burlington & Quincy Railroad Papers, Harris' In-Letters, CBQ-31B1.5, NL.

88. Stevenson, "The Brotherhood of Locomotive Engineers," p. 67; Lightner, "Labor on the Illinois Central Railroad," p. 178; Cochran, *Railroad Leaders,* pp. 33, 374. The last quarter of the nineteenth and first quarter of the twentieth centuries also witnessed increased application of state power to order and stabilize relations within industry. Two standard works on the subject are Gerald G. Eggert, *Railroad Labor Disputes: The Beginning of Federal Strike Policy* (Ann Arbor, Michigan, 1967), and Leonard Lecht, *Experience under Railway Labor Legislation* (New York, 1955).

89. D.W. Hertel, *History of the Brotherhood of Maintenance of Way Employees* (Washington, D.C., 1955), p. 53.

90. Cited in Jesse C. Burt, Jr., "The Savor of Old-Time Southern Railroading," *The Railway and Locomotive Historical Society Bulletin,* no. 84 (Oct. 1951), pp. 38–39.

91. In the past few years, a number of studies on other industries have been published that also emphasize the critical role played by foremen in industrial conflict and labor process development (these works appeared after my own discoveries in the railroad industry and were encouraging corroborations of the major argument of this paper). These studies include Daniel Nelson, *Managers and Workers: Origins of the New Factory System in the United States, 1880–1920* (Madison, Wisc., 1975); Edwards, *Contested Terrain;* and Michael Burawoy, *Manufacturing Consent: Changes in the Labor Process under Monopoly Capitalism* (Chicago, 1979).

92. The form of worker power achieved by railwaymen—control over the work experience, if not the productive process—has not been amply highlighted in recent studies and debates on worker control movements. For various sides to the debate, see Montgomery, *Workers' Control in America,* Burawoy, *Manufacturing Consent,* and Jean Monds, "Workers' Control and the Historians: A New Economism," *New Left Review,* 97 (May–June, 1976), pp. 81–104.

93. Lightner, "Labor on the Illinois Central Railroad," pp. 108, 141; James Whiton,

Railroads and Their Management (Concord, N.H., 1856), p. 65; Gutman, "Trouble on the Railroads," p. 229; Cochran, *Railroad Leaders*, p. 383; Peter Kingsford, *Victorian Railwaymen: The Emergence and Growth of Railway Labour, 1830–1870* (London, 1970), pp. 14–19.

94. Cochran, *Railroad Leaders*, pp. 229, 537.

95. *American Railroad Journal*, Sept. 10, 1853, p. 583; documents accompanying letters of William Osborne to J.W. Brooks, March 31, 1862, Illinois Central Papers, W. Osborne Out-Letters, IC 106.1, NL.

96. Kingsford, *Victorian Railwaymen*, pp. 65–87.

97. On the changing social origins of American railway executives, see Cochran, *Railroad Leaders*, pp. 28–29, 52–53, and Stuart Morris, "Stalled Professionalism: The Recruitment of Railway Officials in the United States, 1885–1940," *Business History Review*, 42 (Autumn 1973), pp. 320–26.

98. Alfred Chandler, Jr., *Henry Varnum Poor: Business Editor, Analyst and Reformer* (Cambridge, Mass., 1956), p. 321; Charles F. Carter, *When Railroads Were New* (New York, 1926), p. 145; Ray Morris, *Railroad Administration* (New York, 1910), pp. 264–65; *Colburn's Railroad Advocate*, August 11, 1855, p. 3; *American Railroad Journal*, Sept. 1, 1855, p. 555.

99. For a recent study on railwaymen and republican ideology, see Nick Salvatore, "Railroad Workers and the Great Strike of 1877: The View from a Small City," *Labor History*, 21 (Fall 1980), pp. 522–45.

Chapter Seven: Notes

1. These verses are taken from *Drill, Ye Tarriers*, a song written in 1888 by an Irish-American vaudeville team, Connelly and Casey. The wording of this song has changed, in true folk song fashion, since 1888. I have followed the version given by Alan Lomax, in his authoritative *The Folk Songs of North America in the English Language* (Garden City, New York: Doubleday & Company, Inc., 1960), pp. 408, 417. A version of the song written to apply to the work of miners can be found in Richard E. Lingenfelter, Richard A. Dwyer and David Cohen, eds., *Songs of the American West* (Berkeley: University of California Press, 1968), pp. 158–59.

2. United States Department of Labor and Commerce, *Bulletin of the Bureau of Labor*, no. 90, (Sept. 1910), p. 447; H.G. Prout, "Railroad Accidents in the United States and England," *North American Review*, 157 (Dec. 1893), pp. 707–15.

3. *Seattle Union Record*, Jan. 21, 1911, p. 7; Texas Bureau of Labor Statistics, *Biennial Report, 1912*, p. 171–173; *Minutes of Evidence Accompanying the Second Report to the Legislature of the State of New York by the Commission Appointed under Chapter 518 of the Laws of 1909 to Inquire into the Question of Employers' Liability and Other Matters, April 20, 1911* (Albany: State Printer, 1911), p. 281 (hereafter *Minutes, 1911*). Other complaints by railroad workers included the danger from steam that escaped from improperly maintained engines, the practice of pushing trains without coupling the engine to the cars, the high proportion of freight cars without functioning air brakes, and the hiring of incompetent workers. Iowa Bureau of Labor Statistics, *Biennial Report, 1903*, pp. 506–8, 523.

4. United States Strike Commission, *Report on the Chicago Strike, 1894*, Sen. Executive Doc. no. 7, 53rd Cong., 3rd sess. (Washington, D.C.: U.S. Government Printing Office, 1895), p. 118; Iowa *Report, 1903*, p. 523.

5. James Oneal, *A History of the Amalgamated Ladies' Cutters' Union Local 10* (New York: Local 10, 1922), p. 146; *Minutes, 1911*, pp, 40, 42; *Minutes of Evidence Accompanying the First Report to the Legislature of the State of New York by the Commission Appointed under Chapter 518 of the Laws of 1909 to Inquire into the Question of Employers' Liability and Other Matters, Mar. 16, 1910* (Albany: State Printer, 1910), pp. 425–27 (hereafter, *Minutes,*

1910); Knisley versus Pratt, 148 NY 372; Andrew M. Prouty, "Logging with Steam in the Pacific Northwest: The Men, the Camps and the Accidents, 1885–1918" (M.A. thesis, University of Washington, 1973), p. 168.

6. Colorado Bureau of Labor, *Report, 1888*, pp. 301–2; *Joint Convention of the Illinois Coal Operators Association and the United Mine Workers of America District 12, February, March, April 1908* (Springfield, 1908), pp. 321–25, 373 (hereafter, *Joint Convention*).

7. Wisconsin Commissioner of Labor Statistics, *Report, 1887*, pp. 65, 68, 81; Ohio Employers' Liability Commission, *Report*, 2 (Columbus, 1911), p. 213.

8. A New York construction worker claimed that there was a building code "violation on every job, every building in New York City." *Minutes, 1911*, pp. 93, 122; Ohio *Report*, 2, p. 214; Iowa *Report, 1903*, p. 498; *Chicago InterOcean*, Jan. 12, 1910, in Deneen Scrapbooks, Charles S. Deneen Papers, Illinois State Historical Society; John A. Fitzpatrick to John B. Andrews, Feb. 17, 1911, John B. Andrews Papers, Labor–Management Documentation Center, New York State School of Industrial and Labor Relations.

9. *Minutes, 1911*, pp. 124, 259; Commonwealth of Massachusetts, "Hearings before the Joint Special Committee on Labor on Bills Relating to Employers' Liability," Oct. 17–28, 1907 (typed transcript), p. 289, Massachusetts State Library; Colorado Bureau of Labor, *Report, 1888*, pp. 300–1.

10. Iowa *Report, 1907*, p. 195. Railroad workers also knew that even if they were not punished for complaining, their protests about unsafe conditions were likely to be ignored. Ibid., p. 196; Ohio *Report*, 2, pp. 329–30.

11. Interview with retired miner, Vermillion, Minn., Mar. 1971.

12. *Minutes, 1910*, p. 331; Prouty, "Logging with Steam," pp. 172–73; Ruth A. Allen, *East Texas Lumber Workers: An Economic and Social Picture, 1870–1950* (Austin: University of Texas Press, 1961), p. 177.

13. Prouty, "Logging with Steam," p. 116.

14. In exchange for their $1 per month, workers were often given tickets called "life savers," which entitled them to hospital benefits. Agnes M. Larson, *History of the White Pine Industry in Minnesota* (Minneapolis: University of Minnesota Press, 1949), pp. 214, 358–59.

15. Testimony of E. Smith, Minnesota Legislature, Committee on Labor and Legislation, "Labor Troubles in Northern Minnesota" (typed hearing transcript), pp. 48–49, John Lind Papers, Box 8, Minnesota Historical Society.

16. National Civic Federation, *Proceedings of the Department for Compensation for Industrial Accidents and Their Prevention, December 8, 1911*, p. 100, copy in Seth Low Papers, Box 99, Columbia University; "Minutes of Meeting of the National Civic Federation in a National Conference on Workmen's Compensation at the Rooms of the New York Board of Trade and Transportation, New York City, November 25, 1912" (typed transcript), pp. 276–77, National Civic Federation Papers, New York Public Library.

17. Wisconsin *Report, 1887*, p. 106; Commonwealth of Massachusetts, Committee on Relations between Employer and Employee, "Hearing before the Commission on Relations between Employer and Employee, August 18 to November 7, 1903" (typed transcript), p. 301, Massachusetts State Library.

18. Minnesota Bureau of Labor, *Report, 1911*, p. 160; *Chicago Daily News*, Dec. 28, 1906.

19. Minnesota State Bar Association, *Proceedings*, 1912, p. 97; Ohio *Report*, 2, pp. 102, 219.

20. United States Strike Commission, *Report, 1894*, pp. 126–28. For other references to the firing of workers who initiated tort action against their employers, see "Meeting of National Civic Federation, 1912," p. 104.

21. Illinois State Federation of Labor, *Proceedings, 1912*, p. 135.

22. Iowa *Report, 1903*, p. 496; Ohio *Report*, 2, p. 219.

23. *Third Annual Report of the Commissioner of Labor, 1887*. (Washington, D.C.: U.S.

Government Printing Office, 1888), pp. 994–1017; *Twenty-First Annual Report of the Commissioner of Labor, 1906* (Washington, D.C.: U.S. Government Printing Office, 1907), pp. 60–64.

24. *Twenty-First Annual Report*, pp. 559–60.

25. Vernon H. Jensen, *Heritage of Conflict: Labor Relations in the Nonferrous Metals Industry up to 1930.* (Ithaca, N.Y.: Cornell University Press, 1950), p. 55; Anthracite Coal Strike Commission, *Report to the President on the Anthracite Coal Strike of May–October 1902*, Sen. Doc. 6, 58th Cong., special sess., 1903 (Washington, D.C.: U.S. Government Printing Office), p. 93.

26. *Joint Convention*, pp. 26–28, 158–64, 321–22; William Graebner, *Coal-Mining Safety in the Progressive Period: The Political Economy of Reform* (Lexington: The University Press of Kentucky, 1976), ch. 3, 4. Graebner feels that the national leaders of the UMWA were remiss in not consistently stressing safety issues in its newspaper and in national contract negotiations. Undoubtedly coal miners were torn between the desire for maximum earnings and the desire for safety. Sometimes the former took precedence over the latter. Graebner may be asking too much of the national leaders to expect them to have negotiated safety issues in national contracts. As he notes, these points were often a serious issue in local contract negotiations. Variation in mining conditions may have made it more feasible to negotiate safety issues on a district and local level. Graebner is too hard on the UMWA when he argues that they were more concerned about who was to pay the wages of shot firers than they were about the greater mine safety to be obtained by using such specialists to detonate explosives. A close reading of the sources indicates that the squabbles over the economic issue of paying the shot firers came only after the UMWA had forced operators to concede the more important principle, that to make mines safer shot firers would be used. As a UMWA official pointed out during negotiations in 1908 over the payment of shot firers in Illinois, the employment of shot firers had reduced the death rate from underground explosions by 38%. *Joint Convention*, p. 324. Although the UMWA could have done a better job on safety, my reading of union convention proceedings and newspapers suggests that the coal miners' union stressed safety more than any other union in the United States, including the railroad brotherhoods.

27. Jensen, *Heritage*, pp. 16, 96, quoting G.H. Smith, *The History of the Comstock Lode, 1850–1920* (Reno: State Printing Office, 1943), pp. 389–90.

28. Ibid., pp. 98–99.

29. Texas *Report, 1915*, p. 99; Iowa *Report, 1909*, p. 248; Michigan Bureau of Labor and Industrial Statistics, *Annual Report*, 1903, p. 159. See also Michigan *Report*, 1907, p. 200 for the remark of a railroad telegrapher: "Look at the wrecks caused by overworked men in railroad service."

30. Illinois Bureau of Labor, *Biennial Report, 1902*, pp. 497–501.

31. Minnesota *Report, 1913*, p. 438. A study of coal mine strikes in Missouri in 1889 listed safety as the cause in three of thirty strikes. Missouri Bureau of Labor Statistics and Inspection, *Annual Report, 1890*, pp. 120–22.

32. Wisconsin State Federation of Labor, *Proceedings, 1914*, p. 42.

33. United States Industrial Commission, *Reports*, 8 (Washington, D.C.: U.S. Government Printing Office, 1901), pp. 280–81.

34. Prouty, "Logging with Steam," pp. 117, 155–57.

35. Thomas W. Gavett, *Development of the Labor Movement in Milwaukee* (Madison: University of Wisconsin Press, 1965), p. 24.

36. Herbert Gutman, "The Braidwood Lockout of 1874," *Journal of the Illinois State Historical Society*, 53 (Spring 1960), p. 10; Robert W. Smith, *The Coeur d' Alene Mining War of 1892* (Corvallis: Oregon State College, 1961), pp. 20–26; *Chicago Tribune*, Nov. 19, 1909, p. 3, and Nov. 22, 1909, p. 1. In Illinois early in the twentieth century, miners used

the wildcat strike to force coal operators to comply with the state law requiring shot firers. *Joint Conference*, p. 325.

37. *New York Times*, June 11, 1972, p. 75; George Vecsey, *One Sunset a Week: The Story of a Coal Miner* (New York: Dutton, 1974), p. 100.

38. Clark Kerr and Abraham Siegel, "The Interindustry Propensity to Strike—An International Comparison," in Arthur Kornhauser, et al., eds., *Industrial Conflict* (New York: McGraw-Hill, 1954), p. 192.

39. Leonard Berkowitz and E. Rawlings, "Effects of Film Violence on Inhibitions against Subsequent Aggression," *Journal of Abnormal and Social Psychology*, 66 (May 1963), pp. 405–12; Leonard Berkowitz, et al., "Film Violence and Subsequent Aggressive Tendencies," *Public Opinion Quarterly*, 27 (Summer 1963), pp. 217–29; Leonard Berkowitz, "Some Aspects of Observed Aggression," *Journal of Personality and Social Psychology*, 2 (Sept. 1965), pp. 359–69; Leonard Berkowitz and R.G. Green, "Film Violence and the Cue Properties of Available Targets," *Journal of Personality and Social Psychology*, 3 (May 1966), pp. 525–30; Leonard Berkowitz and R.G. Green, "Stimulus Qualities of the Target of Aggression: A Further Study," *Journal of Personality and Social Psychology*, 5 (Mar. 1967), pp. 364–68; Leonard Berkowitz and A. Le Page, "Weapons as Aggression-Eliciting Stimuli," *Journal of Personality and Social Psychology*, 7 (Oct. 1967), pp. 202–7; Leonard Berkowitz and D.A. Knurek, "Label-Mediated Hostility Generalization," *Journal of Personality and Social Psychology*, 13 (Nov. 1969), pp. 200–6; Leonard Berkowitz, "The Contagion of Violence: An S-R Mediational Analysis of Some Effects of Observed Aggression," in William J. Arnold and Monte M. Page, eds., *Nebraska Symposium on Motivation 1970* (Lincoln: University of Nebraska Press, 1970), pp. 95–135.

40. *Chicago Record Herald*, Mar. 2, 1903, in Scrapbook of Writing, 1903–1907, John H. Gray Papers, Carleton College.

41. Harry Rosenberg, "Packing Industry and the Stockyards," c. 1904, Mary McDowell Papers, Box 3, Chicago Historical Society.

43. John Brophy, *A Miner's Life* (Madison: University of Wisconsin Press, 1964), p. 34.

44. *Chicago Tribune*, Nov. 14, 1909, p. 1, Nov. 15, 1909, pp. 1–3, Nov. 16, 1909, pp. 1, 2, Nov. 17, 1909, pp. 1–2, Nov. 18, 1909, p. 3, Nov. 20, 1909, p. 6, Nov. 21, 1909, pp. 2–3, Nov. 23, 1909, p. 2, Nov. 24, 1909, p. 3.

45. Melvyn Dubofsky, "The Origins of Working Class Radicalism, 1890–1905," *Labor History*, 7 (Spring 1966), pp. 131–54.

46. It should be emphasized that occupational hazards were not the exclusive cause of the high level of violence in labor relations in these areas. They were a contributory factor, along with the high incidence of gun ownership, the use of private armies by employers, and the hostility of the middle classes, politicians and large entrepreneurs to trade unionism and especially to radical trade unionism aimed at overthrowing the free-enterprise system.

CHAPTER EIGHT: NOTES

1. "Boycotting," *The Nation*, 41 (Dec. 24, 1885), p. 527; all other quotations from "Capital and Labor: Boycotting," *Public Opinion*, 1 (1886), pp. 47–50.

2. *Providence Star*, Apr. 23, 1886, quoted in "Capital and Labor," p. 48. The last book-length study was Leo Wolman's doctoral dissertation from Johns Hopkins University in 1914, published as *The Boycott in American Trade Unions* (Baltimore, 1916).

3. Quotation in "Capital and Labor," p. 48.

4. "The Genesis of Boycotting," *The Nation*, 31 (Dec. 23, 1880), p. 437.

5. Ibid., p. 437; also William Hammond, "The Evolution of Boycotting," *The Forum*, 1 (June 1886), pp. 369–76.

6. E.P. Cheyney, "Decision of the Courts in Conspiracy and Boycott Cases," *Political Science Quarterly,* 4 (June 1889), pp. 264–78; Harry W. Laidler, *Boycotts and the Labor Struggle: Economic and Social Aspects* (New York, 1913).

7. For types of boycotts, see Laidler, *Boycotts,* and Wolman, *The Boycott,* pp. 13–15.

8. Michael Gordon, "The Labor Boycott in New York City, 1880–1886," *Labor History,* 16 (Spring 1975), pp. 206–11; Victor Greene, *The Slavic Community on Strike* (Notre Dame, Ind., 1968), and Wolman, *Boycott,* p. 83.

9. Minute Book of the Toledo Central Labor Union, Nov. 11, 1897 (hereafter CLU Minute Book); estimate based on figures from the 1900 manufacturing census and Labor Day estimate in the *Toledo Blade,* Sept. 7, 1896; on origins of the CLU, see the *Blade,* Oct. 24, 1890, and *Official Yearbook 1918: The Central Labor Union of Toledo and Vicinity* (Toledo, 1918), pp. 1–9, and more generally, William M. Burke, *History and Functions of Central Labor Unions* (New York, 1899).

10. The *Blade,* Aug. 25, 1888, Sept. 2, 1889, May 7 and 24, 1890, Dec. 30, 1892; Randolph Downes, *Industrial Beginnings,* 4, Lucas County Historical Series (Toledo, 1954), p. 128; and on building trades councils, Barbara Newell, *Chicago and the Labor Movement: Metropolitan Unionism in the 1930's* (Urbana, Ill., 1961), p. 21.

11. E.W. Fairfield, *Fire and Sand: The History of the Libbey-Owens Sheet Glass Co.* (Cleveland, 1960), pp. 15–18; The *Blade,* Aug. 18, 1888, Apr. 2, 1894; CLU Minute Books, Nov. 20, 1890, Oct. 6, 1892.

12. The *Blade,* Apr. 1, 1891, CLU Minute Books, Feb. 22 and 26, July 16, Dec. 3, 1891.

13. The *Blade,* Feb. 1 and 8, Mar. 15–18, 1897; CLU Minute Books, Apr. 28, 1898.

14. Stanley Baron, *Brewed in America: A History of Beer and Ale in the United States* (Boston, 1962), pp. 284–85; CLU Minute Books, Feb. 12, July 2, 1891, May 19, 1892, Feb. 23, Apr. 20, 1893, Feb. 23, 1897; Toledo Central Labor Union Business Agent's Reports, Apr. 25, 1901.

15. *Bradstreet's,* 12 (Dec. 19, 1885), pp. 394–95.

16. CLU Minute Books, Feb. 18, May 27, June 10 and 24, July 8, 1897.

17. Ibid., Aug. 5, Sept. 2, 16, and 30, 1897.

18. Business Agent's Reports, Mar. 27, Dec. 4, 1902.

19. Ibid., Aug. 27, 1903, June 19, 1902; CLU Minute Books, May 7, June 18, Dec. 17, 1891, June 1, 1893.

20. CLU Minute Books, June 10, 1897, Nov. 23, 1899.

21. Business Agent's Reports, Jan. 30, 1902, Mar. 14, 1901.

22. Ibid., Aug. 1, 1901; CLU Minute Books, Jan. 26, Feb. 23, Apr. 20, 1893.

23. Business Agent's Reports, Nov. 5, 1903; The *Blade,* Apr. 24, 25, 1896.

24. Business Agent's Reports, Jan. 26, 1905, Apr. 23, 1903, July 13, 1905; Andrew Carnegie, "Results of the Labor Struggle," *The Forum,* 1 (Aug. 1886), pp. 549–50.

25. Business Agent's Reports, Nov. 10, 1900, Sept. 26, 1901; CLU Minute Books, Feb. 18, 1897, Mar. 9, 1893.

26. Clay McShane, *Technology and Reform: Street Railways and the Growth of Milwaukee, 1887–1900* (Madison, 1974), p. 106; Melvin Holli, *Reform in Detroit: Hazen S. Pingree and Urban Politics* (New York, 1969), pp. 38–41; Hoyt L. Warner, *Progressivism in Ohio, 1897–1917* (Columbus, 1964), pp. 305–11, 72–73; Graham Adams, Jr., *Age of Industrial Violence: The Activities and Findings of the U.S. Commission on Industrial Relations* (New York, 1966), pp. 182–89; the *Blade,* Nov. 17, 1890.

27. Theodore Dreiser, *Sister Carrie* (1900; reprint New York, 1970), p. 306.

28. The *Blade,* July 15 and 16, 1891.

29. Ibid., July 15, 16, 17, 18, 1891.

30. Ibid., July 18, 20, 21, and 31, 1891.

31. Ibid., Mar. 20 and 21, 1894.

32. Ibid., Mar. 23, 1894.

33. Ibid., Mar. 22 and 23, 1894.

34. Ibid., Mar. 24, 1894.

35. Ibid., Mar. 22 and 23, 1894.

36. Ibid., Mar. 22, 26 and 31, 1894.

37. CLU Minute Books, Nov. 20 and 23, 1890, Mar. 26 and 31, Apr. 9, 1891; the *Blade,* Nov. 28, 1890, Apr. 6, 1891.

38. CLU Minute Books, July 2 and 30, Oct. 28, 1891, Oct. 20, 1892, Mar. 9, 1893; the *Blade,* Apr. 4, 1893, Apr. 2, 1894, Apr. 2, 1895, Apr. 6, 1897.

39. Randolph Downes, "Watered Securities and the Independent Revolution in Toledo Politics, 1901–1907," *Northwest Ohio Quarterly,* 28 (Spring 1956), pp. 88–105; Downes, *Industrial Beginnings,* pp. 114–22; the *Blade,* Nov. 13, 1896.

40. On Jones's career, see Warner, *Progressivism in Ohio,* pp. 27–54; Downes *Industrial Beginnings,* pp. 154–63; Peter J. Frederick, *Knights of the Golden Rule: The Intellectual as Christian Social Reformer in the 1890's* (Lexington, Ky., 1976), pp. 239–77; Morgan J. Barclay, "Reform in Toledo: the Political Career of Samuel M. Jones," *Northwest Ohio Quarterly,* 50 (Summer 1978), pp. 78–89.

41. Harvey S. Ford, "The Life and Times of Golden Rule Jones" (unpub. doctoral dissertation, University of Michigan, 1953), pp. 90–94; the *Blade,* Feb. 2, Mar. 15, Apr. 6, 1897; CLU Minute Books, Apr. 1, 1897, Mar. 16, 1899.

42. For a European assessment of American boycotting, see August Sartorius von Waltershausen, *Die nordamerikanischen Gewerkschaften unter dem Einfluss der Fortschreitenden Productionstechnik* (Berlin, 1886), pp. 237–61, and G. Schwittau, *Die Formen des wirtschaftlichen Kempfes* (Berlin, 1912), pp. 237–75.

43. For evidence of class solidarity among Toledo workers during the 1930s, see Roy Rosenzweig, "Radicals and the Jobless: The Musteites and the Unemployed Leagues, 1932–1936," *Labor History,* 16 (Winter 1975), pp. 52–77.

CHAPTER NINE: NOTES

This article is a revised version of a chapter from my book, *Eight Hours for What We Will: Workers and Leisure in an Industrial City, 1879–1920* (Cambridge: Cambridge University Press, 1983). That volume contains fuller documentation as well as acknowledgements of the numerous people who have assisted me in developing the analysis presented here. I would, however, like particularly to thank Betsy Blackmar for her always insightful comments on my continuing work in the social history of urban parks.

1. Downing, quoted in Jon Alvah Peterson, "The Origins of the Comprehensive City Planning Ideal in the United States, 1840–1911" (Ph.D. dissertation, Harvard University, 1967), p. 76; Frederick Law Olmsted, Jr., and Theodora Kimball, eds., *Frederick Law Olmsted: Landscape Architect, 1822–1903,* 2 vols. (New York, 1928), 2, p. 171.

2. Lawrence A. Finfer, "Leisure as Social Work in the Urban Community: The Progressive Recreation Movement, 1890–1920" (Ph.D. dissertation, Michigan State University, 1974), pp. 143–44. For even more sweeping indictments, see Joel Spring, "Mass Culture and School Sports," *History of Education Quarterly* 14 (Winter 1974), p. 483; Cary Goodman, *Choosing Sides: Playground and Street Life on the Lower East Side* (New York, 1979). For discussions of parks framed in terms of social control, see Paul Boyer, *Urban Masses and Moral Order in America, 1820–1920* (Cambridge, Mass., 1978), pp. 238, 356–57; Galen Cranz, "Changing Roles of Urban Parks: From Pleasure Garden to Open Space," *Landscape,* 22 (Summer 1978), p. 9. On the use of social control theory by historians, see William A. Muraskin, "The Social-Control Theory in American History: A Critique," *Journal of Social History,* 9 (Summer 1976), pp. 559–80; Gareth Stedman Jones, "Class Expression Versus Social Control? A Critique of Recent Trends in the Social History of 'Leisure,'" *History Workshop,* no. 4 (Autumn 1977), pp. 163–70.

3. For a more detailed portrait of Worcester's industrial and ethnic history, see Rosenzweig, *Eight Hours for What We Will*, pp. 9–32.

4. Commission on Shade Trees and Public Grounds, Minutes, Jan. 11, 1870 (hereafter, PC Minutes), Parks Commission Manuscripts, Green Hill Park, Worcester. Worcester Commission on Shade Trees and Public Grounds, *Annual Report for the Year Ending November 30, 1896* (Worcester, 1897), p. 5 (variously titled annual reports of Parks Commission hereafter *Park Report*); *Park Report, 1897*, pp. 3–5; unidentified clipping, Dec. 15, 1896, Clipping File, Worcester Historical Museum (WHM); Waldo Lincoln, *History of the Lincoln Family* (Worcester, 1923).

5. Olmsted, quoted in Geoffrey Blodgett, "Frederick Law Olmsted: Landscape Architecture as Conservative Reform," *Journal of American History*, 62 (Mar. 1976), pp. 872, 877, 878, and Roy Lubove, "Social History and the History of Landscape Architecture," *Journal of Social History*, 8 (Winter 1975), p. 274. Whether Olmsted was a "conservative" or a "democratic" thinker remains a subject of debate. Compare, for example, the essays by Geoffrey Blodgett and Albert Fein in Bruce Kelly, et al., eds., *Art of the Olmsted Landscape* (New York, 1981). On Olmsted, see Laura Wood Roper, *FLO: A Biography of Frederick Law Olmsted* (Baltimore, 1973), and Albert Fein, *Frederick Law Olmsted and the American Environmental Tradition* (New York, 1972).

6. *Worcester Evening Gazette*, Sept. 15, 1870 (hereafter, WEG). *Park Report, 1884*, pp. 189–90. On the state of Worcester's parks before Lincoln, see *Park Reports, 1867–1870*.

7. See *Park Reports, 1870–1885;* James Draper, "The Parks and Playgrounds of Worcester," *Worcester Magazine*, 1 (Apr. 1901), p. 239.

8. PC Minutes, Dec. 30, 1874, Jan. 23, 1878; *Park Report, 1873*, pp. 12–13; Olmsted quoted in Blodgett, "Frederick Law Olmsted," p. 881. On Olmsted's hostility to active recreation in his scenic parks, see also Steve Hardy, "'Parks for the People': Transforming the Concept of Parks in Boston, 1870–1915" (paper presented at the Annual Convention of the North American Society for Sport History, Banff, Alberta, May 26, 1980); John F Kasson, *Amusing the Million* (New York, 1978), pp. 12–15.

9. John Brinckerhoff Jackson, *American Space* (New York, 1972), pp. 214–15. See also Joseph Kett, *Rites of Passage: Adolescence in America, 1790 to the Present* (New York, 1977), p. 227.

10. *Park Report, 1876*, pp. 9–10; *Park Report, 1878*, p. 19; *Park Report, 1880*, p. 10; *Worcester Spy*, Apr. 19, 1885 (hereafter, WS).

11. *Park Report, 1884*, pp. 209–14. See also *Boston Sunday Herald*, June 28, 1884; WS, July 12, 1884.

12. Robert A. Roberge, "The Three-Decker: Structural Correlate of Worcester's Industrial Revolution" (M.A. thesis, Clark University, 1965), pp. 19–21.

13. *Annual Report of the City Marshal, 1882* (Worcester, 1883), p. 427; *Worcester Daily Times*, July 5, 1887, see also May 5, 1883 (hereafter WDT). Paul Faler describes a similar process of "enclosure" of recreational space in early nineteenth-century Lynn, Massachusetts, in "Cultural Aspects of the Industrial Revolution: Lynn, Massachusetts, Shoemakers and Industrial Morality, 1826–1860," *Labor History*, 15 (Summer 1974), p. 384.

14. *Worcester Sunday Telegram*, July 7, 1889 (hereafter WST).

15. WDT, Jan. 25, June 23, Jan. 12 and 6, 1885. See also WDT editorials of Feb. 17, March 25, April 30, and May 25, 1885. For a similar French-Canadian complaint, see *Le Travaillleur* (Worcester), Oct. 24, 1882.

16. *Worcester Evening Star*, Aug. 5 and 7, 1879. See also June 25, July 25, Aug. 1 and 14, 1879; WDT, Mar. 18, 1881.

17. George O'Flynn, "Richard O'Flynn—A Founder," *Publications, Worcester Historical Society*, n.s. 2 (Apr. 1936), p. 55; Petition of Richard O'Flynn, et al., Aug. 10, 1882, Board of Aldermen Petitions (hereafter, Board of Ald. Petitions), Board of Aldermen Manuscripts, Worcester City Hall.

18. The occupations of petitioners have been identified through the *Worcester Directory.*

19. *WDT,* Dec. 3, 1883. On tension between O'Flynn and Mellen, see Richard O'Flynn Manuscripts, HCC, especially Folio 1, p. 211, where O'Flynn observes: "Mellen's character is well known to the unfortunate who *trust* him for *large* or small accounts." For the second petition drive led by O'Flynn, see Petitions of Walsh et al., O'Flynn et al., Duggan et al., and Creamer et al., June 23, 1884, Board of Ald. Petitions. The signers of these petitions were also overwhelmingly Irish and working-class, based on listings checked in the *Worcester Directory.*

20. On Thayer, see unidentified clipping, Dec. 19, 1916, Clipping File, WHM; *WDT,* July 7, 1889. On Athy, see Franklin P. Rice, ed., *The Worcester of Eighteen Hundred and Ninety-Eight* (Worcester, 1899), pp. 549–51, and Vincent E. Powers, "'Invisible Immigrants': The Pre-Famine Irish Community in Worcester, Massachusetts, from 1826–1860" (Ph.D. dissertation, Clark University, 1977), pp. 437–40.

21. "Report of Finance Committee," Dec. 17, 1883, and "Common Council Records," June 16 and 18, 1884, both in Board of Aldermen Manuscripts; *WDT,* July 1, 1884; *Boston Sunday Herald,* June 21, 1884. See similar analyses, in *WS,* June 28, 1884; *Boston Sunday Herald,* June 28, 1884.

22. *WST,* Dec. 28, 1884.

23. On the relative weakness of unions and radical parties in Worcester, see Rosenzweig, *Eight Hours,* pp.18–26.

24. *Boston Sunday Herald,* June 21, 1884.

25. *Park Report, 1884,* p. 208; *Park Report, 1879,* p. 23.

26. Gilman Bigelow Howe, *Genealogy of the Bigelow Family* (Worcester, 1890), pp. 412–13; *Worcester Evening Post,* Nov. 10, 1935; "Horace H. Bigelow," *Worcester Magazine,* 14 (Sept. 1911), p. 591; *WDT,* Sept. 4, 6, and 10, 1879, Apr. 11, 1882; *WEG,* May 6, 1875, June 1, 1907.

27. *Park Report, 1879,* pp. 22–23. On the rise of land values in other cities see Peterson, "Origins," pp. 103–5. See F.W. Beers, *Atlas of the City of Worcester* (New York, 1870), p. 11, and *Worcester House Directories* for Lincoln family holdings. (Timothy J. Meagher suggested this point to me.)

28. Unidentified clipping, July 28, 1901, Clipping File, WHM; *Worcester Telegram,* Nov. 16, 1886 (hereafter, *WT*).

29. For continuing East Side pressure, see *WDT,* Mar. 31, Apr. 30, May 25, June 23 and 30, July 13, 1885, May 1, 5, and 7, June 8 and 12, July 19, Nov. 30, 1886.

30. *WEG,* Sept. 25, 1886; *Park Report, 1886,* p.24. Of course, working-class residents also argued for the health benefits of parks. See, for example, *WDT,* Jan. 6, 1885.

31. David Montgomery, "Trade Union Practice and Syndicalist Theory," unpublished essay, 1969.

32. J.F. Roche, "Historical Sketch of the Parks & Playgrounds of Worcester," (M.A. thesis, Clark University, 1910), pp. 9–30.

33. *WT,* June 15, July 12, 1899; unidentified clipping, Sept. 1904; *WEG,* undated clippings [Sept. 1904]; *WT,* undated clippings [Sept. and Oct. 1904, 1905]; and Dec. 19, 1904; all in Parks Commission Scrapbooks, Worcester City Hall (hereafter, PC Scrapbooks); Petition of R.H. Mooney et al. for a park in Quinsigamond Village, Sept. 12, 1898, Board of Ald. Petitions.

34. Petition of John G. Hagberg et al., July 1, 1901, Board of Ald. Petitions. See also *WT,* Dec. 24, 1901.

35. *Labor News,* June 22, 1907 (hereafter *LN*). See also unidentified clipping, 1897, PC Scrapbooks; *WT,* Dec. 8, 1894.

36. *WS,* undated clipping [probably 1897], unidentified clipping [1897], both in PC Scrapbooks.

37. *Park Report, 1904*, pp. 14–15. See also *Park Report, 1908*, p. 1044.

38. "Our Common," *Light*, 4 (Nov. 7, 1891), p. 6; *WT*, July 16,1895; *WEG*, Jan. 13, 1908; *WST*, July 3, 1910; *Park Report, 1894*, p. 5; *Park Report, 1914*, p. 835; *Park Report, 1902*, p. 7; WST, Aug. 5, 1893 (found in the materials developed in the Assumption College Community Studies Program). G.F. Hoar to City Council, June 22, 1887, Board of Ald. Petitions; *WDT*, July 5, 1887. See also *WT*, July 4, 1893; *WEG*, Mar. 26, 1910.

39. Olmsted, Jr., and Kimball, *Frederick Law Olmsted*, 2, p. 171; Kasson, *Amusing the Million*, p. 15; *WDT*, June 22, 1880, May 13, 1886, July 2, 1887.

40. *WT*, undated clipping [c. 1947] on "Lake Quinsigamond's Great Days," Scrapbook on Lake, WHM; *WT*, Apr. 30, 1888, May 6, 1889. See also controversy about liquor at the lake in 1877, *WEG*, Apr. 30 and May 1, 1877.

41. Unidentified clipping, Aug. 12, 1898, PC Scrapbooks; *WT*, April 11, 1901. See also *WT*, May 2, 1901.

42. *WES*, Aug. 1, 1879; *LN*, July 8, 1916.

43. PC Minutes, May 5, 1913; *Park Report, 1913*, p.881; interview, Louis Lomatire, Worcester Bicentennial Oral History Project, Worcester, 1976 (typescript in author's possession). On Italian use of East Park, see also *Park Report, 1913*, p. 868; PC Minutes, May 5,1913; *Park Report, 1916*, p. 921; PC Minutes, May 14, 1917; "Cosmopolitan Worcester," *Worcester Magazine*, 18 (Aug. 1915), p. 180.

44. *Park Report, 1914*, p. 829; *WT*, June 12, 1910. For comments on conflicts over park design and use in other cities, see Robert D. Lusiak, "From the Grand Plaza to the Electric City: A Review of the Planning Heritage of Buffalo, N.Y., 1604–1920." (M.S. thesis, State University of New York at Buffalo, 1972), pp. 18–35; Kasson, *Amusing the Million*, pp. 11–17; Hardy, "'Parks for the People'"; Irving Howe, *World of Our Fathers* (New York, 1976), p. 212.

45. Henry Seidel Canby, *The Age of Confidence: Life in the Nineties* (New York, 1934), p.28; Harold Frederic, *The Damnation of Theron Ware*, Everett Carter, ed., (1896; reprint Cambridge, Mass., 1960), pp. 242, 244, 246.

46. "Editorial," *Light*, 1 (July 19, 1890), p. 3. On the growth of active sports and recreation in the 1890s, see John Higham, "The Reorientation of American Culture in the 1890's," in John Higham, *Writing American History: Essays on Modern Scholarship* (Bloomington, Ind., 1970), pp. 78, 80; Foster Rhea Dulles, *America Learns to Play—A History of Popular Recreation, 1607–1940* (1940; reprint Gloucester, Mass., 1963), p. 199. On the midcentury roots of this change in attitude, see Daniel T. Rodgers, *The Work Ethic in Industrial America, 1850–1920* (Chicago, 1978), p. 102.

47. R.M. Washburn, *Smith's Barn—"A Child's History" of the West Side of Worcester, 1880–1923* (Worcester, 1923), pp. 33–34, 40–41; George H. Haynes, *The Life of Charles B. Washburn* (Boston, 1931), p. 228; Charles A. Nutt, *History of Worcester and Its People*, 4 vols. (New York, 1919), 3, pp. 62–64. An important recent account of the shift in the leisure habits of the rich is Lewis A. Erenberg, *Steppin' Out: New York Nightlife and the Transformation of American Culture, 1890–1930*, (Westport, Conn., 1981).

48. Washburn, *Smith's Barn*, pp. 88–96; *WEG*, Apr. 6, 1945, Dec. 8, 1954; Nutt, *History of Worcester*, 3, pp. 283–86.

49. *WT*, Apr. 26, 1916. See also *WT*, Mar. 27 and Apr. 20, 1916.

50. Nutt, *History of Worcester*, p. 285; Higham, "Reorientation of American Culture," p. 78; Jean-Christophe Agnew, "The Struggle for Existence" (lecture, Yale University, Oct. 13, 1980); Rodgers, *Work Ethic in Industrial America*, p. 109.

51. For a Worcester reformer on the uses of leisure, see U. Waldo Cutler, "City and Citizen: Studies in Community Organization as Illustrated in a Typical American City" (lectures, [c. 1917], typescript, WHM). On the Vrooman incident, see Rosenzweig, *Eight Hours*, p. 106.

52. Dorothy Ross, *G. Stanley Hall: The Psychologist as Prophet* (Chicago, 1972), p. 300. See also Dominick J. Cavallo, *Muscles and Morals: Organized Playgrounds and Urban*

Reform, 1880–1920 (Philadelphia, 1981); Bernard Mergen, "The Discovery of Children's Play," *American Quarterly,* 27 (Oct. 1975), pp. 399–420; Kett, *Rites of Passage,* pp. 217–21.

53. Finfer, in "Leisure as Social Work in the Urban Community," examines the playground movement from the perspective of its social control intentions. Cavallo, in *Muscles and Morals,* focuses more on its personality models. Richard Knapp offers an institutional history of the Playground Association in "Play for America: The National Recreation Association, 1906–1950" (Ph.D. dissertation, Duke University, 1971). A good recent overview is Boyer, *Urban Masses and Moral Order,* pp. 242–51. Local studies include Goodman, *Choosing Sides;* Benjamin McArthur, "The Chicago Playground Movement: A Neglected Feature of Social Justice," *Social Service Review,* 49 (Sept. 1975), pp. 376–95; Richard Knapp, "Parks and Politics: The Rise of Municipal Responsibility for Playgrounds in New York City, 1887–1905" (M.A. thesis, Duke University, 1968); Gerald Marsden, "Philanthropy and the Boston Playground Movement, 1885–1907," *Social Service Review,* 35 (Mar. 1961), pp. 48–58. Clarence Rainwater's *The Play Movement in the United States: The Study of Community Recreation* (Chicago, 1922) is an excellent overview by a partisan of the play movement.

54. Robert Sklar, *Movie-Made America: A Social History of American Movies* (New York, 1975), p. 124.

55. *WT,* June 22 and 29, 1910; *WST,* July 12, 1908.

56. *Park Report, 1907,* p. 3; "An Interpreter of Nature," Light, 2 (Sept. 13, 1890), p. 6. The wealth of a fourth, long-term parks Commissioner, Stephen Salisbury, was also in real estate, although he was also closely connected to the city's manufacturing families.

57. This is based on a collective biography of the city's parks Commissioners developed from information in Nutt, *History of Worcester;* Rice, *Worcester;* and the *Worcester Directory.*

58. "Inaugural Address of Mayor James Logan," Jan. 6, 1908, in *Worcester City Documents, 1907* (Worcester, 1980), pp. 17–18; *WEP,* Dec. 9, 1908.

59. *Park Report, 1905,* p. 13; *Park Report, 1898,* p. 17; *Park Report, 1909,* p. 611.

60. *Park Report, 1903,* p. 7; *Park Report, 1911,* p. 571; Henry S. Curtis, quoted in Jean-Christophe Agnew, "American Intellectuals and the Drama of Social Control, 1870–1915" (paper presented at Mid-Atlantic Radical Historians Organization Conference, New York, N.Y., Apr. 1977).

61. *Park Report, 1907,* p. 6; John J. McCoy, *The Playground Movement* (New York, n.d., [probably 1911]), pp. 10–11. See also Board of Trade, Minutes, Oct. 10 and 14, 1909, Feb. 10, 1910 (at Worcester Chamber of Commerce); William Francis Hyde, "Who Shall Have Our Jacks and Jills—Satan or Society?", *Worcester Magazine,* 12 (Aug. 1909), pp. 269–71.

62. The list of Playground Association directors is from the Parks Commission Manuscripts. The biographical profile is based on Nutt, *History of Worcester* and the *Worcester Directory.* See also Washburn, *Smith's Barn,* p. 95.

63. "Report of George Booth for 1910" (typescript, Parks Commission Manuscripts); *WT,* May 20, 21, 23, 26–8, 30 and 31, June 1–5, 8, 10–12, 14, 15, 22, 23, and 30, 1910.

64. W.F. Hyde, "Report on Playgrounds, 1910," May 8, 1911; Emmett Angell, "Report on Playgrounds, 1910," Dec. 4, 1910; both letters to George F. Booth, Parks Commission Manuscripts.

65. *WEG,* Feb. 15, 1913; *WT,* July 28, 1912, *WEG,* [Jan. ?] 1914, in PC Scrapbooks.

66. Playground Association of America, Leaflet No. 2, Oct. 11, 1909, in Playground Association of America, *Miscellaneous Publications, 1907–09,* Gund Library, Harvard University; "Third Inaugural Address of Mayor James Logan," Jan. 1910, in *Worcester City Documents, 1909* (Worcester, 1910), p. 46.

67. McCoy, *Playground Movement,* p. 8; Ellen Murphy, "Report on Sewing," Parks Commission Manuscript; *WT,* Oct. 10, 1910.

68. Ada S. Glickman, "The Delinquent Girl in Worcester" (M.A. thesis, Clark Univ., 1932), pp. 13–26; *WT,* Oct. 10, 1910. McCoy, *Playground Movement,* 7. See also Emmett

Angell, *Play* (Boston, 1910), p. 26. On the assimilationist strand in the playground movement, see David Glassberg, "Restoring a 'Forgotten Childhood': American Play and the Progressive Era's Elizabethan Past," *American Quarterly,* 32 (Fall 1980), pp. 359–61.

69. "Playground Census" (typed sheets, Parks Commission Manuscripts). Since there is no way to know how the Playground Association determined ethnicity, it is possible that these figures may overstate the percentage of foreign-stock children using the playgrounds. For example, third-generation children may have been counted as foreign stock. Nevertheless, the playgrounds still received heavy immigrant use.

70. Interestingly, the English and the English Canadians—the largest ethnic groups to be underrepresented at playgrounds—were also the groups most likely to be under-counted (i.e., counted as "American") by the Playground Census. The overall patterns may also have been distorted because of the differences in the age structures of the different ethnic communities, but there is no systematic evidence on this point.

71. The names of the playground supervisors (and some background information on them) were found in the Parks Commission Manuscripts.

72. Dominock J. Cavallo, "The Child in American Reform," (Ph.D. dissertation, State University of New York at Stony Brook, 1976), p. 135; Paul W. Shankweiler, "A Sociological Study of the Child Welfare Program of Worcester, Massachusetts" (Ph.D. dissertation, University of North Carolina, 1934), pp. 555–56.

73. Mergen, "Discovery of Children's Play," p. 416.

74. *WST*, Aug. 4, 1912, although the articles were politically motivated by the *Telegram's* opposition the playgrounds, the comments seem authentic.

75. Quoted in *Park Report, 1890*, p. 40.

CHAPTER TEN: NOTES

I wish to thank Mari Jo Buhle, Lewis Erenberg, Dee Garrison, and David Green for their comments on earlier versions of this essay, and Robert Asher for his editorial assistance.

1. Belle Lindner Israels, "The Way of the Girl," *Survey,* 22 (July 3, 1909), p. 494; M.M. Davis, *The Exploitation of Pleasure: A Study of Commercial Recreations in New York City* (New York: Russell Sage Foundation, n.d.), p. 15.

2. Using dance as a means of interpreting culture and social relations is discussed in Anya Peterson Royce, *The Anthropology of Dance* (Bloomington: Indiana University Press, 1977), and Frances Rust, *Dance in Society* (London: Routledge and Kegan Paul, 1969).

3. John M. Oskison, "Public Halls of the East Side," University Settlement Society, *Report, 1899*, p. 40. On rackets, see Verne M. Bovie, "The Public Dance Halls of the Lower East Side," University Settlement Society, *Report, 1901*, p. 32; Elsa Herzfeld, *Family Monographs; The History of Twenty-Four Families in the Middle West Side of New York City* (New York: James Kempster, 1905), pp. 17–18; Ruth S. True, *The Neglected Girl* (New York: Russell Sage Foundation, 1914), pp. 68–69. On the variety of halls, see Davis, *Exploitation,* p. 15; Belle Lindner Israels, "Diverting a Pastime," *Leslie's Weekly,* 113 (July 27, 1911), pp. 94, 100; George Kneeland, *Commercialized Prostitution in New York City* (New York: Century, 1913), p. 56.

The interrelationship between work and leisure in 19th-century working-class organizations is discussed in Susan Hirsch, *Roots of the American Working Class: The Industrialization of Crafts in Newark, 1800–1860* (Philadelphia: University of Pennsylvania Press, 1978); John T. Cumbler, *Working-Class Community in Industrial America: Work, Leisure and Struggle in Two Industrial Cities, 1880–1930* (Westport, Conn.: Greenwood, 1979); and

John Alt, "Beyond Class: The Decline of Industrial Labor and Leisure," *Telos*, no. 28 (Summer 1976), pp. 55–80.

4. Israels, "Diverting a Pastime," pp. 94, 100; Bovie, "Public Dance Halls," pp. 32–33. On the social club, see University Settlement Society, *Report*, 1889, pp. 23, 32; Davis, *Exploitation*, p. 9; *New York Times Illustrated Magazine*, June 27, 1897, p. 4, clipping in J.G.P. Stokes Collection, Rare Book and Manuscripts Library, Columbia University; Herbert Asbury, *The Gangs of New York* (New York: 1927; reprint Capricorn Books, 1970), p. 269; New York, Special Committee . . . to Investigate the Condition of Female Labor in the City of New York, *Report and Testimony* (Albany: Wynkoop Hallenbeck Crawford, 1896), 1, p. 86.

5. Davis, *Exploitation*, p. 16; Israels, "Diverting a Pastime," p. 100; True, *Neglected Girl*, p. 70; Oskison, "Public Halls of the East Side," p. 39.

6. Maria Ward Lambin, *Report of the Advisory Dance Committee of the Women's City Club and the City Recreation Committee* (New York, 1924); Israels, "Way of the Girl," p. 494. A general indication of the expansion in dance halls is evidenced in New York City business directories. These do not list dance halls separately, nor do they account for the numerous saloons with attached dancing rooms. However, they show that the number of large general-purpose halls increased 50% from 1895 (130 halls) to 1910 (195 halls). See *Trow Business Directories of New York City, 1895* and *1910* (New York: Trow Directory Co.).

7. George E. Bevans, *How Workingmen Spend Their Spare Time* (New York: Columbia University Press, 1913), pp. 27, 33; Oskison, "Public Halls of the East Side," pp. 39–40; Hutchins Hapgood, *Types from City Streets* (New York: Funk and Wagnalls, 1910), pp. 135, 21.

8. Dorothy Richardson, *The Long Day*, reprinted in William L. O'Neill, ed., *Women at Work* (New York: Quadrangle, 1972), pp. 94–95. See also True, *Neglected Girl*, pp. 69–72.

9. Bovie, "Public Dance Halls," pp. 31–32; Belle L. Mead, "The Social Pleasure of East Side Jews" (M.A. thesis, Columbia University, 1904), p. 6; Israels, "Way of the Girl," p. 494; Herzfeld, *Family Monographs*, p. 18; Thomas Jesse Jones, *Sociology of a New York City Block* (New York: Columbia University, 1904), p. 45; Trinity Church Men's Committee, *A Social Survey of the Washington Street District of New York City* (Oct. 1914), p. 48.

10. See, for example, Investigator's Report, Excelsior Cafe, 306 Eighth Avenue, Dec. 21, 1916, Committee of Fourteen Papers, (hereafter, COFP) New York Public Library. Discussing women on the balcony of this cafe-dance house, the investigator observed that "2 appeared to be respectable Italian girls." The Committee of Fourteen studied vice and prostitution in New York in the Progressive Era. Their investigators looked into saloons and dance halls throughout New York; their manuscript reports provide a revealing picture not only of underworld life, but also of "respectable" working-class behavior in New York's dance halls.

The finest discussion of the importance of cultural traditions in women's lives is in Joan W. Scott and Louise A. Tilly, "Women's Work and the Family in Nineteenth-Century Europe," *Comparative Studies in Society and History,* 17 (Jan. 1975), pp. 36–64. On women in Italian culture, see Virginia Yans McLaughlin, "Patterns of Work and Family Organization: Buffalo's Italians," in Herbert Gutman and Gregory Kealey, eds., *Many Pasts: Readings in American Social History,* 2 (Englewood Cliffs, N.J.: Prentice-Hall, 1973), pp. 195–207.

11. Israels, "Diverting a Pastime," p. 94; True, *Neglected Girl*, pp. 62–63; Sue Ainslie Clark and Edith Wyatt, *Making Both Ends Meet: The Income and Outlay of New York Working Girls* (New York: Macmillan, 1911), p. 21; Lillian W. Betts, "Tenement House Life and Recreation," *Outlook* (Feb. 11, 1899), p. 366; *Boyhood and Lawlessness; West Side Studies*, Pauline Goldmark, ed., (New York: Survey Associates, 1914), p. 155; Mary S. Fergusson, "Boarding Homes and Clubs for Working Women," *Bulletin of the U.S. Department of Labor*, no. 15 (Washington, D.C.: U.S. Government Printing Office, 1898); Esther

Packard, *A Study of Living Conditions of Self-Supporting Women in New York City* (New York: Metropolitan Board of the YWCA, 1915), p. 51; Mary K. Maule, "What is a Shopgirl's Life?" *World's Work*, 14 (Sept. 1907), p. 9314.

The percentage of working women living alone in American cities varied from 10% to 25% in the early 20th century. According to the New York Factory Investigating Commission, 15% of New York City's working women lived independent of family or employers in 1914. See New York State, Factory Investigating Commission, *Fourth Report Transmitted to Legislature, February 15, 1915*, Sen. Doc. 43, 4 (Albany: J.B. Lyon, 1915), pp. 1738, 1676. See also Leslie Woodcock Tentler's discussion of working women "on their own" in *Wage-Earning Women: Industrial Work and Family Life in the United States, 1900–1930* (New York: Oxford University Press, 1979), pp. 115–35.

12. Betts, "Tenement House Life and Recreation," p. 365. See also Robert A. Woods and Albert J. Kennedy, *Young Working Girls: A Summary of Evidence from Two Thousand Social Workers* (Boston: Houghton Mifflin, 1913), p. 61; Belle Lindner Israels, "The Dance Problem," *Proceedings of the National Conference of Charities and Corrections, 1912* (Fort Wayne, Ind., 1912), p. 144. A fictional account of such generational conflict is Anzia Yezierska, *Bread Givers* (1925; reprint New York: Persea Books, 1975).

13. True, *Neglected Girl*, pp. 54–55. Leslie Woodcock Tentler, in *Wage-Earning Women*, pp. 107–14, argues that young women found an illusory freedom in social life, and she ties this to the creation of an urban marriage market which simply reconstituted traditional methods of courtship. She concludes that such social freedom still entailed economic dependence and did not fundamentally change the lives of working women. This interpretation tends to reduce the history of working women to a continuum of economic dependence; I prefer to explore the social and cultural changes, however small, that affected the texture of everyday life and the *context* in which economic dependence occurred.

14. Investigator's Report, Remey's, 917 Eighth Avenue, Feb. 11, 1917, COFP.

15. Investigator's Report, Jim Coffey's, 2923 Eighth Avenue, Feb. 17, 1917, and Manhattan Casino, 2926 Eighth Avenue, Aug. 19, 1917, COFP.

16. Kneeland, *Commercialized Prostitution*, p. 68; Louise de Koven Bowen, "Dance Halls," *Survey*, 26 (July 3, 1911), p. 384.

17. Julian Ralph, "Coney Island," *Scribner's*, 20 (July 1896), p. 18.

18. Julia Schoenfeld, unpublished report, quoted in Richard Henry Edwards, *Popular Amusements* (New York: Association Press, 1915), p. 78. See also Bovie, "Public Dance Halls," p. 33. For waltz instructions, see *The Perfect Art of Modern Dancing*, 7, no. 2 (May 1894), pp. 19–20.

19. For an excellent analysis of the middle-class dance craze, see Lewis A. Erenberg, "Everybody's Doin' It: The Pre-World War I Dance Craze, The Castles, and the Modern American Girl," *Feminist Studies*, 3, nos. 1/2 (Fall 1975), pp. 155–70; and *Steppin' Out: New York Nightlife and the Transformation of American Culture, 1890–1930* (Westport, Conn.: Greenwood Press, 1981).

20. Committee on Amusements and Vacation Resources of Working Girls, two page circular, Box 28, Parks and Playgrounds—Correspondence, Lillian Wald Collection, Rare Book and Manuscripts Library, Columbia University.

21. Ibid. See also Julian Street, *Welcome to Our City* (New York: John Lane, 1913), pp. 9–10.

22. On the impact of the Castles on "modern" social behavior, see Erenberg, "Everybody's Doin' It." In addition to his work, culture before the First World War has been acutely explored by James R. McGovern, "The American Woman's Pre-World War I Freedom in Manners and Morals," *Journal of American History*, 55 (Sept. 1968), pp. 315–33; and Larry May, *Screening Out the Past: The Birth of Mass Culture and the Motion Picture Industry* (New York: Oxford University Press, 1980).

23. Vernon and Irene Castle, *Modern Dancing*, foreword, Frank L. Clendennen, *Dance*

Mad or the Dances of the Day (St. Louis: Arcade Printing, 1914), p. 8; J.S. Hopkins, *The Tango and Other Up-to-Date Dances* (Chicago: Saalfield, 1914), p. 39.

24. Investigator's Report, The Ritz Cabaret, 2114–2118 Seventh Ave., June 9, 1917, COFP.

25. Investigator's Report, Princess Cafe, 1203 Broadway, Jan. 1, 1917, COFP; Kneeland, *Commercialized Prostitution*, p. 70; Investigator's Report, Excelsior Cafe, 306 Eighth Ave., Dec. 21, 1916, COFP.

26. Israels, "Dance Problem," p. 141; True, *Neglected Girl*, pp. 70, 72; Investigator's Report, Manhattan Casino, 2828 Eighth Ave., Aug. 19, 1917, and Weimann's, 1422 St. Nicholas Ave., Feb. 11, 1917, COFP; Israels, "Diverting a Pastime," p. 94.

27. Investigator's Report, The Parisian, 945 Eighth Ave., May 18, 1917, p. 2, COFP; see Erenberg, *Steppin' Out*, pp. 113–45.

28. True, *Neglected Girl*, p. 72.

29. Helen S. Campbell, *Prisoners of Poverty* (1887; reprint Westport, Conn.: Greenwood, 1970), p. 175; Bowen, "Dance Halls," p. 385. On young women's clothing expenditures, see New York State, Factory Investigating Commission, *Fourth Report*, pp. 1519–28; "Tentative Quantity-Cost Budget Necessary to Maintain Family of Five in Washington, D.C.," *Monthly Labor Review*, 9, no. 1 (Dec., 1919), p. 6.

30. Israels, "Diverting a Pastime," p. 100; Kneeland, *Commercialized Prostitution*, p. 70.

31. Israels, "Way of the Girl," p. 489; True, *Neglected Girl*, p. 59.

32. For an overview of women's working conditions and their effect on wages, see Barbara Mayer Wertheimer, *We Were There, The Story of Working Women in America* (New York: Pantheon, 1977), pp. 209–43; and Tentler, *Wage-Earning Women*, pp. 13–25. One extensive study that found women's wages to be far below the living wage is New York State Factory Investigating Commission, *Fourth Report*, 1, pp. 35, 1509; on spending money, see also 4, pp. 1581–82. According to another study, 84% of women in stores and 88% of those in factories contributed all their earnings to the family. U.S. Bureau of Labor, *Report on the Condition of Woman and Child Wage-Earners in the U.S.*, 5, Sen. Doc. 645, 61st Cong., 2nd sess. (Washington, D.C.: U.S. Government Printing Office, 1913), p. 15. For evidence of the dependence of women on men in their leisure time, see Esther Packard, "Living on Six Dollars a Week," pp. 1675–94 and Marie S. Orenstein, "How the Working Girl of New York Lives," pp. 1695–1714, in Factory Investigating Commission, *Fourth Report*, 4; "A Salesgirl's Story," *Independent*, 54 (July, 1902), p. 1821; Woods and Kennedy, *Young Working Girls*, pp. 105–6; Lillian Betts, *The Leaven in a Great City* (New York: Dodd, Mead, 1902), pp. 251–52.

33. Factory Investigating Commission, *Fourth Report*, 4, pp. 1585–86. Also Clark and Wyatt, *Making Both Ends Meet*; and Clara E. Laughlin, *The Work-A-Day Girl; A Study of Some Present Conditions* (1913; reprint New York: Arno, 1974), p. 50.

34. See Woods and Kennedy, *Young Working Girls*, pp. 85–87 (quote on p. 85); Betts, *Leaven*, pp. 81, 218–19; True, *Neglected Girl*, p. 69.

35. Mary Bularzik, "Sexual Harassment at the Workplace: Historical Notes," pamphlet (Somerville, Mass.: New England Free Press, 1979); also, Factory Investigating Commission, *Fourth Report*, 5, p. 2809. On work cultures, see Dorothy Richardson, *The Long Day*, p. 73 and passim; *Thought and Work* (Siegel-Cooper Department Store), 1903–1906; Laughlin, *Work-A-Day Girl*; Clark and Wyatt, *Making Both Ends Meet*, pp. 187–88; Amy E. Tanner, "Glimpses at the Mind of a Waitress," *American Journal of Sociology*, 13 (July 1907), p. 52.

36. Investigator's Report, 2150 Eighth Ave., Jan. 12, 1917, COFP. For other reports of "charity girls," see Woods and Kennedy, *Young Working Girls*, p. 85; Committee of Fourteen, *Annual Report, 1917*, p. 15, and *1918*, p. 32; Factory Investigating Commission, *Fourth Report*, 1, "Memoranda on Vice Problem," p. 403. Charity girls should also be distinguished from "occasional prostitutes," who slipped in and out of prostitution,

but accepted money. See Laughlin, *Work-A-Day Girl*, pp. 51–52, and U.S. Bureau of Labor, *Report on Condition of Woman and Child Wage-Earners*, 15, p. 83.

37. Investigator's Report, La Keunstler Klause, 1490 Third Ave., Jan. 19, 1917, and Bobby More's, 252 West 31st Street, Feb. 3, 1917; see also Manhattan Casino, 2926 Eighth Ave., Feb. 17, 1917, and May 20, 1917, COFP.

38. Investigator's Report, Clare Hotel and Palm Gardens/McNamara's, 2150 Eighth Ave., Jan. 12, 1917; see also, Manhattan Casino, 2926 Eighth Ave., Mar. 19, 1917, COFP.

39. Investigator's Report, Manhattan Casino, 2926 Eighth Ave., March 19, 1917, COFP.

40. Investigator's Report, Semprini's, 145 West 50th Street, Oct. 5, 1918, COFP. For an extended discussion of the dimensions of working women's sexuality in these years, see Kathy Peiss, "'Charity Girls' and City Pleasures: Historical Notes on Working-Class Sexuality, 1880–1920," in Ann Snitow, et al., eds. *Powers of Desire: The Politics of Sexuality* (New York: Monthly Review Press, 1983).

41. Investigator's Report, Manhattan Casino, 2926 Eighth Ave., May 20, 1917, COFP. For other evidence of female friendships, see Hapgood, *Types from City Streets*, p. 131; True, *Neglected Girl*, pp. 60–61; Richardson, *The Long Day*, p. 68 and passim; Israels, "Diverting a Pastime," pp. 94, 100; Woods and Kennedy, *Young Working Girls*, pp. 8, 35.

42. Judith R. Walkowitz, "The Politics of Prostitution," *Signs: Journal of Women in Culture and Society*, 6, no. 1 (Autumn 1980), p. 123–35.

43. See Kathy L. Peiss, "Cheap Amusements: Gender Relations and the Use of Leisure Time in New York City, 1880 to 1920" (Ph.D. dissertation, Brown University, 1982).

44. Christina Simmons, "The Dream World of Confession Magazines, 1920–1940," Fifth Berkshire Conference of Women Historians, Vassar College, June 16, 1981. On the new sexuality, see Simmons, "Marriage in the Modern Manner: Sexual Radicalism and Reform in America, 1914–1941," (Ph.D. dissertation, Brown University, 1982); and Mary P. Ryan, *Womanhood in America*, 3rd ed. (New York: Franklin Watts, 1983), pp. 220–44.

45. See Lillian Breslow Rubin's evocative discussion in *Worlds of Pain: Life in the Working-Class Family* (New York: Basic Books, 1976), 114–33; see also Mirra Komarovsky, *Blue-Collar Marriage* (New York: Vintage Books, 1962), and Lee Rainwater, et al., *Working-Man's Wife* (New York: MacFadden Books, 1959).

CHAPTER ELEVEN: NOTES

The author wishes to thank Cindy Costello, Susan Porter Benson, and Micaela di-Leonardo for their comments on my analysis of women cigar workers.

1. *Tobacco Leaf*, Oct. 1, 1902, p. 24.

2. The Census Bureau lumped together several different groups of tobacco factory operatives, so it is impossible to determine the precise proportion of cigar makers who were women. The percentages I use, however, are drawn from census data. See U.S. Department of Commerce, Bureau of the Census, *Census of Manufacturers: 1900*, 9, *Special Reports on Selected Industries* (Washington, D.C., 1902), p. 653; *Census of Manufacturers: 1919*, 8, *General Report and Analytical Tables* (Washington, D.C., 1923), p. 490; *Census of Occupations: 1900, Special Reports* (Washington, D.C., 1904), p. 12; *Census of Population: 1920*, 4, *Occupations* (Washington, D.C., 1923), p. 38.

3. The concept of work culture has been used and defined in many different ways, but I have been most influenced by the work of Barbara Melosh, *The Physician's Hand: Work Culture and Conflict in American Nursing* (Philadelphia, 1982), pp. 5–6, and Susan Porter Benson, "'The Clerking Sisterhood': Rationalization and the Work Culture of Saleswomen in American Department Stores, 1890–1960," *Radical America*, 12 (Mar.–

Apr. 1978), pp. 41–55. I see work culture as a matrix of values, traditions, beliefs, and practices of workers in a particular work place or occupation. Work culture, however, is more than a description of shop floor life—it is the meaning and function of those patterns. Work culture is created in the dynamic struggle between those who work and those who buy their labor. It relates both to the work process itself and to workers' interpretation of that work. See also David A. Bensman, "Artisan Culture, Business and Union: American Hat Finishers in the Nineteenth Century," (Ph.D. dissertation, Columbia University, 1977); David Montgomery, *Workers' Control in America* (Cambridge, 1979); Ken Kusterer, Know-How on the Job: The Important Knowledge of "Unskilled" Workers (Boulder, Colo., 1978); Herbert Guman, *Work Culture and Society in Industrializing America: Essays in American Working-Class and Social History* (New York, 1977).

4. My own work, "From Hand Craft to Mass Production: Men, Women and Work Culture in American Cigar Factories, 1900–1919," (Ph.D. dissertation, University of Maryland, 1981), examines and compares the work cultures of union men and non-union women during these years. I found that while the goals and concerns of the two work cultures were fundamentally similar, their operation and content diverged sharply. The differences in work and work culture, I believe, are rooted in the system of male domination, which some have labeled patriarchy. Heidi Hartmann has defined this system as "a set of social relations between men, which have a material base, and which, through hierarchy, establish or create interdependence and solidarity among men that enable them to dominate women. Though patriarchy is hierarchical, and men of different classes, races or ethnic groups have different places in the patriarchy, they also are united in their shared relationship of dominance over their women; they are dependent on each other to maintain that domination." See Hartmann, "The Unhappy Marriage of Marxism and Feminism: Towards a More Progressive Union," in Lydia Sargent, ed., *Women and Revolution: A Discussion of the Unhappy Marriage of Marxism and Feminism* (Boston, 1981).

5. Willin N. Baer, *The Economic Development of the Cigar Industry in the United States* (Lancaster, Penn., 1933), pp. 13–50, 74–75, 81, 89, 107, 119, 257; John P. Troxell, "Labor in the Tobacco Industry in the United States" (New York, 1907), pp. 1–8, 46, 78–79; Meyer Jacobstein, *The Tobacco Industry in the United States* (New York, 1907), pp. 11–42, 86–89; U.S. Bureau of Corporations, *Report of the Commissioner of Corporations on the Tobacco Industry*, part 1 (Washington, D.C., 1909), pp. 149–64, 266, 423–24; U.S. Congress, Senate, *Report on Condition of Woman and Child Wage-Earners in the United States*, 18, *Employment of Women in Selected Industries*, Sen. Doc. 645, 61st Cong., 2nd sess. (Washington, D.C.: U.S. Government Printing Office, 1913), pp. 95–102; U.S. Department of Commerce, Bureau of the Census, *Census of Manufacturers: 1900*, 9, *Special Reports on Selected Industries* (Washington, D.C., 1904), 669–71.

6. U.S. Bureau of Corporations, *Report of the Commissioner*, part 1, pp. 149–64, 423–27; U.S. Bureau of the Census, *Census of Manufacturers: 1919*, 8, *General Report and Analytical Tables* (Washington, D.C., 1923), p. 490.

7. Carl Werner, *A Textbook on Tobacco* (New York, 1909), pp. 39–43, 47–61; Baer, *Economic Development*, pp. 41–43, 74–75, 85–89, 119, 257; *Tobacco*, Apr. 24, 1909, p. 2; Edith Abbott, *Women in Industry: A Study in American Economic History* (New York, 1913), pp. 194–97, 186–214; Troxell, "Labor in the Tobacco Industry," p. 59; Elizabeth Faulkner Baker, *Technology and Women's Work* (New York, 1964), pp. 32–35, 162–68.

8. *Tobacco*, Nov. 8, 1906, p. 22; *Tobacco Leaf*, July 23, 1908, p. 18; Abbott, *Women in Industry*, p. 212; U.S. Bureau of Corporations, Tobacco Investigation, file 1073, "Labor Conditions in the Cigar Industry," Record Group (R.G.) 122, National Archives (hereafter, NA), Washington, D.C.; Alice Gannett, "Bohemian Women in New York: Investigation of Working Mothers," *Life and Labor*, Feb. 1913, pp. 49–52; E.P. Hutchinson, *Immigrants and Their Children, 1850–1950* (New York, 1956), pp. 172–75, 182; Barbara Mary

Klaczynska, "Working Women in Philadelphia, 1900–1930," (Ph.D. dissertation, Temple University, 1975), p. 85, 119–21; U.S. Congress, Senate, *Woman and Child Wage-Earners*, 18, pp. 88–91, 106.

9. Jacobstein, *The Tobacco Industry*, p. 140; U.S. Commissioner of Labor, *Nineteenth Annual Report, 1904, Wages and Hours of Labor* (Washington, D.C., 1904), p. 59; U.S. Bureau of Labor Statistics, bulletin 135, *Wages and Hours of Labor, 1911 and 1912* (Washington, D.C., 1913), pp. 14–24; U.S. Bureau of Labor Statistics, "Wages and Hours of Labor in the Cigar and Men's Clothing Industries," *Monthly Labor Review*, 10 (Mar. 1920), p. 81–87; U.S. Congress, Senate, *Reports of the Immigration Commission, Immigrants in Industries*, part 14, *Cigar and Tobacco Manufacturing*, Sen. Doc. 633, 61st Cong., 2nd sess., 1911, pp. 17, 28, 44–45; U.S. Congress, *Woman and Child Wage-Earners*, 18, pp. 109–10, 464–71.

10. *Detroit City Directory, 1908* and *1909; Tobacco Leaf*, Sept. 20, 1905, p. 44, and Mar. 11, 1909, p. 7; George B. Catlin, *The Story of Detroit* (Detroit, 1926), p. 468; Richards Oestreicher, "Changing Patterns of Class Relations in Detroit, 1880–1900," *Detroit in Perspective*, 3 (Spring 1979), p. 146; *Cigar Makers' Official Journal* (hereafter, *CMOJ*), Apr. 1908, p. 5; "Tendency of Industries Employing Largely Women and Child Labor to Locate in the Vicinity of Industries Employing Exclusively Male Labor" (typescript), Commission of Industrial Relations, U.S. Department of Labor, R.G. 174, NA.

11. *Tobacco*, June 8, 1900, p. 4, and July 20, 1900, p. 8; U.S. Industrial Commission, *Report on Immigration*, 15 (Washington, D.C., 1901), p. 388; *Tobacco Leaf*, Nov. 24, 1910, p. 4; June 15, 1911, p. 4; Lucy Winsor Killough, *The Tobacco Products Industry in New York and Its Environs, Present Trends and Probable Future Developments*, Regional Plan of New York and Its Environs, Monograph no. 5 (New York, 1924), pp. 20–30; *CMOJ*, Mar. 1901, p. 12; Report of Conciliator, May 3, 1922, file 170/1677, Federal Mediation and Conciliation Service (hereafter, FMCS), R.G. 280, NA.

12. U.S. Commissioner of Labor, *Eleventh Special Report*, "Regulation and Restriction of Output" (Washington, D.C., 1904), pp. 568–69; U.S. Commissioner of Labor, *Thirteenth Annual Report, 1898, Hand and Machine Labor* (Washington, D.C., 1899), pp.392–95; Baer, *The Cigar Industry*, p. 84; U.S. Congress, *Woman and Child Wage-Earners*, 18, pp. 85–88, 97–100; Reavis Cox, *Competition in the Tobacco Industry, 1911–1932: A Study of the Effects of the Partition of the American Tobacco Company by the United States Supreme Court* (New York, 1933), p. 58; U.S. Bureau of Labor Statistics, bulletin 135, *Rates of Wages in the Cigar and Clothing Industries*, p. 7; "Machinery in Cigar Manufacture," U.S. Bureau of Corporations, Tobacco Investigation, file 3073, R.G. 122, NA; *Tobacco Leaf*, Jan. 15, 1902, p. 23, and Nov. 26, 1909, p. 20.

13. *CMOJ*, June 1906, p. 11; July 1910, p. 8; U.S. Commissioner of Labor, "Regulation and Restriction of Output," p. 572; U.S. Bureau of Corporations, Tobacco Investigation, file 3073, section 9, R.G. 122, NA; *Tobacco Leaf*, Jan. 24, 1906, p. 9; June 26, 1907, p. 6; May 18, 1911, p. 6; Nov. 8, 1910, p. 6; Jan. 7, 1915, p. 4; Jan. 14, 1915, pp. 6–7; Jan. 31, 1918, p. 3; *U.S. Tobacco Journal*, Apr. 21, 1906, p. 7.

14. *U.S. Tobacco Journal*, 21, Apr. 1906, p. 7; *Tobacco*, July 6, 1900, p. 8; Feb. 7, 1902, p. 7; Nov. 21, 1902, p. 2; *CMOJ*, May 1900, p. 9; Oct. 1909, p. 10; May 1911, p. 4; Dec. 1912, p. 25; *Tobacco Leaf*, Aug. 7, 1907, p. 38; Nov. 2, 1902, p. 2; Dec. 21, 1902, p. 28; Nov. 1, 1905, p. 58; Jan. 31, 1906, p. 11; Feb. 7, 1906, p. 32; Sept. 26, 1906, p. 34; Dec. 7, 1911, p. 3.

15. U.S. Congress, Senate, *Report on Condition of Woman and Child Wage-Earners*, 18, p. 95; New Orleans Factory Inspection Department, *Report* (New Orleans, 1912), p. 2; Annette Mann, *Women Workers in Factories: A Study of Working Conditions in 275 Industrial Establishments in Cincinnati and Adjoining Towns* (1918; reprint New York, 1974), p. 22; Kansas Board of Public Welfare, Bureau of Labor Statistics, *Report on the Wage-Earning Women in Kansas City* (Kansas City, 1913), p. 25; Young Women's Christian Association

Papers, Tulane University; U.S. Public Health Service, bulletin 73, *Tuberculosis among Industrial Workers: Report of Investigation Made in Cincinnati with Special Reference to Predisposing Causes* (Washington, D.C., 1915), p. 131; author's interview, Anna Bartasius, Mar. 31, 1982, Philadelphia, Penn. Bartasius is one of about fifty people I interviewed in the course of my research concerning the cigar industry between 1900 and 1940. Tape recordings of all interviews are in my possession.

16. *Tobacco Leaf*, Mar. 25, 1903, p. 11; Nov. 7, 1906, p. 31; U.S. Bureau of Labor, bulletin 82, *Mortality from Consumption in Certain Occupations* (Washington, D.C., 1909), pp. 545–67.

17. U.S. Bureau of Labor Statistics, bulletin 135, *Rates of Wages in the Cigar and Clothing Industries, 1911 and 1912*, p. 10; author's interviews; Helen Piwkowska, and Rose Purzon, Sept. 21, 1978, Detroit, Mich. My description of the work process comes from interviews with both men and women and from my own observations in numerous cigar factories since 1976.

18. Author's interviews; Purzon; Frances Salantak, Sept. 20, 1978 and Cecelia Chromki, Sept. 21, 1978, Detroit, Mich.; *CMOJ*, Dec. 1911, p. 3; *Detroit Labor News*, July 10, 1914, and July 14, 1916; interview, Bartasius, Mar. 31, 1982.

19. Interview, Agnes, Feb. 4, 1982, Evansville, Ind., by Glenda Morrison for the Indiana Labor History Project, Indiana State University–Evansville.

20. *Report of the Michigan State Commission of Inquiry into Wages and the Conditions of Labor for Women and the Advisability of Establishing a Minimum Wage* (Lansing, Mich., 1915), p. 422; author's interviews; Purzon; Natalie Nietupski, Sept. 19, 1978, Detroit, Mich.; Salantak; Piwkowska; T. Grier Miller, "A Sociologic and Medical Study of Four Hundred Cigar Workers in Philadelphia," *The American Journal of the Medical Sciences*, 155, (Feb. 1918), p. 165; New Orleans Factory Inspection Department, *Report, 1923*, p. 2; author's interview, Pauline McKenney Stauffer, June 21, 1977, Hanover, Penn.; William A. Mara, "Have a Cigar; Facts about the Mildness of Black Tobacco—And the Story of Detroit's Great Cigar Industry," *The Detroiter*, June 1925, p. 8. All of the women I interviewed explained the importance of team members' being compatible—both in personality and speed.

21. The practice of removals was notorious in Detroit. See *Detroit Labor News*, July 10, 1914.

22. Cigar makers in 1906 at the I. Lewis Company in Newark, N.J., formed the United Ladies Protective Association and successfully resisted a wage cut, but an unsuccessful strike two years later crushed the organization. Cigar makers in Cincinnati in 1910 had an organization, as did women in Philadelphia in 1916. Certainly other organizations may have been formed which are lost from the record. Lack of resources and hostility from the CMIU might have contributed to the apparent scarcity of such organizations. See *Tobacco Leaf*, Aug. 6, 1908, p. 9; Feb. 3,1910, p. 26; July 28, 1910, p. 28; *Newark Star*, Aug. 5, 1908; *Newark Evening News*, Oct. 3, 1908; New Jersey Bureau of Statistics, *Report, 1908*, p. 348; *U.S. Tobacco Journal*, Apr. 20, 1908, p. 20; May 4, 1908, p. 14; author's interview, John R. Ograin, Aug. 11, 1976, and Sept. 15, 1978, Chicago, Ill.; *CMOJ*, Jan. 1916, p. 43; Feb. 1916, p. 20.

23. Three of the most comprehensive discussions of why male unionists have an interest in excluding women workers can be found in: Ruth Milkman, "Organizing the Sexual Division of Labor; Historical Perspectives on 'Women's Work' and the American Labor Movement," *Socialist Review*, 49 (1980), pp. 95–150; Heidi Hartmann, "Capitalism, Patriarchy, and Job Segregation by Sex," Zillah R. Eisenstein, ed., *Capitalist Patriarchy and the Case for Socialist Feminism* (New York: Monthly Review Press, 1979), pp. 206–47; Alice Kessler Harris, "Where Are the Organized Women Workers?" *Feminist Studies*, 3 (Fall 1975), pp. 92–109. See also Ann Scholfield, "The Rise of the Pig-Headed Girl: An Analysis of the American Labor Press for Their Attitudes towards Women, 1877–1920,"

(Ph.D. dissertation, State University of New York at Binghamton, 1980). My own view is that we must understand the differences in men's and women's work cultures before we can fully map out the complexity of this relationship.

24. *CMOJ*, July 1900, p. 4; Oct. 1900, p. 6; May 1902, pp. 8, 9; Oct. 1906, p. 4; Nov. 1906, p. 16; David S. Jones, *Sight Seeing in Detroit's Foreign District*, CMIU pamphlet, 1912, Vertical File, Labor Collection, Detroit Public Library. The CMIU in Detroit referred to women's employment in the cigar factories as "Detroit's Shame," and accused manufacturers of hiring "poor, half-grown girl laborers." Wages were insufficient for women to live on or "retain their virtue." See: Circular, CMIU Local 22 to Organized Labor, Aug. 1, 1916, file 33/290, FMCS, R.G. 280, NA; "SAFETY FIRST! Beware of Your American Rights," flyer, 1916, attached to letter from Louis F. Post to David S. Jones, Jan. 18, 1918, file 68/1-a, Office of the Chief Clerk, U.S. Department of Labor, R.G. 174; NA; *Detroit Labor News*, Aug. 4, 1916, Oct. 6, 1916; *CMOJ* Oct. 1916, p. 19; May 1910, p. 8.

25. For a more thorough explanation of these differences, see Cooper, "From Hand Craft to Mass Production."

26. Ibid. Temma Kaplan has demonstrated the utility of the cultural constructions of womanhood or "female consciousness" to women initiating collective action in Barcelona, Spain, in the early twentieth century. See Kaplan, "Female Consciousness and Collective Action: The Case of Barcelona, 1910–1918," *Signs*, 7 (Spring 1982), pp. 545–66. For an explanation of women's quiescence, see Leslie Tentler, *Wage-Earning Women: Industrial Work and Family Life in the United States, 1900–1930* (New York, 1979).

27. Miller, "A Sociologic and Medical Study," p. 165; New Orleans Factory Inspection Department, *Report, 1923*, p. 2; interviews, Stauffer, and Salantak; *Tobacco Leaf*, July 20, 1900, p. 7; June 10, 1903, p. 26; Aug. 29, 1906, p. 46; Mar. 27, 1907, p. 28; *Tobacco*, July 6, 1900, p. 8; July 13, 1900, p. 6.

28. *Report of the Michigan State Commission of Inquiry*, p. 422; interviews; Chromki, Purzon, Salantak; Ken Kusterer, *Know-How on the Job*, pp. 59–60.

29. Interviews; Nietupski; Salantak; Stauffer, Feb. 25, and June 21, 1977.

30. Interviews; Salantak, Nietupski, Purzon, Stauffer, June 21, 1977, Editha Mattingly, June 21, 1977, Hanover, Penn.; group interview, Mattingly and Stauffer, Feb. 25, 1977; interview, Raymond Markle, Feb. 26, 1977, Hanover, Penn.; Miller and Smyth, "Health Hazards of Cigar Manufacturing," p. 360.

31. Author's interviews; Neva Fake, Dec. 17, 1982, Red Lion, Penn.; Schmidt, Aug. 20, 1982, and Pearl Hume, Aug. 23, 1982, Lima, Ohio.

32. Interview, Salantak; *Tobacco Leaf*, Jan. 7, 1903, p. 12; author's interview, Fred Brinkman, Aug. 24, 1982, Lima, Ohio. Brinkman had been first a cigar maker and then a foreman at the Deisel-Wemmer factory in Lima.

33. Author's interview, Anna Bartasius, Apr. 1982; *Tobacco Leaf*, Nov. 1, 1905, p. 58; Jan. 21, 1909, p. 40; Oct. 1910, p. 28; Nov. 3, 1910, p. 34; *Tobacco*, Apr. 1900, p. 5; interview, Purzon; U.S. Council on National Defense, Committee on Women's Defense Work, Louisiana Division, Women in Industry Committee, *Conditions of Women's Labor in Louisiana* (New Orleans, 1919), p. 125.

34. Michael Burawoy has argued in his study, *Manufacturing Consent: Changes in the Labor Process under Monopoly Capitalism* (University of Chicago Press, 1979), that modern management has organized work in ways to emphasize workers' common interests with employers and their differing interests from other workers. The organization of work thus produces "consent" at the point of production. It is important that we not make the mistake of attributing worker acquiescence and silence to repression. The cigar industry's managerial techniques during this period were relatively unsophisticated, and while they often did produce the desired effect in the short run, ultimately they did not. See also Yves Lequin, "Social Structure and Shared Beliefs: Four Worker

Communities in the 'Second Industrialization,'" *International Labor and Working Class History,* 22 (Fall 1982), pp. 1–17.

35. New Jersey Bureau of Statistics of Labor and Industries, *Annual Report* (Camden, 1900–1917), New York Board of Mediation and Arbitration, *Annual Report* (Albany, 1901), p. 125; *Tobacco Leaf,* May 14, 1902, p. 30; May 21, 1902, p. 30; June 4, 1902, p. 26; Dec. 17, 1902, p. 3. See also *Tobacco Leaf,* June 24, 1903, p. 18; Feb. 3, 1910, p. 26; July 28, 1910, p. 28; *Tobacco,* Feb. 6, 1902, p. 3; Apr. 25, 1902, p. 3; *CMOJ,* June 1912, p. 9.

36. *CMOJ,* Feb. 1907, p. 10.

37. *Tobacco Leaf,* Nov. 1909, p. 8; New Jersey Bureau of Statistics, *Report, 1908,* pp. 258–59; *1915,* p. 264; Henry Hilfers to Samuel Gompers, Jan. 24, 1916, and Frank Morrison to Hugh Frayne, Jan. 25, 1916, Papers of the American Federation of Labor, "Cigar Makers, 1901–1937," Reel 36, *American Federation of Labor Records: The Samuel Gompers Era,* microfilm (Sanford, N.C., 1979).

38. *Tobacco,* May 18, 1900, p. 7; May 25, 1900, p. 4; *Tobacco Leaf,* June 24, 1903, p. 18; Mar. 27, 1907, p. 5; *CMOJ,* Nov. 1909, p. 8; New Jersey Bureau of Statistics, *Report, 1915,* p. 264; *Newark Evening News,* Aug. 5, 1908, p. 1. See "Labor Chronology" in New Jersey Bureau of Statistics, *Report, 1900–1917.*

39. A.L. Faulkner to William B. Wilson, Oct. 10, 1916, file 33/290, FMCS R.G. 280, NA; *Detroit Labor News,* July 7, 1916; *Tobacco Leaf,* May 16, 1918, p. 26; July 18, 1918, p. 3; *CMOJ,* Mar. 1917, p. 13; Aug. 1918, p. 12.

40. See Chapter 7, "War in the Cigar Industry, 1917–1919," of Cooper, "From Hand Craft to Mass Production."

41. *Tobacco,* July 17, 1919, p. 20; Aug. 7, 1919, pp. 6, 22; Aug. 14, 1919, pp. 5–6; Sept. 4, 1919, p. 5; *U.S. Tobacco Journal,* July 5, 1919, p. 4; July 12, 1919, p. 3; Aug. 2, 1919, p. 3; *Tobacco Leaf,* June 26, 1919, p. 4; Sept. 4, 1919, p. 11.

42. Circular, Aug. 5, 1919, and Circular to Members of Local Unions, Aug. 16, 1919, Papers of Cigar Makers' Local 162, Green Bay, Wisc., folder 3, Box 1, and folder 3, Box 2, respectively, State Historical Society of Wisconsin, Madison, Wisc.; author's interview, John Ograin, July 8, 1977, Chicago, Ill.; U.S. Bureau of Labor Statistics, "Technological Changes in the Cigar Industry and Their Effects on Labor," *Monthly Labor Review,* 33 (Dec. 1931), p. 12; "Rufus Lenoir Patterson's Cigar Machine," *Fortune,* June 1930, p. 58; *New York Call,* Sept. 9, 23, 30, and 31, 1919; *Tobacco,* Oct. 30, 1919, p. 6; *CMOJ,* Nov. 1919, p. 2.

43. Report of Conciliator, May 3, 1922, FMCS, file 170/1677, NA.

CHAPTER TWELVE: NOTES

1. Len DeCaux, *Labor Radical,* (Boston, 1970), p. 230.

2. Staughton Lynd, "The Possibility of Radicalism in the Early 1930's: The Case of Steel," *Radical America,* 6 (Nov.-Dec. 1972), pp. 37–64, and "Guerilla History in Gary," *Liberation,* 14 (Oct. 1969), pp. 17–20; for a revised version of Lynd's views of the 1930s, one more in consonance with what actually happened, not what might have been, see "The United Front in America: A Note," *Radical America,* 8 (July-Aug. 1974), pp. 29–37.

3. David Brody, "Labor and the Great Depression: The Interpretive Prospects," *Labor History,* 13 (Spring 1972), pp. 231–44; and "Radical Labor History and Rank-and-File Militancy," ibid., 16 (Winter 1975), p. 122.

4. Karl Marx and Frederick Engels, *Selected Works* (London, 1968), p. 97.

5. E.P. Thompson, *The Making of the English Working Class* (London, 1965), p. 12.

6. Ronald Radosh, "The Corporate Ideology of American Labor Leaders from Gompers to Hillman," in James Weinstein and David W. Eakins, eds., *For a New America*

(New York, 1970), pp. 125–52; and *American Labor and United States Foreign Policy* (New York, 1969), pp. 18–29; James Weinstein, *The Corporate Ideal in the Liberal State* (Boston, 1968).

7. Stanley Lebergott, *Manpower in American Economic Growth* (New York, 1964), p. 512.

8. Stephan Thernstrom, *The Other Bostonians* (Cambridge, Mass., 1973), pp. 56, 59, 90, 203, 207, 233, 240, 249.

9. Bernard Sternsher, *Hitting Home: The Great Depression in Town and Country* (Chicago, 1970), p. 10; John A. Garraty, "Radicalism in the Great Depression," in Leon B. Blair, ed., *Essays on Radicalism in Contemporary America,* (Austin, 1972), p. 89; Roy Rosenzweig, "Radicals and the Jobless: The Musteites and the Unemployed Leagues, 1932–1936," *Labor History,* 16 (Winter, 1975), pp. 52–77; Daniel J. Leab, "United We Eat: The Creation and Organization of the Unemployed Councils in 1930," *Labor History,* 8 (Fall 1967), 300–15.

10. Irving Bernstein, *Turbulent Years* (Boston, 1969). Ch. 6 remains the best description of the 1934 "Eruption." New York *Times,* July 17, 20, 21, 27, and 28, 1934.

11. Lynd, "The Possibility of Radicalism," pp. 38–40, 49–51; Sidney Fine, *The Automobile under the Blue Eagle* (Ann Arbor, 1963), pp. 298–315.

12. Sidney Fine, *Sit-Down: The General Motors Strike of 1936–1937* (Ann Arbor, 1969), p. 331.

13. Ibid., p. 201.

14. Ibid., p. 201.

15. Horace R. Cayton and George S. Mitchell, *Black Workers and the New Unions* (Chapel Hill, 1939), pp. vi, viii.

16. E. Wight Bakke, *The Unemployed Worker* (New Haven, 1940), p. 87.

17. Cayton and Mitchell, *Black Workers,* p. 268.

18. DeCaux, *Labor Radical,* p. 303.

19. Powers Hapgood to Sweetheart, July 24, 1935, Powers Hapgood Papers, Lilly Library, Indiana University.

20. Adolph Germer to Harry Hauser, Oct. 29, 1937, Adolph Germer Papers, Box 4, State Historical Society of Wisconsin, Madison.

21. Gardner Jackson, *Columbia Oral History Collection* (hereafter, COHC), pp. 727–28; Lee Pressman, COHC, pp. 96–97.

22. See Paul Kleppner, *The Cross of Culture: A Social Analysis of Midwestern Politics* (New York, 1970), chs. 5, 7; Richard J. Jensen, *The Winning of the Midwest* (Chicago, 1971), chs. 9–10.

23. "Notes on CIO Meeting, November 7–8, 1938," Katherine Pollack Ellickson Papers, Franklin D. Roosevelt Library, Hyde Park.

24. Alfred Winslow Jones, *Life, Liberty, and Property* (Philadelphia, 1941), pp. 250–79, 350–51, 354.

25. Walter Galenson, *The CIO Challenge to the AFL* (Cambridge, Mass., 1960), p. 585; Philip Taft, *The A. F. of L. from the Death of Gompers to the Merger,* (New York, 1959), pp. 199–200; W. Jett Lauck Diary, Dec. 13, 1937, W. Jett Lauck Papers, University of Virginia Library; John Frey to W.A. Appleton, Apr. 13 and Aug. 1, 1938, John Frey Papers, Box 1, File 8, Library of Congress.

26. See, for example, James R. Green, "Working Class Militancy in the Depression," *Radical America,* 6 (Nov.-Dec. 1972), pp. 2–3.

27. Isidore Lubin, Memorandum to the President, August 29, 1934, Franklin D. Roosevelt Papers, OF407B, Box 10, Roosevelt Library.

28. Calculated from *Historical Statistics of the United States, Colonial Times to 1957* (Washington, 1960), Series D 764–778, p. 99.

29. R. Rosenzweig, "Radicals and the Jobless," p. 60.

30. E. Wight Bakke, *The Unemployed Worker,* and *Citizens Without Work* (New Haven, 1940); Robert S. and Helen M. Lynd, *Middletown in Transition* (New York, 1937).

31. Lynd and Lynd, *Middletown* (New York, 1929), pp.3–6.

32. Lynd and Lynd, *Middletown in Transition,* pp. 42–43, 73, 203, 447–48.

33. Ibid., pp. 26–28; compare with *Middletown,* p. 254.

34. *Middletown in Transition,* pp. 41, 44. Emphasis in original.

35. Bakke, *Citizens without Work,* p. 102; compare to pp. 89–99.

36. Ibid., pp. 59–66.

37. Ibid., p. 69.

38. Eugene D Genovese, *Roll, Jordan, Roll: The World the Slaves Made* (New York, 1974), p. 115.

39. Bakke, *Citizens without Work,* pp. 57–59.

40. Ibid., p. 64.

41. Edward Shorter and Charles Tilly, *Strikes in France, 1830–1968* (London, 1974), passim.

42. Fine, *Sit-down,* p. 117. The UAW had signed up 1,500 out of more than 12,000 auto workers. Compare to Adolph Germer to John Brophy, Dec. 8, 1935. Germer Papers, Box 2.

43. Hapgood to Lewis, Mar. 29, 1936, Hapgood Papers.

44. Lee Pressman, COHC, pp. 193–94; David J. MacDonald, Oral History Transcript, p. 11, Pennsylvania State University Labor Archives.

45. Fine, *Sit-Down,* p. 331.

46. Peter Freidlander, *The Emergence of a UAW Local, 1936–1939: A Study in Class and Culture* (Pittsburgh, 1975), xiii–xx, pp. 27–28, 119–31, and passim.

47. Brody, "Labor and the Great Depression," p. 241.

48. See note 6 above, and also Lynd, "The Possibility of Radicalism," pp. 50–51; "Guerilla History in Gary," pp. 17–20; and "Personal Histories of the Early CIO," *Radical America,* (May-June 1971), p. 50; Alice and Staughton Lynd, *Rank and File* (Boston, 1973), pp. 4–5, 89–90; compare with Mark Naison, "The Southern Tenant Farmers Union and the CIO," *Radical America,* 2 (Sept.-Oct. 1968), pp. 36–54; and Art Preis, *Labor's Giant Step* (New York, 1964), passim.

49. J.B.S. Hardman, "Union Objectives and Social Power," in J.B.S. Hardman, ed., *American Labor Dynamics* (New York, 1928), p. 104.

50. Melvyn Dubofsky and Warren Van Tine, *John L. Lewis: A Biography* (New York, 1977), is a study of precisely that process and the dilemma of trade-union leadership. Compare to Friedlander, *The Emergence of a UAW Local,* pp. 119–31, passim.

51. Fine, *Sit-Down,* p. 307; Brody, "Radical Labor History," p. 125.

52. For the Edwardian British analogy, see Paul Thompson, *The Edwardians* (Bloomington, Ind. 1975), pp. 260–62. On the working-class core of the Democratic party, see Samuel Lubell, *The Future of American Politics* (New York, 1965 ed.), pp. 179–82 and passim; A.W. Jones, *Life, Liberty, and Property,* pp. 314–17; and Friedlander, *The Emergence of a UAW Local,* pp. 112–14.

53. DeCaux, *Labor Radical,* p. 295; Pressman, COHC, pp. 91, 96–97, 188, 191, 352.

54. Pressman, COHC, p. 380; Statement, John L. Lewis, June, 1940, Herbert Hoover Papers, Post-Presidential Files, Box 98, Herbert Hoover Library, West Branch, Iowa.

55. United Mine Workers of America, *Convention Proceedings, 1938,* p. 172; *1940,* p. 14; Jones observes of Akron's workers in 1939, even the highly politicized ones, "Our measurements of opinion and the comments of workers indicate clearly that most of them do not want to feel that they have isolated themselves from the general run of 'middle class opinion.' The general climate of opinion bears in upon them and would make it impossible for them to turn decisively away into a workers' world, even if such a thing existed." *Life, Liberty, and Property,* p. 297.

CHAPTER THIRTEEN: NOTES

1. U.S. Department of Commerce, Bureau of the Census, *Thirteenth Census of the United States: Population: 1910*, 4, *Occupation Statistics*, pp. 590–91.

2. Dennis C. Dickerson, "Black Steelworkers in Western Pennsylvania, 1900–1950," *Pennsylvania Heritage*, 4, no. 1 (Dec. 1977), p. 53.

3. Dickerson, "Black Steelworkers," p. 57.

4. Dickerson, "Black Steelworkers in Western Pennsylvania, 1915–1950," (Ph.D. dissertation, Washington University, 1978), pp. 76–94, and "The Black Church in Industrializing Western Pennsylvania, 1870–1950," 64, no. 4 (Oct. 1981), pp. 329–44.

5. See Neil A. Wynn's *The Afro-American and the Second World War* (New York, 1975). In "Racial Militancy and Interracial Violence in the Second World War," *Journal of American History*, 58, (1971–1972), pp. 661–81, Harvard Sitkoff argues that the government's need for the loyalty and participation of Blacks, both in the military and in civilian life, "stimulated racial militancy" unprecedented in Afro-American history. Richard Dalfiume's article is also useful: "The 'Forgotten Years' of the Negro Revolution," *Journal of American History*, 55 (June 1968), pp. 90–106.

6. Author's interviews: William See, Apr. 22, 1975, Glen Hazel, Penn.; Ashton Allen, Sept. 6, 1975, Homestead, Penn.; Edward Lipscomb, Sept. 8, 1975, Duquesne, Penn.

7. George E. DeMar, "Pittsburgh's Potential Labor Supply," *Opportunity*, Jan. 1942, pp. 18–19; author's interview, James Wilson, Apr. 23, 1975, West Mifflin, Penn.

8. Author's interview, Calvin Ingram, Sept. 8, 1975, Duquesne, Penn.

9. Author's interview, Bartow Tipper, Mar. 4, 1980, Aliquippa, Penn.

10. DeMar, "Pittsburgh's Potential Labor," pp. 18–19.

11. "Additional Information on the Carnegie–Illinois Steel Company, Farrell, Pennsylvania," *War Manpower Commission Records*, Bureau of Placement, Division of Industrial Allocation, Carnegie–Illinois File, Box 1470, National Archives (hereafter, NA), Washington, D.C.

12. Bert Hough to Harold Ruttenberg, Jan. 22, 1943, Harold Ruttenberg Collection, War Production Board Correspondence, Statistics, and Press Releases, Box 7, Labor Archives, Pennsylvania State University, University Park, Penn.

13. Telegram Patrick J. Fagan to War Manpower Commission, Mar. 2, 1945(?), Steel Plants File, *War Manpower Commission Records*, Bureau of Placement, Industrial Allocation Division, Box 1471, NA.

14. DeMar, "Pittsburgh's Potential Labor," pp. 18–19.

15. *Allegheny County Race Relations Survey*, 1946, Charles S. Johnson, Director, Archives of Industrial Society, University of Pittsburgh Libraries, Folder H, p. 1.

16. Ruttenberg to H.G. Batcheller, Jan. 25, 1943, Ruttenberg Collection, Box 7.

17. M.W. Reid to Edwin Brown, Jan. 14, 1943, Ruttenberg Collection, Box 7.

18. *Homestead Messenger*, Jan. 26, and Feb. 3, 1942.

19. Reid to Brown, Ruttenberg Collection.

20. *Duquesne Times*, Aug. 15, 1941.

21. Florence Murray, ed., *The Negro Handbook*, pp. 195–96.

22. "Additional Information on the Carnegie–Illinois Steel Company," Box 1070.

23. Murray, *The Negro Handbook*, pp. 195–96.

24. Federal Security Administration, "Minutes of Meeting between the Urban League of Pittsburgh and War Production Board," Records of the Fair Employment Practices Committee, Regional Files, Region III, Active Cases, Unarranged, Clairton, Penn., File, Box 598, NA.

25. *Allegheny County Race Relations Survey*, p. 31.

26. Ibid., p. 23.

27. George E. DeMar to Robert C. Weaver, Sept. 15, 1942, FEPC Records, Regional Files, Region III, Closed Cases, NA.

28. *Allegheny County Race Relations Survey,* p. 28.
29. G. James Fleming to Will Maslow, Aug. 24, 1944, FEPC Records, Regional Files, Region III, Box 596, NA. Mackintosh & Hemphill Company File, FEPC Records, Regional Files, Region III, Box 598, NA.
30. Author's interview, J.Burrell Reid, Sept. 6, 1975, Pittsburgh, Penn.
31. George M. Johnson to Reginald A. Johnson, Mar. 31, 1945, Jones & Laughlin Steel Company File, FEPC Records, Regional Files, Region III, Box 597, NA.
32. Joseph Krivan to Reginald A. Johnson, Feb. 22, 1943, Jones & Laughlin File, FEPC Records, Box 597, NA.
33. Frances Stanton to Franklin D. Roosevelt, Apr. 5, 1943, Carnegie–Illinois File, FEPC Records, Regional Files, Region III, NA.
34. Mrs. William J. Scott to Franklin D. Roosevelt, Apr. 22, 1944, FEPC Records, Box 610, NA.
35. Ruth L. Boyd et al. to Franklin D. Roosevelt, July 26, 1943, FEPC Records, Box 610, NA.
36. National Malleable & Steel Casting Company File, FEPC Records, Region III, Box 612, NA.
37. Interview, Tipper.
38. Ethel M. Cotton File, FEPC Records, Region III, Box 559, NA.
39. Farrell & Sharon Penn. File, FEPC Records, Region III, Box 599, NA.
40. George C. DeMar to R.J. Greenly, May 4, 1943, FEPC Records, Region III, Box 604, NA.
41. Milo A. Manly to G. James Fleming, Mar. 7, 1944, FEPC Records, Region III, Carnegie–Illinois File, Box 604, NA.
42. Manly to Fleming, Oct. 13, 1944, and Manly to Fleming, Oct. 16, 1944, FEPC Records, Region III, Clairton, Penn. File, Box 598, NA.
43. *First Report,* p. 82.
44. Manly to Fleming, Dec. 28, 1944, "Reports on Pittsburgh Area Field Trips," FEPC Records, Region III, Box 600, NA.
45. Milo A. Manly to Will Maslow, April 28, 1945, Jones & Laughlin Boiler Firemen, Water Tenders and Stokers File, FEPC, Region III, Box 599, NA.
46. Author's interview, Roger Payne, Apr. 12, 1976, Philadelphia, Penn.
47. *1557 Labor Journal,* Clairton, Penn., Dec. 15, 1962.
48. Joseph Krivan to Reginald Johnson, Feb. 22, 1943, FEPC Records, Region III, Jones & Laughlin File, Box 597, NA.
49. Viola Twyman to G. James Fleming, Mar. 11, 1944, FEPC Records, Region III, Box 611, Mackintosh–Hemphill File, NA.
50. Interview James McCoy, Nov. 7, 1968, Pittsburgh, Penn. by Mark B. Lapping; U.S.W.A. Oral History Project, Labor Archives, Pennsylvania State University.
51. See my sketch of Boyd L. Wilson in the second edition of Gary M. Fink, ed., *Biographical Dictionary of American Labor Leaders,* (Westport, Conn., 1984).
52. *Pittsburgh Courier,* May 30, 1942.
53. Crucible Steel Company of America File, FEPC Records, Region III, Box 598, NA.
54. Fleming to Maslow, June 22, 1944, Carnegie–Illinois Steel Corporation File, FEPC Records, Region III, Box 604, NA.
55. George M. Johnson to American Steel Band Company, Sept. 26, 1942, to Joseph Bowman, Feb. 11, 1943, and to John Brophy, Jan. 8, 1942, American Steel Band File, FEPC Records, Region III, NA.
56. *First Report,* pp. 8, 11.
57. Manly to Maslow, Apr. 28, 1945, Roger Williams File, FEPC Records, Region III, Box 600, NA.
58. Manly to Maslow, Mar. 29, 1945, John A. Anderson File, FEPC Records, Region III, Box 599, NA.

59. G. James Fleming to Frank L. McNamee, Aug. 8, 1944, FEPC Records, Region III, Box 610, NA.

60. Milo A. Manly to G. James Fleming, June 8, 1944, FEPC Records, Region III, Box 600, NA.

61. G. James Fleming to James E. Matthews [1944], FEPC Records, Region III, Box 598, NA.

62. John E. Peoples et al. to Director of War Mobilization and Reconversion, Feb. 12, 1945; Mae Patterson to FEPC, May 9, 1945; and Karly Keen Klinger to Mae Patterson, June 16, 1945; all in FEPC Records, Region III, Box 600, NA.

63. *New Jersey Afro-American*, Dec. 29, 1944.

64. Louis C. Kesselman, *The Social Politics of F.E.P.C.*, (Chapel Hill, N.C., 1948), pp. 15–24, 166–77, 222–28.

65. *Allegheny County Race Relations Survey*, p. 28.

66. Author's interview, John Hughey, Sept. 8, 1975, Rankin, Penn.

67. Thomas Augustine, "The Negro Steelworkers of Pittsburgh and the Unions," M.A. thesis, University of Pittsburgh, 1948, p. 41.

68. Author's interview, Milton Croom, Mar. 6, 1980, Clairton, Penn.

CHAPTER FOURTEEN: NOTES

1. Allen Nevins, *Ford: Expansion and Challenge, 1915–1933* (New York, 1957), p. 288.

2. *The Rouge: the Image of Industry in the Art of Charles Sheeler and Diego Rivera* (Detroit Institute of the Arts, 1978), pp. 7–10; Nevins, *Ford: Expansion and Challenge*, pp. 200–16, 279–99.

3. Richard Edwards, *Contested Terrain: the Transformation of the Workplace in the Twentieth Century* (New York, 1979), pp. 111–29.

4. W. Ellison Chalmers, "Industrial Relations in the Automobile Industry" (Ph.D. dissertation, University of Chicago, 1935), pp. 171–75; *The Rouge*, p. 68.

5. Stephen Meyer, *The Five Dollar Day: Labor Management at the Ford Motor Company, 1906–1921* (Albany, 1981), pp. 169–202.

6. Chalmers, "Industrial Relations," 155–71; National Industrial Recovery Administration Hearings on Regularizing Employment and Otherwise Improving the Conditions of Labor in the Automobile Industry," Detroit, Dec. 15, 1934, (mimeo.), p. 51; author's interview with Robert Robertson, Ford labor relations, Dec. 16, 1981 (by phone); author's interview with Theodore Bonaventura, Ford foreman, Washington, D.C., Feb. 12, 1982.

7. Keith Sward, *The Legend of Henry Ford* (New York, 1949), pp. 293–313, 390–94.

8. C.L.R. James, *State Capitalism and World Revolution* (Detroit: Facing Reality, 1963), p. 40.

9. Ford Motor Company, "Rouge Plant: Place of Birth and Citizenship of Persons at Present Employed," Apr. 22, 1940, Box 37, Martindale papers, Henry Ford Museum.

10. Steve Babson, "Pointing the Way: the Role of British and Irish Workers in the Rise of the UAW" (unpub. seminar paper, Wayne State University); author's interview, Walter Doroch, Oct. 14, 1982.

11. August Meier and Elliott Rudwick, *Black Detroit and the Rise of the UAW* (New York, 1980), pp. 3–33; interview, Ed Lock, Plastics Building Union chairman, by Peter Friedlander, 1976.

12. Ford Organizing Committee, folder, Ken Bannon Collection, "Ford Department," Box Archives of Labor History, Wayne State University (hereafter ALHWSU); author's interview, Saul Wellman, Nov. 10, 1983.

13. Nevins, *Ford: Decline and Rebirth, 1933–1968* (New York, 1963), pp. 159–64; Sward, *Legend of Henry Ford*, pp. 398–408.

14. Sward, *Legend of Henry Ford,* pp. 417–21.

15. Nevins, *Ford: Decline and Rebirth,* pp. 162–67; Sward, *Legend of Henry Ford,* pp. 421–24; *Detroit News,* June 22, 1941; Percy Llewellyn, first president of Local 600, claimed that CIO President Philip Murray agreed to drop the UAW's NLRB case against Ford in return for the union shop. This enabled Ford to protect from exposure its many undercover loyalists in the shop. Bennett hoped to use these agents eventually to take over the local. Author's interview, Percy Llewellyn, Oct. 20, 1982, Dearborn, Mich.

16. Frank Marquart, *An Auto Worker's Journal: The UAW from Crusade to One-Party Union* (College Park, Pa., 1975), p. 94.

17. Harry Elmer Barnes, "Labor policies of the Ford Motor Company" (unpub. manuscript, 1944), Henry Ford Museum; Ford Motor Company, "Study of Work Stoppages, 1955" Bannon Collection, "Ford Department" Box, ALHWSU.

18. For a more detailed study of these wildcat strikes, see Lichtenstein, "Auto Worker Militancy and the Structure of Factory Life, 1937–1955," *Journal of American History,* 67 (September 1980), pp. 335–53. The argument that these strikes were not a product of "union consciousness" is advanced by Martin Glaberman, in *Wartime Strikes: The Struggle against the No-Strike Pledge in the UAW during World War II,* pp. 35–61, 125–27.

19. "Complete Report of March 7 and March 14, 1944 Incidents," UAW Executive Board Minutes, Sept. 7–18, 1944, pp. 52–64, ALHWSU, *Ford Facts,* Mar. 15, 1944.

20. Roger Keeran, *The Communist Party and the Auto Workers Unions* (Bloomington, Ind., 1980), pp. 40, 55, 71–75, 218–19; Maurice Sugar, *The Ford Hunger March* (Berkeley, 1980), pp. 29–45; "Ford Organizing Committee" Bannon Collection, "Ford Department" Box, ALHWSU; author's interview with Saul Wellman, Nov. 15, 1983.

21. William D. Andrew, "Fractionalism and Anti-Communism: Ford Local 600," *Labor History,* 20 (Spring 1979), pp. 227–36; Keeran, *The Communist Party and the Auto Workers,* pp. 234–35; U.S. Congress, House Committee on Un-American Activities, *Hearings, Investigation of Communist Activities in the State of Michigan,* 83rd Cong., 2nd sess., pp. 5090–99; "Building Units in Ford Local," Association of Catholic Trade Unionists Collection, Box 24, ALHWSU.

22. Interview, Wellman.

23. George Heliker, "Ford Labor Relations," (unpub. manuscript), p. 323, Frank Hill Papers, Henry Ford Museum.

24. Author's interview, Robert Robertson, Oct. 9, 1983, Stirling Heights, Mich. Shelton Tappes remembered that in the foundry 90 straw bosses were eliminated: half joined foreman ranks, the rest were incorporated into the UAW. Author's interview, Shelton Tappes, Oct. 12, 1982, Detroit.

25. Charles P. Larrowe, "A Meteor on the Industrial Relations Horizon: The Foreman's Association of America," *Labor History,* 2 (Fall, 1961), pp. 259–87; author's interviews, Theodore Bonaventura and Bertram Fenwick, FAA leader, Aug. 3, 1982, Livonia, Mich.

26. U.S. Congress, House Committee on Education and Labor, *Hearings, Amendments to the National Labor Relations Act,* 80th Cong., 1st sess., p. 868.

27. Herbert R. Northrup, "The Foreman's Association of America," *Harvard Business Review,* 23 (Winter 1945), 187–91.

28. Malcolm Denise, "Labor Relations and Implementation of Policy—1943, 1944, 1945," quoted in George Heliker, "Ford Labor Relations," p. 303.

29. Heliker, "Grievance Arbitration in the Automobile Industry: A Comparative Analysis of its History and Results in the Big Three," (Ph.D. dissertation, University of Michigan, 1954), p. 118–30.

30. Harry Shulman and Neil Chamberlain, *Cases on Labor Relations* (Brooklyn, 1949), p. 434.

31. Ibid., p. 45.

32. Henry Ford II, "The Challenge of Human Engineering: Mass Production, a Tool

for Raising the Standard of Living," *Vital Speeches of the Day,* 12 (Feb. 15, 1946), p. 273.

33. Benjamin Selekman et al., *Problems in Labor Relations* (New York, 1958), pp. 288–98; "Production Standards: Chronological Review of Current Language," Bannon Collection, Box 17.

34. Larrowe, "Meteor on the Industrial Relations Horizon," pp. 287–99; author's interview with Malcolm Denise, Ford Labor Relations, Oct. 21, 1982, Detroit.

35. Quoted in Howell John Harris, *The Right to Manage: Industrial Relations Policies of American Business in the 1940s* (Madison, Wisc., 1982), p. 85.

36. Heliker, "Labor Relations Report," pp. 345–51; interview, Carl Brown, FAA President, by Howall Harris and Dennis East, Nov. 13, 1974, ALHWSU.

37. "An Auto Empire Decentralizes and Reorganizes," *Business Week,* October 17, 1953, pp. 130–34; "Factory Counts," December 1939, Dec. 1944, Martindale Papers, Henry Ford Museum.

38. Ford Motor Company "Press Release," Mar. 8, 1956, Bannon Collection, Ford Motor Company Box; "Rouge Hourly Employment," and "Ford Rouge Employment Statistics," Mar. 1960, Walter P. Reuther Collection, Boxes 96 and 250, respectively; ALHWSU; author's interview, Paul Boatin, Motor Building Union chairman, Oct. 6, 1983, Dearborn.

39. Joseph Gerchelin, "Revolutionary Automation at Ford," *Automotive Industries,* 99 (Nov. 15, 1984), pp. 24–27; Rupert LeGrand, "Ford Handles Automation," *American Machinist,* Oct. 21, 1948, p. 107.

40. Author's interview, John Sarri, Motor Building Union committeeman, Oct. 11, 1982, Dearborn; interview, Boatin. The UAW also set up an engineering department which helped train workers and committeemen in time-study techniques and was used in conjunction with the grievance procedure to spot-check Ford industrial engineers. But without an effective committeeman system such union time study efforts were ineffective and merely served to legitimize Taylorist practice. At Chrysler, by way of contrast, a dense shop-steward system enabled union workers there to hold Chrysler management in check until the recession of 1957–1958. For a superb study of Chrysler, especially Dodge Main, see Steve Jefferys, "Management and Managed: the Movement of Managerial Authority and Workplace Legitimacy in Chrysler Corporation since 1933." (forthcoming, Cambridge University Press)

41. For an overview of these issues see Richard Herding, *Job Control and Union Structure* (Rotterdam, 1972); and David Brody, *Workers in Industrial America* (New York, 1980), p. 188–95.

42. Ford Motor Company, "Executive Communication," Mar. 4, 1948, UAW Research Department Collection, Box 12, ALHWSU; Al Comons, "The 1949 Ford Strike—Beginning of an Era" (unpublished seminar paper), Department of History, Wayne State University; "Ford Provoked Strike: Reuther Faces Hard Test," *Labor Action,* May 10, 1949.

43. Martin Halpern, "The Disintegration of the Left–Center Coalition in the UAW, 1945–1950" (Ph.D. dissertation, University of Michigan, 1982), pp. 513–17; *Labor Action,* July 4, 1949.

44. *Detroit Free Press,* May 7, 1949.

45. Ford Motor Company and UAW-CIO, "Arbitration Award," Bannon Collection, Box "FMC"; Local 600 leaflet, "Strike Betrayal," Local 600 vertical file, ALHWSU; Comons, "The 1949 Ford Strike."

46. Ford Motor Company "Study on Work Stoppages" (1955), 5, Bannon Collection, "Ford Department" Box.

47. Andrew, "Factionalism and Anti-Communism: Ford Local 600," pp. 239–49; "We Accuse," Nat Ganley Collection, Box 11, ALHWSU.

48. Carl Stellato, "My Differences with Walter Reuther" (unpub. manuscript, Sept. 1951, Reuther Collection, Box 97; Phil Schatz, "Ford Workers Win Victory," *The Worker,*

Fall 1950, Ganley Collection, Box 11; also Andrew, "Factionalism and Anti-Communism: Ford Local 600," pp. 247–53.

49. Interviews: Sarri and Wellman.

50. Jack Steiber, *Governing the UAW* (New York, 1962), p. 148.

51. John DeMotte, "The 1955 Ford–UAW Contract," (Bureau of Industrial Relations), 24 (1956) 2.

52. Author's interviews: Sarri and Robertson; interview, Billie Sunday Farmer by William J. Eaton and Frank Cormier, Oct. 16, 1967, John F. Kennedy Library, Cormier and Eaton Collection, Boston.

53. Author's interview, Walter Dorach; Robert MacDonald, *Collective Bargaining in the Automobile Industry* (New Haven, 1963), pp. 160–205; "Lines of Demarcation" (1964), Reuther Collection, Box 98.

54. Ford Motor Company, "Collective Bargaining Review and Proposals," July 16, 1964, pp. 21–22, Bannon Collection, Box 18.

55. Jack Crellin, "Local Differences Block Ford Return to Work," *Detroit News,* Oct.13, 1961; Ford Motor Company, "Remarks by Malcolm Denise, vice president for labor relations, 13th Annual Union–Management Conference," Notre Dame University, Feb. 27, 1965.

56. Author's interviews: Dorach and Wellman. Boatin, who had left the Party in the late 1940s, but had nevertheless been barred from holding office after the International briefly took over the Local, was reinstated by the UAW as a unionist in good standing by the International Executive Board in May 1956. He was promptly reelected president of the Dearborn Engine Plant (the old Motor Building); see memorandum, Victor Reuther to Jack Conway, May 13, 1957, Reuther Papers, Box 250.

CHAPTER FIFTEEN: NOTES

1. U.S. Department of Commerce, Bureau of the Census, *Report on the Population of the United States at the Eleventh Census: 1890;* Part 2, *Statistics of Population,* Table 118, Total Males and Females 10 Years of Age and Over Engaged in Selected Occupations Classified by General Nativity, Color, Age Periods, . . . Providence, R.I. (Washington, D.C.: U.S. Government Printing Office, 1892), p. 714; Rhode Island Bureau of Industrial Statistics, Rhode Island Wage Earners, Bulletin 1, Part 2 of the *Annual Report for 1908* (Providence, R.I.: E.L. Freeman, 1908), pp. 471–74; U.S. Departments of Commerce and Labor, Bureau of the Census, *Fifteenth Census of the United States: 1930,* 4, *Population: Occupation by States,* Rhode Island, Table 6, Number and Proportion of Persons 10 Years Old and Over Gainfully Occupied, By Color, Nativity, and Sex (Washington, D.C.: U.S. Government Printing Office, 1933), p. 1459.

2. Elyce Rotella, *From Home to Office: U.S. Women at Work, 1870–1930* (Ann Arbor, Michigan: UMI Research Press, 1981), p. 115.

3. Analysis of the collection made by Gail Sansbury, Director, Oral History Project, Rhode Island Working Women, Providence, R.I.

4. Rotella, *From Home to Office,* p. 69.

5. Judith Smith, "The 'New Woman' Knows How to Type: Some Connections between Sexual Ideology and Clerical Work, 1900–1930," paper presented at the Berkshire Conference on Women's History, 1974. Quoted in Elyce Rotella, *From Home to Office,* p. 162.

6. Rotella, *From Home to Office,* p. 24.

7. Rhode Island Bureau of Industrial Statistics. *Third Annual Report, 1889.* Table 6, Average Annual and Weekly Wages of Each Occupation (Providence: E.L. Freeman, 1890), p. 145.

8. U.S. Departments of Commerce and Labor, Bureau of the Census, *Sixteenth Census*

of the United States: 1940. Population, 3, *The Labor Force*, part 5, Rhode Island, Table 16, Wage and Salary Income Received in 1939 by All Experienced Persons in the Labor Force (Washington, D.C.: U.S. Government Printing Office, 1943), p. 190.

9. U.S. Departments of Commerce and Labor, Bureau of the Census, *Census of the Population: 1950*, 2, *Population*, Part 39: Rhode Island, Table 78, Income in 1949 of the Experienced Civilian Labor Force, by Occupation and Sex, for the State (Washington, D.C.: U.S. Government Printing Office, 1952), pp. 39–101.

10. Roslyn Feldberg and Evelyn Glenn, "Clerical Work: The Female Occupation," in Jo Freeman, ed., *Women: A Feminist Perspective*, (Palo Alto, Calif.: Mayfield Publishing, 1979), p. 322. See also Rotella, *Home to Office*, p. 159.

11. United States Department of Labor, Special Report, Jan. 1981, cited in *Office Work in America*, Report by Working Women (Cleveland, Ohio: 1982), pp. 3–4.

12. Oral Histories of Clerical Workers in Rhode Island, 1981–1983, Archives of Rhode Island Working Women, Providence, R.I. All oral histories quoted or referred to are contained in this collection. Initials are used to protect narrators; many are employed currently and discuss current job situations.

13. Garrett D. Byrnes, "A Long Trail to the Groves of Academe," *Providence Sunday Journal*, Apr. 23, 1972, pp. B-4 and B-5.

14. Bryant and Stratton Business College, circular, 1877.

15. Janice Hart Weiss, "Educating for Clerical Work: A History of Commercial Education in the United States since 1850" (Ph.D. dissertation, Harvard Graduate School of Education, 1978), p. 75.

16. *Rhode Islander* (magazine of the *Providence Sunday Journal*), Mar. 23, 1969, p. 13.

17. Providence Public Schools, *Courses of Study in the High Schools* (Providence: Snow and Farnham, 1909); *School Report, Pawtucket, R.I. 1905–1906* (Pawtucket: John Whittle, 1906).

18. "The Dictation Phonograph," advertisement, *Providence Board of Trade Journal*, Feb. 1908, end page.

19. *Bulletin of Bryant College, Catalog, 1947–1953* (Providence: Bryant College, 1946), p. 49.

20. Roslyn Feldberg and Evelyn Glenn, "Clerical Workers," in Ann Seidman, ed., *Working Women: A Study of Women in Paid Jobs* (Boulder, Colo.: Westview Press, 1979), p. 318.

21. Rotella, *From Home to Office*, pp. 123, 144.

22. Florence Parker Simister, *The First Hundred Years* (Providence: Rhode Island Hospital Trust, 1967), p. 82.

23. Margery Davies, *Woman's Place Is at the Typewriter: Office Work and Office Workers, 1870–1930* (Philadelphia: Temple University Press, 1982), p. 100.

24. Lee Galloway, *Office Management: Its Principles and Practices* (New York: Ronald, 1920); William Henry Leffingwell, *Office Management: Principles and Practice* (New York: Shaw, 1925).

25. Harry Braverman, *Labor and Monopoly Capital* (New York: Monthly Review Press, 1974), p. 325.

26. Author's informational interview, Prof. Eileen Rafferty, Community College of Rhode Island, Apr. 8, 1983.

27. Ida Russakoff Hoos, *Automation in the Office* (Washington, D.C.: Public Affairs Press, 1961), p. 57.

28. C. Wright Mills, *White Collar*, ch. 9, "The Enormous File" (New York: Oxford University Press, 1953).

29. Roslyn Feldberg and Evelyn Glenn, "Proletarianizing Clerical Work," Andrew Zimbalist, ed., *Case Studies on the Labor Process* (New York: Monthly Review Press, 1979), p. 58.

30. Feldberg and Glenn, "Clerical Workers," p. 329.

31. Jon M. Shepard, *Automation and Alienation: A Study of Office and Factory Workers* (Boston: MIT Press, 1971), p. 63.

32. Joel Makover, *Office Hazards* (New York: Tilden Press, 1981), p. 96.

33. Makover *Office Hazards*, pp. 23–26.

34. Makover, *Office Hazards*, pp. 23–26.

35. *Women's Work*, (published by Rhode Island Working Women), May–June 1982.

36. Olov Ostberg, Central Organization of Salaried Employees, Sweden, "Occupational Health and the Computerized Office," International Conference on Office Work and New Technology, Boston, Oct. 28, 1982.

37. Author's informational interviews: Professor Leger Morrison, Bryant College, Mar. 9, 1983; Prof. Lee Chalek, Johnson & Wales College, Mar. 22, 1983; Mr. Troiano, Director of the Evening Division, Johnson & Wales College, Mar. 22, 1983; Prof. Diane LaSala, Johnson & Wales College, Mar. 22, 1983; Mrs. Harlow, Katharine Gibbs School, Apr. 4, 1983, Providence; and Rafferty.

38. *Woman's Work*, May–June 1982.

39. Lisbet Hjort, Government Office of Organizational and Managerial Development, Norway, Report to Panel on "Occupational Health and the Computerized Office," International Conference on Office Work and New Technology.

40. "VDTs—A New Social Disease?" *The Harvard Medical School Health Letter*, 3, no. 5, p. 5.

41. Berit Westman, Swedish Telephone, Report to Panel on "The Redesign of Computerized Work," International Conference on Office Work and New Technology.

42. Janine Morgall, Lund University, Denmark, Report to Panel on "Impact of Office Automation on Secretaries and Word-Processing Operators," International Conference on Office Work and New Technology.

Authors' Biographies

PATRICIA COOPER is Assistant Professor in the Department of History and Politics at Drexel University. She is the author of several articles and of *Smoke and Fire: Gender, Class and Work Culture in American Cigar Factories, 1900-1919* (forthcoming). Currently she is working on labor and labor organization in the Philadelphia radio industry, 1930-1945.

DENNIS CLARK DICKERSON is Associate Professor of History at Rhodes College. He is the author of numerous articles on Black history, and of *Black Workers and Smokey Cities: Black Labor in the Iron and Steel Industry of Western Pennsylvania, 1875–1980* (forthcoming). He has held grants from the American Council of Learned Societies and the National Endowment for the Humanities, and in 1985–86 held a Guggenheim Fellowship to write a biography of Civil Rights leader Whitney Young, Jr.

MELVYN DUBOFSKY is Professor of History and Sociology at the State University of New York at Binghamton. He is author of numerous articles and books, including *We Shall Be All: The Industrial Workers of the World* and, with Warren Van Tine, *John L. Lewis: A Biography.*

BRIAN GREENBERG is Associate Professor of History at the University of Delaware and Coordinator of the Hagley Graduate Program in the History of Industrial America at the Hagley Museum and Library. He is the author of several articles on labor and social history, and has written two books: *Worker and Community: Response to Industrialization in a Nineteenth-Century American City—Albany, New York 1850–*

1884 (1985) and (with Leon Fink) *Union Power, Soul Power: The Making of a Union in the Hosptials* (forthcoming), a study of the organization of hospital workers in the United States.

THOMAS E. LEARY is Director of Interpretation at the Buffalo and Erie County, New York Historical Society, where projects about the local steel and automobile industries are underway. Previously he served as Curator of the Slater Mill Historic Site in Pawtucket, Rhode Island. He has been active in the fields of labor history, industrial archaeology, and public history since receiving his Ph.D. in American Civilization from Brown University; his dissertation focused on workers at an early textile machinery shop in western Massachusetts. He has directed an inventory of historic industrial sites in western New York, documented the production process inside an antique steel-rolling mill prior to its shutdown, and supervised compilation of oral histories involving Rhode Island machinists. Currently he is writing a book on the history of the Lackawanna, New York steel plant owned by the Bethlehem Steel Company.

WALTER LICHT teaches American economic and labor history at the University of Pennsylvania where he also is director of the Penn Institute for Local History. He is the author of *Working For the Railroad: the Organization of Work in the Nineteenth Century* (1983), which was awarded the Philip Taft Labor History Prize for 1984, and numerous articles. Most recently he authored (with Philip Scranton) *Work Sights: Industrial Philadelphia in Photography, 1890–1945* (1985).

NELSON LICHTENSTEIN is Associate Professor of History at Catholic University. He is the author of numerous articles and of *Labor's War at Home: The CIO During World War II* (1984). He is Co-Editor (with Steven Meyer III) of a collection of essays about American automobile workers. Currently he is writing a biography of Walter Reuther.

WILLIAM H. MULLIGAN, JR. is Director of the Clarke Historical Library and Adjunct Professor of History at Central Michigan University. He received his Ph.D. from Clark University. Previously he was Assistant to the Director at the Regional Economic History Research Center of the Eleutherian Mills-Hagley Foundation. His publications include several articles on the family during industrialization and two books: *Northborough During the American Revolution* (1974) and *Northborough: the Town and Its People* (forthcoming).

KATHY PEISS is Associate Professor of History and Womens' Studies at the University of Massachusetts at Amherst. She is the author of

Cheap Amusements: Working Women and Leisure in New York City, 1880 to 1920 (1986) and articles on sexuality, leisure and gender.

ROY ROSENZWEIG is Associate Professor of History and Director of the Oral History Program at George Mason University. He is the author of several essays on social and labor history and of *Eight Hours for What We Will: Workers and Leisure in an Industrial City, 1870–1920* (1983), co-editor of *Experiments in History Teaching*, and co-producer of *Mission Hill and the Miracle of Boston*, a documentary film. Currently he is co-authoring (with Betsy Blackmar) a social history of Central Park, and co-editing (with Sue Benson and Steve Brier) *Presenting the Past: Essays on History and the Public* (1985).

VALERIE QUINNEY received her Ph.D. in history from the University of Wisconsin and taught at Brooklyn College and the University of Rhode Island and directed the Oral History Project at Wheaton College. Currently she is teaching part-time at Northern Illinois University, and indulging a long-time desire to write drama based on oral history. Her first play, *In the Service of Others*, was produced at Northern Illinois University in 1984. She is author of articles based on oral history research into the lives of three generations of women workers in a mill village in North Carolina and is co-author of a manual of oral history methodology, *How to Find Out By Asking*. The research for this article on clerical workers was carried out by a collective composed of women clerical workers from Rhode Island Working Women. Quinney was in charge of training sessions and participated in the project as an interviewer. The project, directed by Gail Sansbury, was partially funded by a grant from the Rhode Island Committee for the Humanities.

GREGORY ZIEREN is Visiting Assistant Professor of History at the University of Iowa. He has worked with the Iowa Labor History Project. His article on Cedar Rapids, Iowa packinghouse workers' organizational efforts in the 1930s will appear in *The Palimpsest*.

EDITORS' BIOGRAPHIES

CHARLES STEPHENSON is Assistant Professor of History at Central Connecticut State University; his fields of emphasis are American economic, political and labor history, and quantitative methodology. He served as Chair of the Network on Workers and Industrialization from 1978 to 1983 and as a General Editor of the American Social History Series for the State University of New York Press from 1979 to

1983. He is the author of numerous articles and of *The Real Democrats: The Democrats of Texas in Texas Politics*. He is editor (with Michael Hanagan) of *Proletarians and Protest: The Roots of Class Formation in an Industrializing World* (1986), of *Confrontation, Class Consciousness and the Labor Process: Studies in Proletarian Class Formation* (1986), and of a special issue of *Social Science History* (IV:1 [Fall 1980]) on "The Skilled Worker and Working-Protest"; he has completed editing (with Robert Asher) a collection of essays on ethnicity and the American working class. He is General Editor, with Robert Asher, of the American Labor History Series for the State University of New York Press. Currently he is completing a manuscript on American migration and economic development.

ROBERT ASHER is Associate Professor of History at The University of Connecticut. He has written numerous articles on the history of workmen's compensation, ethnicity and trade union structure, and the psychology of corporate paternalism. He is the author of *Connecticut Workers and Technological Change* (1983). Asher wrote the introduction to the collection *American Federation of Labor and Congress of Industrial Organization Pamphlets, 1889–1955* (1977). He was the Principal Investigator of the Connecticut Workers and A Half Century of Technological Change Project which was funded by the National Endowment for the Humanities (1981–1983). With Bruce M. Stave, Asher produced the microfiche edition of the interviews conducted by the staff of the Technological Change Project—*The Worker and Technological Change 1930–1980: Interviews With Connecticut Workers* (1984). Asher's essay on "The Limits of Big Business Paternalism: Relief for Injured Workers in the Years Before Workmen's Compensation" will appear in David Rosner and Gerald Markowitz, eds., *Dying for Work* (forthcoming, Indiana University Press). Asher is a member of the editorial collective that has prepared an anthology of original essays, *Women, Work and Technology*, which will be published by the University of Michigan Press. With Charles Stephenson, he has completed editing a collection of original essays on ethnicity and the American working class. He is currently finishing a book on the history of industrial safety and workmen's compensation in the U.S., 1840–1940 and is writing a series of essays on collective bargaining over production standards. With Charles Stephenson, he is a General Editor of the American Labor History Series published by the State University of New York Press.

Index